Corporate Working Capital Management

Corporate Working Capital Management

A Vijayakumar
N Pasupathi

AUTHORSPRESS
Publishers of Scholarly Books

Worldwide Circulation through Authorspress Global Network
First Published 2010
by
Authorspress
E-35/103, Jawahar Park
Laxmi Nagar, Delhi-110 092
e-mail: authorspress@yahoo.com

Corporate Working Capital Management
ISBN 978-81-7273-553-1

Printed in India at Tarun Offset, Delhi.

Preface

Fixed capital and working capital are the dominant contributors to the total capital of a developing country. Fixed capital investments generate production capacity whereas working capital makes the utilisation of that capacity possible. A firm can exist and survive without profitability but cannot survive without working capital. In a period of rising capital casts and scarce funds, the working capital is one of the most important areas requiring management review. It consumes a great deal of time to increase profitability as well as to maintain proper liquidity at minimum risk.

Working capital management is a very important component of corporate finance because it directly affects the liquidity and profitability of the company. It deals with current assets and current liabilities. Working capital management is important due to many reasons. For one thing, the current assets of a typical manufacturing firm accounts for over half of its total assets. Excessive levels of current assets can easily result in a firm's realising a substandard return of investment. However, firms with too few current assets may incur shortages and difficulties in maintaining smooth operations. Working capital management involves planning and controlling current assets and current liabilities in a manner that eliminates the risk of inability to meet due short-term obligations on the one hand and avoid excessive investment in these assets on the other hand. Viewed in this perspective, the study devoted to working capital management may be rewarding one.

The automobile industry is a major constituent of surface transport. It plays a significant role in the GDP of the country.

India has growing market potential for automobiles due to rise in demand. Therefore, the present study was undertaken for a proper insight in to the management of working capital in the automobile industry.

This book contains various aspects of working capital management in the Indian automobile industry. Further, in order to cater to the needs of research scholars, teachers and financial executive, the subject matter in the book has been treated in a conceptual-cum-analytical manner. The book is intended to be useful for practicing managers, financial executives working in the service sectors, students of M.Com., M.B.A., M.F.C. and other banking professional examinations. Further, this book is of special interest to Ph.D. and M.Phil. scholars of various universities, colleges and research institutions. The contents of the book may be much useful to researchers pursuing research in the field of working capital management.

We earnestly hope that it would serve its purpose and meet the market needs. However, we would gratefully welcome suggestions and feedback from colleagues, students and practitioners. Any constructive criticism will undoubtedly help us greatly to enhance our research capability. We express our heartfelt gratitude to God Almighty whose blessings guided us in carrying out the research successfully. The work presented in this book could be possible only because of the cooperation, guidance and assistance given by a number of persons and a few institutions. It is difficult to recount them all and we tender due apologies to all those contributions we have not been able to recount. However, we cannot afford not to mention a few.

In the preparation of this book, We have received help and encouragement from different sources. We shall forever cherish the kind permission and encouragement given to us by Mr. K.M.Dhandapani, President, The Mudaliar Educational Trust. We are grateful to K.K.Balusamy, our most beloved Secretary and Correspondent, Erode Arts College, for his encouragement and inspiration given to use. I would like to thank Mr. K.N.Murugesan, Vice-President, Mr.U.N.Murugesan, Vice-President, Mr. L.Kumaravel, Treasurer and other management committee members for their encouragement. We would like to thank Dr. V.Venkateswaran, Principal, Erode Arts College, Erode for the necessary help we required in completing this work. We also express our deep sense of gratitude to faculty members of Department of Commerce, Erode Arts College, Erode for their co-operation and assistance for completing this task. We are grateful to our colleagues and friends for their help and support in the completion of this book. We also extend our profound thanks to Authors Press, New Delhi, for giving shape to our ideas by publishing this book in record time.

A. Vijayakumar and N. Pasupathi

List of Abbreviations

CA	:	Current Assets
CL	:	Current Liabilities
NWC	:	Net Working Capital
TA	:	Total Assets
FA	:	Fixed Assets
CV	:	Co-efficient of Variation
CAGR	:	Compound Annual Growth Rate
CR	:	Current Ratio
LR	:	Liquid Ratio
WTR	:	Working Capital Turnover Ratio
ITR	:	Inventory Turnover Ratio
RTR	:	Receivable Turnover Ratio
CTR	:	Cash Turnover Ratio
QNWC	:	Quick Net Working Capital
PBT	:	Profit Before Tax

Contents

1

Introduction

Developing economies are confronted with the problem of inefficient utilisation of resources available to them. Capital is the limited productive resource in such economies, and proper utilisation of these resources promotes the rate of growth, cuts down the cost of production and, above all, improves the efficiency of the productive system. The total capital of a country comprises fixed capital and working capital. Fixed capital investment generates production capacity whereas working capital makes the utilisation of that capacity possible. Thus, the study of working capital occupies an important place in financial management.

Since the fifties, there have been concerted efforts by theoretical economists to analyse the financial decisions of business firms within the context of equilibrium models of financial markets. While these models have been employed to analyse the long-term corporate investment and financial decisions, virtually no research has been conducted in an attempt to apply them to working capital decisions.[1] It shows that the earlier emphasis of financial management was more on long-term financial decisions. Working capital management which is concerned with short-term financial decisions appears to have been relatively neglected in the literature of finance. Even in recent years, major theoretical developments have been made with respect to long range financial decisions of the firm but research devoted to short-range or working capital decisions making would appear to have been less productive.[2]

Funds are needed in every business for carrying on day-to-day operations. Working capital funds are regarded as the life-blood of a business firm. A firm can exist and survive without making profit but cannot survive without working capital funds. If a firm is not earning profit, it may be termed as 'sick', but not having working capital may cause it bankruptcy and closure over a period of time. In addition, working capital has acquired a great significance and sound position for the twin objects of "Profitability and Liquidity". It consumes a great deal of time to increase profitability as well as to maintain proper liquidity at minimum risk. Leslie R. Howard[3] rightly pointed out that a deeper understanding of the importance of working capital and its satisfactory provision can lead not only to material savings in the economical use of capital but can also assist in furthering the ultimate aim of a business, namely, that of maximising financial returns on the minimum amount of capital which need to be employed.

All the above factors clearly indicated the crucial importance of working capital in the management of finance. Thus, need for skilled working capital management has become very essential in recent years. Viewed in this perspective, the study devoted to working capital management may be a very rewarding one.

Statement of the Problem

The working capital management is the most critical problem in financial management. Most of the time financial executives are devoted towards managing the current assets and current liabilities which are the main constituents of working capital. Importance of the working capital management stems from two reasons, viz., (i) substantial portion of total investment is invested in current assets and (ii) the level of current assets and current liabilities will change quickly with the variation in sales. Hence, this study makes an attempt to analyse the size, composition, circulation of working capital, and whether such an investment has increased or declined over a period of time. Knight[4] pointed out that not only working capital components are interdependence on each other but also on net sales and profit. Hence, this study also makes an attempt to evaluate some of the linkages between the different components of working capital and their relationships with the variables like sales, value of output, earnings cashflow, etc.

The mismanagement of working capital will lead to loss of profits in the short-run but it will ultimately lead to the downfall of the enterprises in the long-run. An excessive investment in working capital will lower the rate of return while inadequate investment will hamper the solvency position and growth thereby affecting the operation of business. The adequacy of working capital together with its efficient handling virtually determines the survival or demise of an enterprise.[5] Thus this study attempts to determine the operational adequacy of working capital with the use of Bivariate Discriminant Analysis. In working capital analysis, the direction of change over a period of time is of crucial importance. It is, therefore, very essential for an analyst to make a study about the trend and direction of working capital. Not only that, analysis of working capital trends provide a base to judge whether the practice and prevailing policy of the management with regard to working capital is good enough or an improvement is to be made in managing the working capital funds. Hence, in this study, an attempt is made about the trend of the components of the working capital movements to provide a deep and broad base while examining the working capital management of the selected enterprise.

After determining the requirements of current assets, one of the important tasks of the financial manager is to select as assortment of appropriate sources of finance for the current assets. Normally, the current assets of a firm are supported by a combination of long-term and short-term sources of financing. The short-term financing is less costly than the long-term financing but the former is more risky than the latter. Thus, the choice should naturally involve a trade-off between risk and return. Normally the excess of current assets over current liabilities should be financed by long-term sources; precisely it is not possible to find out which long-term source has been used to finance current assets, but it can be examined as to what proportion of current assets has been financed by long-term funds. Therefore, an attempt has been made in the study in this regard.

It is observed that different authors have approached the study of working capital management in different ways. The major inferences of almost all the studies concerning the approaches of working capital management centres around risk-return trade off. Based on these approaches, this study also attempts to develop an approach with the help of which risk-return analysis of working capital position can be conducted for the selected enterprises.

Lack of liquidity implies lack of freedom of choice as well as constraints on management's freedom of movements. If liquidity continues to be a problem, it may ultimately lead to bankruptcy. Thus, in the study of working capital management, one frequently occurring problem is to determine the short-term liquidity position which has been accomplished in this study. The investment decisions in the current assets deal with a number of problems from the working capital management point of view because the profitability and liquidity of the business very much depend upon the nature and style of current assets management. An appropriate level of current assets and current liabilities in the business enterprise determine the level of working capital affecting ultimately the firm's liquidity and solvency. To have higher profitability, the firms may sacrifice solvency and maintain a relatively low level of current assets. When the firms do so, their profitability will improve as less funds are tied up in the idle current assets, but their solvency will be threatened. In this study an attempt is made to study the association of profitability with the working capital ratios.

One of the important areas of working capital management is to study the nature of short-run behaviour of the demand for working capital and its components. The study of the demand for cash has been stimulated by Baumol, Tobin and Friedman. However, this study is not only limited to the study of the demand for cash but it has also been extended to the study of demand for inventories, receivables, gross working capital and net working capital as well.

Selection of Automobile Industry

Transport sector is the backbone of country's economic growth and development. Transportation throughout the world has made possible an unprecedented level of mobility across the geographical boundaries. The mobility has given many people more options about where to live and work than they had years ago. Similarly, mobility has broadened the access of business to new markets and more choices by increasing the available pool of resources. From the economic point of view, transportation is a vital factor for steady economic growth and development. The trade facilitated by transportation has been a growing component of national income in all the countries. Studies show that the contribution of transportation in GDP has a positive impact. The structure of the economy also influences the transport system because consumer expenditure on transportation contributes to national economy. The transport sector is equally important for both industrialised and developing economics. The transport sector including water transport, aviation and surface transports are major players of Gross Domestic Product (GDP), which includes the value of all goods and services. Being the largest transport networking in the world, particularly in road transportation, the automobile industry plays a significant role in the GDP of the country.

The automobile industry is a major constituent of surface transport. Automobile as a commodity includes passenger cars, commercial vehicles, three wheelers and two wheelers. India has a growing market potential for automobiles due to rise in demand.

As a result more and more manufacturers are bringing in new forms of the existing product because diffusion of a new product depends upon demand statistics. Automobile manufacturers, particularly car manufacturers, are attracting buyers with new model shopping to tap the growing demand for automobiles. Utility vehicles also posted significant growth. Further, two- and three-wheeler industries, especially the motor cycle segments, have shown a steep jump, while the volume growth of all the players has recorded a pretty good market share. Therefore, the automobile industry has been selected for this study in order to determine its working capital performance during the study period. In this study the researcher focuses on automobiles such as commercial vehicles, passenger cars and multiutility vehicles, and two - and three- wheelers.

Significance of the Study

The management of working capital is of special importance in industries and automobile industry is one such industry. From the point of view of the socio-economic development of the country, the automobile industry is significant enough in terms of investment and employment. The sales and working capital function in the automobile industry differ from that of other industries. Even though many studies in this direction have been conducted, the present one would be of greater significance to many. It would help to understand the pattern and the structure of financial variable of leading companies apart from identifying the financial relationship of companies with their respective industries. The change in the economic policy of the government certainly has had an impact on the performance of corporate units in India. A need at present is therefore felt to study the impact of such changes on the performance of the corporate sector and hence the research problem has to be changed to "Working Capital Management of Indian Automobile Industry". This particular topic has been selected for the study because effort has been made to examine the changes that might have occurred in the performance of the automobile industry due to the changes in the government policy.

As such, the study is expected to help the corporate management, the financiers, the investors and the government at large, to take valuable decisions at their own. The study has academic relevance too in so far as new theoretical and practical knowledge would be added to the existing stock of knowledge undoubtedly. The present study will act as a masterpiece on the subject for further research and development. There is no study on working capital management of the Indian automobile industry after liberalisation. Therefore, to cover the gaps in the earlier studies, the present study is undertaken to give an insight into the working capital management of selected sectors of Indian automobile industry. It would also enable shareholders, investors and investment analysts to identify the determinants of corporate performance. Further, it would provide insight to banks, financial institutions and long-term lenders to understand the financial capability and effectiveness of the companies. Moreover, it would open up new vistas to the industry association and the government in understanding the characteristics of the companies for their and intra-firm comparison. It might also help the academic researchers in securities, industry and company by providing different perspective of the analysis.

REFERENCES

1. Cohn, R.A. and Pringle, J.J. (1975), Steps Towards an Integration of Corporate Financial Theory, in *Management of Working Capital: A Reader*, Keith V. Smith (ed.), New York: West Publishing Co., p.369.
2. Smith, K.V. (1976), State of the Art of Working Capital Management, in Issues in *Managerial Finance*, Eugene F. Brigham and Ramom E.Johnson, (ed.), Illinois: The Dryden Press, p. 63.
3. Howard, L.R. (1971), *Working Capital – Its Management and Control*. London: Mac Donald & Evans Ltd, p. 2.

4. Knight, W.D. (Spring 1972), Working Capital Management - Satisficing versus Optimisation, *Financial Management,* pp. 33-40.

5. Donnell, O. and Goldberg (1964), *Elements of Financial Administration,* New Delhi: Prentice Hall of India Pvt. Ltd., p. 55.

2

Approaches to the Study of Working Capital Management

This chapter presents the review of literature relating to the study undertaken. The collection of reviews has been made from various studies undertaken by the academicians, practitioners, researchers, etc., from time to time. These reviews will enlighten the existing knowledge of the researcher. Besides this, the reviews of empirical studies explore the avenues for present and future research related to the subject matter. In order to understand the research problem the earlier attempts made by the academicians, economist, socialist, etc., are needed to be studied. The review of literature guides the researchers for getting better understanding of methodology used, limitations of various available estimation procedures, database, lucid interpretation and reconciliation of the conflicting results. In case of conflicting and unexpected results, the researcher can take the advantage of knowledge of other researchers simply through the medium of their published works.

A large number of research studies had been carried out on different aspects of the working capital management by the researchers, economists and academicians in India and abroad. Different authors had analysed working capital management in different perspectives. A review of these analyses is important in order to develop an approach that can be employed in the context of the study of the automobile industry in India. Therefore, the present chapter reviews the various approaches to the study of working capital management.

Risk-Return Trade-off

Sagan (1955)[1] in his study discussed mainly the role and function of the money manager who is directly concerned with the management of cash that is generated in the course of business transactions. He stressed that more emphasis was laid on the money manager's job. He suggested that the preparation and analysis of a cashflow schedule was a basic factor to achieve a successful programme of money management. He also pointed out that the level of operational cash needs depends primarily on the level of sales.

The Walker (1964)[2] study towards a theory of working capital is a lot more improvement upon the Sagan study. His main argument was that it was possible to develop a theory of working capital. In this connection, he developed the following propositions, which imply a risk-return trade-off of working capital management.

i) If working capital is varied to sales, amount of risk that a firm assumes is also varied and the opportunity for gain or loss is increased.

ii) Capital should be invested in each component of working capital as long as the equity-network position of the firm increases.

iii) The type of capital used to finance working capital directly affects the amount of risk that a firm assumes.

iv) The greater the disparity between the maturities of a firm's short-term debt instruments and its flow of internally generated funds, the greater the risk and vice versa.

He indicated that changes in working capital in certain industries cause the rate of return on investment to react more favourably than in others. It showed a kind of negative relationship that exists between the level of working capital and the rate of return. If the Sagan study states that the level of working capital is a function of sales, the Walker study states that it is a function of output. Therefore, both the studies do not differ significantly so far as the major determinant of the level of working capital is concerned. However, Walker goes beyond it by indicating that the working capital level also varies directly with management's attitude towards risk.

The Van Horne (1969)[3] study examined separately the level of a firm's liquid assets and the maturity composition of its debt in order to illustrate the respective trade off between risk and return. The study emphasized the fact that the lower the level of liquid assets the greater the risk of not being able to meet current obligations. The risk of technical insolvency can be minimised by maintaining a high proportion of liquid assets. However, this strategy would affect the return on investment. Thus, the decision concerning a liquid asset balance is a matter of risk-return trade off. Generally, the longer the maturity schedule of debt, the less risky would be the debt financing of the firm. However, his study added to it by stating that the relationship also exists between the maturity schedule and the cost of debt. The longer as maturity schedule, the more costly is likely to be the financing and vice versa.

Lesile R. Howard (1971)[4] described that working capital may be regarded as the lifeblood of a business; its effective provision can do much to ensure the success of a business, while its inefficient management can lead not only to loss of profits but also to the ultimate downfall of what otherwise might be considered as a promising concern. A deeper understanding of the importance of working capital and its satisfactory provisions can lead not only to material savings in the economical use of capital but can also assist in furthering the ultimate aim of a business, i.e., maximising financial returns on the minimum amount of capital which need be employed.

Knight (1972)[5] in his study basically argued that optimising models dealing with single working capital accounts independently may produce inconsistent results as compared to the models that give simultaneous treatment to each working capital account. He presented reserve-stock models, applied successfully to inventories, simultaneously to inventories and receivables, and to cash, to disclose their implications which are found in their simultaneous interrelationship of variables. He suggested that the area of simultaneously must be extended to all the elements including revenue, cost and risk factor involved in profit planning.

Chakraborthy (1973)[6] opined that working capital is a segment of capital employed. Since the return on the capital employed is an aggregate measure of the overall efficiency in conducting a business, it pointed out the excessive working capital would lower the capital turnover ratio and so bring down the overall return on capital employed. Similarly, a too small amount of working capital, though yields an immediate higher return on capital employed, may reduce the earning capacity of the fixed capital employed over the succeeding periods. He suggested that operating cycle concept draws attention towards the need for concerted credit management against the broader perspective of better working capital management and higher return on capital employed.

The first study of Smith (1974)[7] described dual goals of profitability and liquidity and suggested that the job of financial managers is to achieve a trade off between the two. He illustrated his idea by using the rate of return on equity investment as a measure of profitability and net working capital and current ratio as a measure of liquidity. His study also indicated simulating future financial statements of a firm based on a set of simultaneous equations. He presented their model, in which Current Assets (CA) and Current Liability (CL) are directly related to firm sales (S),

$$CA = f_1 (S) \quad \text{.........} \quad (1)$$

$$CL = f_2 (S) \quad \text{.........} \quad (2)$$

The second study of Smith (1974)[8] relates to profitability versus liquidity trade off in working capital management. The study suggested that parallel monthly forecasts of liquidity and profitability can be useful in evaluating trade off between these two goals. He stressed that such forecast can also be useful in estimating the impact of certain working capital policies on these goals and in reflecting the uncertainty of the future. This study also discussed individual and collective effects of accounts receivables, inventories, accounts payable and other accruals on profitability and liquidity.

The Bierman, Chopra and Thomas (1975)[9] study was an attempt to interrelate working capital and capital structure decisions with the working capital used not only as a buffer to avoid ruin but also to affect sales. The study assumed that working capital level affects both the expected earnings and the variance of earnings. The study states that if W is the amount of working capital, W* is the optimum level of it, S_0 is the initial amount of equity, the loss of W* is the ruin which would reduce equity to $S_0 - W^*$ and the firm is made to borrow $g(S_0 - W^*)$, where g is a constant between 0 and 1. It is assumed that W = W* before the ruin occurs. After the firm borrows $g(S_0 - W^*)$, the firm will again return to W*. Given a certain level of revenues, dividends can be paid only after paying interest on long-term debt and reaching W*.

John J. Hampton (1983)[10] described that the working capital management is the functional area of finance that covers all the current accounts of the firm. It is concerned with the adequacy of current assets as well as the level of risk posed by current liabilities. He also viewed that the firm's policies for managing its working capital should be designed to achieve three goals such as adequate liquidity, minimisation of risk and contribute to maximising firm value.

Arthur J. Keown, David F. Scoh, Jr, John D. Martin and J. William Petty (1985)[11] viewed that working capital management involves managing the firm's liquidity, managing the firm's investment in current assets and its use of current liabilities. Each of these problems was shown to involve risk-return trade off, investing in current assets was found to reduce the firm's risk of liquidity at the expense of lowering its overall rate of return on its investment in assets. Furthermore, the use of long term sources of financing was found to enhance the firm's liquidity while reducing its rate of return on assets.

Mall and Singh (1989)[12] examined the working capital management in Fertiliser Corporation of India for the period of six years from 1979-80 to 1984-85. It includes size, distribution and financing pattern of working capital. They concluded to increase in current assets investment with corresponding decrease in net working capital, which leads to decrease in profitability and increase the risk of technical insolvency of the company. The large proportion of inventories had been one of the important causative variables responsible for the poor profitability during the period under investigation and the adverse effect of financing large part of gross working capital through current liabilities.

Chang, Dandapani and Prakash (1995)[13] in their study, that a comparison of working capital management amongst European and US firms are discussed. Statistics cover six industry sectors. Particular attention was paid to the financing and investment of working capital; the relationship between financing and investment; and the effect on working capital policies of growth. Findings showed that similar working capital investment policies between European and US firms. US companies take a more conservative approach to current asset financing than do European firms. US industries generally have shorter cash conversion cycles than those of Europe. Comparisons between individual countries are also made and the implications of study findings are assessed.

Sahu (2002)[14] in his analysis identified the effective of liquidity management with usefulness and develops a simple model for current and quick ratios of 12 Indian paper companies for the period of 1989-90 to 1996-97. This study revealed the effective management of liquidity in the paper companies.

Shanmugam (2006)[15] in his study revealed that the trend of working capital, overall profitability ratios, interrelationships between working capital accounts and selected financial variables and interrelationship between liquidity and profitability in the engineering industry in India for the period 1991-2000. It concluded that the interrelationship between sales and working capital accounts are found to be significant for the industry aggregate data and profitability is associated with the liquidity as shown by the two out of six categories.

Liquidity Analysis

Management of working capital is crucial for the success of an enterprise. The adequacy of current asset, together with their efficient handling, virtually determines the survival (liquidity) of a business concern. Working capital is said to be life-blood and nerve centre of an undertaking. A brief review of the dispersed efforts as research in the field of liquidity is attempted in the following paragraphs.

The Welter (1970)[16] study is quite a distinct one from the earlier studies on working capital. It was devoted to the calculation of savings possible through reduction of working capital. His study first requires to specify the delay centres along with costs borne by them. After specifying the delay centres and costs borne by them, the study requires to calculate the working capital tied up in each delay centre with the help of additional information regarding average delay and added value. In order to assess whether saving is possible through reduction of working capital or not, the study suggested the working out of the possibility of reducing the various delays occurring in delay centres. The study further highlighted the fact that the firm could reduce average delay so as to generate savings possible through reduction of working capital if it could change the distribution of average delays favourably.

Cossaboom (1971)[17] in his study described that the profitability-liquidity trade off has been getting top billing by many management teams lately. The study suggested that there are four aspects such as Liquidity, Flexibility, Sensitivity innovation and Segmental financing which financial managers should examine to reduce their firms' vulnerability to further liquidity squeezes. Among the four approaches, financing flexibility and innovation by financial managers may be the best approach for further liquidity management.

The linkages between credit, inventory or short-term borrowing policies in order to determine optimal working capital policies were also indicated by the Merville and Tavis (1973)[18]. They rightly pointed out that the current liabilities of a firm are the stock reflection of closely interrelated operational and financial cashflows and unless the net effect of these combined flows is recognised, the search for optimal credit, inventory or short-term borrowing polices will not become complete.

Weston and Brigham (1975)[19] rightly stated that there are many aspects of working capital management which make it an important function of the financial manager. On the one hand, it maintains proper liquidity, while on the other hand, it helps in increasing the profitability of the concern.

James E.Gentry (1976)[20] hypothesized a relationship between profitability and liquidity as perceived by business managers unlike the frequently assumed negative relationship. This relationship may not be continuously linear but rather have the shape of an inverted tea cup.

The Yardeni (1978)[21] study relates to the application of the portfolio-balance framework to an empirical study of the portfolio behaviour with special focus on management of the working capital portfolio of non-financial corporations. For this model, the study assumed that current assets and liabilities as well as equity were treated as exogenous variables and current assets and current liabilities were treated as indigenous. This study indicated that it is often required to determine the optimal composition of the portfolio of current assets and current liabilities with the help of the following:

$$1 = DD/W + LAPT/W + INV/W + NAR/W - BL/W$$

Where		
	W	= DT + E – NCA
	LAPT	= LA – PTL
	NAR	= AR – AP
	DD	= Cash and Demand Deposits
	DT	= Bonded Debt
	E	= Equity
	NCA	= Non-Current Assets
	LA	= Interest Tax Liability
	INV	= Inventory
	AR	= Accounts Receivables
	AP	= Accounts Payable
	BL	= Bank Loans

After computing the short-term and long-term co-efficient of the model, the Yardeni study pointed out the short run changes in independent variables as sales, new orders and interest rates do influence current assets and current liabilities significantly.

Ramamoorthy (1978)[22] described that profitability and solvency are the twin objectives of working capital management. Survival and growth of the company thus depend on its ability to meet the two sets of profitability and solvency. He also viewed that if liquid assets are adequate to pay off current liabilities, a feeling of confidence in the financial strength of the company is automatically created and its credit reputation is sustained.

Lambrix and Singhvi (1979)[23] suggested that the financial executives of firms should understand the factors that determine the length of working capital cycle and consequently try to optimise the level of their working capital investment. They also suggested that the "Predetermined decision" level of working capital must be examined in relation to profitability measured by the return on net assets. They developed check-lists that are classified by components of the working capital cycle with the objective of assisting a firm in identifying and resolving working capital problem areas.

Kulshrestha (1980)[24] in his study, stressed that corporate liquidity is a vital factor in business. Excess liquidity, through a guarantor of solvency would reflect lower profitability, deterioration in managerial efficiency through complacency, increased speculation and unjustified expansion, extension of too liberal credit and dividend policies. Too little liquidity then may lead to frustration of business objections, reduced rate of return, business opportunities missed and weakening of morale. The control of liquidity requires active working capital management.

Pancras (1981)[25] develops a system for the time adjustment of current assets through the process of discounting and close selection to arrive at real liquidity position, illustrating his point with balance sheet figures of an engineering company. The calculation of discount factor is given below.

$$\text{Discount factor} = 1/(1 + r/100)^n$$

n= Total cycle time taken to convert cash to Raw material then to finished goods and immediately back to cash.

r= Annual earning rate or the borrowing rate whichever is higher.

He stressed that to the banker the time adjusted current ratio would provide invaluable information relating to the quality of the financial management with regard to working capital.

Banerjee (1982)[26] conducted a study on the corporate liquidity and profitability in India. The study related to the periods 1970-71 to 1977-78. The purpose of the study was to analyse the trend of liquidity position and its relationship with the profitability in the medium and large public limited companies in the corporate sector in India. The study concluded that liquidity will lead to rise in profitability and viceversa; there are others, where increase in liquidity will be associated with a decline in profitability.

Johnson, Campbell and Savoie (1983)[27] in their study analysed that the liquidly management practices of major US corporations during the 1975 and 1982 recessions are compared so as to determine whether liquidity management tools remain consistent over time. Three liquidity management issues are evaluated, comprising factors used in managing liquidity: factors used in identify liquidity problems; and factors used in resolving these problems. The overall conclusion is that far more similarities than difference may be noted.

Sharma and Reddy (1985)[28] made a study on the liquidity position of the Nizam Sugar Factories Limited (NSF) during the years 1972-73 and 1981-82 and to identify the factors influencing the liquidity. The study concluded that the major element that is affecting the liquidity position of the firm is the government policies with respect to the input and output as well.

Mukherjee (1988)[29] conducted a study on working capital management in public sector enterprises and concluded that in eleven enterprises out of the selected twenty, liquidity and profitability were found to be adversely correlated while in the rest the positive correlation between these two variables was observed. This study however concluded that as a whole the liquidity and profitability were adversely correlated.

Reddy (1988)[30] in his study, stressed that the cooperative sugar mills have to go a long way in the proper management of the working capital. Problems may arise on account of seasonal character of the industry, but the absence of networking capital is a grave danger for the mills. He also stressed that sustained efforts have to be made to maintain liquidity and sufficient amount of net working capital in order to avoid the potential danger of technical insolvency.

John J. Hampton and Cecilia, Wagner (1989)[31] in their study used the techniques of financial analysis to address issues of working capital adequacy. Guidelines have been developed on methods of evaluating cash, current assets, current liabilities, and overall adequacy. Their study also developed an Electronic spreadsheet model to bring all the measures together and allow the analyst to compare the firm's ratios with norms taken from similar firm.

Vijayakumar and Venkatachalam (1995)[32] conducted an empirical study on the interrelationship between working capital management and profitability. In this study thirty-one sugar companies in Tamil Nadu were selected. This study shows that the liquidity was negatively associated with profitability while the inventory turnover and debtor's turnover had positive influence on profitability.

Mallik and Sur (1999)[33] conducted a study on the working capital management of a leading fast-moving consumer goods company and observed that a very high degree of positive relationship between liquidity and profitability.

Dutta and Joginder Singh (2000)[34] conducted the study on "Working Capital Management of Horticulture Industry in Himachal Pradesh" – a case study of Himachal Pradesh Horticulture Produce Marketing and Processing Corporation (HPMC), for the period from 1990-1991 to 1997-1998. It also attempted to analyse and evaluate working capital management by throwing light on financing pattern of working capital. The study revealed that the working capital position worsened drastically during the study period. It was also found out that, despite suffering huge losses, the firm was holding huge idle inventories and hence miserably failed to trade off between liquidity and profitability. The regression results of the study have revealed that there was no significant correlation between gross working capital and sales.

Sarvanan (2001)[35] made a study on working capital management in ten selected non-banking financial companies. He concluded that the sample firms, with the help of statistical tools, had placed importance on the liquidity aspect compared to that of the profitable aspects.

Debasish Sur, Joydeep Biswas and Prasenjit Ganguly (2001)[36] studied the association between the liquidity and profitability of Indian private sector enterprises as a case study of Aluminium Producing Industry. They had identified a very high degree of positive correlation between liquidity and profitability of selected companies. They also observed that liquidity variables jointly influenced the profitability of the selected companies.

Debasish Sur (2001)[37] in his study discussed that the liquidity with Motaal's comprehensive test and the association between liquidity and profitable of four companies in Indian Power Sector i.e., AEC Ltd, BSES Ltd, CESC Ltd and SEC Ltd for the period from 1987-88 to 1996-97. He concluded that the current assets and current liabilities level was satisfactory in AEC Ltd and BSES Ltd, liquid assets were inadequate and the instant capacity of the companies to meet its quick liabilities was not at all satisfactory, variation of investment in current assets was high in BSES Ltd and low in AEC Ltd and inventory and debtors management were quite encouraging. Further, he revealed that the association liquidity and profitability was positive, the degree of influence of liquidity of these two enterprises on their profitability was very low and insignificant. He confirmed the inefficiency of their liquidity management as a whole.

Sathyamoorthi (2003)[38] in his work attempted to ascertain how the current assets were financed and also attempted to discover the relative importance of various current assets components. The study covered four years data of selected co-operative organisations in Botswana. The study revealed that the liquidity ratios played a vital role to evaluate the short-term efficiency of the organisation. The study showed that the co-operatives had low liquidity resulting their weak position to pay short-term debts. The survey also revealed that co-operatives were in action working towards a break-through to be achieved.

Khatik and Pradeep Kumar Singh (2003)[39] in their study made an attempt to examine the liquidity position of Eicher Limited by using various financial ratios. The results of the study showed that the liquidity management of Eicher Limited was not satisfactory due to poor current assets management. The company should give special attention to management of current assets and debtors collection period, because debtor directly affects liquidity position of the company. The study suggested that all the techniques of current assets management should be employed by the company to maintain overall control over liquidity position.

Bardia (2004)[40] in his study on the liquidity management in a Navarathna Steel manufacturing public sector enterprise reported a favourable influence of the liquidity of the company on its profitability.

Chakraborty (2004)[41] stated that the conventional method of measuring liquidity would not be sufficient to cover the extended view of liquidity and new framework must be developed to cover analysis of amount and trend of internal cashflow which is the better proposition to focus on a firm's liquidity position based on financial ratios. He discussed about the theory of corporate liquidity and flexibility backed by Net Liquid Balance (NLB) of Shulman and Cow concluded that NLB is definitely a better approach to measure liquidity than the conventional method of ratio analysis.

Reddy and Patkar (2004)[42] studied the size and its components and liquidity management in factoring companies. They also studied the correlation between liquidity and profitability of factoring companies. They concluded that debtors and amount due to creditors are the major components of current assets and current liabilities respectively in determining the size of the working capital.

Narware and Vivek Sharma (2004)[43] in their study made an attempt to examine and highlights the efficiency of the liquidity management in Hindustan Petroleum Corporation Limited. The study concluded that the short-term liquidity was not at all satisfactory. Liquid assets are insufficient to meet obligations and a major part of fund was cumbersome in form of inventories. Thus it can be concluded that the liquidity management of HPCL was very poor and was not satisfactory. The study suggested that excessive liquidity position was bad, idle assets earn nothing and affect firm's profitability. So, better management of company it required to maintain an efficient liquidity position.

Subhas Chandra Sarkar and Amalendu Bhunla (2004)[44] in their study made an attempt to examine the various aspects of liquidity trend analysis of the Tata Iron and Steel Company. The results of the study showed that the direction of change in liquidity position in the light change in current assets, current liabilities and working capital was not correlated positively. The study suggested that increase in working capital might have been necessitated by the new business environment in general and to counter the challenges from its counterparts in the scale of production and distribution in particular.

Singh's (2004)[45] study on working capital in Lupin Laboratories Ltd attempted to assess the significance of management of working capital through working capital ratios and operating cycle. Having analysed seven years data (1995-2002), he concluded that the liquidity position of the company compared to the percentage of net fixed assets and the operating cycle showed declining trend. The element wise analysis of working capital also revealed that trade debtors constituted the highest percentage of current assets followed by loans and advances, inventories and cash and bank balances. The study brought out the need for efficient management of debtors, the percentage of which was the highest.

Pandey (2005)[46] viewed that the two important aims of the working capital management are profitability and liquidity. Solvency refers to the company's ability to meet their obligations. To ensure the solvency, the company should be very liquid, which means large amount of current assets holdings. If the company maintains relatively larger current assets than the requirements, the company's profitability will suffer to the extent the investment was idle. To have higher profitability, the company had to sacrifice the liquidity position. Maintaining these two in the same direction was challenging and difficult task which the finance managers encounter.

Amit K. Mallik, Debasish Sur and Debdas Rakshit (2005)[47] examined the relationship between working capital and profitability of some selected companies in Indian pharmaceutical industry during the period 1990-91 to 2001-02. The study concluded that the joint influence of the liquidity, inventory management and credit management on the profitability were very significant in the selected companies for the study.

Santimoy Patra (2005)[48] in the study made an attempt to examine the impact of liquidity on profitability between ROI and each of the selected liquidity ratios. The data of TISCO Limited during the period 1990-91 to 1999-2000 were used in this study. The study of the impact of liquidity ratios on profitability showed both negative and positive association. Out of seven liquidity ratios selected for this study, four ratios namely current ratio, acid test ratio, current assets to total assets ratio, inventory turnover ratio showed negative correlation with profitability ratio. The remaining three ratios namely working capital turnover ratio, receivable turnover ratio and cash turnover ratio have shown positive association with the profitability ratio, all of which are statistically significant at 5 per cent level of significance. It can be inferred from this study that profitability of the company was influenced by its liquidity. So, the hypothesis that there is an adverse effect of liquidity on profitability is true in case of TISCO Ltd.

Rajendran and Ramesh (2006)[49] in their study made an attempt to examine the efficiency of liquidity management of Tamilnadu Tourism Development Corporation Limited (TTDC). The data of TTDC Limited used in this study have been collected from published annual reports of the company. The study covers a period of ten years from 1994-1995 to 2003-2004. The results of the study showed that the liquidity management TTDC was very poor and was not satisfactory. The study suggested to improve the liquidity position, the government should allot required funds to TTDC Limited in the forthcoming period.

Sushma Vishnani and Bhupesh Kr Shah (2006)[50] in their study made an attempt to examine the Liquidity Vs Profitability – a detailed study in perspective of Indian consumer electronics industry. The results of the study showed that no established relationship between liquidity and profitability exists for the industry as a whole; the various companies of the industry depicted different type of relationship between liquidity and profitability, although majority of them revealed positive association between liquidity and profitability.

Kannadhasan (2007)[51] in his study discussed many organisations that are profitable on paper are forced their operations due to on inability to meet their short-term debt obligations. In order to sustain the business, it is essential for any organisations to successfully manage its working capital. Though much research has already been conducted, this area requires further attention and care. Ineffective management of working capital is the important factors causing industrial sickness. This study, by using the data available in the annual reports for the period from 1998-99 to 2004-05, examines the working capital management of Titan Industries Limited. The study revealed that the liquidity position of Titan Industries Limited is good as it remained above the standard norms throughout the period of study. The turnover ratios reveal that the company's ability to manage the current assets for generation of sales has improved further during the study period.

Sam Luther (2007)[52] in his study made an attempt to study the liquidity, profitability and risk-return trade off of Madras Cements Limited (MCL). The study concluded that there was a linear relationship between liquidity and profitability. The study further revealed that the high degree of aggressive policy adopted by MCL has made a negative impact on its profitability. The study suggested that MCL was to formulate certain policies to control the working capital so as to meet any sort of financial distress which may occur in future.

Structure and Utilisation of Working Capital

In addition to the above studies, there are also studies on working capital management which deal exclusively with structure and utilisation of working capital in the context of Indian Industries. The major findings of the approaches used in these important studies are presented briefly in this section.

The National Council of Applied Economic Research (NCAER) (1966)[53] carried out a study on the structure of working capital with special reference to three industries namely, fertilisers (8), Cement (9) and Sugar (15). The study was mainly devoted to the analysis of composition of working capital during 1959-1963. The study pointed out that an indication of the effective utilisation of working capital and its requirements for an industry should increase less than in proportion to the increase in the volume of output. But it is difficult to quantify that optimum rate at which the demand for working capital should increase in response to an increase in the volume of output. The study also pointed out that the control of inventory had not received proper attention. However, NCAER failed to put into sharp focus the various problems involved in the management of different components of working capital.

Nalini Ambegaokar (1969)[54], Economic Department, Reserve Bank of India, conducted a study on working capital requirements and availability of bank credit in Indian processing and manufacturing industries. The main findings may briefly be stated as follows:

i) Industries have increasingly relied on bank credit for financing a large part of their working capital requirements.

ii) Although it is difficult to determine a 'norm' for the quantum of inventories, some relationships in the growth of inventories and output / sales has been indicated.

iii) The growing industries, appeared to be out of proportion with the increase in their output.

Mishra (1975)[55] studied the problems of working capital in the selected Indian public enterprises. The study pointed out that the selected enterprises have not been able to utilise working capital efficiently. In all the selected enterprises, an excess inventory was noticed. For the reduction of over-stocking, the study suggested installing an "Integrated Inventory Management" from the very inception of the enterprises. The study also pointed out that the size of cash was on the high side in terms of operational requirements. Its main reason was stated to be the lack of proper planning on control of cash.

Chakraborty (1976)[56] who examined the association between working capital turnover and profitability in Indian cement, sugar and fertiliser industries, reported a positive relationship.

To determine the effectiveness of working capital management, Bhattacharya and Raghavachari (1977)[57] conducted a study taking 721 large Indian Companies and 14 large Indian banks and financial Institutions. Using eleven ratios namely current ratio (x_1), quick ratio (x_2), average finished goods inventory as number of days' sales (x_3), average raw material as number of days of raw material consumption (x_4), average receivable as number of days' sales (x_5), cash flow as percentage of sales (x_6), creditors as percentage of raw material consumed (x_7), profit after tax as percentage of sales (x_8), sales as number of times of total assets (x_9), profit after tax as percentage of total assets (x_{10})

and debt as percentage of equity (x_{11}), The computed discriminant function is given by

$$D = -0.31\ x_1 + 0.154\ x_2 - 0.010\ x_3 - 2.555\ x_4 + 11.196\ x_5 - 0.022\ x_6 + 0.211\ x_7 + 0.002\ x_8 - 0.130\ x_9 - 0.035\ x_{10} - 0.043\ x_{11}.$$

$$\bar{D}_1 = 18.604 \quad \bar{D}_2 = 5.013 \text{ and}$$

$$D^* = (\bar{D}_1 + \bar{D}_2)/2 = 11.8$$

If the value of the discriminant function is greater that D^*, the company is said to be effective one in managing its working capital. The probability of misclassification based on the computed discriminant function is 0.065. The analysis further identified the following four factors having substantial importance.

1. Profit after tax as percentage of sales (25.2 per cent).
2. Sales as number of times of total assets (25.2 per cent).
3. Quick assets as percentage of current liabilities (15.5 per cent).
4. Average receivables as number of days' sales (15.3 per cent).

The study by Vijaya Saradhi (1980)[58] attempted to highlight the problems of working capital management based on the study of aggregate financial data of public enterprises and as revealed by a few case studies of individual units. The study pointed that the share of inventories in the total current assets investment was the highest and increased. Cash inflows are affected by delays in realisation of bills receivable. In the event of shortage of cash, payment to supplier is delayed. These findings clearly indicate that the study was concerned more with a fact-finding process rather than applying techniques or building up models concerning working capital management. The study does not take into account the current liabilities which form an important part of working capital.

Mishra (1980)[59] in his study states that the management of working capital occupies an important place in almost all the text books on finance. However, the problem of working capital management during inflation are yet to receive due attention from authors on financial management. His study pointed out that the measures which a financial manager would be required to tackle the problems relating to the management of working capital during inflation includes accounting for price changes, controlling costs, managing inventories, controlling new investment, improving turnover, managing credit and collection, managing creditors, managing cash and exploring other possibilities. The study concluded that under present inflationary conditions management of working capital is perhaps more important than even the management of profits and this problem requires greatest attempt and effort from the financial manager.

Agarwal (1983)[60] in his study also threw some light on the state of working capital management in selected large manufacturing and trading public limited companies in the private sector. The main findings may briefly be stated as follows:

1. In the majority of industries, the working capital per rupee of sales has shown a declining trend over the years.
2. The majority of industries have not been able to control liquid resources effectively.
3. The average annual percentage growth rate in receivables exceeded the average growth rate in sales.
4. In the majority of industries, long-term funds as a percentage of total working capital have registered an upward trend which mainly due to restrictive flow of bank credit to the industries.

The above findings are based on the computation of a few traditional ratios. It seems as if the limitation of these ratios has not been recognised properly during the study. This study has also revealed that firms in majority of industries under study have failed to plan their working capital requirements properly. In most of the industries, liquid resources have not been controlled and utilised effectively.

Mukherjee (1985)[61] in his explanatory study analysed 20 Central Government Undertakings in India for the period from 1974-75 to 1978-79. It covered the following areas size, relationship between size of business and size of working capital, output and working capital, adequacy of working capital, operational adequacy of working capital, working capital leverage, working capital turnover and components of current assets. Finally, the researcher advised the government to make a liberal policy for internal sources of financing, take care of project economies, run on commercial lines and lay down the minimum rate of return.

Yadav (1986)[62] in his study described that ineffective management of working capital is one of the important factors causing industrial sickness. The rationale of his argument springs from the fact that unless the working capital is managed effectively, monitored efficiently, planned properly and reviewed periodically at regular intervals to remove bottlenecks if any, the company cannot earn profits and increases its turnover.

Sharma and Agarwal (1986)[63] in their study of working capital as an important aspects of management of finance in relation to a specific business undertaking seems worthwhile as the working capital management has an effect on the liquidity position, inventories and profitability. An attempt has been made in this paper to study the working capital management of the Rajasthan State Road Transport Corporation for the period form 1997-78 to 1981-82. This study concluded that corporation has not been able to manage its liquidity resources.

Sarkar (1987)[64] studied that the various aspects of liquidity management with the indices of various ratios, net working capital to flow of funds from operations (Bierman's measure) and defensive assets to projected expenditure (Benson and Sotter's measure). The unit selected for the analysis is the Durgapur Project Ltd for the period of eight years from 1977-78 to 1984-85. The resultant effect was that the firm was required to meet high amount of debt-service charges year to year. This may be one of the reasons for their recurring losses. It seems that the company assumes a non-risk position in terms of the liquidity almost deliberately at the cost of its profitability. There is no proper trade-off between risk and profitability, which is necessary for any firm in connection with its liquidity management.

Sarkar and Saha (1987)[65] made an attempt to assess the relationship between profitability crisis and working capital management in the Indian public sector. This study revealed that owing to poor management of working capital, the profitability of the selected public enterprises suffered.

Panda and Satapathy (1988)[66] carried out a research study regarding the effects of working capital on profitability in Indian cement industry. This study revealed that the positive influence of working capital on profitability of the selected companies was highly significant.

Mukherjee (1988)[67] conducted a study in 1988 on the management of working capital in public enterprises in respect of Central Government Industrial Undertakings. The study related to the period from 1974-75 to 1978-79. The main findings may briefly be stated as follows.

1. Increase in current assets was mainly due to accumulation of inventories and liabilities due to increase in financing through payables.
2. Overall size of sales and output had significant effect on overall size of working capital.
3. The working capital requirements of the units are not ascertained on objective grounds, they are based on consideration other than those suggested for prudent financial management.
4. The overall profitability and size of working capital were negatively correlated by significant extent.
5. There was a very significant negative correlation in between liquidity and owners profitability.

Garai and Mallik (1988)[68] in their study stated that the role of working capital looked from the other side of the ratio of fixed capital in total capital employed. The income generation process of an industry is studied by taking this ratio as a regressor in non-linear regression model. From their results of the analysis of cross-sectional data for all States and Union Territories of India for six industries for three years, it was found that this ratio plays an important role in income generating processes and an optimum value for this ratio (0.48) may be obtained.

Harbans Lal Verma (1989)[69] made a study in 1989 at the Punjabi University on the Management of Working Capital in respect of Iron and Steel Industry in India. The sample of study covered both the public sector and the private sector. The study related to the period from 1978-79 to 1985-86. Verma observed that the problem of working capital in this industry is related more to surplus investments than to inadequacy in the inventory and receivables. But as far as cash is concerned, almost all the units have experienced inadequacies during the period. He also suggested that this can be tackled through improved co-ordination in the function of some strategic departments such as purchase, production, marketing and finance.

Harbir Singh (1990)[70] in his study stated that there are certain areas in which substantial efforts are urgently required to keep the company on an even keel. The company can improve its financial health, if it adopts a technique of more scientific control on raw materials, stores and spares and strives to reduce the unprofitable investment blocked in loans and advances and other current assets. To regulate the cash flow, it is imperative that a weekly cashflow statement and a cash budget be prepared on a regular basis. These measures will hopefully enable the company to make a real breakthrough and place it in the forefront of the sugar industry.

Panigrahi (1990)[71] in his study discussed with the objectives of working capital analysis and its impact on profitability. The study reveals that liquidity position is not satisfactory. The impact of working capital ratios on profitability showed that both negative and positive impact on profitability in transport sector.

Agarwal (1991)[72] has developed a multi-objective criterion to the problem of working capital decisions by making use of the potentials of goal programming which allows a simultaneous solution of complementary and conflicting objectives rather than a single objective only. The goal programming model may be used for different profit targets, with varying levels of current assets, in order to obtain a satisfying level of the various components of working capital and the profitability and liquidity goals. It may be concluded that the goal programming model formulated for the management of working capital serves to illustrate the need for a solution where conflicting objectives are defined.

Gupta (1991)[73] has argued in favour of working capital control through variance analysis. He was of the opinion that variance analysis may provide useful and relevant information to the management enabling it to exercise timely and effective control over working capital.

Rao and Chinta Rao (1991)[74] in their study stated that the traditional liquidity ratios could not help us to find out the real position regarding the adequacy of the working capital amount involved, but simple regression model is powerful enough to identify the in brooding prevailing in the working capital position and to highlight the ineffective planning and control of working capital.

Sushil K. Jain (1991)[75] in his article focused that the importance of working capital, working capital cycle, determinants, optimum level and components of working capital. It concluded that all precautions should be taken for the efficient and effective management of working capital. The financial manager should pay special attention to the levels and financing of each components of working capital. To decide the levels and financing of the components of working capital, the risk-return/cost-benefit implications must be evaluated.

Banerjee and Hazra (1992)[76] analysed through a case that the amount, importance, variation, sources, components and estimation of working capital in Grasim Industries Limited for a periods of five years from 1985 to 1990. They have been used the tools like percentages, averages, ratios, trend analysis, linear regression etc. They concluded that investment in working capital was moderate and an increase in dependency of long term finance as source, high variation in working capital, investment in outside trade and steep increasing trend in working capital was not reflected in the trading results of the company.

Basu (1992)[77] in his study revealed that the working capital analysis and its impact on the profitability and short-term solvency of tyre companies in India for a period of three years from 1987-88 to 1989-90. It observed that the mixed results but requires to be monitored closely in view of working management in current business and may have to sacrifice solvency and maintain relatively low level of current assets in order have higher profitability.

Vijayakumar, Sivasubramanian and Venkatachalam (1994)[78] in their case study discussed that the components, estimating, financing of working capital and its impact on profitability. This study concluded that a moderate trend in the financial position and the utilisation of working capital. The impact of working capital on profitability shows a mixed trend indicating both positive and negative trends.

Vijayakumar (1996)[79] in his study examined the structure, sources, components and utilisation of working capital and liquidity position, risk-return, impact on profitability, demand for working capital and effect of inflation on working capital of 31 companies in the sugar Industry in Tamil Nadu for a period 1982-83 to 1991-92. The study concluded that a lot of funds invested in inventory and receivable can be released for alternative uses, increasing funds through internal sources and under utilisation of capacities of the industry will be solved to a large extent. The study suggested that the selected units improve their overall performance in the management of working capital.

Indrasena Reddy and Someshwar Rao (1996)[80] conducted a study on working capital management in HCL. They used seven important working capital ratios and statement of changes in working capital and concluded that the company's working capital management is not up to the expected level. The study suggested that working capital management needs to be improved by effective utilisation and control of current assets.

Vijayakumar (1996)[81] analysed in his study the nature of short-run behaviour of the demand for working capital and its components, its economies and diseconomies of scale in Indian Public Sector Enterprises for the period of 13 years from 1981-82 to 1993-94 with econometric models. He concluded that the results presence of diseconomies of scale with respect to the demand for working capital and its components except inventory. He suggested that the demand for working capital and its components is a function of both sales and their holding costs. The capital cost co-efficients are all with theoretically correct signs but it is statistically significant only in the case of inventory.

Shankar (1996)[82] discussed about new working capital finance instruments like commercial paper, factoring, forfeiting, debt securitisation and norms for working capital finance in detail. Finally he recommended a new concept in working capital management called zero working capital which means at all times the current assets shall equal the current liabilities. This concept would ensure a smooth and uninterrupted working capital cycle and it would put pressure on the finance managers to improve the quality of current assets at all times which means current ratios is one and quick ratio below one.

Mishra and Kar (1997)[83] in their paper analysed the trend, sources and variance of working capital, operating cycle and inventory and its components in ECIL for a period of five years from 1983-1984 to 1987-88. The study concluded that the significant improvements in its profitability and financial position during last three years. In the area of working capital, it has adopted scientific methods for controlling inventories and debtors.

Carg (1997)[84] in his in depth study identified the financing pattern and utilisation of working capital in State-owned eight public sector industrial enterprises in Haryana covers a period of ten years ranging from 1978-79 to 1987-88. The study depicts that except two enterprises, all other units financed their working capital from borrowed funds and this trend has continuously increased, most of the units have weak financial base and limited access to financial institutions to support their scarce resource and their risk bearing capacity has become very low.

Mallik and Sur (1998)[85] made an attempt of analyse the impact of working capital management on profitability in Indian tea industry using relevant statistical tools and techniques. The study on the inter-relation between the nine selected ratios in the area of working capital management and the selected profitability measure revealed both negative and positive associations. Out of the nine ratios relating to working capital management, five ratios registered negative correlation with the profitability indicator while the remaining four ratios witnessed positive association.

Khan Mohd Amir (1998)[86] conducted a study on working capital management at Escorts Limited with a thrust on analysing financing of working capital, management of cash, management of accounts receivables and management of inventory. The study revealed that the company did not use real professional assistance and expertise, which inturn impaired the overall performance of the company. Financial decisions taken were found to be short-term perspective ignoring the effect in the long run. The cash planning was found to be very ineffective and hence the company found it to be very difficult to procure the cash from operations even though there was enough cash generated from operations. It was also found out that apart from following hedging approach the company depended on ordinary share capital, preference share capital and debentures as the long-term sources of working capital.

Sarma and Chary (1999)[87] study on VST Industries Ltd revealed that working capital management in the sample unit was inefficient. A disproportionate investment in current asset in relation to sales resulted in declining working capital turnover ratio. The company did not follow any consistent policy with respect to investment and financing of working capital. Though there existed many opportunities to make use of trading on equity and hedging for appropriate management of working capital, the company never made use of the same. Having analysed working capital in terms of current ratio, quick ratio, working capital turnover ratio, inventory turnover ratio, debtor's turnover ratio and average collection period, the study revealed that the company failed to manage inventory efficiently which inturn has resulted in lower profitability.

Sivaram Prasad (1999)[88] studied on working capital management in Indian paper industry laying emphasis on individual current assets like cash, receivables and inventory. The study revealed that the working capital formed 47.2 per cent of the total net assets during 1984-93. The rate of return on current assets was negative or insignificant in all selected mills indicating inefficient management of working capital. The results of correlation analysis indicated a close relationship between profitability and working capital efficiency emphasising the need to exercise better control over working capital.

Anand (2001)[89] attempted to develop quantitative benchmarks at the firms and the industry level, so as to evaluate the working capital management performance of corporate India from time to time. The study finds very little evidence on the positive relationship between working capital management and firm profitability. The findings of the study capture the dynamic of risk-return trade-off, which will help the performance evaluation of working capital management of corporate India.

Yadav, Jain and Rastogi (2001)[90] in their study examined and compared the effectiveness of working capital management and the specific problems and deficiencies faced in the management of different components of working capital of three major oil sector companies in India, namely, IOCL, HPCL and BPCL for 10 years from 1988 to 1997. They reveals that these companies managed their working capital well. They have to continue doing well and improve upon the present to face the ensuing competition from other players, including multinationals.

Rabiul Alam and Syed Zabid Hossain (2001)[91] in their study made an attempt to examine the inventory management scenario with particular reference to impact on working capital in ship building industry in Bangladesh. The data of Khulna Shipyard Limited (KSL) used in this study have been collected from published annual reports of the company. The study covers a period of ten years from 1987-1988 to 1996-1997. The results of the study showed that inventory in terms of months cost of production showed over investment in inventory, as it was above the suggested norm during the whole period of study. Such over-stocking would have adversely affected the profitability of KSL during the period under review. Gradual reduction of investment in the volume of inventory, quality of sales has to be increased through sales drive to improve inventory turnover and cash flows, reduction of cost of sales by increasing capacity utilisation, reduction of overhead expenditure were the measures suggested to improve the inventory management of KSL.

Anand and Gupta (2003)[92] in their study discussed the cash conversion efficiency, days operating cycle and days of working capital in 427 Indian manufacturing companies for the period of three years from 1988-99 to 2000-01. They concluded that there exists some relationship between cash conversion efficiency and day of operating cycle with working capital financing strategy of firms and working capital performance and the firm's value.

Parmar (2003)[93] in his study made an attempt to evaluate the performance with respect to inventory management in two selected units such as the Gujarat State Fertiliser Company Limited (GSFC) and the Gujarat Narmada Valley Fertiliser Company Limited (GNFC). The study reveals that the overall performance regarding inventory management at GNFC was better in terms of efficient utilisation of inventories where as GSFC was not able to do so during the study period. The results of the study concluded that the overall performance of GNFC was encouraging while that of GSFC was not alarming.

Ghosh and Maji (2003)[94] made an empirical study on the relationship between utilisation of current assets and operating profitability in Indian cement and tea industries. This study based on twenty two companies (eleven selected from each of the two industries) concluded that the degree of utilisation of current assets was positively associated with the operating profitability of all the companies under study.

Satyanarayana Chary and Venkateshwarlu (2003)[95] in their study made an attempt to examine the need, sources, components, estimation of working capital and its impact on profitability with special reference to Sri Venkata Narasimha Solvent Oils Limited for the period of six years from 1996-1997 to 2001-2002. The results of the study showed that the company has not utilised its long-term funds more effectively by investing them in fixed assets. Further, impact of the working capital and profitability ratios showed completely positive impact over the study period. The study suggested that correct estimation of working capital should be made and fluctuation in quantum of working capital in relation to sales should be avoided.

Narware (2004)[96] in his empirical study envisaged to assess the impact of working capital on profitability, the combine effect of the ratios relating to working capital management and profitability and determination the working capital leverage in National Fertiliser Limited for the period ten years from 1991 to 2000. This study concluded that working capital management and profitability has both the negative and positive association, three ratios registered negative correlation with profitability ratio (ROI) and in working capital leverage increase in the profitability of the company was less than proportion to decrease in working capital.

Sanjay J. Bhayani (2004)[97] in his study made an attempt to examine the empirical study of Gujarat Ambuja Cements Limited, a cement producing enterprise in Gujarat, for assessing the impact of working capital on its profitability during the period from 1993-94 to 2002-03. The results of the study showed that the working capital leverage of the company recorded a fluctuating trend during the period under study. In ranged between 0.04 in the year 1999-2000 and 0.24 in the year 1994-1995. The working capital leverage was always less than unity. Hence, the increase in the profitability of the company was less than the proportion to decrease in working capital. The study suggested that there may be a negative relationship between working capital and profitability.

Parasuram (2004)[98] studied the working capital practices in leading pharmaceutical companies. He concluded that the working capital management practices are seen to be quit different for the larger companies (companies with larger turnover) compared to others. Sales investigated the usefulness of current and quick ratios and builds a needs involving those ratios to determine whether liquidity management position in Indian paper industry is effective or not. He concluded that most of the large producing companies in India have been caught in a vicious down cycling the treat to their viability.

Ghosh and Maji (2004)[99] examined the efficiency of working capital management of the Indian cement companies from 1992-93 to 2001-02. Instead of using the common method of analysing different working capital management ratios, three index values representing the average percent of the components of current assets, the degree of utilisations of the total assets in relation to sales and the efficiency in managing the working capital been computed for the selected firms over ten years' study period. The study concluded that the Indian cement industry did not perform remarkably during study period.

Khatik and Singh (2004)[100] in their study concluded that the short-term liquidity was very much satisfactory, higher investment in current assets, good position of debtors and higher the age of inventory. The overall positions of the working capital of Indian Farmers' Fertiliser Cooperative Limited (IFFCO) are satisfactory but there is a need of improvement in inventory. Because inventory are not properly utilised and maintain by IFFCO during the study period. It also suggested to the management should be trying to proper utilisation of inventory and also try to maintain the inventory as per their requirement so liquidity will not be interrupted.

Rabiul Alam and Hossain (2004)[101] in their field survey examined that the strengths and weaknesses of working capital of Khulna Shipyard Limited for a period of ten years from 1987-88 to 1996-97. They concluded that the company does not estimate the working finance requirements, which is essential for better working capital management. In this regard, the concept of operating cycle period (OCP) has to be given due weightage in estimating the working capital requirements of the enterprise. Effective use of OCP eliminates, to a great extent, unnecessary blocking of funds in various components of current assets. They suggested that the company should consider source of working finance and should try to increase working capital from the sources like trade credit, which would help reduce the interest burden.

Santanu Ghosh and Santi Gopal Maji (2004)[102] in their study examined that the efficiency of working capital management practice and ability to improve their efficiency up to the industrial average in 20 large cement companies operating in India for a period of ten years from 1992-93 to 2001-02 with three index suggested by Bhattacharya. The study observed that the Indian cement industry did not perform remarkably well during this period. Some of the sample firms had successfully improved efficiency during these years; the existence of a very high degree of inconsistency in this matter clearly points out the need for adopting sound working capital management policies by these firms and identifies the forces for inefficiency.

Sudarshan (2004)[103] examined the status of inventory holding in Chemicals and Pharmaceutical Central Public Enterprises. The analysis reveals that could reduce the enterprises inventory holding in terms of number of days of consumption, cost of production and cost of sales in order to improve their working capital efficiency. Further, the enterprises did not enjoy economics of scale in respect of inventory holding in relation to sales. However, still there is scope for further improvement. The study suggested that the proper control over inventories improves the operational efficiency and profitability of the enterprises.

An investigation in to the effectiveness of working capital management of an organisation with particular reference to its short-term liquidity and solvency and impact on commercial operations of the organisation was made by Mukhopadhyay (2004)[104] in his study entitled "Working Capital Management in Heavy Engineering Firm". The study concluded that working capital management should not be treated as an isolated management function but it is part and parcel of the overall corporate management functions and impact of corporate management policy and strategy effects of working capital management practice of the firm. It is thus necessary to work out and analyse cause-effect relationship of every function of the management to assess its impact on the working capital management.

Sudarsana Reddy, Sivarami Reddy and Mohan Reddy (2004)[105] in their study evaluated the performance of the debtors' management of the paper industry in Andhra Pradesh. For this purpose, the analysis of trends in sales and debtors, debtors' size, turnover, collection period and aging of receivables had been carried out. The forgoing analysis reveals that the sample mills adopted liberal credit policy, which had a favourable effect on sales with the exception of Sirpur. The size of trade debtors as a percentage of current assets has shown declining trend. But the collection period of debtors slowly increased in all the mills except in Sirpur. The increasing debtors' collection period was an indication of slackness in collection efforts of the mills. To reduce the collection period, the collection and follow up efforts of trade debtors shall be rationalised and the slackness should altogether be removed.

Sudipta Ghosh (2005)[106] in his study made an attempt to evaluate the performance of Stewarks & Lloyds of India Limited. The data of Stewarks & Lloyds of India Limited used in this study have been collected from published annual reports of the company. The study covers a period of five years from 1996-97 to 2000-2001. The results of the study showed the overall performance of the company regarding inventory management is satisfactory in terms of efficient utilisation of inventories during the period of study. The study suggested that to have an efficient inventory management, a proper balance between these two extreme situations should be maintained for smooth operation of the business.

Amit K. Chakraborty (2005)[107] in his study made an attempt to examine the working capital management of Andrew Yule and Company Limited during the period from 1993-94 to 2002-03. The study revealed that the short-term liquidity position of the company was not satisfactory at all. But the acid test ratio indicates very good short-term liquidity position of the company. The cause of this attitude of the ratio was due to exclusion of the inventory from the total current assets. Further the study concluded that the inventory contributes only (average) 17.92 per cent in gross working capital, which indicates proper utilisation and maintenance of inventory.

Patel (2005)[108] in his study made an attempt to analysis of working capital of Colour-Chem Limited. A ratio analysis and Altman's 'Z' score model has been used. It studied the position and efficiency of working capital for a period of 19 years from 1981 to 1999. The study concluded that the company was in a position to pay its current obligations and efficiently utilises its current assets. The model suggests that the company never become sick in future.

Rais Abramd and Ali Ghufran (2005)[109] in their analytical study indicated that components, financing and structure of working capital and impact of working capital on profitability in eight marketing cooperative societies for a period of three years from 1997-98 to 1999-2000. The study concluded that six societies for their investment in working capital following aggressive approach, low dependencies for their financing of working capital as long-term funds, the liquidity position of all the societies was not satisfactory except one and negative impact on working components.

Ioannis Lazaridis and Dimitrios Tryfonidis (2006)[110] investigated the relationship of corporate profitability and working capital management. The purpose of this study was to establish a relationship that is statistically significant between profitability, the cash conversion cycle and its components for listed firms in the Athens Stock Exchange. The results of the study showed that there was statistical significance between profitability, measured through gross operating profit, and the cash conversion cycle. The study concluded that managers can create profits for their companies by handing correctly the cash conversion cycle and keeping each different component (account receivables, accounts payables and inventory) to an optimum level.

Amir Jafar and Debasish Sur (2006)[111] concluded the study on the efficiency of the working capital management in the National Thermal Power Corporation (NTPC), the only 'Navarathna' Public Enterprise in the Indian power sector, during the period 1983-84 to 2002-03. This study reveals that the company achieved a higher level of efficiency in managing its working capital during the post-liberalisation era by adapting itself to the new environment emanated from liberalisation, globalisation and competitiveness.

Sanjay J. Bhayani (2006)[112] made an attempt to study the impact assets utilisation on profitability of Indian industry. For the purpose of study 24 Indian industries have been selected which comprises 641 Indian firms. The results of the study indicated that fixed assets turnover and profitability has shown a positive relationship. So, it indicates that high fixed assets turnover higher profitability. Further, the results of analysis of multiple determinations make it clear that 40.70 per cent of total variation in the corporate profitability was accounted for by the joint variation in the efficiency of inventory and receivable management.

Sukhdev Singh (2006)[113] in his study made an attempt to examine the Inventory control practices in Indian Farmers Fertiliser Cooperative Limited (IFFCO) by using various financial ratios. The inventory control practices revealed that correlation between sales and inventory ranges from very high to moderate among inventory items and the correlation was significant in case of all the components of inventory except stores and spares. The growth rate of stock of raw material, work-in-progress, finished goods and total inventory was more than the ideal situation and provides clues for improvements. The stock of stores and spares requires the immediate attention of management in order to stop ruthless purchases.

Anand and Malhotra (2007)[114] in their study discussed the cash conversion efficiency, days operating cycle and days of working capital in 339 India non-financial companies for a period of three years from 2001-02 to 2003-04 for each company and for 98 industry groups. They concluded that there exists some relationship between working capital management and profitability on an aggregate basis suggest that there was a significant negative relation between cash flows from operating activities and average days of account receivables.

Ghosh (2007)[115] in his study reviewed that the four different industries, namely, pharmaceutical industry, cement industry, national fertiliser limited and textile industry. The objectives of the study was to determine size and source of working capital with a survey made in 98 small scale textile firms of Punjab. It concluded that in addition to the own capital, bank loans was the most prominent source of working capital among most of the survey units.

Sharma (2007)[116] in his study analysis that various procedures and techniques of financial analysis adopted by the textile industry of the accounting and control of various constituents of current assets in all aspects of textile units in India for a period from 2002-2006. It may be remarked that the existing system of current assets accounting in all the textile companies selected for this study was not been satisfactory and needs improvement in all the directions immediately. Today, manufacturing units of several other industries are using modern techniques of current assets accounting and the textile industry should not lag behind.

Azhagaiah and Gejalakshmi (2007)[117] in their study make an attempt to examine the working capital management efficiency of the Indian textile companies during 1995-1996 to 2005-2006. For measuring the efficiency of working capital management three-index values-performances, utilisations and efficiency indexes are calculated. Using industry norm as target–efficiency level of the individual firms, this study also tests the speed of achieving that target level of efficiency by an individual firm during the period of study. Findings of the study indicate that Indian textile industry as a whole performs remarkably well during the period. The liquidity is strong, performance and utilisation of current assets are satisfactions and adoption of sound working capital policy has been successful.

Pradeep Singh (2008)[118] in his study made an attempt to examine the inventory and working capital management of Indian Farmers Fertiliser Co-operative Limited (IFFCO) and National

Fertiliser Limited (NFL). He concluded that the overall position of the working capital of IFFCO and NFL is satisfactory. But there was a need for improvement in inventory in case of IFFCO. However inventory was not properly utilised and maintained by IFFCO during study period. The management of NFL must try to properly utilise the inventory and try to maintain the inventory as per the requirements, so that liquidity will not be interrupted.

Kaushik Chakraborty (2008)[119] in his study to evaluate the relationship between working capital and profitability of twenty five selected companies in the Indian pharmaceutical industry during the period 1996-97 to 2007-08. He concluded that no definite relationship between liquidity and profitability specially regarding its nature can be established from the empirical results obtained from the study. However, the consolidated position reveals that a higher liquidity position was associated with higher profitability. He suggested that efficient management of working capital is an integral part of the overall corporate strategy to improve corporate profitability.

Empirical Works on the Demand for Cash and Inventories

The object of this section is to present how the demand for cash and inventories by business firms has been approached by the different authors. The hypotheses concerning the demand for working capital and its various components by the selected Indian automobile industry have been formulated on the basis of the review of these empirical works on the demand for cash and inventories.

Studies on the Demand for Cash

The study of short-run behaviour of the demand for cash has been encouraged by the earlier studies of Baumol, Tobin and Friedman.

Baumol (1952)[120] indicated the applicability of the inventory model in determining the level of cash to be held by the business firms. He described the ordering costs and holding costs of cash in a fashion similar to those costs associated with inventory. His conclusion was that the rational individual will, given the price level, demand cash in proportion to the square root of the value of this transactions. As per his model, the average long-run cash balance is given by

$$C = (bT / Zi)^2$$

where, C is the cash balance, b is the transaction cost, T is the dollar value of transactions at a constant price level and i is the capital cost.

James Tobin (1956)[121] in his study explains liquidity preference as behaviour towards risk. His analysis transforms the problem of uncertainty into one involving risk, for liquidity preference may be interpreted as preference for less risky forms of investment. In his model the individual's interest earnings net of transactions costs were maximised. Both Baumol and Tobin mainly indicated that there are important economies of scale in cash holding and an inverse relationship between interest rates and the demand for money.

According to Friedman (1959)[122] the determinants of the demand for money are bonds yields (r_b), equity (r_e), the rate of change of the price level (1/p, dp/dt), the ratio of non-human to human wealth (W), the level or real income per capita (Y/P), tastes and preferences of wealth owning units and all other factors (U). The demand for money function may be written as:

$$Y/M = V (r_b, r_e, 1/p, dp/dt, W, Y/P, U)$$

His empirical results indicated that the permanent income elasticity was 1.8 and the effect of interest rates on the demand for money was too small to be statistically significant. He concluded that the demand for money is not statistically sensitive to changes in the rate of interest.

The study of Allan. Meltzer (1963)[123] was based on 14 industries for nine different years. He specified the following function as a first approximation to the theory.

$$M = f (r, w)$$

where, M is money, the sum of currency and demand deposits of the public, r is the market ratio of interest and w is the net wealth of the public. He used sales as a proxy for the firms' wealth. In order to arrive at conclusion, he tested three functional forms.

$$\log M = a + b \log S' \quad \text{.................. (1)}$$

$$M = KS' \quad \text{.................. (2)}$$

$$M = b + bS'^2 + dS' \quad \text{.................. (3)}$$

where M and S′ were defined as cash and sales per firm by dividing the mean value of M and S; by the relevant number of firms. He concluded that the demand for money by business firms is a function of sales, linear in logarithms and the rejection of the model of transactions demand with economies of scale suggested by Baumol and Tobin and Friedman's position that cash balance increase more than proportionately with permanent income.

Frazer (1964)[124] conducted a study of corporate financial structure and the demand for money where he used quarterly cross-section data for the period 1956 to 1961. He concluded that there do appear to be significant economics in precautionary balances since cash varies less than proportionately with the assets of firms.

Whalen's (1965)[125] in his attempt to analyse business demand for cash utilised the cross section data for the single year, 1958-59. He estimated the parameters of:

$$M/MA = a_1 + b_1 S' / MA \quad \text{.................. (I)}$$

$$M/MA = a_1 + b_2 S' / MA + C\, S' / MA \quad \text{........... (II)}$$

where M is money, S′ is sales, and MA is total of money and income-earning monetary assets. Besides, he also estimated the parameters of two other equations:

$$\text{Log } M = \log a + b \log S' \quad \text{............... (III)}$$

$$\text{Log } M = \log a + b \log W/S' + C \log S' \quad \text{......... (IV)}$$

where W is the total assets of the firm. His results for equations (I) and (II) indicated the presence of substantial diseconomies in the transactions demand for cash, but, when equation (IV) was used, the regression co-efficient relating to cash and sales was less than 1.

De Allessi (1966)[126] studied the demand for money for British business firms by applying a methodology very much similar to Meltzer's. He used the market value of each firm's common stock instead of sales as a proxy for wealth as shown below:

$$\ln M_t = a_1 + b_1 \ln W_t + m_i$$

where M is the cash balances, W is wealth and m_i is the error term. The study mainly revealed that the quantity of money held by firm was positively related to its wealth and the wealth elasticity of money appears to be about one, supporting the results of Meltzer.

The study by Nadiri (1969)[127] was also based on quarterly time series data. According to Nadiri the demand for real cash balance is given by

$$M^* = f\ (C/W,\ V,\ X)$$

where M^* is the desired level of real cash balances, C is the user cost of capital services, W is the price of labour services, X is the expected level of output, and V is the opportunity cost of holding money. Nadiri observed that the income elasticities of real cash balances were consistently less than unity. This finding supported the theoretical propositions on Baumol and Tobin and contradicted Friedman's high income elasticity. The interest rate elasticity had a negative co-efficient and was statistically significant at the 5 per cent level of significance.

Ramamurthy (1976)[128] in his Working Capital Management had stressed the importance of maintaining adequate cash position planning the sources of cash and utilisation of cash is of paramount importance for successful cash management. Proper cash planning shall be applied for predicating cash inflow and outflow. The designing and implementation of cash control system calls for a variety of planning decisions like location of bank facilities, information process, transfer of funds and similar measures. The cash management system should be modified, at any time, to meet new and changing situations.

Bhole (1979)[129] made an empirical study of liquidity preference of corporate sector in India for the period 1951-74. He used the data relating to the functioning of the sample of non-financial, non-government medium and large public limited Companies in India. In this study regression models were fitted to the data to estimate the magnitudes of elasticities of different variables viz., sales income, rate of interest, price level, inventory holding and net receivables. He concluded that the income elasticity and price elasticity on corporate demand for money falls in Friedman's line of evidence on this subject.

Kamta Prasad and Sampath (1979)[130] investigated empirically the transactions demand for cash in the corporate sector of the Indian economy during the period 1950-51 to 1970-71. They observed that since the estimated value of transactions elasticity demand for majority of industries was less than unity, it indicates that there exists significant economics of scale in holding cash balances in the corporate sector.

Ashok Kumar Lahiri's (1981)[131] study on "Liquidity behaviour of Indian business firms" presents some independent evidence for the period, 1971-74 in support of the existence of economics of scale and inter-industry differences. He found that in majority of the industries the elasticity co-efficient is substantially less than unity. This indicates the existence of economics of scale in money.

Radhe S. Pradhan (1986)[132] in his work on Working Capital Management of Nepal Enterprise used econometric models to describe the demand for working capital and its various components. In this study, the demand for working capital has been viewed in a way similar to the demand for cash and inventories. The models used in this study are

$$Y^{*} = f(W) \quad \text{................ (I)}$$

$$Y^{*} = f(W, i_2) \quad \text{............... (II)}$$

$$Y^{*} = f(W, i_2, Cu) \quad \text{.............. (III)}$$

where W – Wealth

i_2 – Interest rate

Cu – Capacity utilisation rate

The regression results show that the levels of working capital and its components, an enterprise desired to hold depend not only on sales but on holding costs also. However, the inclusion of capacity utilisation in the models does not seem to have contributed much to the demand functions of working capital and its various components.

Studies on the Demand for Inventories

There is no controversy as to the fact that target inventory levels are functions of expected sales as indicated by almost all the studies on the demand for inventories by firms. The controversy arises about the cost of capital and other effects on inventory demand. Theoretically, the level of inventories of a firm would depend on the costs associated with holding the inventories.

Newton Robinson (1959)[133] studied interest rate effect on departmental store inventory holdings, but he did not find any effects of interest rate. Lovell (1964)[134] also reported incorrect signs of interest rate co-efficients in his regression explaining deflated durable and non-durable manufacturing inventory levels. Jon Joyce (1973)[135] in his cross section study found a negative co-efficient for short-term bank interest rate but the results were not statistically significant. Similarly, the two studies by T.C. Liu (1963)[136] and Paul V. Kuznets (1964)[137] also reported a negative statistically significant co-efficient on the interest rate.

Liberman (1980)[138] in his study examined the size and significance of the theoretically important cost of capital effect on inventory investment by utilising firm specific cost of capital measures in a pooled cross-section econometric analysis of inventory behaviour. The study hypothesized that desired inventories are a function of sales, the opportunity cost of holding inventories and in the case of goods produced to order, order back logs. The estimated equation was as:

$$\text{In } I_t = b_0 + b_1 \text{ In } S'_t + b_2 \text{ In } CK_t + b_3 \text{ In } OB_t + m_i$$

where I_t was the firms real inventory level in period t, S'_t was the level of sales, CK_t was the real cost of capital and OB_t was the real order backlog. His result showed that cost of capital co-efficients was statistically significant with theoretically correct signs. Similarly, sales co-efficient demonstrated support for economies of scale.

The Irvin Study (1981)[139] noticed that the estimated co-efficient on the capital cost measures were not only negatively signed but also they were statistically significant. The Akhtar study (1983)[140] also noticed that nominal interest rates had significant effects on the behaviour of inventories.

Recommendations of Working Capital Committees

In recent years banks have placed several restrictions on the flow of bank credit for working capital requirements to the industries. For this purpose of regulating and control of working capital loans, the RBI has taken several measures. Various committees and study groups were appointed to look into the matter and to suggest measures to regulate and control the liberal flow of bank credit for working capital requirements.

The Dehejia study (1969)[141] group found that in the absence of any restraint on bank credit, industry used to avail of bank credit much more than justified by production performance. The excessive dependence of industry on bank credit for working capital requirements is undesirable and the industry must find alternative means, particularly internal long-term sources for meeting a large portion of working capital. The study group also suggested that this would be possible for correcting the shortcomings of the present lending system of banks by introducing the mush needed discipline in credit disbursement and utilisation.

To achieve this object the Reserve Bank of India appointed the Tandon committee (1974)[142] to frame guidelines for follow up bank credit for working capital requirements. The committee has suggested norms for inventory and receivables. It suggested three methods for calculation of permissible bank credit limit for working capital.

I. Method : MPBF = 75% of (CA – CL_E)

II. Method : MBF = (75% OF CA) – (CL_E)

III. Method : MPBF = 75% of (CA – CCA) – (CL_E)

MPBF: Maximum Permissible Bank Finance, CA: Current Assets, CL_E: Current Liabilities Excluding Bank Finance, CCA: Core current Assets.

The methods are based on the principle that the working capital should increasingly be financed by the industries out of their own funds (internal long-term sources), this would bring about gradual reduction in bank credit. An analysis of the Tandon Committee suggestions leads to the conclusion that the norms suggested by the committee for holding of inventory levels were not suitable for the textile mills. To solve this problem the Indian Cotton Mills Federation (ICMF) submitted a memorandum which suggested changes in the norms to the Reserve Bank of India.

In July 1983, the Reserve Bank of India appointed the Pathak Committee (1983)[143] to examine the need for revision of the inventory norms laid down by the Tandom Committee. The committee has suggested revised norms in respect of composite, spinning and processing mills wherever applicable.

The Chore Committee (1979)[144] was appointed to review the cash credit system and to examine the prevailing style of bank credit and consider the effectiveness of the monitoring and follow-up system adopted by banks. The committee has suggested that in assessing bank credit limits, banks should follow the second method of lending recommended by the Tandon Committee.

The Marathe Committee (1983)[145] was appointed to review the working of cash authorisation scheme from the point of view of its operational aspects. The committee has observed that the basic purpose of the Credit Authorisation Scheme (CAS) is to ensure orderly credit management and improve the quality of bank lending so that all borrowings are in conformity with the policies and priorities laid down by the Reserve Bank of India.

Approaches Chosen for the Study

It is clear that the various authors have developed the various propositions such as management attitude towards risk, maturity schedule of debt, material savings in the economical use of capital, simultaneous treatment to each element of working capital, operating cycle concept, parallel monthly forecasts of liquidity and profitability and capital structure decisions, which can be useful in evaluating risk-return trade off of working capital management. In addition, the authors are of the view that the level of working capital is a function of sales and output.

It is also clear from the above references that various authors have viewed that maintaining proper liquidity together with its efficient handling should have favourable effects on long-run returns and it determines the survival or demise of an enterprise. Further, financial strength of the company is created and its credit reputation is sustained. Inadequate liquidity creates potential danger of technical insolvency. The various models such as, relation with operational and financial cashflows, discounted current ratio and portfolio-balance framework model are suggested to have better liquidity management. Further, the studies suggested that financial flexibility, sensitivity, innovation by financial managers and segmental financing are the best approach for future liquidity management. Further majority of the studies which deal exclusively with structure and utilisation of working capital in the context of Indian industries suggest that excessive investment in inventory, receivables and inadequacy of cash, and over-dependence of industries on bank credit are the main causes for the ineffective working capital management.

Further it is clear that the interest in the study of demand for money was aroused by Baumol, Tobin and Friedman, Frazer, Nadiri, Kamta Prasad and Ashok Kumar Lahiri observed economics of scale thereby supporting Baumol and Tobin, while Meltzer, Whalen, De Allessi and L.M. Bhole observed diseconomies of scale thereby supporting Friedman as far as the transaction demand for cash is concerned. Similarly, there is no unanimous finding as regards the effect of capital costs on the demand for cash. Among others, De Allessi and Nadiri showed the statistically significant effect of capital costs on the demand for cash, while Friedman did not find the same. Similarly it may be seen that effect of capital cost on inventory demand has been a controversial subject. Liu, Kuznets, Liberman, Irvine and Akhtar observed significant effects of capital costs on the demand for inventories, which Robinson, Lovell, Joyce did not observe the same. Similarly, some reported economies of scale with respect to holding inventories, while others did not report the same.

From the above discussion, it is clear that the different authors including economists, financial theorists, management scientists, and practising business executives have approached working capital management in different ways and at varying levels of analysis. These different approaches to working capital management improve with the emergence of more and more literature on the subject over time. Though there are various approaches, only a few of them can be considered in this study. The approaches that are included in the study cover assessing the structure and utilisation of working capital, structural determinants of working capital, assessing the financial liquidity position, impact of working capital ratio on profitability and estimating demand for working capital, in the selected automobile industry of India.

References

1. Jhon Sagan (May 1955), Towards a Theory of Working Capital Management, *The Journal of Finance*, pp. 121-129.
2. Walker, E.W. (Winter 1964), Towards a Theory of Working Capital, *The Engineering Economist*, pp. 21-35.
3. Van Horne, J.C. (Winter 1969), A Risk-Return Analysis of a firm's Working Capital Position, *The Engineering Economist*, pp. 71-88.
4. Howard, L.R. (May 1971), *The Engineering Economist*, p.1.
5. Knight, W.D. (Spring 1972), *The Engineering Economist*, pp.33-40.
6. Chakraborthy, S.K. (August 1973), Use of Operating Cycle Concept for Better Management of Working Capital, *The Economic and Political Weekly*, pp. 69-76.
7. Smith, K.V. (1974), An Overview of Working Capital Management, in *Management of Working Capital: A Reader*. New York: West Publishing Company, pp. 3-20.
8. Smith, K.V. (1974), Profitability Versus Liquidity Trade off in Working Capital Management, in *op.cit.*, pp. 409-422.
9. Bierman, H., et al. (March 1975), Ruin considerations: Optimal Working Capital and Capital Structure, *The Journal of Financial and Quantitative Analysis*, pp. 119-128.
10. Hampton, J.J. (June 1983), *Financial Decision Making*, New Delhi: Prentice Hall of India Pvt. Ltd, p.18.
11. Keown, A.J. et al. (1985), *Basic Financial Management*, New Delhi: Prentice Hall of India Pvt. Ltd, p.131.
12. Mall, C.P. and S.K.Singh (April-June, 1989), Management of Working Capital in a Public Sector Corporation – A Case Study, *IPE Journal*, pp. 23-33.

13. Chang, C.H., Dandapani, K and Prakash, A .J (1995), Aspects of Financial Management in Europe and Asia, *Management International Review,* Vol.35, special issue No. 2, pp. 105-117.
14. Sahu, R.K.(November 2002), A Simplified model for liquidity analysis of Paper companies, *The Management Accountant,* pp. 805-808.
15. Shanmugam, R. (July-September 2006), Liquidity – Profitability International ships: A Sectoral Analysis, *Udyog Pragati – The Journal for Practicing Managers,* pp. 38-43.
16. Paul Welter (1970), How to calculate savings possible through reduction of working capital?, *Financial Executive,* pp. 50-58.
17. Cossaboom, R.A. (May 1971), Let's Reassess the Profitability-Liquidity Trade off, *Financial Executive,* pp. 46-51.
18. Merville, J. and Tavis, L.A. (January, 1973), Optimum Working Capital Policies: A Chance Constrained Programming Approach, *The Journal of Financial and Quantitative Analysis,* pp. 47-59.
19. Fred Weston, J. and Engene Brigham, F. (1975), *Managerial Finance,* New York: The Dryden Press, pp.185.
20. Gentry, J.E. (1976), Management Perceptions of the Working Capital Process, *Faculty Working Paper,* College of Commerce and Business Administration, University of Illinois, Urbana.
21. Yardeni, E.E. (May, 1978), A Portfolio-Balance Model of Corporate Working Capital, *The Journal of Finance,* pp. 535-552.
22. Ramamoorthy, V.E. (1978), *Working Capital Management,* Institute of Financial Management Research, Madras.
23. Lambrix, R.L. and Singhvi, S.S. (June, 1979), Managing the Working Capital Cycle, *Financial Executive,* pp. 32-41.
24. Kulshreshta, N.K. (August 1980), Corporate Liquidity – X -Rayed, *The Management Accountant,* Vol. 15, No. 8, pp. 331-34.
25. Pancras, U. (November 1981), Time Adjusted Current Ratio, *The Management Accountant,* pp. 524-526.
26. Banerjee, B. (July 1982), Corporate Liquidity and Profitability in India. *Research Bulletin,* Institute of Cost Works Accountant of India, pp. 225-234.
27. Johnson, J.M, Campbell, D.R. and Savoie, I.M. (October 1983), Corporate liquidity: A comparison of two recessions, *Financial Executive,* pp. 18-22.
28. Sharma, S.N. and Reddy, A.V. (Auguest 1985), Corporate Liquidity; A Case Study, *The Management Accountant,* pp. 415-419.

29. Mukherjee, A.K. (1988), *Management of Working Capital in Public Enterprises*, Vohra publishers & Distributors, Allahabad.

30. Reddy, B.R. (January and July 1988), Working Capital Management in Co-operative Sugar Mills in Tamil Nadu, *Research Bulletin*, pp. 37-45

31. Hampton, J.J. and Wagner, C. (1989), *Working Capital Management*. New York: John Wiley & Sons.

32. Vijayakumar, A. and Venkatachalam, A. (1995), Working capital and profitability – An empirical analysis, *The Management Accountant*, pp. 748-750.

33. Mallik, A. K. and Sur, D. (1999), Working Capital Management: A Case Study of Hindustan Lever Ltd, *Finance India*, pp. 857-871.

34. Dutta and Joginder Singh, (2000), "Working Capital Management of Horticulture Industry in H.P – A Case Study of HPMC", Unpublished thesis, Himachal Pradesh University.

35. Sarvanan, P. (2001), A Study of Working Capital Management in Non-Banking Finance Companies, *Finance India*, Vol.XV, No.3, pp. 987-994.

36. Debasish Sur, Joydeep Biswas and Prasenjit Ganguly (2001), Liquidity Management in Indian Private Sector Enterprises: A case study of Indian alumium producing industry, *Indian Journal of Accounting*, Vol.32, pp.68-76.

37. Debasish Sur, (June 2001), Liquidity Management : An overview of four companies in Indian Power Sector, *The Management Accountant*, pp. 407-412.

38. Sathyamoorthi, C.R. (2002), Management of Working Capital in Selected Co-operatives in Botswana, *Finance India*, Vol.16, No.3, pp.105-125.

39. Khatik, S.K and Pradeep Kumar Singh (2003), Liquidity Management in EICHER Ltd., – A case study, *The Management Accountant*, pp. 217-220.

40. Bardia, S.C. (2004), Liquidity Management – A case study of Steel Authority of India Ltd, *The Management Accountant*, pp. 463-467.

41. Chakraborty, P.K. (2004), Managing Corporate Liquidity and Financial Flexibility: Different Approach, *The Management Accountant*, Vol.39, No.8, pp. 653-655.

42. Reddy, Y.V. and Patkar S.B. (2004), Working Capital and Liquidity Management in Factoring: A comparative study on SBI and Canbank Factors, *The Management Accountant*, Vol. 39, No.5, pp. 373-378.

43. Narware, P.C. and Vivek Sharma (2004), Liquidity Management of Hindustan Petroleum Corporation Ltd., - An empirical study, *The Management Accountant,* Vol.39, No.3. pp. 201-203

44. Subhas Chandra Sarkar and Amalendu Bhunla (2004), Liquidity Trend Analysis: A case study of TISCO, *Southern Economist,* Vol.43, No.9, pp.15-17.

45. Singh, P.K. (2004), Working Capital Management in Lupin Laboratories Ltd – A Case Study, *The Management Accountant,* pp.534-539.

46. Pandey, I.M. (2005), *Financial Management,* (9th Edition), New Delhi: Vikas publishing House Pvt Ltd., pp. 579-592.

47. Amit K.Mallik, Debasish Sur and Debdas Rakshit (2005), Working Capital and Profitability: A study on their relationship with reference to selected companies in Indian Pharmaceutical Industry, *GITAM Journal of Management,* Vol.3, No:2, pp. 51-62.

48. Santimoy Patra (2005), Liquidity Vs Profitability, *Indian Journal of Accounting,* Vol.xxxv(2), pp.39-43.

49. Rajendran, P. and Ramesh, D. (March 2006), Liquidity Management of Tamilnadu Tourism Development Corporation Ltd –An Empirical Study, *The Management Accountant,* pp. 205-208.

50. Sushma Vishnani and Bhupesh Kr Shah (2006), Liquidity Vs Profitability – A detailed study in perspective of Indian consumer electronics industry, *Pranjana,* Vol.9, No.2, pp.13-19.

51. Kannadhasan, M. (2007), Working capital management in a Public Limited Company – A case study, *The ICFAI Journal of Management Research,* Vol. VI, No.5, pp. 20-33.

52. Sam Luther, C.T. (2007), Liquidity, risk and profitability analysis – A case study of Madras Cements Ltd, *The Management Accountant,* Vol.42, No.10, pp. 784-789.

53. National Council of Applied Economic Research (NCAER, 1966), Structure of Working Capital, New Delhi.

54. Nalini Ambegaokar (October 1969), Working capital requirements and availability of bank credit (Indian Processing and Manufacturing Industries), *Reserve Bank of India Bulletin,* pp. 1535-1553.

55. Mishra, R.K. (1975), *Problems of Working Capital* (With special reference to selected public undertakings in India), Bombay: Somaiya Publications Pvt. Ltd.

56. Chakraborty, P.K. (2004), Managing Corporate Liquidity and Financial Flexibility: Different Approach, *The Management Accountant*, Vol.39, No.8, pp. 653-655.

57. Bhattcharya, S.K. and Raghavachari, M. (March 1977), Determinants of effective Working Capital Management: A Discriminant Analysis Approach, *Working paper No. 151*, Indian Institute of Management, Ahmedabad.

58. Vijaya Saradhi, S.P. (June-December 1980), Problems of Working Capital Management in Public Enterprises, *The Indian Journal of Accounting*, Vol. X, pp. 65-75.

59. Mishra, M. (October 1980), Problems of Working Capital Management during Inflation, *The Chartered Accountant*, pp.298-302.

60. Agarwal, N.K. (1983), *Management of Working Capital*, New Delhi: Sterling Publishers Pvt. Ltd.

61. Mukherjee, A.K (Jan-March 1985), Management of Working Capital of Central Government Undertakings in India, *IPE Journal*, pp.36-48.

62. Yadav, R.A. (1986), Working Capital Management – A Parametric Approach. *The Chartered Accountant*, pp. 952-955.

63. Sharma, K.K and Agarwal, R.K (January 1986), Working Capital Management in State Transport Undertaking, *Journal of Transport Management*, pp. 17-20.

64. Subir Nath Sarkar (July 1987), Liquidity Management in the Public Sector – a Case Study of a Government of West Bengal Undertaking, *The Management Accountant*, pp. 496-498.

65. Sarkar, J.B. and Saha, S.N. (1987), Profitability crisis and working capital management in the public sector in India: A Case Study, *The Management Accountant*, pp. 328-333.

66. Panda, J. and Satapathy, A.K (1988), *Working capital structure of Private Enterprises: A study of cement industry*, New Delhi, Discover Publishing House.

67. Mukherjee, A.K. (1988), *Management of Working Capital in Public Enterprises*, Allahabad: Vohra Publishers & Distributor.

68. Garai, S. and Mallik, A. (July, 1988), Role of Working Capital in Manufacturing Industries—Case Study in Indian perspective, *Research Bulletin*, pp. 46-54.

69. Verma, H.L. (1989), *Management of Working Capital*, New Delhi: Deep & Deep Publications.

70. Harbir Singh (1990), Management of Working Capital: A case study of Modi Sugar Mills, Modinagar, Ph.D. Dissertation, Meerut

University, Published in A survey of Research in Commerce and Management, pp. 477-483.

71. Panigrahi, J. (October 1990), Working capital management of large Indian companies *The Management Accountant,* pp. 653-656.
72. Agarwal, J.D. (1991), Goal programming Model for Working Capital Management, in *Working Capital Management* (Analysis & Cases), Jaipur: Research Development Association, pp. 67-80.
73. Gupta, S.P. (1991), Working Capital Control through Variance Analysis, in *Working Capital Management* (Analysis & Cases), Jaipur: Research Development Association, pp. 143-145.
74. Rao, K.V. and Chinta Rao (April-June 1991), Evaluating Efficiency of Working Capital Management – Are the conventional techniques adequate?, *Decision,* Vol. 18, No. 2, pp. 81-98.
75. Sushil.K.Jain (May, 1991), Working Capital Management, *The Management Accountant,* pp. 507-509.
76. Banerjee, D and Hazra, M.K (May, 1999), Working capital Management in Grasim Industries Limitied: A case study, *The Management Accountant,* pp. 336-340.
77. Basu, S.N. (May 1992), Working Capital Management –Type Companies, *The Management Accountant,* pp. 331-333.
78. Vijayakumar, A., Sivasubramanian, K. and Venkatachalam, A. (April 1994), Working Finance in National Cooperative Sugar Mills Ltd, Tamilnadu – A case study, *Management & Labour Studies,* Vol. 19, No. 2. pp. 132-143.
79. Vijayakumar, A. (1996), Working Capital Management in Sugar Industry in Tamilnadu, Ph.D Dissertation, Bharathiar University, Coimbatore.
80. Indrasena Reddy, P. and Someswar Rao, K. (1996), Working capital Management in Public Sector Undertaking – A case study, *The Management Accountant,* Vol.31, No. 9, pp. 643-645.
81. Vijayakumar, A. (April-June 1996), The Transactions Demand for Working Capital in Indian PSUs: Some theoretical and empirical results, *IPE Journal,* pp. 92-100.
82. Shankar, K. (1996), Developments in Working Capital Finance, *The Management Accountant,* Vol.31, No. 9, pp. 689-694.
83. Mishra, R.K. and Kar, N.C. (1997), Management Working Capital in ECIL, *Working Capital Management,* pp. 327-334.

84. Carg, P.K (1997), Financing and Utilisation of WC in Public Sector Industrial Enterpreises, *Working Capital Management*, pp. 127-135.

85. Mallik, A.K and Sur, D. (1998), Working capital and profitability: A case study in interrelation, *The Management Accountant*, pp. 805-809.

86. Khan Mohd Amir (1985), Working Capital Management at Escorts Ltd, Unpublished thesis, Aligarh Muslim University, Aligarh.

87. Subramanya, Sarma.M and Thiruvengala Chary (1999), Working Capital Management in VST – An Appraisal, *Finance India* Vol.XIII, No.1, March 1999, pp.71-79.

88. Sivaram Prasad R.(1999), Working Capital Management in Indian Paper Industry, Unpublished thesis, Nagarjuna University, Nagarjuna Nagar.

89. Anand, M. (2001), Working capital performance of corporate India: An Empirical Survey, *Management & Accounting Research*, Vol. 4, pp. 35-65.

90. Surendra S.Yadav, Jain P.K. and Ashish K.Rastogi, (July 2001), Working Capital Management in oil industry in India, *The Management Accountant*, pp.511-516.

91. Rabiul Alam, S.M. and Syed Zabid Hossain (2001), Aspects of Inventory Management in shipbuilding industry in Bangladesh, *The Management Accountant*, September, pp.699-706.

92. Manoj Anand and Gupta, C.P (January-June 2003), Working Capital Management of Corporate India: An Empirical Survey for the year 2000-2001, *Management & Accounting Research*, pp. 11-45.

93. Parmar (2003), Performance evaluation through inventory management (A comparative study of G.S.F.C & G.N.F.C), *Indian Journal of Accounting*, Vol.xxxiii, June, pp.64-68.

94. Ghosh, S.K and Maji, S.G. (2003), Utilisation of current assets and operating profitability: An Empirical study on Cement and Tea industries in India, *Indian Journal of Accounting*, pp. 52-55.

95. Satyanarayana Chary and Venkateshwarlu (2003), Working Capital Analysis (A case study of Sri Venkata Narasimha Solvent Oils Ltd), *Udyog Pragati*, Vol.27, No.3, pp.38-50.

96. Narware, P.C. (June 2004), Working Capital and Profitability – An empirical analysis, *The Management Accountant*, pp. 491–495.

97. Sanjay J. Bhayani (2004), Working capital and Profitability Relationship (A case study of Gujarat Ambuja Cement ltd), *SCMS Journal of Indian Management*, Vol.1, No.2, pp. 98-107

98. Parasuram, N.R. (2004), Working Capital Practices in Leading Pharmaceutical Companies – A view of the credit policy and profitability, *The Management Accountant,* Vol. 39, No. 12, pp. 998-1005.

99. Ghosh and Maji (2004), Working Capital Management Efficiency: A study on the Indian Cement Industry, *The Management Accountant,* Vol. 39, No.5, pp. 363-372.

100. Khatik, S.K and Singh, P.K. (January 2004), Working Capital Management in Indian Farmers Fertiliser Cooperative Limited – A case study, *The Management Accountant,* pp. 19-25.

101. Rabiul Alam, S.M. and Zabid Hossain, S. (February 2004), Management of Working Finance: A study on the Shipbuilding Industry in Bangladesh, *The Management Accountant,* pp. 111-117.

102. Santanu Kr.Ghosh and Santi Gopal Maji, (May 2004), Working Capital Management Efficiency: A study on the Indian Cement Industry, *The Management Accountant,* pp. 363-372.

103. Sudarshan, R. (2004), Analysis of inventory behaviour-an application model for Chemicals and Pharmaceutical enterprises, *The Management Accountant,* pp.868-872.

104. Mukhopadhyay, D (2004), Working Capital Management in Heavy Engineering Firms – A case study, *The Management Accountant,* pp.317-323.

105. Sudarsana Reddy, G., Sivarami Reddy, C., and Mohan Reddy, P. (2004), Debtors' management: A case study of Andhara Pradesh paper industry, *The Management Accountant,* pp. 265-274.

106. Sudipta Ghosh (2005), Performance Appraisal through Inventory Management (A case of study of Stewarks and Lloyds of India Ltd), *The Management Accountant,* pp.560-562.

107. Amit K. Chakraborty (2005), Working Capital Management: An Empirical Study, *Southern Economist,* Vol. 43, No.19, pp. 23-27.

108. Patel, D.M (January 2005), Analysis of Working Capital (A Case study of Colour-Chem Limited), *ACCST Research Journal,* pp. 13-21.

109. Rais Abmad and Ali Ghufran (June-December 2005), Analytical study of Working Capital Management of Marketing Cooperative Societies, *Management & Account Research,* pp. 35-51.

110. Ioannis Lazaridis and Dimitrios Tryfonidis (2006), Relationship between Working Capital Management and Corporate profitability, *Journal of Financial Management and Analysis,* Vol. 19, No.1, pp. 26-35.

111. Amir Jafar and Debasish Sur (2006), Efficiency of Working Capital Management in Indian Public Enterprises during the post liberalisation Era, A case study of NTPC, The ICFAI *Journal of Management Research,* Vol. V, No. 6, pp. 56-63.

112. Sanjay, J.Bhayani (2006), Assets Turnover and Profitability, *Indian Journal of Accounting,* Vol.xxxvi (2), pp. 1-7.

113. Sukhdev Singh (2006), Inventory Control Practices in IFFCO, *The Management Accountant,* July, Vol.41, No.7, pp.577-580.

114. Manoj Anand and Keshav Malhotra, (January 2007), Working Capital Management Performance of Corporate India: An Empirical Study, *Applied Finance,* pp. 46-80.

115. Arindam Ghosh, (January 2007), Working Capital Management Practices in some selected industries in India, *The Management Accountant,* pp. 60 –67.

116. Nand Kishore Sharma, (May 2007), Current Assets Accounting and Control, *The Chartered Accountant,* pp. 1706-1712.

117. Azhagaiah, R. and Gejalakshmi, S. (2007), Working–Capital Management–Efficiency, Udyog Pragan, Vol.31, No.3, pp. 15-20

118. Pradeep Singh (2008), Inventory and Working Capital Management: An Empirical Analysis, The ICFAI *Journal of Accounting Research,* Vol.VII, No.2, April, pp.53-73.

119. Kaushik Chakraborty, G. (2008), Working Capital and Profitability: An Empirical Analysis of their Relationship with Reference to Selected Companies in the Indian Pharmaceutical Industry, *The ICFAI University Press,* pp.41-59.

120. Baumol, W. (November 1952), The Transaction Demands for Cash: An Inventory Theoretic Approach, *The Quarterly Journal of Economics,* pp. 545-566.

121. Tobin, J. (August 1956), The Interest Elasticity of Transactions Demand for Cash, *The Review of Economics and Statistics,* pp. 241-247.

122. Friedman, M. (August 1959), The Demand for Money: Some Theoretical and Empirical Results, *The Journal of Political Economy,* pp. 327-351.

123. Meltzer, A.H. (August 1963), The Demand for Money: A Cross Section study of Business firms, *The Quarterly Journal of Economics,* pp. 405-422.

124. Frazer, W.J. (April, 1964), Financial Structure of Manufacturing Corporations and the Demand for Money: Some Empirical Findings, *The Journal of Political Economy,* pp. 176-183.

125. Whalen, E.L. (September 1965), A Cross-Section Study of Business Demand for Cash, *The Journal of Finance,* pp. 423-443.

126. Louis De Allessi (Auguest 1966), The Demand for Money: A Cross-Section study of British Business Firms, *Economica,* pp. 288-302.

127. Nadiri, M.I. (May, 1969), The Determinants of Real Cash Balance in the US Total Manufacturing Sector, The Quarterly Journal of Economics, pp. 173-196.

128. Ramamurthy. V.E. (1976), *Working Capital Management,* Institute for Financial Management and Research, Madras, pp. 78-86.

129. Bhole, L.M. (1979), An Empirical Study of Liquidity Preference of Corporate Sector in India, 1951-1974, *The Indian Economic Journal,* Vol. 27, No. 1, pp. 65-80.

130. Kamta Prasad and Sampath, R.K. (July-September 1979), Business Demand for Money in India—A Temporal Cross-Section Analysis, *The Indian Economic Journal,* Vol. 27, No. 1, pp. 43-62.

131. Ashok Kumar Lahiri (1981), Liquidity Behaviour on Indian Business Firms, *The Indian Economic Journal,* Vol. 29, No. 1, pp. 1-9.

132. Pradhan, R.S. (1986), *Management of Working Capital,* New Delhi: National Book Organisation, pp. 86-94.

133. Robinson, N.Y. (June 1959), *The Acceleration Principle: Review,* pp. 348-358.

134. Lovell, M.C. (1964), Determinants of Inventory Behaviour, *In Models of Income Behaviour* (Ed.) Edward F. Denison and Lawrence R. Klein, New York.

135. Joyce, J.M. (October 1973), Cost of Capital and Inventory Investment: Further Evidence, *The Southern Economic Journal,* pp. 323-329.

136. Liu, T.C. (July 1963), An Exploratory Quarterly Model of Effective Demand in the Post-war US Economy, *The Econometrica,* pp. 301-308.

137. Kuznets, P.W. (1964), Financial Determinants of Manufacturing Inventory Behavour; A Quarterly Study Based on US Estimates, *Yale Economic Essays,* pp. 331-369.

138. Charles Lieberman (August 1980), Inventory Demand and Cost of Capital Effects, *The Review of Economics and Statistics,* pp. 348-356.

139. Qwen Irvine, F. (September 1981), Retail Inventory Investment and the Cost of Capital, *The American Economic Review,* p. 633.

140. Akhtar, M.A. (June 1983), Effects of Interest Rates and Inflation on Aggregate Inventory Investment in US, *The American Economic Review,* pp. 319-328.

141. Dehejia, V.T. (November 1969), Report of the Committee. Reserve Bank of India Bulletin, Bombay: Reserve Bank of India, pp. 1972-1978.

142. Prakash Tandon (1974), *Report of the Study Group to Frame Guidelines for Follow-up of Bank Credit,* Bombay: Reserve Bank of India, pp. 20-21.

143. Pathak, J.N. (1983), *Report of the Committee,* Reserve Bank of India Bulletin. Bombay, Reserve Bank of India, pp. 15-22.

144. Chore, K.B. (1979), *Report of the Working Group to Review the System of Cash Credit,* Bombay: Reserve Bank of India, pp. 26-52.

145. Marathe, S.S. (1983), *Report of the Committee to Review the Working of the Credit Authorisation Scheme,* Bombay: Reserve Bank of India, pp. 20-27.

3

Method of Analysis

In research, the methodology needs to be cautiously designed to capitulate results that are as objective as realistic. An able-bodied comprehensible *modus operandi* empowers the new-fangled research investigator re-examine the study milieu. Good methodology follows the standards of the established conventions. For the present study, a number of indispensable inimitabilities of the research methodology skirmishing the application magnitude and research rationalisation of each one are defined here in this chapter.

The ensuing paragraphs in this chapter deal with the methodology adopted in selection and analysis of data for this study. It outlines the objective and scope of the study, procedure followed for selection of the sample and the collection of data, classification of the sample and the technique followed in analysing the data for the period of study. Further, the hypotheses set and limitations of the study have also been dealt herein.

Objectives of the Study

The present study in general aims at making a comparative study of working capital management performance in commercial vehicles, passenger cars and multiutility vehicles and two and three wheelers sectors of Indian automobile industry. The specific objectives of the study are:

1. To examine the structure, source and utilisation of working capital and its components;

2. To estimate the risk-return analysis of working capital position;
3. To assess the liquidity position;
4. To assess the impact of working capital ratios on profitability; and
5. To estimate transactions demand functions of working capital and its various components on efficiency in utilisation of working capital in the selected units of the automobile industry in India.

Research Design

It is not possible in practice for an individual research worker to approach all the bits and pieces in the universe. Researchers select only a small amount of bits pieces from the universe for the purpose of the study on the basis of stratified sampling. The sample so selected constitutes the sample design for the purpose. A research design is a definite plan for obtaining a sample from a given population. Research design means a sketch or a drawing of a research project's structure. It comprises a series of prior pronouncements that, taken together, provide a roadmap for carrying out a research project. The research design of the present study is outlined hereunder.

Selection of Sample

Keeping in view the scope of the study, it is decided to include all the companies under automobile industry working before or from the year 1992-93 to 2006-07. But, owing to several constraints such as non-availability of financial statements or non-working of a company in a particular years etc., the researcher is compelled to restrict the number of sample companies to 17. Therefore, this study is *expost facto* based on survey method making a survey of seventeen companies in Indian automobile industry. There are 26 companies operating in the Indian automobile industry. The companies under automobile industry are classified into three sectors namely; commercial vehicles, passenger cars and multiutility vehicles and two- and three-wheelers. The details of the sector with the available companies of Indian automobile industry are presented in Table 3.1.

Table 3.1

Total Number of Companies Available in Indian Automobile Industry

S.No	*Sectors*	*Total companies available*	*15 years data available companies*
1	Commercial vehicles	5	5
2	Passenger cars and Multiutility vehicles	8	3
3	Two- and three-wheelers	13	9
	Total	26	17

Source: Prowess Database, 2007.

All the three sectors have been selected for the purpose of the study. The selected sectors include 26 companies. Out of 26 companies, five are under commercial vehicles, eight under passenger cars and multiutility vehicles and 13 under two and three wheelers sector. Out of 26 companies of the selected sectors, 15 years data is available for 17 companies only. Therefore, all the 17 companies are included in the sample. It accounts for 69.23 per cent of the total companies available in the Indian automobile industry. The selected 17 companies include five under commercial vehicles, three under passenger cars and multiutility vehicles and nine under two- and three-wheelers sectors. A list of companies selected included in the present study along with the year of incorporation, ownership and its market share is presented in Table 3.2..

It is evident from Table 3.2 that the sample company represents 98.74 percentage of market share in commercial vehicles, 87.08 percentage in passenger cars and multiutility vehicles and 99.81 percentage in two- and three-wheelers. Thus, the findings based on the occurrence of such representative sample may be presumed to be true representative of automobile industry in the country.

Table 3.2
List of Sample Companies included in the Present Study

S.No	Sectors / companies	Year of incorporation	Ownership	Market share (%)	Total market share (%)
Commercial Vehicles (5)					
1.	Ashok Leyland Ltd	1956	Hinduja Group	35.62	
2.	Tata Motors Ltd	1956	Tata Group	34.22	
3.	Bajaj Tempo Ltd	1958	Firodia Group	11.50	
4.	Eicher Motors Ltd	1982	Eicher Group	10.65	
5.	Swaraj Mazda Ltd	1983	State and Private Sector	6.75	98.74
Passenger Cars and Multiutility Vehicles (3)					
6	Hindustan Motors Ltd	1942	Birla C.K.Group	8.31	
7	Mahindra & Mahindra Ltd	1945	Mahindra and Mahindra	42.17	
8	Maruti Udyog Ltd	1981	Private (Foreign)	36.60	87.08
Two- and Three-Wheelers (9)					
9	Bajaj Auto Ltd	1945	Bajaj Group	18.80	
10	LML Ltd	1972	LML Group	11.58	
11	Maharastra Scooters Ltd	1975	Bajaj Group	7.80	
12	TVS Motor Company Ltd	1982	TVS Group	12.93	
13	Kinetic Motors Ltd	1984	Firodia Group	11.75	
14	Hero Honda Motors Ltd	1984	Hero (Munsals) Groups	10.54	
15	Kinetic Engineering Ltd	1970	Firodia Group	9.72	
16	Majestic Auto Ltd	1986	Hero Group	9.04	
17	Scooters India Ltd	1972	Central Govt. Commercial Enterprise	7.65	99.81

Period of Study

The period 1992-93 to 2006-07 is selected for this study of the Indian automobile industry. This 15 years period is chosen in order to have a fairly long, cyclically well balanced period, for which a reasonably homogeonous, reliable and uptodate financial data would be available. Further, the span chosen for the study is the period of the beginning of liberalisation measures introduced by the Government of India. Hence, the period 1992-93 to 2006-07 is an era of growth of working capital management in the manufacturing sector, particularly automobile industry and has got genuine economic significance of its own.

Source of Data

The study is mainly based on secondary data. The major source of data analysed and interpreted in this study related to all those companies selected is collected from "PROWESS" database, which is the most reliable on the empowered corporate database of Centre for Monitoring Indian Economy (CMIE). It contains a highly normalised database built on a sound understanding of disclosure in India on around 12,000 companies, which include public, private, cooperative and joint sector companies. The database provides financial statements, ratio analysis, funds flow, cash flow, product profiles, returns and risk on the stock market, etc.

Besides prowess databases, relevant secondary data have also been collected from BSE Stock Exchange Official Directory, CMIE Publications, Annual Survey of Industry, Business newspapers, Reports on Currency and Finance, Libraries of various Research Institutions, through Internet etc. The study required variety of data therefore, websites like http://indiainfoline.com, www.indiastat.com and www.google.com have been comprehensively searched.

For this study, a major part of data come from secondary sources. Data have been collected in raw form and then it is made suitable for analysis as per the methodology defined for the purpose.

Data Analysis

The financial and statistical analysis approach plays a vital role in the financial environment. To enjoy the benefit of financial and statistical analysis researcher has collected, assembled and correlated the data, classified the data appropriately and condensed them into a related data series; stated the resultant information in a comprehensive form, text, tables and analysed and interpreted the reported data. The financial and statistical techniques applied in the study are given below.

In the course of analysis in this study, use of various accounting and statistical techniques have been made. Accounting technique includes ratio analysis, while among statistical techniques the arithmetic mean ($\overline{X}$), co-efficient of variation (CV), test of significance ('t' test), trend indices, simple growth rates, correlation co-efficient (*r*), co-efficient of determination (R^2), linear regression equations, analysis of times series, chi-square test and analysis of variance have been applied through EXCEL, SX and SPSS statistical software. In addition, multiple regression and discriminant analysis were also applied using financial ratio as variables. Econometric models are used to describe the demand for working capital and its various components.

Ratio Analysis

Ratio analysis is regarded as one of the best tools in analysis and comparing the time series accounting data of different firms. That is why it has been extensively used in the present study. Various ratios are computed in order to analyse the size, composition and circulation of working capital and its various components (inventory, receivables and cash) have been explained at the relevant places in different chapters. However, in this study the use of ratios has not been made in the course of analysis directly. To make the analysis and interpretation more precise and accurate, the values of X, CV and '*t*' have been computed from the ratios.

Arithmetic mean (X)

It gives a single value to describe the whole data. It has been obtained by adding the values of all observations and dividing it by the number of observations.

$$\overline{X} = \Sigma x/N$$

where Σx – Sum of variables and N- Number of observations.

Co-efficient of variations (CV)

It is used in problems which requires to compare the variability of two or more than two series. The series, for which the co-efficient of variations is greater, is said to be more variable or conversely less consistent, less uniform, less stable or less homogeneous. On the other hand, the series for which co-efficient of variations is less, is said to be less variable or more consistent, more uniform, more stable or more homogeneous. In ratio analysis of financial data, less co-efficient of variation in a ratio is taken to mean relatively better control of the management on that ratio.

$$CV = \sigma/\overline{X}$$

where σ – Standard deviation and $\overline{X}$ is the mean.

't' test

Along with the $\overline{X}$ and C.V values for each group of ratios, the values of 't' static have been computed in order to determine whether the mean of a sample (particular unit) deviates significantly from population (Industry) mean.

$$t = \frac{(\overline{X} - \mu)}{S} \times \sqrt{N}$$

where $\overline{X}$ is the mean and S is the standard deviation of the sample with size N and μ is the population mean.

If the calculated value of 't' exceeds the tabulated value, it indicates that the difference between $\overline{X}$ and μ is significant. If it is less than the table value, the difference between $\overline{X}$ and μ is not significant; hence, the sample distribution closely resembles the population distribution with mean μ.

SIMPLE GROWTH RATES

In order to see at what rate the growth has taken place in the working capital and its various components in relation to sales during the period under study, simple growth rates and average growth rates have been computed.

$$g = \frac{Y_t - Y_{t-1}}{Y_{t-1}} \times 100$$

where g is the growth rate and Y_t and Y_{t-1} are the values of variable Y in time *t* (current year) and time $_{t-1}$ (previous year) respectively.

TREND INDICES

In order to compute the index of change in variable, the following formula has been used:

$$I_t \frac{Y_t}{Y_0} \times 100$$

where Y_t is the value of the variable in the year *t* for which the index is to be computed, Y_0 is the value of the variable in the base year. In order to measure the change in the relative proportion of various components of the working capital to the total, such indices have been computed.

ANALYSIS OF TIME SERIES

Time series analysis is used to detect patterns of change in statistical information over regular intervals of time. For the analysis of working capital of automobile industry of India, the secular trend values are proposed to be computed by the method of least square at relevant places.

CHI-SQUARE TEST

The chi-square test is the simplest and most widely used non-parametric test in statistical work. Symbolically,

$$\text{Chi-square} = \Sigma\ (O - E)^2 / E$$

where 'O' refers to the observed frequencies and 'E' refers to the expected frequencies. The calculated value of chi-square is compared with the table value of chi-square for given degrees of freedom at a certain specified level of significance. If at the stated level the calculated value of chi-square is more than the table value of chi-square, the difference between expected and observed values is considered to be significant, i.e., it could not have arisen due to chance factor. The technique of chi-square is applied for the analysis of working capital trend.

Analysis of Variance

The analysis of variance has been developed specially to test the hypothesis whether the means of several samples have significant difference or not. From this technique, one is able to determine whether the samples have the same mean as the population from which they have been drawn. The technique of analysis of variance is proposed to be applied for the analysis of working capital trends and liquidity analysis.

Linear Regression Analysis

To make future projections of dependent variables (such as working capital, inventory and receivables) for a given value of independent variable (sales) possible, the linear regression equation ($Y = a + bX$) has been used. Further, in this part of the analysis, the values of correlation co-efficient (r), co-efficient of determination (R^2) and 't' test have been computed in order to ascertain the closeness or relationship between dependent and independent variables.

The Discriminant Analysis

The use of ratio analysis to judge the liquidity position of the enterprises is not free from certain limitations. The limitations arise from the fact that the methodology is basically univariate; that is, each ratio is examined in isolation. Due to this, the financial analyst has to use his own judgement to assess the combined effects of two or more ratios[1]. A linear multiple discriminant analysis has been applied in finance to problems involving more than two groups. Altman[2] has applied the discriminant analysis in predicting bankruptcy but here it is applied in operational adequacy of working capital and liquidity predication context. This study considers a simple case in which two variables X_1 and X_2 are used to discriminate between two groups – good and poor risks. The two variables used are networking capital in terms of monthly operational requirements (X_1)and net working capital in terms of monthly sales requirements (X_2) in the case of operational adequacy of working capital and also current ratio (X_1) and liquid ratio (X_2) in the case of liquidity assessment. Let

$$Z = aX_1 + bX_2 \qquad \text{... (1.1)}$$

be a linear combination of X_1 and X_2. The problem is to determine the values of 'a' and 'b' by means of past data and some criterion that proves 'Z' useful as an index for discriminating among members of the two groups[3]. In this study, discriminate analysis has been performed for all the selected years. However, its limitation is that only two variables are being considered.

Econometric Models

In this study, econometric models are used to describe the demand for working capital and its various components by Indian automobile industry. The demand for working capital has been viewed in a way similar to the demand for cash and inventories. Following Keynes[4], it is assumed that there are three motives for holding working capital: (i) the transaction motive; (ii) the precautionary motive; and (iii) the speculative motive. Other things remaining same, transactions and precautionary working capital balances are both similar functions of the volume of sales and therefore are treated as a single variable. For convenience, the demand for 'transactions and precautionary working capital balances' henceforth will be referred to as 'transactions demand for working capital'. Having established the motives for holding working capital, the next step is to specify the variables which influence them. The decisions about the aggregate amount working capital and its various components to be held may be regarded as subject to wealth constraint. In this study, wealth is defined in terms of sales (S). As a first approximation to the theory, the function may be written as

$$Y_1 = f(S) \quad \ldots (1.2)$$

$$Y_2 = f(S) \quad \ldots (1.3)$$

$$Y_3 = f(S) \quad \ldots (1.4)$$

$$Y_4 = f(S) \quad \ldots (1.5)$$

$$Y_5 = f(S) \quad \ldots (1.6)$$

where

Y_1 - Real cash
Y_2 - Real inventories
Y_3 - Real receivables
Y_4 - Real gross working capital
Y_5 - Real net working capital
S - Real sales

In an empirical investigation, equations (1.2) to (1.6) take the following form.

$$Y^* = KS^b e^u \quad \ldots (1.7)$$

where Y^* denotes Y_1 to Y_5. Taking the logarithm of this equation (1.7) gives

$$\text{Log } Y^* = \log K + \log S + u_i \quad \ldots (1.8)$$

So far the opportunity cost of working capital to enterprises has been ignored. A review of the empirical works on the demand for cash and inventories suggests that the opportunity cost of capital should be included as an explanatory variable in the models. Therefore, the opportunity cost of working capital and its various components measured by the short-term interest rates of Indian commercial banks (i_2), has been included in the models. Equations (1.2) to (1.6) can now be stated as

$$Y^* = f(S, i_2) \quad \ldots (1.9)$$

Similarly, equation (1.7) takes the form

$$Y^{*} = KS^{b}\, i_2^{\,b}\, e^{u} \qquad \ldots (1.10)$$

Taking the logarithm of this equation (1.10) gives

$$\text{Log } Y^{*} = \log K + b_1 \log S + b_2 \log i_2 + u_i \qquad \ldots (1.11)$$

Where b_1 and b_2 are elasticities of Y^{*} with respect to the explanatory variable of the models. The above models assume reasonable a priori hypothesis of

$$\partial y/\partial S > 0 \text{ and } \partial y/\partial i2 < 0 \qquad \ldots (1.12)$$

Moreover, the model recommended on the basis of the findings may prove to be a signpost in the field of corporate finance since the data and information likely to be tested and analysed with the help of latest available quantitative techniques. Furthermore, researchers in particular are concerned with a change and likely contribution to the field of knowledge by their research so carried out. Similarly, it is expected that the findings of the present study would certainly become an addition to the present knowledge as far as Indian context is concerned. Hence, the scope of the present study is quite wide.

Scope of the Study

The present study includes the empirical analysis of working capital management of Indian automobile industry. The scope of working capital is very wide and broad-based. For the theoretical understanding, the meaning and definition of working capital and various concepts have come under the purview of the study. The second part of the study is confined to the various approaches to the study of working capital management. For the analytical and technical study, tools and techniques, such as ratios, mean, standard deviation, co-efficient of variation, compound annual growth rate, t-test, ANOVA, chi-square test, correlation, regression and their interpretation are included in the study. It also contains the analysis of impact of working capital on profitability. The period of study has been confined to the years between 1992-93 and 2006-07. The year 1992-93 has been selected as the beginning year of the study period because the tempo of liberalisation has actually been started from the year 1990-91.

Limitations of the Study

However, there are some limitations of the study, which are generally inherent in all such studies conducted at human being level. The most important among them are:

1. The study is based on secondary data obtained from the published annual reports and as such its finding depends entirely on the accuracy of such data.
2. In order to make a study on working capital management more fruitful, it is essential that data should be of frequent time intervals. But, such type of weekly or monthly data could not be obtained and due to this the study has been forced to use the annual data which are available in profit and loss accounts and balance sheets. The use of annual data in this study is thus likely to make the conclusions somewhat less valid and less reliable.
3. The present study is largely based on ratio analysis which has its own limitations.
4. Statistical test used in the study to interpret the analysed data to generalise the findings of the study for the entire population has got their own limitations and result in the analysis is subject to some constraints as are applicable to statistical tools.
5. The analysis of financial statement of business enterprise gives diagnostic indicators. Researchers being outside external analyst obviously have no access to internal data. Therefore, inside view of the organisation cannot be characterised in the study.
6. The financial statement does not keep pace with the changing price level.

However, all these limitations, do not, in any way, affect the worth of this research work.

References

1. Fred Weston, J. and Brigham, E.F, (1981), Managerial Finance, New York: The Dryden Press, p.185.

2. Altman, E.I, (September 1968), Financial ratios, Discriminant analysis and the Prediction of Corporate Bankruptcy, *The Journal of Finance*, pp.589-609.
3. Fred Weston, J. and Brigham, E.F, (1981), op. cit., p.186.
4. John Maynard Keynes (1936), The General Theory of Employment, Harcount Brace and Company, p.201.

4

Structure, Sources and Utilisation of Working Capital

Working capital is the portion of an enterprise's total capital which is employed in short-term operations, i.e., current assets. A typical list of these assets in order of liquidity includes cash in hand and at bank, short-term investment, payments in advance, accounts receivables, raw materials inventory, inventory of goods in process and finished goods inventory.[1] The management of all these current assets assumes greater importance because the sum total of investment in current assets forms over one-half of an enterprise's total assets.[2] Besides, liquidity and profitability, the two desired goals of financial management, are directly affected by working capital management performance. As the size of working capital increase, both the enterprise's risk and return would decrease and vice-versa[3]. Since, the current assets (working capital) affect the risk return trade off to be achieved by the enterprise, the study of structure, sources and utilisation appears to be one of the important areas of investigation on working capital management.

The purpose of the present chapter is to examine the issues like how large is the investment in working capital and its various components, how the quality of current assets has evolved over time, and whether working capital and its various components have been utilised efficiently by the selected automobile industry of India during the period under study.

SIZE OF WORKING CAPITAL

It is evident from Appendix I that the size of Current Assets (CA), Current Liabilities (CL) and Net Working Capital (NWC) in the automobile industry have been on the increasing trend during the period under review. The CA increased from Rs. 6,090.06 crores in 1992-93 to Rs.36,780.33 crores in 2006-07, i.e., 6.04 times. CL during the same period rose from Rs. 4,483.09 crores to Rs. 25,170.81 crores; the rise comes to 5.61 times. As the increase in CA is more than that in CL, the NWC has been able to increase from Rs.1,606.97 crores to Rs.11,609.52 crores in the same period, the increase being approximately 7.22 times. Moreover, the increase in NWC has been gradual throughout the period except in 1993-94, 1998-99, 1999-2000, and 2000-01 when it had fallen. The reason for decrease in NWC in 1993-94, 1998-99, 1999-2000 and 2000-01 were more decrease in finished goods components of current assets.

On comparing the changes that have taken place in the size of CA, CL and NWC in the commercial vehicles sector, the passenger cars and multiutility vehicles sector, and the two- and three-wheelers sector, it is observed that increases are more in the case of two- and three-wheelers sector than in passenger cars and multiutility vehicles sector and the commercial vehicles sector. In the commercial vehicles sector, the CA, CL and NWC have increased by 4.30, 5.75 and 1.46 times from 1992-93 to 2006-07 whereas in the passenger cars and multiutility vehicles sector the rise has been 5.06, 4.18 and 7.25 times in the same period. The two- and three-wheelers sector they have increased by 13.22, 6.97 and 485.36 times in all the three variables. In the year 1993-94, 1998-99 and 1999-2000 all the sectors showed the decrease in NWC due to fall in the size of CA and CL.

The rate of increase in the size of CA, CL and NWC in all the selected units has been found to be fairly good during the period under review. It is evident from the analysis that Swaraj Mazda Ltd, Eicher Motors Ltd in commercial vehicles sector; Hindustan Motors Ltd in the passenger cars and multiutility vehicles sector; LML Ltd, Majestic Auto Ltd and Scooters India Ltd in the two- and three-wheelers sector have the smaller size of working capital. The growth had taken place at a high rate in Ashok Leyland Ltd in the commercial vehicles sector, Mahindra and Mahindra Ltd in the passenger cars and multiutility vehicles sector, and Bajaj Auto Ltd and Hero Honda Motors Ltd in the two- and three-wheelers sector in proportion to other units. It is also evident from the analysis that two out of five units in commercial vehicles (Ashok Leyland Ltd and Tata Motors Ltd), one out of three units in passenger cars and multiutility vehicles (Maruti Udyog Ltd) and four out of nine units in two and three wheelers (Bajaj Auto Ltd, LML Ltd, TVS Motor Company Ltd and Hero Honda Motors Ltd) registered more growth in current liabilities than in current assets during the period under study.

Tables 4.1 to 4.4 which contains the values of mean, co-efficient of variations and 't' values (to test the significance of sample means in relation to population mean) of ratios concerning the size of working capital of commercial vehicles sector, passenger cars and multiutility vehicles sector and two- and three-wheelers sector.

Table 4.1 indicates that CA has formed a high proportion of total assets in the industry. The industry average of the ratio of CA to TA comes to 55.47 per cent. Commercial vehicles sector has the share of CA to TA 53.53 per cent on an average whereas the passenger cars and multiutility vehicle sector and two- and three-wheelers sector have the mean values at 50.80 and 62.00 per cent for this ratio respectively. Interestingly, the variations in mean values of this ratio for all the sectors are statistically significant from industry mean.

The mean values for CA to TA ratios vary from 49.47 per cent to 92.00 per cent among the commercial vehicles sector, 49.13 per cent to 55.47 per cent among the passenger cars and multiutility vehicles sector and from 44.20 per cent to 81.53 per cent among the two- and three-wheelers sector during the period under study. It is inferred from the analysis that four out of five units in commercial vehicles (Ashok Leyland Ltd, Bajaj Tempo Ltd, Eicher Motors Ltd and Swaraj Mazda Ltd), one out of three units in passengers cars and multiutility vehicles (Maruti Udyog Ltd) and three out of nine units in two- and three-wheelers (Bajaj Auto Ltd, Kinetic Motors Ltd and Scooters India Ltd) have higher mean values for this ratio than sector mean. The high CV values of this ratio in all the sector reveals that high variations have taken place in this ratio during the study period (Tables 4.2, 4.3 and 4.4).

Table 4.1: Statistical Values of Ratios Relating to the Size of Working Capital (For the Period 1992-93 to 2006-07)

(Total Industry)

Particulars	*Statistics*	*Commercial vehicles sector*	*Passenger cars and multiutility vehicles sector*	*Two- and three-wheelers sector*	*Total Industry*
Current assets to total assets (%)	Mean	53.53	50.80	62.00	55.47
	CV	0.17	0.11	0.11	0.12
	7t	-1.98 ***	-3.38 **	5.68 *	
Current assets to fixed assets (%)	Mean	281.19	159.13	250.47	180.87
	CV	0.30	0.27	0.26	0.25
	t	-2.64 **	-5.05 *	7.97 *	
Current assets to sales (in days)	Mean	712.53	887.20	694.67	742.93
	CV	0.25	0.14	0.12	0.15
	t	–1.26	6.58*	–1.71	
Current ratio	Mean	1.38	1.38	1.32	1.36
	CV	0.12	0.18	0.11	0.07
	t	0.44	0.35	–1.16	
Liquid ratio	Mean	0.53	0.64	0.60	0.59
	CV	16.81	0.33	0.27	0.20
	t	–1.87 ***	1.67	0.53	

* Significant at 0.01 level; ** Significant at 0.05 level; *** Significant at 0.10 level

Source: Computed from the annual reports of the respective units.

Table 4.2: Statistical Values of Ratios Relating to the Size of Working Capital (For the Period 1992-93 to 2006-07)

(Commercial vehicles sector)

Particulars	*Statistics*	*Ashok Leyland Ltd*	*Tata Motors Ltd*	*Bajaj Tempo Ltd*	*Eicher Motors Ltd*	*Swaraj Mazda Ltd*	*Total*
Current assets to total assets (%)	Mean	62.27	49.47	69.00	58.20	92.00	53.53
	CV	0.08	0.24	0.12	0.19	0.20	0.17
	t	4.66 *	-5.65 *	5.02 *	2.16 **	7.02 *	
Current assets to fixed assets (%)	Mean	187.40	153.67	273.20	170.67	621.02	281.19
	CV	0.18	0.38	0.38	0.31	0.32	0.30
	t	2.24 **	–3.64 **	4.02 *	0.42	5.08 *	
Current assets to sales (in days)	Mean	576.27	754.87	800.27	1181.27	989.80	712.53
	CV	0.34	0.27	0.15	0.30	0.16	0.25
	t	–4.81 *	2.91 **	2.69 **	7.05 *	–0.43	
Current ratio	Mean	2.16	1.07	1.27	1.25	1.20	1.38
	CV	0.21	0.21	0.17	0.17	0.17	0.12
	t	9.42 *	–5.49 *	–1.54	–3.94 *	–3.01 *	
Liquid ratio	Mean	0.95	0.45	0.25	0.50	0.50	0.53
	CV	0.32	0.49	0.56	0.28	0.36	16.81
	t	6.99 *	–1.59	–6.49 *	–1.10	–0.48	

* Significant at 0.01 level; ** Significant at 0.05 level

Source: Computed from the Annual reports of the respective units.

Table 4.3: Statistical Values of Ratios Relating to the Size of Working Capital (For the Period 1992-93 to 2006-07)

(Passengers cars and multiutility vehicles sector)

Particulars	*Statistics*	*Hindustan Motors Ltd*	*Mahindra and Mahindra Ltd*	*Maruti Udyog Ltd*	*Total*
Current assets to total assets (%)	Mean	50.87	49.13	55.47	50.80
	CV	0.08	0.16	0.18	0.12
	t	0.05	-1.13	2.05 ***	
Current assets to fixed assets (%)	Mean	116.73	169.87	181.53	159.13
	CV	0.21	0.28	0.31	0.27
	t	–2.94	1.02	2.54 **	
Current assets to sales (in days)	Mean	735.87	814.00	998.33	887.20
	CV	0.12	0.20	0.25	0.14
	t	–5.25 *	–1.70	2.59 **	
Current ratio	Mean	1.17	1.54	1.56	1.38
	CV	0.20	0.21	0.49	0.18
	t	–2.12 ***	1.71	0.86	
Liquid ratio	Mean	0.39	0.72	0.80	0.64
	CV	0.28	0.33	0.85	0.33
	t	–3.27*	1.33	1.32	

* Significant at 0.01 level; ** Significant at 0.05 level; *** Significant at 0.10 level

Source: Computed from the annual reports of the respective units.

Table 4.4: Statistical Values of Ratios Relating to the Size of Working Capital (For the Period 1992-93 to 2006-07)

(Two and three wheelers sector)

Particulars	*Statistics*	*Bajaj Auto Ltd*	*LML Ltd*	*Maharastra Scooters Ltd*	*TVS Motor Company Ltd*	*Kinetic Motors Ltd*	*Hero Honda Motors Ltd*	*Kinetic Engi-neering Ltd*	*Majestic Auto Ltd*	*Scoot-ers India Ltd*	*Total*
Current assets to Total assets (%)	Mean	65.20	54.00	50.07	47.47	64.47	58.13	60.13	44.20	81.53	62.00
	CV	0.16	0.19	0.42	0.19	0.11	0.25	0.11	0.19	0.19	0.11
	t	2.37 **	-2.53 **	-1.90 ***	-4.83 *	0.79	-1.11	-0.82	-9.96 *	4.33 *	
Current assets to Fixed assets (%)	Mean	357.27	152.80	1227.80	107.73	201.60	189.53	203.67	92.07	801.93	250.47
	CV	0.48	0.40	0.83	0.36	0.21	0.55	0.35	0.32	0.26	0.26
	t	3.66 **	-4.31 *	3.69 **	-7.67 *	-2.08 ***	-2.65 **	-1.89 ***	-9.67*	8.77 *	
Current assets to sales (in days)	Mean	464.27	724.67	376.93	1598.93	1029.33	1548.40	504.13	924.27	469.87	694.67
	CV	0.28	0.24	0.44	0.24	0.30	0.38	0.23	0.26	0.22	0.12
	t	-8.00 *	0.59	-7.07 *	9.05*	4.20 *	5.68 *	-5.11 *	3.62 *	-6.53 *	
Current ratio	Mean	1.87	0.91	1.57	1.10	1.20	1.32	1.43	1.03	1.54	1.32
	CV	0.16	0.25	0.40	0.18	0.29	0.29	0.20	0.23	0.64	0.11
	t	6.76 *	-6.95 *	1.76 ***	-4.04 *	-1.16	-0.06	1.32	-3.42 *	1.02	
Liquid ratio	Mean	0.95	0.29	0.85	0.37	0.44	0.76	0.51	0.45	0.78	0.60
	CV	0.38	0.41	0.78	0.46	0.30	0.67	0.45	0.22	0.81	0.27
	t	4.37 *	-5.36 *	1.77 ***	-4.07 *	-2.65**	1.42	-1.17	-2.92 **	1.41	

* Significant at 0.01 level; ** Significant at 0.05 level; *** Significant at 0.10 level

Source: Computed from the annual reports of the respective units.

With regard to CA to FA ratio also, commercial vehicles sector has to maximum share at CA to FA i.e., 281.19 per cent, whereas the passenger cars and multiutility vehicles sector and two and three wheelers sector have the mean value of 159.13 per cent and 250.47 per cent respectively for this ratio. The industry average for the ratio of CA to FA worked out to 180.87 per cent. The variations in mean values of this ratio for all the sectors are statistically significant from industry mean. The mean values for CA to FA ratios vary from 153.67 per cent to 621.02 per cent among the commercial vehicles sector and 116.73 per cent to 181.53 per cent and 92.07 per cent to 1,227.80 per cent among the passenger cars and multiutility vehicles sector and two and three wheelers sector respectively during the study period. It is evident from the analysis that four out of five units in commercial vehicles (Ashok Leyland Ltd, Bajaj Tempo Ltd, Eicher Motors Ltd and Swaraj Mazda Ltd and), two out of three units in passenger cars and multiutility vehicles (Mahindra and Mahindra Ltd and Maruti Udyog Ltd) and three out of nine units in two and three wheelers (Bajaj Auto Ltd, Maharashtra Scooters Ltd and Scooters India Ltd) have higher mean values for this ratio than sector mean. The high CV values of all the sectors reveals high variation in this ratio during the study period.

The ratio of CA in terms of number of days of sales brings out that the passenger cars and multiutility vehicles sector have high value for the ratio compared to the commercial vehicles sector and the two and three wheelers sector. The industry mean for this ratio comes to 742.93 days as against 712.53 days for the commercial vehicles sector, 887.20 days for the passengers car and multiutility vehicles sector and 694.67 days for two and three wheelers sector. This ratio reflects upon the utilisation of working capital which happen to certainly better in the two and three wheelers sector than in the commercial vehicles sector and the passenger cars and multiutility vehicles sector in the Indian automobile industry of India. Moreover, the CV which works out to 0.25 for the commercial vehicles sector, 0.14 for the passenger cars and multiutility vehicles sector and 0.12 for the two and three wheelers sector, indicates moderate variation in this ratio during the study period.

It is evident from the analysis that Ashok Leyland Ltd in commercial vehicles sector and Hindustan Motors Ltd in the passenger cars and multiutility vehicles sector, Maharastra Scooters Ltd., Bajaj Auto Ltd and Scooters India Ltd in the two and three wheelers sector are certainly better than the other sector units as far as the ratio of CA to sales is concerned. The mean values for this ratios vary from 576.27 days to 1,181.27 days among the commercial vehicles sector, 735.86 days to 998.33 days among the passenger cars and multiutility vehicles sector and 376.93 days to 1,598.93 days among the two and three wheelers sector during the study period. It is also evident from the analysis that all the selected units in the commercial vehicles sector (except Swaraj Mazda Ltd), the passenger cars and multiutility vehicles sector (except Mahindra and Mahindra Ltd) and the two and three wheelers sector (except LML Ltd), the mean value of this ratio vary significantly from the sector mean. The high CV values of all the sector units reveal high variations in this ratios during the study period.

The CR and LR, which are regarded as the tests of liquidity seem to be very strong in the industry where the mean values for these ratio have been 1.36 and 0.59 respectively. The mean of CR in the commercial vehicles sector (1.38) happens to be higher than industry mean. The mean of LR in commercial vehicles sector (0.53) is lower than industry mean. The mean values of CR (1.38) and LR (0.64) in the passenger cars and multiutility vehicles sector are higher than the industry mean. The mean value of CR in the two and three wheelers sector (1.32) is lower than industry mean. The mean value of LR in the two and three wheelers sector (0.60) is higher than the industry mean. From this, it may be inferred than the passenger cars and multiutility vehicles sector enjoyed slightly better liquidity than commercial vehicles sector and the two and three wheelers sector. Moreover, the CV values of all the sectors units revealed high variations in this ratio during the study period under review.

Among commercial vehicles sector, the mean values of CR and LR of Ashok Leyland Ltd is comparatively high and vary significantly from the sector mean. Similarly among passenger cars and multiutility vehicles sector, the mean value of CR and LR of Mahindra and Mahindra Ltd and Maruti Udyog Ltd are comparatively high and vary significantly from the sector mean. Among the two and three wheelers units the mean value of CR of Bajaj Auto Ltd (1.87), Maharashtra Scooters Ltd (1.57), Kinetic Engineering Ltd (1.43) and Scooters India Ltd (1.54) are comparatively high and vary significantly from the sector mean and LR of Bajaj Auto Ltd (0.95), Maharashtra Scooters Ltd (0.85), Hero Honda Motors Ltd (0.76) and Scooters India Ltd (0.78) are comparatively high and vary significantly from the sector mean. Moreover the high CV value of all the sector units indicates high variation in these ratios during the period under study. All this analysis leads to the conclusion that during the period under study, the passenger cars and multiutility vehicles units have enjoyed relatively good liquidity. Moreover, the wide gaps in CR and LR in all the units further indicate that inventory forms quite a large proportion of total current assets in the industry.

To conclude, it may be said that the size of working capital in the Indian automobile industry has been quite large and current assets have constituted a considerable proportion to total investment. The two and three wheelers sector are definitely better than the commercial vehicles sector and passenger cars and multiutility vehicles sector as far as the utilisation of working capital is concerned as its current assets to sales ratio has been found to be the lowest. As far as the liquidity is concerned, the passenger cars and multiutility vehicles sector have maintained comparatively sound liquidity position than the commercial vehicles sector and the two and three wheelers sector during the study period.

Composition of Working Capital

After assessing the size of working capital in the automobile industry of India, the size of each component of working capital relative to total is calculated and presented in tables 4.5 to 4.8. Tables 4.5 to 4.8 contain the statistical values (Mean, CV and CAGR) relating to the proportion of each component of working capital to total current assets during the period under review.

It has been observed from the tables that inventory constitutes second major components of working capital in all the units in Indian automobile industry. The industry average of inventory as proportion to total current assets amount to 35.61 per cent against

39.15 per cent for the commercial vehicles sector, 36.39 per cent for the passenger cars and multiutility vehicles sector and 31.34 per cent for the two and three wheelers sector during the period under study. The mean values of inventory to total current assets vary from 32.13 per cent to 59.87 per cent among the commercial vehicles sector units, 29.01 per cent to 48.19 per cent among the passenger cars and multiutility vehicles sector units and 7.33 per cent to 48.03 per cent among the two and three wheelers sector units during the study period. It is inferred from the analysis that Ashok Leyland Ltd in commercial vehicles sector, Maruti Udyog Ltd in the passenger cars and multiutility vehicles sector and Maharashtra Scooters Ltd in the two and three wheelers sector have been able to make some reductions in inventory percentage to total current assets (decreasing trend value) during the study period. The high CV values indicate that, throughout the period high fluctuations have taken place in the ratio of inventory to total current assets.

Receivables, the major components of working capital in the automobile industries comprises, on an average, 48.84 per cent of total current assets in the industry as against 52.26 per cent for commercial vehicles sector, 46.86 per cent for the passenger cars and multiutility vehicles sector and 47.37 per cent for the two and three wheelers sector. The compound annual growth rate value has been maximum in the case of commercial vehicles sector. The mean values of receivable to current assets ratio oscillate between 33.92 per cent and 60.16 per cent in the commercial vehicles sector, 44.65 per cent and 49.64 per cent in passenger cars and multiutility vehicles sector units and it ranged between 30.52 per cent and 68.56 per cent in the two and three wheelers sector units during the study period. However, the CAGR, which has improved in all the units, has the highest rate in Swaraj Mazda Ltd in the commercial vehicles sector, Hindustan Motors Ltd in the passenger cars and multiutility vehicles sector and Kinetic Motors Ltd in the two and three wheelers sector.

The table further brings out that cash, third component of working capital, has claimed 9.51 per cent of current assets in the industry as against 7.31 per cent for commercial vehicles sector, 11.72 per cent for the passenger cars and multiutility vehicles sector and 9.29 per cent for the two and three wheelers sector on

Table 4.5: Statistical Values of Composition of Working Capital
(For the Period 1992-93 to 2006-07)
(Total Industry)

(% to total CA)

Particulars	Statistics	Commercial vehicles sector	Passengers cars and multiutility vehicles sector	Two- and three-wheelers sector	Total Industry
Inventory	Mean	39.15	36.39	31.34	35.61
	CV	0.13	0.15	0.14	0.13
	CAGR	-2.93	-3.57	-3.03	-3.14
Receivables	Mean	52.26	46.86	47.37	48.84
	CV	0.07	0.13	0.11	0.06
	CAGR	2.07	-1.00	-1.48	-0.07
Cash and bank	Mean	7.31	11.72	9.29	9.51
	CV	0.44	0.52	0.21	0.32
	CAGR	3.80	8.91	3.80	6.21
Other current assets	Mean	1.35	5.13	12.00	5.96
	CV	1.11	1.12	0.67	0.81
	CAGR	5.98	NIL	14.87	16.43

Source: Computed from the annual reports of the respective units.

Table 4.6

Statistical Values of Composition of Working Capital

(For the Period 1992-93 to 2006-07)

(Commercial vehicles sector)

(% to total CA)

Particulars	*Statistics*	*Ashok Leyland Ltd*	*Tata Motors Ltd*	*Bajaj Tempo Ltd*	*Eicher Motors Ltd*	*Swaraj Mazda Ltd*	*Total*
Inventory	Mean	32.13	39.24	59.87	33.70	40.72	39.15
	CV	0.14	0.25	0.13	0.18	0.36	0.13
	CAGR	0.94	-3.46	-1.16	-3.68	-7.92	-2.93
Receivables	Mean	53.24	60.16	33.92	59.33	54.57	52.26
	CV	0.26	0.17	0.25	0.10	0.27	0.07
	CAGR	-2.35	1.44	1.44	2.07	26.58	2.07
Cash and bank	Mean	11.02	7.85	5.90	6.97	4.71	7.31
	CV	0.95	0.90	0.38	0.66	0.49	0.44
	CAGR	2.88	11.41	5.89	4.59	2.02	3.80
Other current assets	Mean	3.61	5.12	0.35	NIL	NIL	1.35
	CV	1.01	1.75	1.17	NIL	NIL	1.11
	CAGR	12.24	NIL	NIL	NIL	NIL	5.98

Source: Computed from the annual reports of the respective units.

Table 4.7: Statistical Values of Composition of Working Capital
(For the Period 1992-93 to 2006-07)
(Passengers Cars and Multiutility Vehicles Sector)

(% to total CA)

Particulars	*Statistics*	*Hindustan Motors* Ltd	*Mahindra & Mahindra Ltd*	*Maruti Udyog Ltd*	*Total*
Inventory	Mean	48.19	32.00	29.01	36.39
	CV	0.09	0.19	0.39	0.15
	CAGR	-1.73	-3.79	-6.41	-3.57
Receivables	Mean	44.65	49.64	46.42	46.86
	CV	0.10	0.17	0.28	0.13
	CAGR	1.39	-0.92	-3.57	-1.00
Cash and bank	Mean	6.56	15.71	12.93	11.72
	CV	0.31	0.60	0.97	0.52
	CAGR	-2.44	8.15	21.59	8.91
Other current assets	Mean	0.80	5.01	17.45	5.13
	CV	1.95	0.67	0.96	1.12
	CAGR	NIL	NIL	NIL	NIL

Source: Computed from the annual reports of the respective units.

Table 4.8

Statistical Values of Composition of Working Capital (For the Period 1992-93 to 2006-07)

(Two and three wheelers sector)

(% to total CA)

Particulars	*Statistics*	*Bajaj Auto Ltd*	*LML Ltd*	*Maharashtra Scooters Ltd*	*TVS Motor Company Ltd*	*Kinetic Motors Ltd*	*Hero Honda Motors Ltd*	*Kinetic Engineering Ltd*	*Majestic Auto Ltd*	*Scooters India Ltd*	*Total*
Inventory	Mean	11.19	43.34	7.33	39.95	48.03	30.16	27.38	31.43	44.70	31.34
	CV	0.79	0.21	0.67	0.19	0.22	0.54	0.20	0.15	0.38	0.14
	CAGR	-14.23	4.73	2.02	0.20	-3.03	-8.830	-2.83	-1.16	-5.77	-3.03
Receivables	Mean	55.95	37.56	56.72	47.01	47.10	30.52	68.56	64.79	17.85	47.37
	CV	0.25	0.27	0.42	0.19	0.26	0.42	0.10	0.07	0.33	0.11
	CAGR	-3.24	-3.91	-4.39	-2.54	3.14	-4.14	0.99	0.13	0.45	-1.48
Cash and bank	Mean	2.68	17.29	2.08	10.56	12.44	5.02	1.65	3.05	36.89	9.29
	CV	0.98	0.43	0.65	0.74	0.45	2.48	1.32	0.39	0.36	0.21
	CAGR	-10.80	-4.02	-1.73	11.66	2.79	-10.17	16.31	-6.76	12.02	3.80
Other current assets	Mean	30.19	1.91	39.04	5.28	1.72	36.75	2.78	5.70	8.94	12.00
	CV	0.68	1.04	0.58	0.87	1.93	0.80	1.10	0.13	NIL	0.67
	CAGR	NIL	NIL	NIL	NIL	NIL	10.43	NIL	NIL	NIL	14.87

Source: Computed from the annual reports of the respective units.

an average. The mean value of cash to current assets ratio oscillate between 4.71 per cent and 11.02 per cent in the commercial vehicles sector units, 6.56 per cent and 15.71 per cent in the passenger cars and multiutility vehicles sector units and 1.65 per cent and 36.89 per cent in the two and three wheelers sector units. The high value for CV indicate that variations where sharper in the proportion of this component in all the units than in the proportion of inventory or receivables.

In the automobile industry of India, comparatively a low proportion of current assets has been found in the form of other current assets. The mean values of this ratio vary between 0.35 per cent and 5.12 per cent among the commercial vehicles sector units, 0.80 per cent and 17.45 per cent among the passenger cars and multiutility vehicles sector units and 1.72 per cent and 39.04 per cent among the two and three wheelers sector units. Moreover the relative fluctuations in this ratio during the period under study have been very high.

To sum up, it may be inferred from the above analysis that receivables which has formed a major component of working capital in the selected automobile units registered a downward trend during the recent years. The inventory constitutes the second important component of current assets followed by cash and other current assets. The other currents assets are not significant in this industry

Circulation of Working Capital

An analysis of circulation of working capital highlights the efficiency with which it is being utilised. The analysis is done with certain turnover ratio which reflect upon the efficiency in the use of working capital and its components. Generally higher the level of these turnover ratios, the more efficient is the use and the smaller would be the requirements of working capital of an enterprise. These ratios include Inventory Turnover Ratio (ITR), Receivables Turnover Ratio (RTR), Cash Turnover Ratio (CTR) and Working Capital Turnover Ratio (WTR). For the purpose of the present study, the statistical value of these ratios (Mean, CV and 't' value) have been given in Tables 4.9 to 4.12.

Inventory Turnover Ratio

The turnover of inventory directly affects the liquidity and profitability of a firm. The ratio helps to judge the efficiency of inventory management. Ordinarily the higher the rate of inventory turnover, the larger the amount of profit, the smaller the amount of working capital tied up in inventory and the more current the stock of merchandise[4]. Generally it is believed that a high inventory turnover implies more efficient management of inventory. This is however true up to a point beyond that a high inventory turnover may signal problems[5]. It is because inventory turnover can be increased by carrying very small inventories also. But this policy may lead to a large number of stock outs leading to loss of sales. For each industry, there is a range of inventory turnovers that may be considered good[6]. However, while interpreting this ratio, care must be exercise that a very high turnover ratio may be the result of and unduly small size of the inventory which adversely affects smooth operations. A low ratio suggests poor inventory management.

Table 4.9 reveals that the overall ITR is very high in the industry. The industry mean value of ITR 9.75 times as against the commercial vehicles sector 7.50 times, the passenger cars and multiutility vehicles sector 9.60 times and two and three wheelers sector 12.13 times. The mean value ITR in the two and three wheelers sector is the highest and showed good performance in the inventory management. The CV values further indicate that the two and three wheeler units had a better inventory control than the commercial vehicle and passenger cars and multiutility vehicles sectors during the period under study.

Table 4.10 shows that ITR varies widely from one industry to another. The mean values of ITR ranges from 4.59 times to 11.83 times in the commercial vehicles sector units and from 6.04 times to 14.05 times and 3.61 times to 22.42 times in the passenger cars and multiutility vehicles sector units and the two and three wheelers sector units respectively. The average ITR is the highest for Eicher Motors Ltd, followed by Ashok Leyland Ltd, Tata Motors Ltd,. Bajaj Tempo Ltd, Swaraj Mazda Ltd in the commercial vehicles sector. Similarly, the average ITR is the highest for Maruti Udyog Ltd followed by Hindustan Motors Ltd and Mahindra and Mahindra Ltd in the passenger cars and

Table 4.9: Statistical Values of Ratios Relating to Circulation of Working Capital (For the Period 1992-93 to 2006-07)

(Total Industry)

Particulars	*Statistics*	*Commercial vehicles sector*	*Passengers cars and multiutility vehicles sector*	*Two- and three-wheelers sector*	*Total Industry*
Inventory turnover ratio	Mean	7.50	9.60	12.13	9.75
	CV	0.32	0.30	0.08	0.20
	t	-10.58 *	-0.49	7.20 *	
Receivables turnover ratio	Mean	14.83	16.47	23.05	18.11
	CV	0.31	0.36	0.23	0.21
	t	-5.39 *	-1.80 ***	4.22 *	
Cash turnover ratio	Mean	100.51	39.11	102.27	80.63
	CV	0.67	0.57	0.43	0.32
	t	1.55	-6.14 *	1.94 ***	
Working capital turnover ratio	Mean	3.25	-2.68	51.36	17.31
	CV	-0.15	0.22	59.03	-1.50
	t	-0.90	-1.19	1.13	

* Significant at 0.01 level; *** Significant at 0.10 level

Source: Computed from the Annual reports of the respective units.

Table 4.10
Statistical Values of Ratios Relating to Circulation of Working Capital
(For the Period 1992-93 to 2006-07)
(Commercial vehicles sector)

Particulars	*Statistics*	*Ashok Leyland Ltd*	*Tata Motors Ltd*	*Bajaj Tempo Ltd*	*Eicher Motors Ltd*	*Swaraj Mazda Ltd*	*Total*
Inventory turnover ratio	Mean	5.86	9.13	4.59	11.83	6.08	7.50
	CV	0.33	0.37	0.27	0.43	0.35	0.32
	t	-5.40 *	3.79 *	-6.50 *	5.10 *	-7.21 *	
Receivables turnover ratio	Mean	6.18	16.05	33.29	11.19	7.42	14.83
	CV	0.77	1.04	0.82	0.27	0.53	0.31
	t	-6.15 *	0.29	2.88 **	-2.34 **	-5.32 *	
Cash turnover ratio	Mean	152.50	64.89	87.66	149.36	48.15	100.51
	CV	1.67	1.03	0.61	1.65	0.41	0.67
	t	0.95	-1.54	-0.72	0.86	-3.44 *	
Working capital turnover ratio	Mean	3.45	11.20	4.09	-8.09	5.58	3.25
	CV	0.33	0.39	-0.07	-0.08	0.61	-0.15
	t	0.03	1.04	0.19	-0.55	0.35	

* Significant at 0.01 level; ** Significant at 0.05 level
Source: Computed from the annual reports of the respective units.

Table 4.11

Statistical Values of Ratios Relating to Circulation of Working Capital

(For the Period 1992-93 to 2006-07)

(Passenger Cars and Multiutility Vehicles Sector)

Particulars	*Statistics*	*Hindustan Motors Ltd*	*Mahindra & Mahindra Ltd*	*Maruti Udyog Ltd*	*Total*
Inventory turnover ratio	Mean	6.04	8.72	14.05	9.60
	CV	0.25	0.38	0.76	0.30
	t	-6.46 *	-3.71 *	6.24 *	
Receivables turnover ratio	Mean	7.01	11.63	30.39	16.47
	CV	0.13	0.36	0.51	0.36
	t	-5.96 *	-3.34 *	5.47 *	
Cash turnover ratio	Mean	34.93	21.51	60.88	39.11
	CV	0.38	0.85	1.04	0.57
	t	0.61	-3.03 *	1.99 ***	
Working capital turnover ratio	Mean	-8.97	8.67	-7.74	-2.68
	CV	0.18	0.92	-1.54	0.22
	t	-0.48	1.03	-0.26	

* Significant at 0.01 level; *** Significant at 0.10 level

Source: Computed from the annual reports of the respective units.

Table 4.12: Statistical Values of Ratios Relating to Circulation of Working Capital (For the Period 1992-93 to 2006-07)

(Two- and three-wheelers sector)

Particulars	*Statistics*	*Bajaj Auto Ltd*	*LML Ltd*	*Maharashtra Scooters Ltd*	*TVS Motor Company Ltd*	*Kinetic Motors Ltd*	*Hero Honda Motors Ltd*	*Kinetic Engineering Ltd*	*Majestic Auto Ltd*	*Scooters India Ltd*	*Total*
Inventory turnover ratio	Mean	18.75	5.31	22.42	14.52	6.88	21.83	5.74	10.13	3.61	12.13
	CV	0.48	0.30	0.68	0.30	0.23	0.68	0.41	0.18	0.31	0.08
	t	3.14 *	-11.23 *	2.57 *	2.06 *	-8.64 *	2.80 **	-7.79 *	-2.99 **	-28.73 *	
Receivables turnover ratio	Mean	27.01	22.95	18.54	33.99	13.52	54.835.35		7.33	24.41	23.05
	CV	0.24	0.48	0.49	0.65	0.69	0.53	0.56	0.28	1.09	0.23
	t	3.12 *	-0.04	-1.53	2.28 **	-3.03 *	4.73 *	-11.09 *	-10.28 *	0.21	
Cash turnover ratio	Mean	76.24	12.95	69.40	71.84	253.58	151.89	175.54	104.67	4.29	102.27
	CV	0.55	0.50	0.73	0.72	1.04	0.75	0.74	0.61	0.63	0.43
	T	-1.94 ***	-7.64 *	-1.99 ***	-2.27 **	2.62 **	1.69	2.88 **	0.12	-8.33	
Working capital turnover ratio	Mean	3.06	18.57	4.69	-52.94	11.41	476.92	3.62	-5.83	2.73	51.36
	CV	1.64	-8.68	-0.88	-2.67	-2.88	65.33	0.70	0.18	1.54	-59.03
	t	-1.64	-0.75	-1.05	-2.02 ***	-0.90	1.22	-1.06	-1.26	-1.10	

* Significant at 0.01 level; ** Significant at 0.05 level; *** Significant at 0.10 level

Source: Computed from the annual reports of the respective units.

multiutility vehicles sector, and the average ITR is the highest for Maharashtra Scooters Ltd, followed by Bajaj Auto Ltd, LML Ltd, TVS Motor Company Ltd, Kinetic Motors Ltd, Hero Honda Motors Ltd, Kinetic Engineering Ltd, Majestic Auto Ltd and Scooters India Ltd in the two and three wheelers sector units. Further, the high value of CV values reveals quite high fluctuations in this ratio in all the sectors during the period under study. Thus, different industries have employed investment in inventories with varying degrees of efficiency.

Receivables Turnover Ratio

The receivable turnover gives a general measure of the productivity of the receivables investment[7]. It is also a measure of a firm's liquidity or activity. The higher the enterprise's accounts receivable turnover, the more favourable it is[8]. It indicates the speed with which receivable are converted into cash. To maximise profitability, a higher turnover of inventory should be accompanied by prompt collection of receivables.

Table 4.9 indicates that the mean value of RTR for the industry as a whole comes to 18.11 times. As against this, commercial vehicles sector has RTR values of 14.83 times and the passenger cars and multiutility vehicles sector and the two and three wheelers sector have 16.47 times and 23.05 times respectively. It is inferred from the table that the two and three wheelers sector have better performance in receivables management than the commercial vehicles sector and the passenger cars and multiutility vehicles sector.

Table 4.10 indicates that receivables turnover ratio varies widely from one industry to another. The mean values of RTR for the commercial vehicles sector units are high and vary significantly from sector mean except Tata Motors Ltd. It ranged between 6.18 times and 33.29 times for the commercial vehicles sector units. The mean values of RTR of the passenger cars and multiutility vehicles sector units ranged between 7.01 times and 30.39 times and the mean values vary significantly at 1 per cent level in case of all units from sector mean. The mean values of RTR of the two and three wheelers sector units ranged between 5.35 times and 54.83 times and the mean values relatively high and vary significantly at 10 per cent level except LML Ltd, Maharastra

Scooters Ltd and Scooter India Ltd from sector mean. Moreover, the high CV values of all the sectors show relatively high fluctuations in the ratio during the period under study.

Cash Turnover Ratio

The cash turnover ratio indicates the number of times the average cash balance is turned over during the year. It helps to evaluate the cash management performance. While interpreting this ratio, it should be borne in mind that increase in the ratio may be due to inadequate cash balances. The study to CTR provides a deep insight into the cash balance held by a concern.

Table 4.9 brings out that CTR has been quite high in the two- and three-wheeler units as compared to the commercial vehicles sector and the passenger cars and multiutility vehicles sector. The mean value of CTR for the industry as a whole comes to 80.63 times, as against 100.51 times for the commercial vehicles sector, 39.11 times for the passenger cars and multiutility vehicle sector, 102.27 times for the two and three wheelers sector. The mean values of CTR of the commercial vehicles sector units ranged between 48.15 times and 152.50 times and the mean values varies significantly at 1 per cent level in the case of Swaraj Mazda Ltd from sector mean. Moreover, the mean values of CTR of the passenger cars and multiutility vehicles sector units ranged between 21.51 times and 60.88 times and the mean values vary significantly in case of Mahindra and Mahindra Ltd and Maruti Udyog Ltd from sector mean. In the two and three wheelers sector units, the mean values of CTR ranged between 4.29 times to 253.58 times and the mean values relatively high and very significantly at 10 per cent level except Hero Honda Motors Ltd, Majestic Auto Ltd and Scooters India Ltd from the sector mean. The CV values show relatively high fluctuations in the ratio during the period under study.

Working Capital Turnover Ratio

The overall efficiency with which working capital funds are used can be measured by WTR. The higher the working capital turnover, the lower the investment in working capital and the greater the profits. However, a very high WTR may be due to insufficient working capital funds for a given volume of business. The table under discussion further reveals that the mean value of WTR of the commercial vehicles sector has been 3.25 times as against -2.68 times for the passenger cars and multiutility vehicles sector and 51.36 times for the two and three wheelers sector and 17.31 times for the industry as a whole. The mean values of WTR of the commercial vehicles sector units ranged between -8.09 and 11.20 times and the mean values of WTR of the passenger cars and multiutility vehicles sector units ranged between –8.97 and 8.67 times. The mean value of WTR of the two and three wheelers sector units ranged between -52.94 and 476.92 times and the mean values vary significantly in case of LML Ltd from sector mean. The high CV values show relatively high fluctuations in the ratio during the period under study.

It may therefore be concluded that different units in the automobile industry have utilised their working capital with the varying degrees of efficiency.

Growth of Working Capital

Working capital and sales are two functionally related concepts. With the increase in sales, the increase in working capital is also excepted. But in a concern already having excessive investments in current assets, lesser growth in gross working capital than growth in sales is an indication of improved working capital management. For the purpose of comparing the growth of sales with that of current assets in the selected units, during the period under study, progressive base year percentage growth rates have been computed and presented in Table 4.13.

Table 4.13 reveals that the industry has recorded lower growth rates in current assets than in sales. The overall average growth rates in current assets and sales in industry work out to 12.74 per cent and 15.92 per cent respectively. Further, the two and three wheelers sector have more average growth in current assets than in sales compared to the commercial vehicles sector and the passenger cars and multiutility vehicles sector. Among the commercial vehicles sector units, current assets have increased at a significantly higher rate than sales in Swaraj Mazda Ltd during the study period. In all the passenger cars and multiutility vehicles sector units growth rates in current assets have lower than the growth rate of sales. In the two and three wheeler units current assets have increased at a higher rate than sales in five out of nine units (Bajaj Auto Ltd, Maharastra Scooters Ltd, Kinetic Motors Ltd, Kinetic Engineering Ltd and Majestic Auto Ltd) during the study period.

Table 4.13

Average Growth Rates in Gross Working Capital and Sales

(1992-93 to 2006-07)

Units	*Gross Working Capital*	*Sales*
Ashok Leyland Ltd	8.83	15.52
Tata Motors Ltd	10.26	17.22
Bajaj Tempo Ltd	7.28	8.09
Eicher Motors Ltd	17.25	21.31
Swaraj Mazda Ltd	18.86	15.36
Commercial vehicles sector	10.21	16.49
Hindustan Motors Ltd	-2.93	-1.39
Mahindra and Mahindra Ltd	12.66	14.99
Maruti Udyog Ltd	12.99	15.02
Passenger cars and multiutility vehicles sector	11.41	13.85
Bajaj Auto Ltd	21.53	16.00
LML Ltd	1.71	4.37
Maharashtra Scooters Ltd	-10.48	-15.50
TVS Motor Company Ltd	20.12	21.80
Kinetic Motors Ltd	7.43	2.83
Hero Honda Motors Ltd	8.56	9.21
Kinetic Engineering Ltd	5.40	2.92
Majestic Auto Ltd	5.10	2.02
Scooters India Ltd	13.30	13.44
Two and three-wheelers sector	18.78	17.49
Industry (Total)	12.74	15.92

Source: Computed from the annual reports of the respective units.

To conclude, working capital management may be considered efficient in four out of the five units in commercial vehicles (Ashok Leyland Ltd, Tata Motors Ltd, Bajaj Tempo Ltd and Eicher Motors Ltd), all the units of passenger cars and multiutility vehicles and in four out of nine units in the two and three wheelers (LML Ltd, TVS Motor Company Ltd, Hero Honda Motors Ltd and Scooters India Ltd) sector.

Relationship between Gross Working Capital and Sales-Regression Analysis

In order to observe more accurately the behaviour of gross working capital in relation to sales in the selected units, linear regression equations and correlation values have been computed and presented in Table 4.14.

Table 4.14 establishes that gross working capital and sales are significantly correlated at 1 per cent level in respect of all the selected automobile units. The high correlation confirms our theoretical assertion that working capital and sales are functionally related to each other. The correlation has been found closer in all the sectors of the automobile industry.

The values of parameter 'b' indicate that working capital is more sensitive to the change in sales in the selected units in the industry. The values of parameter 'b' are quite high in two and three wheelers sector (0.58) compared with that in the commercial vehicles sector (0.35), and the passenger cars and multiutility vehicles sector (0.35). It reflects upon the efficiency of management in the two and three wheelers sector for a unit increase in sales. The linear regression equations given in the above table can also be used for projecting the requirements of working capital for a given volume of sales in any of the units under study. The value of parameter 'a' which is the lowest in the two and three wheelers sector, points to the capacity of the firm to adjust the size of its working capital according to changes in sales. On the whole, this fact indicates that two and three wheelers sector have an efficient control on working capital as compared to the commercial vehicles sector and the passenger cars and multiutility vehicles sector during the study period.

Table 4.14

Gross Working Capital and Sales-regression Results

(Y= a + bx)

Units	*Linear regression equation*	*Pearson correlation co-efficient*	R^2	*t- Value*
Ashok Leyland Ltd	Y = 887.22 + 0.28X	0.86	0.73	5.953*
Tata Motors Ltd	Y = 991.83 + 0.36X	0.95	0.90	10.936*
Bajaj Tempo Ltd	Y = 96.34 + 0.30X	0.88	0.78	6.738*
Eicher Motors Ltd	Y = 12.35 + 0.28X	0.98	0.97	19.934*
Swaraj Mazda Ltd	Y = -29.80 + 0.69X	0.93	0.87	9.409*
Commercial vehicles sector	Y = 1906.06 + 0.35X	0.97	0.92	11.809*
Hindustan Motors Ltd	Y = 36.45 + 0.45X	0.93	0.86	9.031*
Mahindra and Mahindra Ltd	Y = 446.35 + 0.32X	0.95	0.91	11.431*
Maruti Udyog Ltd	Y = -38.83 + 0.38X	0.93	0.86	9.093*
Passenger cars & multiutility vehicles sector	Y = 562.41 + 0.35X	0.98	0.96	17.354*
Bajaj Auto Ltd	Y = -795.77 + 1.14X	0.98	0.95	15.848*
LML Ltd	Y = 120.16 + 0.25X	0.87	0.76	6.359*
Maharashtra Scooters Ltd	Y = 36.33 + 0.56X	0.91	0.82	7.802*

(Contd...)

(Contd...)

Units	*Linear regression equation*	*Pearson correlation co-efficient*	R^2	*t- Value*
TVS Motor Company Ltd	Y = 11.63 + 0.21X	0.97	0.94	14.074*
Kinetic Motors Ltd	Y = 34.29 + 0.23X	0.58	0.34	2.564*
Hero Honda Motors Ltd	Y = -134.38 + 0.32X	0.97	0.93	13 547*
Kinetic Engineering Ltd	Y = 9.23 + 0.71X	0.78	0.61	4.464*
Majestic Auto Ltd	Y = 40.42 + 0.15X	0.64	0.41	3.000*
Scooters India Ltd	Y -2.13 + 0.83X	0.89	0.79	6.901*
Two- and three-wheelers sector	Y = -425.49 + 0.58X	0.98	0.96	17.995*
Industry (Total)	Y = 1741.75 + 0.43X	0.98	0.97	19.351*

Y - Working Capital; X - Sales;

* Significant at 0.01 level

Source: Computed from the annual reports of the respective units.

Size of Business and Working Capital

In an ordinary sense, growth in a business can be measured by ascertaining growth in production and sales. Growth in production and sales would result in growth in raw material consumption, inventories, man hours, receivables etc., which would require more and more working finance. As a company grows, it is logical to except that larger amount of working capital will be required. Though it is very difficult to draw up firm rules for the relationship between the growth in the volume of a company's business and the growth of capital in a going concern also shifts with economic circumstances and corporate practices, growth industries require more working capital than those that are static, other things being equal.[9]

In this section, the impact of the size of sales and output in terms of cost on working capital has been measured by computing "Multiple Correlation" between networking capital and output in terms of cost and sales value. The results are presented in Table 4.15.

As shown in Table 4.15 in all the cases there was a combined positive impact of sales and output in terms of cost on net working capital. This table further shows that the combined impact of sales and output in terms of cost on net working capital is significantly high in all the passenger cars and multiutility vehicles sector units than in the commercial vehicles sector units and the two and three wheelers sector units. For the industry, the co-efficient is +0.929 which shows that the net working capital is highly affected by the sales and the cost of output. Individually, among commercial vehicles sector units two out of five units (Ashok Leyland Ltd and Swaraj Mazda Ltd), the passenger cars and multiutility vehicles sector units, two out of three units (Hindustan Motors Ltd and Maruti Udyog Ltd) and the two and three-wheelers sector units four out of nine units (Bajaj Auto Ltd, Hero Honda Motors Ltd, Kinetic Engineering Ltd and Scooters India Ltd) the multiple correlation co-efficient were high, remaining cases it is low.

Adequacy of Working Capital

There is no standard by which the adequacy of working capital can be measured. However, as practice suggested the adequacy of working capital can be judged in terms of its relations with firm's debts. In order to establish such relationship generally current ratio and liquid ratio are studied. The current ratio is an

Table 4.15
Size of Business (Cost of Output and Sales) and Working Capital Multiple Correlation Co-efficients

Units	*Correlation co-efficient*			
	r_{12}	r_{13}	r_{23}	$R_{1.23}$
Ashok Leyland Ltd	0.289	0.262	0.998	0.707
Tata Motors Ltd	0.420	0.408	0.999	0.500
Bajaja Tempo Ltd	-0.397	-0.391	0.997	0.408
Eicher Motors Ltd	-0.161	-0.162	0.999	0.224
Swaraj Mazda Ltd	0.707	0.701	0.999	0.707
Commercial vehicles sector	0.435	0.423	0.998	0.447
Hindustan Motors Ltd	0.788	0.756	0.997	0.866
Mahindra and Mahindra Ltd	0.530	0.533	0.998	0.524
Maruti Udyog Ltd	0.873	0.873	0.999	0.866
Passenger cars & multiutility vehicles sector	0.920	0.920	0.999	0.923
Bajaj Auto Ltd	0.939	0.939	0.997	0.931
LML Ltd	0.338	0.327	0.978	0.336
Maharashtra Scooters Ltd	-0.093	0.043	0.952	0.438
TVS Motor Company Ltd	0.566	0.571	0.998	0.570
Kinetic Motors Ltd	0.308	0.263	0.963	0.527
Hero Honda Motors Ltd	0.885	0.885	0.999	0.707
Kinetic Engineering Ltd	0.785	0.727	0.993	0.926
Majestic Auto Ltd	0.073	0.069	0.988	0.065
Scooters India Ltd	0.811	0.805	0.995	0.816
Two- and three-wheelers sector	0.939	0.939	0.995	0.837
Industry (Total)	0.897	0.918	0.999	0.929

X_1 - Net Working Capital X_2 - Output in Terms of cost X_3 - Sales

Source: Computed from the annual reports of the respective units.

index of solvency of the concern. It shows the extent to which current assets may diminish in value carrying any loss in respect of payment of short-term creditors. Thus, it is an indication of the ability of an enterprise to meet its current liabilities.

If the conventional liquidity of 2:1 is considered as a norm for the current ratio, the following inferences can be drawn from Tables 4.1 to 4.4.

1. In industry, all the sectors working capital has been observed to be inadequate.
2. Among the commercial vehicles sector units, in one out of five units (Ashok Leyland Ltd) have excess working capital and in the remaining cases, it is inadequate.
3. Among the passenger cars and multiutility vehicle sector, all the units working capital has been observed to be inadequate.
4. Among the two and three wheelers sector units, in Bajaj Auto Ltd, working capital is found to be adequate and in the remaining cases, it is found to be inadequate.

The current ratios can be used to indicate high or low level of working capital but they are unable to give an exact clue to the quality of current assets. Some current assets, although classified as current, are not easily converted into cash. To offset this weakness, liquid ratios are studied. If the conventional liquidity of 1:1 is considered as a norm, the following inferences can be drawn from Tables 4.1 to 4.4.

i) Among the commercial vehicles sector units, in one out of five units (Ashok Leyland Ltd) has adequate working capital and in the remaining cases, it is found to be inadequate.
ii) In the passenger cars and multiutility vehicles sector, Maruti Udyog Ltd and Mahindra and Mahindra Ltd, it has been adequate and Hindustan Motors Ltd, it is found to be inadequate.
iii) Among the two and three wheelers sector, in two out of nine units (Bajaj Auto Ltd and Maharastra Scooters Ltd) has adequate working capital and in the remaining cases, it is inadequate.

On the whole, all the sectors working capital has been observed to be inadequate.

Operational Adequacy of Working Capital

The current and liquid ratios measure the technical solvency of working capital but the operational adequacy of working capital can be measured by ascertaining the magnitude of working capital in relation to average sales turnover and months cost of operations. Tables 4.16 to 4.19 show the relationship between net working capital in terms of monthly average sales turnover and monthly average cost of operations.

Working Capital in Relation to Cost of Operation

Tables 4.16 to 4.19 reveal that the mean value of overall ratio of net working capital in terms of month cost of production is 20.86. As against this commercial vehicles sector, the passenger cars and multiutility vehicles sector and the two and three wheelers sector have the mean value of 6.93, 3.72 and 17.20 respectively. The table also shows that the mean value of this ratio varies widely from one industry to another. The mean values of this ratio in the commercial vehicles sector units ranged between 0.80 and 5.82 and the mean values varies significantly at 1 per cent and 5 per cent level from the sector mean. The mean values of this ratio of the passenger cars and multiutility vehicles sector units ranged between 0.76 and 2.01 and the mean value varies significantly at 1 per cent level in case of Maruti Udyog Ltd, 5 per cent level in case of Hindustan Motors Ltd and Mahindra and Mahindra Ltd, from sector mean. The mean value of this ratio of the two and three wheelers sector units ranged between -27.09 and 4.71 and the mean value varies significantly at 1 per cent level in case of all the units of two and three wheelers sector. Further, the value of CV which swings between 0.21 and 1.07 in commercial vehicles sector, 0.48 and 1.58 in the passenger cars and multiutility vehicles sector and -7.17 and 2.62 in the two and three wheelers sector, reveals quite high fluctuations in this ratio during the period under study.

Working Capital in Relation to Sales

Tables 4.16 and 4.19 also show that the mean value of the overall ratio of net working capital and month sales turnover is 1.55 as against 1.40 in commercial vehicles sector, 1.34 in passenger cars and multiutility vehicles sector and 1.92 in two and three wheelers sector. Among the commercial vehicles sector units this ratio ranged between 0.53 and 4.51 and the mean value varies significantly at 1 per cent level in case of Tata Motors Ltd and Ashok Leyland Ltd from the sector mean. The mean values of this ratio of the passenger cars and multiutility vehicles sector units ranged between 0.77 and 2.02 and the mean values vary significantly at 10 per cent level in case of Mahindra and Mahindra Ltd and the mean value of this ratio of the two- and three-wheelers sector units ranged between -0.17 and 5.09 and the mean values relatively high and vary significantly at 10 per cent level except LML Ltd and Kinetic Engineering Ltd from the sector mean. The high CV value of this ratio in all the selected units also shows high variations in this ratio during the study period.

To sum up the analysis regarding operational adequacy of working capital, it can be concluded that the size of the working capital of the two and three wheelers units taken together was excessively high in relation to sales and output requirements. It is also true from the analysis that the units under study did not have any fixed policy regarding the size of working capital to meet the operational requirements.

Operational Adequacy of Working Capital – A Bivariate Discriminant Analysis

The present study attempts to apply linear discriminant analysis with only two sets of independent variables. The sample units were classified in two categories as per their liquidity ratios. Group A consisted of those units where current ratios were found to be atleast 1.5:1 and the rest of the units have been classified in Group B. In this study, adequacy of the size of net working capital has been treated as dependent variable and sizes of net working capital in terms of monthly operational requirements (X_1) and sales requirements (X_2) have been treated as independent variables. The object is to determine weights for X_1 and X_2, that is the values of 'a' and 'b' in

$$Z = aX_1 + bX_2$$

where, Z is the discriminant index.

Table 4.16

Statistical Values of Ratios Relating to Operational Adequacy of Working Capital

(Total industry)

Particulars	*Statistics*	*Commercial vehicles sector*	*Passengers cars and multiutility vehicles sector*	*Two- and three-wheelers sector*	*Total industry*
WC in terms of months cost of production	Mean	6.93	3.72	17.20	20.86
	CV	0.81	0.67	0.63	0.33
	t	-8.08*	-11.30*	-1.48	
WC in terms of months sales	Mean	1.40	1.34	1.92	1.55
	CV	0.82	0.57	0.63	0.34
	t	-0.60	-1.46	1.32	

* Significant at 0.01 level

Source: Computed from the annual reports of the respective units.

Table 4.17

Statistical Values of Ratios Relating to Operational Adequacy of Working Capital

(Commercial vehicles sector)

Particulars	*Statistics*	*Ashok Leyland Ltd*	*Tata Motors Ltd*	*Bajaj Tempo Ltd*	*Eicher Motors Ltd*	*Swaraj Mazda Ltd*	*Total*
WC in terms of months cost of Production	Mean	4.49	5.82	0.93	0.80	0.95	6.93
	CV	0.45	0.21	0.63	0.79	1.07	0.81
	t	-2.18 **	-5.50 *	-4.26 *	-4.59 *	-3.84 *	
WC in terms of months Sales	Mean	4.51	0.53	0.93	0.80	0.97	1.40
	CV	0.45	2.53	0.63	0.78	1.05	0.82
	t	8.49 *	-6.88 *	-1.63 ***	-2.72 **	-0.93	

* Significant at 0.01 level; ** Significant at 0.05 level; *** Significant at 0.10 level

Source: Computed from the Annual reports of the respective units.

Table 4.18

Statistical Values of Ratios Relating to Operational Adequacy of Working Capital

(Passenger cars and multiutility vehicles sector)

Particulars	*Statistics*	*Hindustan Motors Ltd*	*Mahindra & Mahindra Ltd*	*Maruti Udyog Ltd*	*Total*
WC in terms of months cost of Production	Mean	0.76	2.01	0.98	3.72
	CV	1.18	0.48	1.58	0.67
	t	-3.62 **	-2.22 **	-8.19 *	
WC in terms of months Sales	Mean	0.77	2.02	1.00	1.34
	CV	1.18	0.48	1.57	0.57
	t	-1.48	1.90 ***	-1.43	

* Significant at 0.01 level; ** Significant at 0.05 level; *** Significant at 0.10 level

Source: Computed from the annual reports of the respective units.

Table 4.19

Statistical Values of Ratios Relating to Operational Adequacy of Working Capital

(Two and three wheelers sector)

Particulars	*Statistics*	*Bajaj Auto Ltd*	*LML Ltd*	*Maharashtra Scooters Ltd*	*TVS Motor Company Ltd*	*Kinetic Motors Ltd*	*Hero Honda Motors Ltd*	*Kinetic Engineering Ltd*	*Majestic Auto Ltd*	*Scooters India Ltd*	*Total*
WC in terms of months cost of Production	Mean	4.71	-0.77	4.71	0.21	0.59	0.71	2.47	-0.18	-27.09	17.20
	CV	0.42	-2.29	1.39	2.62	2.36	1.18	0.49	-7.17	-2.09	0.63
	t	-5.38 *	-6.30 *	-3.75 *	-6.30 *	-5.55 *	-6.01 *	-5.08 *	-6.24 *	-3.55 *	
WC in terms of months Sales	Mean	4.73	-0.74	5.09	0.21	0.56	0.72	2.49	-0.17	1.92	1.92
	CV	0.42	-2.28	1.27	2.62	2.46	1.17	0.50	-7.76	29.73	0.63
	t	10.76 *	-4.89	1.87***	-7.01 *	-2.33 **	-3.62 *	1.13	-4.68 *	-2.02 ***	

* Significant at 0.01 level; ** Significant at 0.05 level; *** Significant at 0.10 level

Source: Computed from the annual reports of the respective units.

Table 4.20

Good and Poor Risk Units in Terms of Current Ratio

(Group A consists of those units whose current ratio is atleast 1.5:1 and remaining units in Group B)

Year	92-93	93-94	94-95	95-96	96-97	97-98	98-99	99-00	00-01	01-02	02-03	03-04	04-05	05-06	06-07
Group A	ALL	ALL	ALL	ALL	ALL	ALL	ALL	ALL	ALL	ALL	ALL	ALL	ALL	ALL	MUL
	HHM	LMML	MML	BAL	HML	EML	EML	MML	BAL	BAL	MUL	MUL	MUL	MUL	BAL
	KEL	BAL	BAL		MML	MML	MML	BAL	MSL	MSL	BAL	MSL	BAL	BAL	HHML
		KML	KML		BAL	BAL	BAL	KEL	KEL	KEL	MSL	HHML	MSL	MSL	SIL
					KEL	TMCL	KEL	SIL	SIL	SIL	SIL	SIL	HHML	HHML	
						KEL	SIL			–			SIL	SIL	
						SIL									
	n_1=3	n_1=4	n_1=4	n_1 = 2	n_1=5	n_1=7	n_1=6	n_1=5	n_1=5	n_1=5	n_1=5	n_1=5	n_1=6	n_1=6	n_1=4
Group B	TML	TML	TML	TML	TML	TML	TML	TML	TML	TML	TML	TML	TML	TML	ALL
	BTL	BTL	BTL	BTL	BTL	BTL	BTL	BTL	BTL	BTL	BTL	BTL	BTL	BTL	TML
	EML	EML	EML	EML	EML	SML	SML	EML	EML	EML	EML	EML	EML	EML	BTL
	SML	SML	SML	SML	SML	HML	HML	SML	SML	SML	SML	SML	SML	SML	EML
	HML	HML	HML	HML	MUL	MUL	MUL	HML	HML	HML	HML	HML	HML	HML	SML
	MML	MUL	MUL	MML	LMLL	LMLL	LMLL	MUL	MML	MML	MML	MML	MML	MML	HML
	MUL	LMLL	LMLL	MUL	MSL	MSL	MSL	LML	LMUL	MUL	LMLL	BAL	LMLL	LMLL	MML
	BAL	MSL	MSL	LMLL	TMCL	KML	TMCL	MSL	LMLL	LMLL	TMCL	LMLL	TMCL	TMCL	LMLL

(Contd...)

(Contd...)

LMLL	TMCL	TMCL	MSL	KML	HHML	KML	TMCL	TMCL	TMCL	KML	TMCL	KML	KML	MSL
MSL	HHML	HHML	TMCL	HHML	MAL	HHML	KML	KML	KML	HHML	KML	KEL	KEL	TMCL
TMCL	KEL	KEL	KML	MAL		MAL	HHML	HHML	HHML	KEL	KEL	MAL	MAL	KML
KML	MAL	MAL	HHML	SIL		MAL	MAL	MAL	MAL	MAL			KEL	
MAL	SIL	SIL	KEL											MAL
SIL			MAL											
n_2=14	n_2=13	n_2=13	n_2=15	n_2=12	n_2=10	n_2=11	n_2=12	n_2=12	n_2=12	n_2=12	n_2=12	n_2=11	n_2=11	n_2=13

ALL – Ashok Leyland Ltd; TML – Tata Motors Ltd; BTL – Bajaj Tempo Ltd; EML – Eicher Motors Ltd; SML – Swaraj Mazda Ltd; HML – Hindustan Motors Ltd; MML – Mahindra and Mahindra Ltd; MUL – Maruti Udyog Ltd; BAL – Bajaj Auto Ltd; LMLL – LML Ltd; MSL – Maharashtra Scooters Ltd; TMCL – TVS Motor Company Ltd; KML – Kinetic Motors Ltd; HHML – Hero Honda Motors Ltd; KEL – Kinetic Engineering Ltd; MAL – Majestic Auto Ltd; SIL – Scooters India Ltd

Source: Computed

Table 4.21

Discriminant Functions for the Period 1992-93 to 2006-07

Year	*Function*	*Remark*
1992-93	Z = 0.319a – 0.068b	a > b
1993-94	Z = 1.279a – 0.393b	a > b
1994-95	Z = 1.492a – 0.459b	a > b
1995-96	Z = 0.388a – 0.052b	a > b
1996-97	Z = 2.485a – 1.036b	a > b
1997-98	Z = 0.692a – 0.484b	a > b
1998-99	Z = 1.633a – 0.891b	a > b
1999-00	Z = 2.675a – 1.115b	a > b
2000-01	Z = 2.295a – 0.956b	a > b
2001-02	Z = 2.811a – 1.171b	a > b
2002-03	Z = 1.505a – 0.627b	a > b
2003-04	Z = 0.935a – 0.389b	a > b
2004-05	Z = 1.515a – 0.631b	a > b
2005-06	Z = 1.799a – 0.981b	a > b
2006-07	Z = 1.605a – 0.494b	a > b

Note: The expression *a* > *b* is to be read "*a* is stronger than *b*".

Source: Computed.

As per the rule, the selected units falling in the good and poor risk group are presented in Table 4.20. After classifying the selected units in to the good and poor risk classes, the discriminant function of the selected years are estimated and presented in Table 4.21 where the co-efficient for 'a' and 'b' indicate the size of net working capital in terms of monthly operational requirements and sales requirements. The table reveals that the size of net working capital in terms of monthly operational requirements appeared to be stronger than sales requirements in all the years.

The discriminant co-efficient given in Table 4.21 was multiplied with the mean values of each industry ratio in order to obtain the discriminant score of each units. Table 4.22 presents the data relating to the discriminant score of all the units. With the help of the discriminant scores, the cut-off value was calculated as follows.

$$\text{Cut of Value} = \frac{n_i\overline{Z}_q + n_2\overline{Z}_q}{n_1 + n_2}$$

where n_1 and n_2 are the size of samples and z_1 and z_2 represent the mean of the discriminant score of group A and group B respectively. The cut-off values have also been presented in Table 4.22. Actual Z scores of the individual units were then compared with the discriminating Z scores. In the case where the Z scores were found to be more than the discriminating Z scores, it can be said that the sizes of net working capital were more than the operational and sales requirements.

It is evident from Table 4.22 that during the year 1992-93 to 1995-96, considering discriminant Z score, in case of Scooters India Ltd, the size of working capital was found to be very low considering the operational and sales requirements. In rest of the cases, size of working capital was found to be in excess in relation to operational and sales requirements.

In 1996-97 the cut-off Z score was found to be 2.23. In the case of Ashok Leyland Ltd, Tata Motors Ltd, Swaraj Mazda Ltd, Hindustan Motors Ltd, Mahindra and Mahindra Ltd, Bajaj Auto Ltd and Kinetic Engineering Ltd, the size of working capital was found to be in excess to meet their operational and sales requirements. In the case of Eicher Motors Ltd, it had satisfactory size of working capital as its Z score was less than 2.23 but was not low to be inadequate. In rest of the cases, size of working capital was found to be inadequate in relation to operational and sales requirements.

In 1997-98, the cut off Z score was 0.41. Considering this discriminant score, in the case of Hindustan Motors Ltd and Tata Motors Ltd, Z scores were found to be less than 0.41 but were not too low to be inadequate. In the case of Bajaj Tempo Ltd, Eicher Motors Ltd, Maruti Udyog Ltd, LML Ltd, Maharashtra Scooters Ltd, TVS Motor Company Ltd, Kinetic Motors Ltd, Hero Honda

Motors Ltd and Majestic Auto Ltd, the size of working capital was found to be very low. In the rest of the cases it was found that working capital was in excess as Z scored by the individual units were more than the cut off Z score.

In 1998-99, the cut off Z score was found to be 1.43. In the case of Eicher Motors Ltd and Maruti Udyog Ltd, the working capital positions was found to be quite satisfactory. In the case of Tata Motors Ltd, Bajaj Tempo Ltd, Hindustan Motors Ltd, LML Ltd, Maharashtra Scooters Ltd, TVS Motor Company Ltd, Kinetic Motors Ltd, Hero Honda Motors Ltd and Majestic Auto Ltd, the size of working capital was found to be too low and in rest of the case the sizes of working capital was in excess to meet their respective operational and sales requirements.

In 1999-2000, the cut-off Z score was 2.81. Considering it as discriminating Z score, it was found that in the case of Ashok Leyland Ltd, Swaraj Mazda Ltd, Mahindra and Mahindra Ltd, Baja Auto Ltd, Kinetic Engineering Ltd and Scooters India Ltd, the size of working capital was found to be in excess to meet their respective operational and sales requirements and in the rest of the cases the size of working capital was found to be too low.

In 2000-01, the cut-off Z score was 2.09. In the case of Ashok Leyland Ltd, Mahindra and Mahindra Ltd, Bajaj Auto Ltd, Maharastra Scooters Ltd, Kinetic Engineering Ltd and Scooters India Ltd, the size of working capital was found to be in excess to meet their respective operational and sales requirements and in the rest of the cases the size of working capital was found to be too low.

In 2001-02, the cut-off Z score was 2.76. In the case of Bajaj Tempo Ltd and Kinetic Motors Ltd, Z score was found to be less than 2.76 but was not too low to be inadequate. In other words the size of the working capital was found to be quite satisfactory. In the case of Tata Motors Ltd, Eicher Motors Ltd, Hindustan Motors Ltd, Maruti Udyog Ltd, LML Ltd, TVS Motor Company Ltd, Hero Honda Motors Ltd and Majestic Auto Ltd, the size of working capital was found to be very low. In the rest of the cases, it was found that working capital was in excess as Z scored by the individual units were more than the cut off Z score.

Table 4.22

Discriminant Z Values for the Selected Units (1992-93 to 2006-07)

Units	*92-93*	*93-94*	*94-95*	*95-96*	*96-97*	*97-98*	*98-99*	*99-00*	*00-01*	*01-02*	*02-03*	*03-04*	*04-05*	*05-06*	*06-07*
Ashok Leyland Ltd	1.86	4.05	7.81	1.91	7.48	1.46	4.17	5.49	5.59	6.73	3.01	1.12	2.79	1.75	1.25
Tata Motors Ltd	0.63	2.07	1.30	0.13	2.38	0.36	0.36	-0.91	-2.51	0.50	-0.95	0.10	0.47	0.90	0.46
Bajaj Tempo Ltd	0.45	1.10	1.47	0.24	1.26	0.17	0.81	1.90	1.71	1.90	1.01	0.52	0.62	-0.40	-0.23
Eicher Motors Ltd	0.29	1.07	1.55	0.50	2.12	0.29	1.13	1.64	0.90	0.18	-0.01	0.21	0.26	-0.02	-0.14
Swaraj Mazda Ltd	-0.13	-0.74	-0.62	0.32	2.66	0.48	1.93	2.98	1.63	2.80	0.33	0.33	0.67	0.45	1.67
Hindustan Motors Ltd	0.17	1.23	1.35	0.48	3.05	0.38	0.80	1.83	1.12	0.88	0.68	-0.04	-0.42	-0.87	-0.25
Mahindra & Mahindra Ltd	0.52	2.95	2.84	0.26	4.20	0.60	2.47	4.18	2.55	3.34	1.43	0.20	0.65	1.05	1.40
Maruti Udyog Ltd	0.47	-0.51	-2.66	-0.01	0.75	0.05	1.08	0.16	0.42	0.79	1.70	1.38	2.54	2.70	2.35
Bajaj Auto Ltd	0.45	1.98	4.17	0.96	5.70	1.00	4.24	11.48	5.54	8.28	3.21	1.52	7.25	6.10	7.12
LML Ltd	-0.50	-1.71	0.06	0.15	0.33	0.07	0.74	1.86	0.50	-2.01	-0.37	-0.44	-0.80	-1.91	-6.65

(*Contd...*)

(Contd...)

Units	*92-93*	*93-94*	*94-95*	*95-96*	*96-97*	*97-98*	*98-99*	*99-00*	*00-01*	*01-02*	*02-03*	*03-04*	*04-05*	*05-06*	*06-07*
Maharashtra Scooters Ltd	0.68	2.41	4.40	0.59	1.58	0.12	0.76	2.62	4.04	9.38	10.71	12.18	7.74	4.89	-8.00
TVS Motor Company Ltd	-0.31	-0.27	0.42	-0.01	0.78	0.24	-0.05	1.00	0.55	0.80	-0.04	-0.03	0.17	-0.34	0.68
Kinetic Motors Ltd	0.21	1.57	1.56	0.22	0.80	0.16	0.81	1.45	1.85	1.13	2.20	0.72	0.13	-1.74	-3.38
Hero Honda Motors Ltd	0.34	0.58	0.29	0.01	0.01	0.12	0.10	-0.37	1.03	-1.51	1.13	0.92	1.54	1.44	1.82
Kinetic Engineering Ltd	0.86	2.59	2.26	0.48	3.41	0.59	1.92	5.54	4.32	6.33	3.00	0.91	1.39	-0.85	2.88
Majestic Auto Ltd	0.03	0.21	0.43	0.55	0.48	0.22	0.42	-1.08	-1.76	-4.02	-1.83	-1.03	1.42	-0.04	-0.30
Scooters India Ltd	-30.03	-141.22	-103.53	-26.67	0.93	0.61	2.62	7.99	7.98	11.50	5.56	2.67	4.76	3.50	6.70
Discriminant Z Score	-1.41	-7.21	-4.52	-1.17	2.23	0.41	1.43	2.81	2.09	2.76	1.81	1.25	1.83	0.98	0.43

Source: Computed

In 2002-03, the cut-off Z score was found to be 1.81. Considering it as discriminating Z score it was found that in the case of Ashok Leyland Ltd, Bajaj Auto Ltd, Maharashtra Scooters Ltd, Kinetic Motors Ltd, Kinetic Engineering Ltd and Scooters India Ltd, the size of working capital was found to be in excess to meet their respective operational and sales requirements and in the rest of the cases, the size of working capital was found to be too low.

In 2003-04, the cut-off Z score was 1.25. Considering it as discriminating Z score it was found that in the case of Maruti Udyog Ltd, Bajaj Auto Ltd, Maharashtra Scooters Ltd and Scooters India Ltd the size of working capital was found to be in excess to meet their respective operational and sales requirements and in the rest of the cases, the size of working capital was found to be too low.

In 2004-05, the cut-off Z score was found to be 1.83. In the case of Ashok Leyland Ltd, Maruti Udyog Ltd, Bajaj Auto Ltd, Maharashtra Scooters Ltd, Scooters India Ltd, the size of working capital was found to be in excess to meet their operational and sales requirements. In case of Hero Honda Ltd it had satisfactory size of working capital as its Z scores was less than 1.83 but was not too low to be inadequate. In rest of the cases, size of working capital was found to be inadequate in relation to operational and sales requirements.

In 2005-06, the cut-off Z score was 0.98 considering it as discriminating. In the case of Ashok Leyland Ltd, Mahindra and Mahindra Ltd, Maruti Udyog Ltd and Bajaj Auto India Ltd, the size of working capital was found to be in excess to meet their respective operational and sales requirements and in the rest of the cases the size of working capital was found to be low.

In 2006–07, the cut-off Z score was 0.43. In the case of Bajaj Tempo Ltd and Eicher Motors Ltd, Z score was found to be less than 0.43 but was not too low to be inadequate. In other words, the size of the working capital was found to be quite satisfactory. In case of Hindustan Motors Ltd, LML Ltd, Maharashtra scooters Ltd, Kinetic Motors Ltd and Majestic Auto Ltd, the size of the working capital was found to be very low. In the rest of the cases it was found that the working capital was in excess as Z scored by the individual units was more than the cut-off Z score.

Table 4.23

Classification Matrix

Year	*As per current ratio*		*As per discriminant score*	
	Adequate	*Inadequate*	*Adequate*	*Inadequate*
1992-93	3	14	16	1
1993-94	4	13	16	1
1994-95	4	13	16	1
1995-96	2	15	16	1
1996-97	5	12	7	10
1997-98	7	10	6	11
1998-99	6	11	6	11
1999-00	5	12	6	11
2000-01	5	12	6	11
2001-02	5	12	7	10
2002-03	5	12	6	11
2003-04	5	12	4	13
2004-05	6	11	5	12
2005-06	6	11	7	10
2006-07	4	13	10	7

Source: Computed

It can be concluded that in the years 1992-93 to 2006-07 Ashok Leyland Ltd in commercial vehicles sector, Mahindra and Mahindra Ltd in passenger cars and multiutility vehicles sector and Bajaj Auto Ltd in two- and three-wheelers sector units maintained adequate size of working capital in relation to sales and output requirements throughout the period under study.

The number of good and risk units as per the current ratio and as per the discriminant score are presented in Table 4.23. It is clear from the table that the misclassification of units is noticed all the years. Generally one unit in the good risk group has been misclassified as poor risk under the criteria of discriminant score. Such industries are Ashok Leyland Ltd in 2003-04, Eicher Motors Ltd in the years 1997-98 and 1998-99, Maruti Udyog Ltd in 2002-03, TVS Motor Company Ltd in 1997-98 and Hero Honda Motors

Ltd in the years 2003-04 and 2004-05. It is also inferred that the poor risk industries appeared to be good risk under the criteria of discriminant score. Such a unit is Ashok Leyland Ltd in the year 2006-07, Tata Motors Ltd in 1992-93, 1993-94, 1994-95, 1995-96, 1996-97 and 2006-07, Bajaj Tempo Ltd in 1992-93, 1993-94, 1994-95 and 1995-96, Eicher Motors Ltd in 1992-93, 1993-94, 1994-95 and 1995-96, Swaraj Mazda Ltd in 1992-93, 1993-94, 1994-95, 1995-96, 1996-97, 1997-98, 1998-99, 1999-2000, 2001-02 and 2006-07, Hindustan Motors Ltd in 1992-93, 1993-94, 1994-95 and 1995-96, Mahindra and Mahindra Ltd in 1992-93, 1995-96, 2000-01, 2001-02, 2005-06 and 2006-07, Bajaj Auto Ltd in 1992-93 and 2003-04, LML Ltd in 1992-93, 1993-94, 1994-95 and 1995-96, Maharashtra Scooters Ltd in 1992-93, 1993-94, 1994-95 and 1995-96, TVS Motor Company Ltd in 1992-93, 1993-94, 1994-95, 1995-96 and 2006-07, Kinetic Motors Ltd in 1992-93, 1995-96 and 2002-03, Hero Honda Motors Ltd in 1993-94, 1994-95 and 1995-96 Kinetic Engineering Ltd in 1993-94, 1994-95, 1995-96, 2002-03 and 2006-07. Majestic Auto Ltd in the years 1992-93, 1993-94, 1994-95, 1995-96.

Working Capital Trend Analysis

In working capital analysis the direction of change over a period of time is crucial importance. Emphasizing the importance of analysis of working capital trends, Man Mohan and Goyal[10] have pointed out that, an analysis of working capital trends provides a base to judge whether the practice and prevailing policy of the management with regard to working capital is good enough or an improvement is to be made in managing the working capital funds. Further, any one trend by itself is not very informative and, therefore, comparison with related trends should also be made by an analyst. An upward trend in working capital, coupled with a downward trend in sales would usually reflect an unfavourable situations; an upward trend of current assets, in concert with a downward trend of current liabilities, would usually be viewed favourably.

Total Industry

The indices of working capital during the period of study from 1992-93 to 2006-07 in the automobile industry of India marked a continuous rising trend except in the years 1993-94, 1998-99, 1999-2000, 2000-01 and 2006-07. It increased from 86.33 in 1993-94 to 824.83 in 2005-06, consisting of a wide difference of 738.50. The high increase in working capital during 2005-06 was the effect of increase in working capital of Ashok Leyland Ltd and Tata Motors Ltd in the commercial vehicles sector and all the passenger cars and multiutility vehicles sector and Bajaj Auto Ltd and Hero Honda Motors Ltd in the two- and three-wheelers sector. The least squares trend values of working capital in the automobile industry in India are shown that the yearly increase in working capital comes to Rs.681.80 crores. The trend values of working capital varied significantly from observed values of working capital in all the years. The deviations were negative in years 1995-96, 1999-2000, 2000-01, 2001-02, 2002-03 and 2003-04 while they were positive in the remaining years. The negative deviation were very significant due to sharp decrease in the working capital of Eicher Motors Ltd in the commercial vehicles sector, Hindustan Motors Ltd in the passenger cars and the multiutility vehicles sector and LML Ltd, Kinetic Motors Ltd and Majestic Auto Ltd in the two- and three-wheelers sector. The difference between the actual and trend values of working capital in the automobile industry is significant because the calculated value of chi-square comes to 44686.83 which highly exceeds the table value 15.5 of chi-square at 5 per cent level of significance.

Commercial Vehicles Sector

It is evident from Table 4.24 that the indices of working capital in commercial vehicles sector marked a fluctuating trend in all the years. It fluctuated from -8.03 in 2000-01 to 262.97 in 2005-06, consisting a wide difference of 343.00. As compared to 1999-2000 (39.78) the indices decreased in 2000-01 (-80.03). The indices during 2003-04 and 2004-05 increased sharply and reached, 110.56 and 178.21 respectively and finally it reached 262.97 in the year 2005-06. The significant increase in working capital indices in 2005-06 was due to substantial increase in the working capital of Ashok Leyland Ltd and Tata Motors Ltd. The least square trend values of working capital in commercial vehicles sector shows that yearly increase in working capital comes to Rs.21.91 crores. The

Table 4.24

Working Capital Indices and Trend Values of the Selected Units

(Total Industry) *(Rs. in crores)*

Units	*92-93*	*93-94*	*94-95*	*95-96*	*96-97*	*97-98*	*98-99*	*99-00*	*00-01*	*01-02*	*02-03*	*03-04*	*04-05*	*05-06*	*06-07*
Commercial Vehicles															
W. Capital (Rs)	1136.04	1020.55	1441.70	1191.73	2375.68	2235.60	1042.22	451.87	-91.17	202.18	-41.43	1256.00	2024.50	2987.41	1652.43
Indices	100.00	89.83	126.87	104.90	209.12	196.79	91.74	39.78	-8.03	17.80	-3.65	110.56	178.21	262.97	145.46
Trend Values	1105.63	1127.54	1149.45	1171.36	1193.27	1215.18	1237.09	1259.00	1280.91	1302.82	1324.73	1346.64	1368.55	1390.46	1412.37
Passenger Cars & Multiutility Vehicles															
W. Capital (Rs)	484.21	375.55	-267.75	255.99	1157.79	1185.95	1744.45	1007.61	822.21	871.76	1687.70	2142.28	3122.00	4349.77	3511.45
Indices	100.00	77.56	-55.30	52.87	239.11	244.92	360.27	208.09	169.80	180.04	348.55	442.43	644.76	898.32	725.19
Trend Values	-242.36	6.09	254.54	502.99	751.44	999.89	1248.34	1496.79	1745.24	1993.69	2242.14	2490.59	2739.04	2987.49	3235.94

(Contd...)

(Contd...)

Units	*92-93*	*93-94*	*94-95*	*95-96*	*96-97*	*97-98*	*98-99*	*99-00*	*00-01*	*01-02*	*02-03*	*03-04*	*04-05*	*05-06*	*06-07*
Two & Three Wheelers															
W. Capital (Rs)	-13.28	-8.86	328.12	163.82	1025.91	1438.73	1633.97	2259.59	1521.79	1402.26	2038.13	2006.53	5169.66	5917.66	6445.64
Indices	100.00	66.72	-2470.78	-1233.58	-7725.23	-10833.81	-12303.99	-17014.99	-11459.26	-10559.19	-15347.36	-15109.41	-38928.16	-44560.69	-48536.45
Trend Values	-791.40	-379.96	31.48	442.92	854.36	1265.80	1677.24	2088.68	2500.12	2911.56	3323.00	3734.44	4145.88	4557.32	4968.76
Total Industry															
W. Capital (Rs)	1606.97	1387.24	1502.73	1611.54	4559.38	4860.28	4420.64	3719.07	2252.83	2476.20	3684.40	5404.81	10316.29	13254.84	11609.52
Indices	100.00	86.33	93.52	100.28	283.73	302.45	275.09	231.43	140.19	154.09	229.28	336.33	641.97	824.83	722.45
Trend Values	71.87	753.67	1435.47	2117.27	2799.27	3480.87	4162.67	4844.47	5526.27	6208.07	6889.87	7571.67	8253.47	8935.27	9617.07

Source: Ccmputed from the annual reports of the respective units

Table 4.25

Working Capital indices and Trend Values of the Selected Units

(Commercial vehicles sector)

(Rs. in crores)

Units	*92 - 93*	*93 - 94*	*94 – 95*	*95 - 96*	*96 - 97*	*97- 98*	*98 - 99*	*99 - 00*	*00 - 01*	*01 - 02*	*02 - 03*	*03 - 04*	*04 - 05*	*05- 06*	*06-07*
Ashok Leyland Ltd															
W. Capital (Rs)	479.03	408.03	859.06	883.82	1046.00	1227.28	728.57	698.87	854.13	860.51	710.59	605.97	1126.05	1078.88	697.57
Indices	100.00	85.18	179.33	184.50	218.36	256.20	152.09	145.89	178.30	179.64	148.34	126.50	235.07	225.22	145.62
Trend Values	703.52	722.68	741.84	761.00	780.16	799.32	818.48	837.64	856.80	875.96	895.12	914.28	933.44	952.60	971.76
Tata Motors Ltd															
W. Capital (Rs)	605.43	559.79	507.62	227.93	1219.90	911.57	217.68	-361.07	-1049.70	-752.26	-831.31	204.93	761.09	1908.64	916.79
Indices	100.00	92.46	83.84	37.65	204.49	150.57	35.95	-59.64	-173.38	-124.25	-137.31	33.85	125.71	315.25	151.43
Trend Values	318.91	321.42	323.93	326.44	328.95	331.46	333.97	336.48	338.99	341.50	344.01	346.52	349.03	351.54	354.05
Bajaj Tempo Ltd															
W. Capital (Rs)	45.32	46.44	58.07	36.72	45.21	47.05	38.75	57.56	56.44	46.29	67.96	74.31	51.20	-39.28	-15.60
Indices	100.00	102.47	128.13	81.02	99.79	103.82	85.50	127.01	124.54	102.14	149.96	163.97	112.97	-86.67	-34.42

(Contd...)

(Contd...)

Units	*92-93*	*93-94*	*94-95*	*95-96*	*96-97*	*97-98*	*98-99*	*99-00*	*00-01*	*01-02*	*02-03*	*03-04*	*04-05*	*05-06*	*06-07*
Trend Values	59.61	5.97	54.33	51.69	49.05	46.41	43.77	41.13	38.49	35.85	33.21	30.57	27.93	25.29	22.65
Eicher Motors Ltd W. Capital (Rs)	9.80	13.32	23.59	29.62	36.43	28.34	28.82	27.30	22.01	4.54	-0.61	46.30	48.65	-4.78	-20.57
Indices	100.00	135.92	240.71	302.24	371.73	289.18	294.08	278.57	224.5	46.33	6.22	472.45	496.43	-48.78	-209.90
Trend Values	26.89	25.84	24.79	23.74	22.69	21.64	20.59	19.54	18.49	17.44	16.39	15.34	14.29	13.24	12.19
Swaraj Mazda Ltd W. Capital (Rs)	-3.54	-7.03	-6.64	14.14	28.14	21.36	28.40	29.21	25.95	43.10	11.94	24.49	37.51	43.95	74.24
Indices	100.00	198.59	187.57	-399.44	-794.92	-603.39	-802.26	-825.14	-733.05	-1217.51	-337.29	-691.81	-1059.60	-1241.53	-2097.18
Trend Values	-3.27	0.68	4.63	8.53	12.53	16.48	20.43	24.38	28.33	32.28	36.23	40.18	44.13	48.08	52.03

Source: Computed from the annual reports of the respective units.

Table 4.26

Working Capital Indices and Trend Values of the Selected Units

(Passenger cars and multiutility vehicles sector)

(Rs in crores)

Units	*92-93*	*93-94*	*94-95*	*95-96*	*96-97*	*97-98*	*98-99*	*99-00*	*00-01*	*01-02*	*02-03*	*03-04*	*04-05*	*05-06*	*06-07*
Hindustan Motors Ltd															
W. Capital (Rs)	30.24	73.26	80.69	108.96	177.78	165.21	109.71	131.52	77.46	38.52	53.66	-3.80	-19.66	-37.59	-8.04
Indices	100.00	242.26	266.83	360.32	587.90	546.33	362.80	434.92	256.15	127.38	177.45	-12.57	-65.01	-124.31	-26.59
Trend Values	128.79	119.70	110.61	101.52	92.43	83.34	74.25	65.16	56.07	46.98	37.89	28.80	19.71	10.62	1.53
Mahindra & Mahindra Ltd															
W. Capital (Rs)	212.20	401.60	333.96	159.53	733.31	876.72	907.33	819.09	567.45	533.24	493.84	157.88	422.06	886.17	1044.94
Indices	100.00	189.26	157.38	75.18	345.57	413.16	427.58	386.00	267.41	251.29	232.72	74.40	198.90	417.61	492.43
Trend Values	384.33	410.85	437.37	463.89	490.41	516.93	543.45	569.97	596.49	623.01	649.53	676.05	702.57	729.09	755.61
Maruti Udyog Ltd															
W. Capital (Rs)	241.77	-99.31	-681.71	-12.50	246.70	144.02	727.41	57.00	177.30	300.00	1140.20	1988.20	2719.60	3501.20	2474.55
Indices	100.00	-41.08	-281.97	-5.17	102.04	59.57	300.87	23.58	73.33	124.08	471.61	822.35	1124.87	1448.15	1023.51
Trend Values	-755.47	-524.45	-293.43	-62.41	168.61	399.63	630.65	861.67	1092.69	1323.71	1554.73	1785.75	2016.77	2247.79	2478.81

Source: Computed from the annual reports of the respective units

Table 4.27

Working Capital Indices and Trend Values of the Selected Units

(Two- and three-wheelers sector)

(Rs. in crores)

Units	92-93	93-94	94-95	95-96	96-97	97-98	98-99	99-00	00-01	01-02	02-03	03-04	04-05	05-06	06-07
Bajaj Auto Ltd															
W. Capital (Rs)	155.69	245.05	603.61	553.71	896.81	1136.80	1393.70	1990.60	1061.30	1509.20	1307.00	1124.40	3975.95	4757.62	5008.02
Indices	100.00	157.40	387.70	355.65	576.02	730.17	895.18	1278.57	681.68	969.36	839.49	722.20	2553.76	3055.83	3216.66
Trend Values	-314.43	-26.47	261.49	549.45	837.41	1125.37	1413.33	1701.29	1989.25	2277.21	2565.17	2853.13	3141.09	3429.05	3717.01
LML Ltd															
W. Capital (Rs)	-29.47	-32.92	1.46	15.42	9.67	17.17	85.13	56.14	16.88	-44.62	-33.46	-66.32	-42.35	-72.10	-151.91
Indices	100.00	111.71	-4.95	-52.32	-32.81	-58.26	-288.87	-190.50	-57.28	151.41	113.54	225.04	143.71	244.66	515.47
Trend Values	30.90	23.90	16.90	9.90	2.90	-4.10	-11.10	-18.10	-25.10	-32.10	-39.10	-46.10	-53.10	-60.10	-67.10
Maharashtra Scooters Ltd															
W. Capital (Rs)	27.32	30.30	49.27	25.97	20.66	12.29	21.50	33.60	38.52	47.24	57.45	65.21	17.88	16.60	-1.75
Indices	100.00	110.91	180.34	95.06	75.62	44.99	78.70	122.99	141.00	172.91	210.29	238.69	65.45	60.76	-6.41
Trend Values	33.01	32.69	32.37	32.05	31.73	31.41	31.09	30.77	30.45	30.13	29.81	29.49	29.17	28.85	28.53
TVS Motor Company Ltd															
W. Capital (Rs)	-18.63	-6.60	13.88	-2.06	36.69	97.30	-7.74	80.48	63.80	77.22	-9.06	-12.06	45.65	113.76	193.88
Indices	100.00	35.43	-74.50	11.06	-196.94	-522.28	41.55	-431.99	-342.46	-414.49	48.63	-64.73	245.03	-610.63	1040.69
Trend Values	-11.13	-3.19	4.75	12.69	20.63	28.57	36.51	44.45	52.39	60.33	68.27	76.21	84.15	92.09	100.03

(Contd...)

(Contd...)

Kinetic Motors Ltd															
W. Capital (Rs)	10.09	20.38	18.41	14.33	13.11	18.72	25.60	23.94	24.56	18.94	60.90	18.94	4.06	-30.93	-55.79
Indices	100.00	201.98	182.46	142.02	129.93	185.53	253.72	237.26	243.41	187.71	603.57	187.71	40.24	-306.54	-552.92
Trend Values	29.23	26.90	24.47	22.04	19.61	17.18	14.75	12.32	9.89	7.46	5.03	2.60	0.17	-2.26	-4.69
Hero Honda Motors Ltd															
W. Capital (Rs)	33.88	19.62	11.89	0.59	0.13	5.26	17.49	-45.91	203.71	-343.75	550.36	808.75	1077.25	1288.12	1354.52
Indices	100.00	57.91	35.09	1.74	0.38	157.20	51.62	-135.51	601.27	-1014.61	1624.44	2387.10	3179.60	3802.01	3997.99
Trend Values	-326.12	-231.63	-137.14	-42.65	51.84	146.33	240.82	335.31	-429.80	524.29	618.78	713.27	807.76	902.25	996.74
Kinetic Engineering Ltd															
W. Capital (Rs)	26.71	25.59	23.40	21.40	37.44	52.90	54.28	81.83	80.29	105.60	71.97	29.03	25.14	-14.11	28.76
Indices	100.00	95.81	87.61	80.12	140.17	198.05	203.22	306.36	300.60	395.36	269.45	108.69	94.12	-52.83	107.68
Trend Values	42.09	42.27	42.45	42.63	42.81	42.99	43.17	43.35	43.53	43.71	43.89	44.07	44.25	44.43	44.61
Majestic Auto Ltd															
W. Capital (Rs)	1.09	2.78	5.55	22.99	5.51	22.89	10.15	-10.92	-22.44	-34.69	-32.83	-17.40	9.45	-0.49	-4.15
Indices	100.00	255.05	509.17	2109.17	505.50	2100.00	931.19	-1001.83	-2058.72	-3182.57	-3011.93	-1596.33	866.97	-44.95	-380.73
Trend Values	8.96	7.04	5.39	3.74	2.09	0.44	-1.21	-2.86	-4.51	-6.16	-7.81	-9.46	-11.11	-12.76	-14.41
Scooters India Ltd															
W. Capital (Rs)	-219.96	-313.06	-399.35	-488.53	5.89	27.40	33.86	49.83	55.17	67.62	65.80	55.92	56.76	59.19	74.06
Indices	100.00	142.33	181.56	222.10	-2.68	12.46	-15.39	-22.65	-25.08	-30.74	-29.91	-25.42	-25.80	-26.91	-33.67
Trend Values	-283.74	-251.48	-219.22	-186.96	-154.70	-122.44	-90.18	-57.92	-25.66	6.60	38.86	71.12	103.38	135.64	167.90

Source: Computed from the annual reports of the respective units.

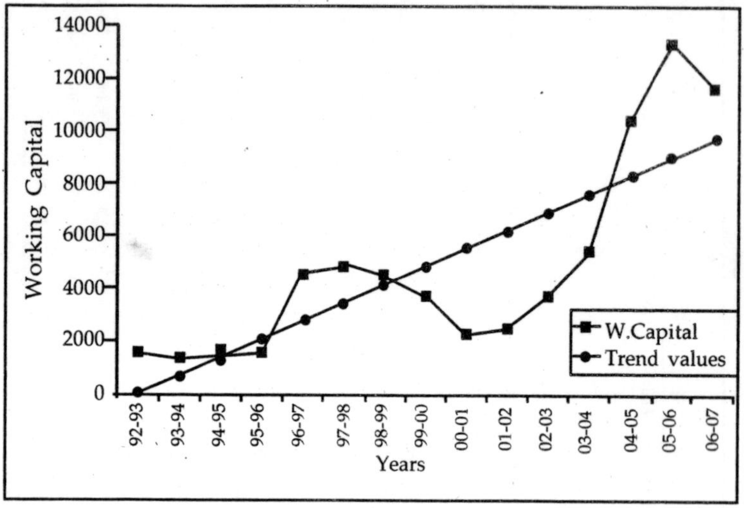

Figure 4.1
Automobile industry in India – trends of working capital (1992-93 to 2006-07)

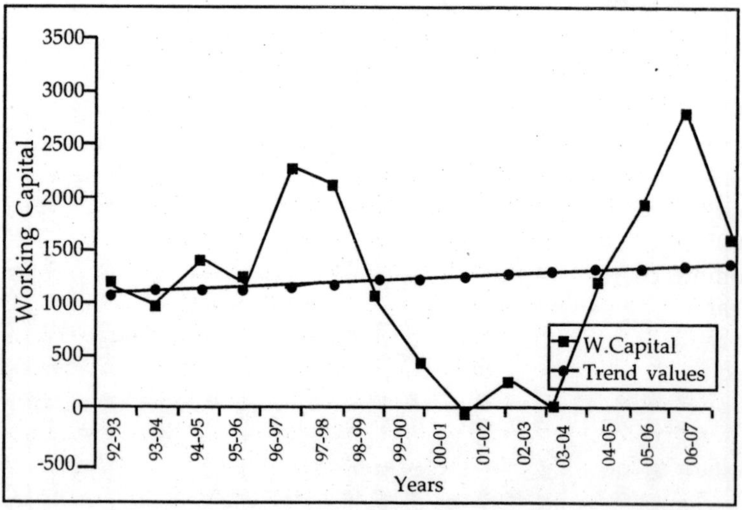

Figure 4.2
Commercial vehicles sector – trends of working capital (1992-93 to 2006-07)

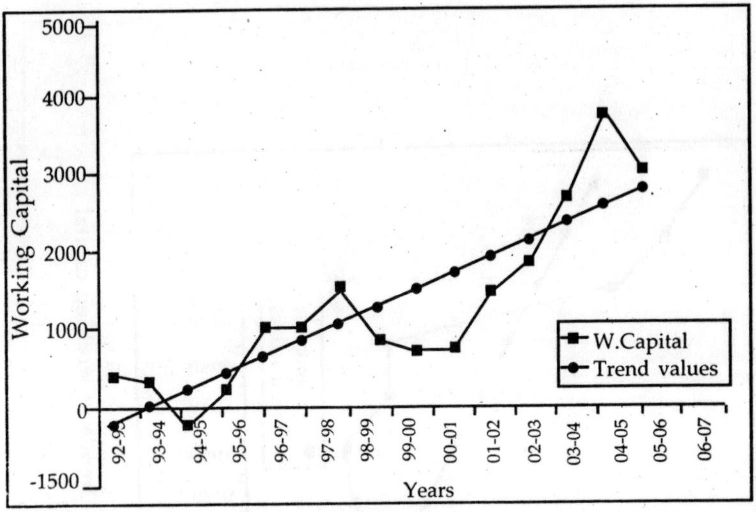

Figure 4.3
Passenger Cars and Multiutility Vehicles Sector–trends of Working Capital
(1992-93 To 2006-07)

trend values of working capital were significantly different from actual values during the period of study from 1993-94 to 2006-07. The deviations were negative in the years 1993-94, 1998-99, 1999-2000, 2000-01, 2001-02, 2002-03 and 2003-04 while they were positive in the remaining years. The positive difference during 2005-06 was very significant because the working capital of the commercial vehicles sector increased significantly during this year as compared to the previous year due to sharp increase in current assets of all the selected units of the commercial vehicles sector. The difference between the actual and values of working capital is significant because the calculated value of chi-square comes to 8665.56, which highly exceeds the table value 15.5 of chi-square at 5 per cent level of significance.

Passenger Cars and Multiutility Vehicles Sector

It is clear from Table 4.24 that the indices of working capital in passenger cars and multiutility vehicles sector have shown an

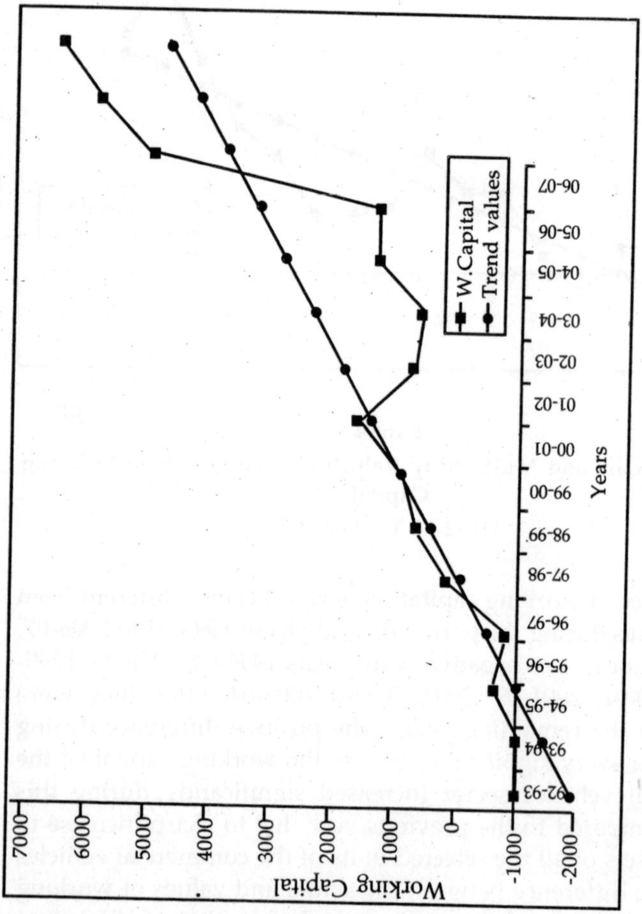

Figure 4.4: Two- and three-wheelers sector – trends of working capital (1992-93 to 2006-07)

increasing trend throughout the period of study, except in the year 1994-95. It increased from -55.30 in 1994-95 to 898.32 in 2005-06. The indices of working capital increased continuously from 1995-96 to 1998-99 and 2001-02 to 2005-06. The significant increase in working capital indices in 2005-06 was due to substantial increase in the working capital of all the selected units of the passenger cars and multiutility vehicles sector. The least square trend values of working capital in the passenger cars and multiutility vehicles sector shows that the yearly increase in working capital comes to 248.45 crores. The trend values of working capital differed significantly in all the years. The differences were negative years in 1994-95, 1995-96, 1999-2000, 2000-01, 2001-02, 2002-03 and 2003-04 while they were positive in the rest of the years. The positive difference during 2005-06 was very significant. This was due to a sharp increase in the working capital of all the units. The difference between the actual and trend values of working capital in the passenger cars and multiutility vehicles sector is significant because the calculated value of chi-square comes to 26096.82, which highly exceeds the table value 15.5 of chi-square at 5 per cent level of significance.

Two- and Three-Wheelers Sector

It is evident from Table 4.24 that the indices of working capital in two and three wheeler units marked a fluctuating trend during study period from 1992-93 to 2006-07. The indices in the years 1993-2000, 2002-03 and 2004-07, the working capital was decreased while they were increased in the remaining years. The main reason for decrease in the working capital is due to decrease in the working capital of LML Ltd, Kinetic Motors Ltd and Majestic Auto Ltd. The least square trend values of working capital in the two- and three-wheelers sector shows that the yearly increase in working capital comes to Rs.411.44 crores. The difference were negative in the years 1995-96, 1998-99 and 2000-04 while they were positive in the rest of the years The positive difference during 2006-07 was very significant. The difference between the actual and trend values of working capital in the two- and three-wheelers sector is significant because the calculated value of chi-square comes to 6186.46 which highly exceed the table value 15.5 chi-square at 5 per cent level of significance.

Analysis of Variance (F-Test) - Working Capital

Total industry

With the view to testing the significance of variations in the indices of working capital between various companies and between various years covered under the study, the F-test (Analysis of Variance) based on two way classification has been applied. It can be seen from Table 4.28 that the calculated value of 'F' ratio between the years is 1.12 and 'F' ratio between the companies is 6.03. The calculated value of 'F' (1.12) between the years is less than the table value of 'F' (1.74) at 5 per cent level of significance. Thus the difference in the indices of working capital between the years among all the selected automobile industries is not significant. But the calculated value of 'F' (6.03) between the companies is more than the table value of 'F' (1.69) at 5 per cent level of significance. Thus, the difference in the indices of working capital between the companies among different years are significant.

Commercial Vehicles Sector

It can be clear from Table 4.28 that the calculated value of 'F' ratio between the years is 1.26 and 'F' ratio between the companies is 25.07. The calculated value of 'F' (1.26) between the years is less than the table value of (1.87) at 5 per cent level of significance. Thus the difference in the indices of working capital between the years among all the selected commercial vehicles sector units is not significant. The calculated value of 'F' (25.07) between the companies is more than the table value of 'F' (2.54) at 5 per cent level of significance. Thus, the difference in the indices of working capital between the companies among different years are significant.

Passenger Cars and Multiutility Vehicles Sector

It can be seen from Table 4.28 that the calculated value of 'F' ratio between the years is 0.53. The calculated value of 'F' (0.53) between the years is less than the table value of 'F' (2.06) at 5 per cent level of significance. Thus, the difference in the indices of working capital between the years among all the selected passenger cars and multiutility vehicle units is not significant.

Table 4.28

Analysis of Variance of Indices of Working Capital

(Total Industry)

Source of variance	*Sum of squares*	*d.f*	*Mean square variance*	*F ratio (Calculated value)*	*Critical values of F (at 5% level)*
Between years	66,09,092.04	14	4,72,078.00	1.12	1.74
Between companies	4,05,97,907.16	16	25,37,369.20	6.03	1.69
Residual	9,42,77,490.10	224	4,20,882.65		
Total	14,14,84,489.30	254			

(Commercial vehicles sector)

Source of variance	*Sum of squares*	*d.f*	*Mean square variance*	*F ratio (Calculated value)*	*Critical values of F (at 5% level)*
Between years	14,44,448.30	14	10,3174.88	1.26	1.87
Between companies	82,08,967.44	4	20,52,241.86	25.07	2.54
Residual	45,84,905.59	56	81,873.31		
Total	1,42,38,321.33	74			

(Passenger cars and multiutility vehicles sector)

Source of variance	*Sum of squares*	*d.f*	*Mean square variance*	*F ratio (Calculated value)*	*Critical values of F (at 5% level)*
Between years	9,55,993.55	14	68,285.25	0.53	2.06
Between companies	1,51,716.67	2	75,858.34	0.59	3.34
Residual	36,02,840.16	28	1,28,672.86		
Total	47,10,550.38	44			

(Two and three wheelers sector)

Source of variance	*Sum of squares*	*d.f*	*Mean square variance*	*F ratio (Calculated value)*	*Critical values of F (at 5% level)*
Between Years	1,05,27,598.74	14	7,51,971.34	1.05	1.78
Between Companies	2,80,88,317.05	8	35,11,040.63	4.92	2.02
Residual	7,99,49,345.41	112	7,13,833.44		
Total	11,85,65,261.20	134			

Source: Computed

The calculated value of 'F' (0.59) between the companies is less than the table value of 'F' (3.34) at 5 per cent level of significance. Thus the difference in the indices of working capital between the companies among different years are not significant.

Two and Three Wheelers Sector

It can be seen from Table 4.28 that the calculated value of 'F' ratio between the years is 1.05 and 'F' ratio between the companies is 4.92. The calculated value of 'F' (1.05) between the years is less than the table value of (1.78) at 5 per cent level of significance. Thus, the difference in the indices of working capital between the years among all the selected two- and three-wheeler units is not significant. The calculated value of 'F' (4.92) between the companies is more than the table value of 'F' (2.02) at 5 per cent level of significance. Thus the difference in the indices of working capital between the companies among different years are significant.

On the basis of this analysis, it may be concluded that the performance of individual automobile companies is significantly different with the standards of industry. Fither the companies are above the industry standards or they are below the company standards with regard to working capital.

Financing of Working Capital

One of the important tasks of the financial manager is to select an assortment of appropriate sources to finance the current assets.

A business firm has various sources to meet its financial requirements. Normally the current assets of a firm are supported by a combination of long-term and short-term sources of financing. The long-term sources of finance provide support for a small part of current assets requirement which is called the net working capital or working capital margin. The short-term sources of finance, referred to also as current liabilities, provide the major support for current assets. In Table 4.29 an attempt has been made to explain the relative importance of long-term and short-term debt in financing working capital.

Table 4.29

Sources of Financing of Working Capital

		(Total Industry)			*(Rs. in crores)*
S. No	*Particulars*	*Commercial vehicles sector*	*Passenger cars & multiutility vehicles sector*	*Two- and three-wheelers sector*	*Total Industry*
1	Working capital (Gross)	6,807.07	4,587.68	6,566.74	17,961.49
2	Sources of working capital				
	a) Short-term funds	3,896.33	2,302.78	1,796.33	7,995.44
	b) Long-term funds	2,910.74	2,284.90	4,770.41	9,966.05
3	Total long-term funds (Net worth + long term borrowings)	7,170.61	5,607.45	7,288.42	20,066.48
4	Percentage of long-term funds used for financing working capital (2b as % of 3)	40.59	40.75	65.45	49.67

Source: Computed from the annual reports of the respective units.

It is evident from Table 4.29 that the average proportion of financing current assets of the Indian automobile Industries from long-term sources was 55.49 per cent, as against 42.76 per cent in commercial vehicles sector, 49.81 per cent in the passenger cars and multiutility vehicles sector and 72.65 per cent in the two- and three-wheelers sector. The table also reveals that the average percentage of long-term funds used for financing working capital in industry was 49.67 per cent, whereas in the commercial vehicles sector, passenger cars and multiutility vehicles sector and two and three wheelers sector, it was 40.59 per cent, 40.75 per cent and 65.45 per cent respectively.

Table 4.30

Sources of financing of working capital

(Commercial vehicles sector) *(Rs. in crores)*

S. No	*Particulars*	*Ashok Leyland Ltd*	*Tata Motors Ltd*	*Bajaj Tempo Ltd*	*Eicher Motors Ltd*	*Swaraj Mazda Ltd*
1	Working Capital (Gross)	1,651.10	4,509.04	281.24	199.87	165.82
2	Sources of working Capital					
	a) Short- Term Funds	587.97	2,893.42	176.82	131.52	106.60
	b) Long -term Funds	1,063.13	1,615.62	104.42	68.35	59.22
3	Total Long-Term Funds (Net worth + Long Term Borrowings)	1,696.85	4,555.32	182.13	661.60	74.71
4	Percentage of Long-term Funds used for financing working capital (2b as % of 3)	62.65	35.47	57.33	10.33	79.27

Source: Computed from the Annual reports of the respective units.

Similarly the average percentage of long term funds used for financing working capital in all the selected units in commercial vehicles sector, the passenger cars and multiutility vehicles sector and the two- and three-wheelers sector is presented in Table 4.30 to 4.32. It is evident from the table that the average percentage of long term funds used for financing working capital is the highest in Swaraj Mazda Ltd, followed by Ashok Leyland Ltd, Tata Motors Ltd, Bajaj Tempo Ltd and Eicher Motors Ltd in the commercial vehicles sector. Among the passenger cars and multiutility vehicle sector, it is the highest in Maruti Udyog Ltd, followed by Hindustan Motors Ltd, Mahindra and Mahindra Ltd and among the two- and three-wheelers sector, it is the highest in Maharashtra Scooters Ltd followed by Bajaj Auto Ltd, LML Ltd, TVS Motor Company Ltd, Kinetic Motors Ltd, Hero Honda Motors Ltd, Kinetic Engineering Ltd, Majestic Auto Ltd and Scooters India Ltd during the study period.

Table 4.31

Sources of Financing of Working Capital

(Passenger cars and multiutility vehicles sector)

(Rs. in crores)

S. No	*Particulars*	*Hindustan Motors Ltd*	*Mahindra & Mahindra Ltd*	*Maruti Udyog Ltd*
1	Working capital (Gross)	406.45	1,613.48	2,567.75
2	Sources of working capital			
	a) Short-term funds	235.85	835.13	1,231.78
	b) Long -term funds	170.60	778.35	1,335.97
3	Total long-term funds (Net worth + long term borrowings)	415.35	2,374.80	2,817.78
4	Percentage of long-term funds used for financing working capital (2b as % of 3)	41.07	32.78	47.41

Source: Computed from the annual reports of the respective units.

It can be observed from the above analysis that the dominance of long-term funds as sources of working capital is more in the two- and three-wheelers sector than in commercial vehicles sector and the passenger cars and multiutility vehicles sector. Theoretically speaking working capital funds of any concern should mainly be financed by short-term funds. In case of necessity sometimes long-term sources may also be used for the purpose. From practical view point a proper balance between the long-term and short-term sources should be maintained as far as possible depending on the respective cost of these sources.

Generally, the long-term debts are costlier than the short-term debts and are taken as the base to comment on the performance of working capital management of the company. Increasing dependence on the long-term sources of financing working capital in all the two and three wheelers sector units, Tata Motors Ltd and Ashok Leyland Ltd in commercial vehicles sector units and Maruti Udyog Ltd and Mahindra and Mahindra Ltd in passenger cars and multiutility vehicles sector units depicts the incapability of the company to make efficient management of its current assets namely receivables and inventories.

Risk Return Analysis of Working Capital

One of the important propositions developed by E.W.Walker[11] states that if amount of working capital is varied relative to fixed capital the amount of risk that a firm assumes is also varied and opportunity for gain or loss increased. This theory assumes that there exists a definite relationship between the degree of risk and rate of return and relationship can be changed by changing the level of working capital. The basic question is to find out percentage reduction in working capital needed in order to result in a more than proportionate increase in return on investment. This can be determined by computation of working capital leverage. Working capital leverage can be defined as effect of change in working capital in relation of fixed capital, on return on investment. If working capital increases in relation to fixed capital there should.be decrease in return on investment and vice versa. The working capital leverage can be expressed in terms of

$$WCL = \frac{\text{Return on Investment (ROI)}}{\text{Working Capital to Fixed Capital}}$$

(or)

Table 4.32: Sources of Financing of Working Capital

(Two and three wheelers sector)

(Rs. in crores)

S. No	Particulars	Bajaj Auto Ltd	LML Ltd	Maharashtra Scooters Ltd	TVS Motor Company Ltd	Kinetic Motors Ltd	Hero Honda Motors	Kinetic Engineering Ltd	Majestic Auto Ltd	Scooters India Ltd
1	Working capital (Gross)	3,484.80	249.05	1,109.14	354.55	88.53	983.61	152.72	63.99	80.35
2	Sources of working capital									
	a) Short-term funds	541.88	230.00	32.13	250.84	49.41	468.22	46.79	48.06	128.96
	b) Long-term funds	2,942.90	19.01	1,077.01	103.71	39.12	515.39	105.93	15.93	Nil
3	Total long-term funds (Net worth + long term borrowings)	3,261.91	818.74	1,141.16	461.71	616.95	804.50	147.24	75.50	-39.24
4	Percentage of long-term funds used for financing working capital (2b as % of 3)	90.22	2.32	94.38	22.46	6.34	64.06	71.94	21.10	Nil

Source: Computed from the annual reports of the respective units.

Table 4.33
Working Capital Leverage of the Sample Units

Units\Years	*92-93*	*93-94*	*94-95*	*95-96*	*96-97*	*97-98*	*98-99*	*99-00*	*00-01*	*01-02*	*02-03*	*03-04*	*04-05*	*05-06*	*06-07*
Ashok Leyland Ltd	0.080	0.141	0.083	0.115	0.118	0.060	0.099	0.153	0.133	0.152	0.197	0.338	0.193	0.248	0.600
Tata Motors Ltd	0.080	0.238	0.707	2.579	0.587	0.459	1.290	-0.511	0.006	-0.316	-0.746	5.628	5.460	1.838	2.143
Bajaj Tempo Ltd	0.147	0.301	0.296	1.357	0.503	0.220	-0.223	-0.018	-0.016	0.157	0.290	0.377	0.065	-0.946	-3.128
Eicher Motors Ltd	–	–	0.440	0.366	0.281	0.216	0.331	0.624	1.090	7.635	-52.560	2.168	1.709	-4.695	-2.179
Swaraj Mazda Ltd	–	–	–0.390	0.189	0.108	0.165	0.088	0.075	0.156	0.121	0.888	0.631	0.343	0.129	0.085
Commercial vehicles sector	0.096	0.240	0.405	0.383	0.207	0.162	0.113	0.147	0.207	0.241	0.872	0.669	0.396	0.339	0.288
Hindustan Motors Ltd	NIL	0.666	0.610	0.586	0.329	0.442	0.341	0.214	-0.146	–	–	–	0.506	–	–
Mahindra & Mahindra Ltd	0.194	0.144	0.293	1.038	0.268	0.225	0.191	0.264	0.221	0.208	0.334	1.824	0.937	0.462	0.450

(Contd...)

Maruti Udyog Ltd	0.310	–2.208	–0.246	–65.240	2.485	3.859	0.654	7.300	0.777	0.469	0.182	0.244	0.220	0.177	0.255
Passenger cars and multiutility vehicles sector	0.239	0.420	2.629	1.865	0.599	0.655	0.366	0.398	0.002	0.226	0.206	0.398	0.335	0.261	0.313
Bajaj Auto Ltd	0.431	0.475	0.260	0.424	0.258	0.193	0.185	0.112	0.127	0.164	0.207	0.241	0.062	0.067	0.070
LML Ltd	–	-0.765	16.165	1.371	4.657	2.655	0.522	0.430	-0.263	–	–	–	–	–	–
Maharashtra Scooters Ltd	0.055	0.045	0.022	0.062	0.119	0.170	0.138	0.110	0.004	0.007	0.006	-0.001	0.021	0.027	-0.142
TVS Motor Company Ltd 0.830	–	0.640	-3.358	2.235	-33.015	2.064	0.912	-15.680	3.104	1.250	1.033	-41.040	-18.340	3.807	1.316
Kinetic Motors Ltd	0.170	0.210	0.291	0.332	0.354	0.268	0.220	0.653	1.262	0.753	0.046	-0.435	0.000	-0.077	-0.049
Hero Honda Motors Ltd	0.455	0.849	2.204	35.660	25.580	1.780	8.882	-5.513	1.441	-1.355	0.910	0.582	0.516	0.520	0.662

(Contd...)

(Contd...)

Kinetic Engineering Ltd	0.172	0.176	0.238	0.564	0.307	0.207	0.161	0.134	0.140	0.090	0.078	-0.529	-0.629	1.011	-0.324
Majestic Auto Ltd	3.640	2.954	1.602	0.320	1.005	NIL	0.829	-0.548	–	–	–	-0.508	0.652	-8.260	-1.320
Scooter India Ltd	–	–	–	–	0.352	0.053	0.031	0.021	0.015	0.007	0.004	0.008	0.008	0.014	0.009
Two- & three-wheelers sector	–0.040	-0.043	-0.035	-0.026	0.455	0.231	0.219	0.218	0.153	0.161	0.135	0.123	0.129	0.138	0.146
Total Industry	-0.717	-0.665	-0.583	-0.525	2.109	1.601	1.300	1.453	1.113	1.296	1.672	1.782	1.388	1.203	1.257

Source: Computed from the annual reports of the respective units

$$WCL = \frac{ROI}{WCFC}$$

Table 4.34

Correlation co-efficient between ROI and WC of the sample unit

Units	*Correlation Co-efficient*
Ashok Leyland Ltd	-0.358 (-1.383) **
Tata Motors Ltd	0.880 (0.320)
Bajaj Tempo Ltd	0.321 (1.221)
Eicher Motors Ltd	-0.178 (-0.651)
Swaraj Mazda Ltd	0.259 (0.966)
Commercial vehicles sector	- 0.184 (0.674)
Hindustan Motors Ltd	0.807 (4.928) *
Mahindra & Mahindra Ltd	0.072 (0.261)
Maruti Udyog Ltd	0.120 (0.435)
Passenger cars & multiutility vehicles Sector	0.132 (0.482)
Bajaj Auto Ltd	-0.025 (-0.089)
LML Ltd	0.305 (1.154)
Maharastra Scooters Ltd	0.541 (2.321) **
TVS Motor Company Ltd	0.226 (0.837)
Kinetic Motors Ltd	0.274 (1.027)
Hero Honda Motors Ltd	0.368 (1.425)
Kinetic Engineering Ltd	0.676 (3.308) ***
Majestic Auto Ltd	0.441 (1.770)
Scooters India Ltd	0.413 (1.637)
Two and three wheelers sector	-0.511 (-2.144) ***
Industry (Total)	-0.101 (-0.368)

Figures in brackets show 't' value

* Significant at 0.01 level; ** Significant at 0.05 level; *** Significant at 0.10 level

Source: Computed from the annual reports of the respective units.

For the purpose of this study working capital means net working capital. Table 4.33 shows the working capital leverage scores of sample units. It is evident from the table that the overall working capital leverage of Indian automobile industries as a whole, in all the fifteen years was low which shows that change in net working capital in relation to fixed capital have less impacts over the profitability position. The same situations were also reflected in the commercial vehicles sector, passenger cars and multiutility vehicles sector and two- and three-wheelers sector. As Walker thinks, leverage must at least be at unity. Coming to the sample units individually, none of the selected units supports the views of Walker, because the working capital leverage of the selected units either may be more than or less than unity during the study period.

Another important aspect of the working capital leverage which is evident from the proposition of Walker is the rate of change in return on investment corresponding with the rate of change in the working capital in relation to fixed capital. As he thinks it must be at unity, i.e., if there is decrease in working capital in relation to fixed capital, there must be an increase in the rate of return to the investors at least by same margin. It can be expressed as

$$\frac{\text{Change in return on investment (ROI)}}{\text{Changes in working capital in relation to fixed capital}} = 1 \text{ or more}$$

Walker thinks that there would be negative relationship in between ROI and WC at least by unity. For the purpose of testing the hypothesis of Walker, simple correlations between ROI and working capital in relation to fixed capital of the sample units have been computed and presented in Table 4.34.

Table 4.34 indicates that three units (Ashok Leyland Ltd and Eicher Motors Ltd in the commercial vehicles sector and Bajaj Auto Ltd in the two- and three-wheelers sector) out of fifteen units had satisfied the hypothesis of Walker, of negative relationship between working capital in relation to fixed capital and profitability in terms of investments. Such negative correlation between ROI and WC has been observed to be decidedly significant in the Ashok Leyland Ltd only. It is also inferred from the table that such correlation co-efficient has been observed to be positive in the remaining units. These units did not satisfy the hypothesis developed by E.W.Walker.

Structural Determinants of Working Capital

Cash, inventories and receivables are the main structural determinants of working capital. Current and quick ratios indicate the relationship between the firm's current obligations, current assets and quick assets respectively. But these ratios do not assess the management of the components of current assets. Therefore, this section deals with the management of structural determinants of working capital, namely, inventories, receivables and cash.

Inventory Management

Inventory constitutes a major component of working capital of most business firms except financial ones. Their size and rate of turnover influence greatly the size and rate of turnover of working capital and, through them, the income and profit of a business. The proper management and control of inventory not only solves the acute problems of liquidity but also increases annual profits and causes substantial reduction in the working capital of a firm. Inventories form a link between production and sales of a product. Therefore, it is essential to have a sufficient level of investment in inventories. Inadequate inventory adversely affects smooth running of business, whereas excess of it involves extra cost, thus reducing profits.

The basic objective of inventory management is to optimise the size of inventory in a firm so that smooth performance of production and sales functions may be possible at the minimum costs. The holding of surplus and slow-moving inventories involves extra cost. Inventory carrying costs alone are estimated to be between 10 and 20 per cer in India while the interest payable on money borrowed from banks for obtaining inventories is around 18 per cent.[12] To what extent the automobile industries of India have been successful in optimising their inventory holdings during the period is evaluated in this section.

Size of Inventory

The size of inventory in the industry average has increased from Rs.190.17 crores in 1992-93 to Rs.520.93 crores in 2006-07, i.e., more than two and half times during the period. Except during the years, 1993-94, 1997-98, 1998-99 and 2000-2004 when investment in inventory has slightly come down, the increase has been regular. Among the firms, the increase in inventory size has been observed more in the two- and three-wheelers sector (3.49 times) compared to the commercial vehicles sector (2.93 times) and the passenger cars and multiutility vehicles sector (2.42 times). On the whole, it may be said that the size of inventory among the firms has increased at a faster rate in the two- and three-wheeler sector than in the commercial vehicles sector and the passenger cars and multiutility vehicles sector.

Table 4.35

Statistical Values of Ratios Relating to the Size of Inventory

(Total Industry)

Particulars	*Statistics*	*Commercial vehicles sector*	*Passengers and cars multiutility vehicles*	*Two- and Three-wheelers sector sector*	*Total Industry*
Inventory to current assets ratio (%)	Mean	39.09	36.11	32.17	35.79
	CV	0.13	0.17	0.20	0.15
	t	4.96 *	0.34	-4.21 *	
Inventory to total assets ratio (%)	Mean	26.32	18.44	18.52	21.09
	CV	0.18	0.22	0.25	0.20
	t	–12.44 *	–10.72 *	-6.73 *	

* Significant at 0.01 level

Source: Computed from the annual reports of the respective units.

Tables 4.35 to 4.38 show the values of mean and co-efficient of variations and 't' value regarding ratios measuring the size of inventory. It reveals that inventory has constituted a very high proportion of total investment in the industry. The mean value of inventory to current assets ratio for the industry amounts to 35.79

per cent whereas it has been 39.09 per cent in the commercial vehicles sector, 36.11 per cent in the passenger cars and multiutility vehicles sector and 32.17 per cent in the two- and three-wheelers sector. The commercial vehicles sector has relatively higher mean value than the passenger cars and multiutility vehicles sector and the two- and three-wheelers sector and its 't' value indicates that the mean value of this sector varies significantly from industry mean. The CV values for inventory to current assts ratio further indicate that variations in this ratio in all the companies during the period under study have been moderate.

It is apparent from the table that the mean value of inventory to total assets ratio for industry amounts to 21.09 per cent whereas it has been 26.32 per cent in the commercial vehicles sector, 18.44 per cent in the passenger cars and multiutility vehicles sector and 18.52 per cent in the two- and three-wheelers sector. The commercial vehicles sector has relatively higher mean value than the passenger cars and multiutility vehicles sector and the two- and three-wheeler units and its 't' value indicates that the mean value of this ratio varies significantly from industry mean. The CV for the ratio of inventory to total assets ratio indicates that variations in this ratio have been high during the period under study.

The proportion of inventory to current assets has been quite high in all the selected units during the period under study. It ranged from 29.27 per cent to 59.73 per cent in the commercial vehicles sector units, 29.27 per cent to 47.00 per cent in the passenger cars and multiutility vehicles sector units and 7.47 per cent to 55.47 per cent in two- and three-wheelers sector units. The mean value of these ratios varies significantly from sector mean except Swaraj Mazda Ltd in the commercial vehicles sector and Hero Honda Motors Ltd and Majestic Auto Ltd in two- and three-wheelers sector. The high CV value of this ratio in all the selected units indicates more variations in this ratio during the study period.

Similarly, the ratio of inventory to total assets has also been quite high in all the selected units during the period under study. It ranged from 14.27 per cent to 41.27 per cent in the commercial vehicles sector, 15.40 per cent to 24.13 per cent in the passenger

Table 4.36

Statistical Values of Ratios Relating to the Size of Inventory

(Commercial vehicles sector)

Particulars	*Statistics*	*Ashok Leyland Ltd*	*Tata Motors Ltd*	*Bajaj Tempo Ltd*	*Eicher Motors Ltd*	*Swaraj Mazda Ltd*	*Total*
Inventory to current assets ratio (%)	Mean	31.93	29.27	59.73	33.67	40.87	39.09
	CV	0.14	0.26	0.13	0.18	0.35	0.13
	t	-4.22 *	-6.38 *	11.78 *	-4.48 *	0.70	
Inventory to total assets ratio (%)	Mean	20.13	14.27	41.27	19.93	36.00	26.32
	CV	0.14	0.37	0.18	0.32	0.27	0.18
	t	-4.35 *	-12.97 *	10.65 *	-7.53 *	6.21 *	

* Significant at 0.01 level

Source: Computed from the annual reports of the respective units

Table 4.37

Statistical Values of Ratios Relating to the Size of Inventory

(Passenger cars and multiutility vehicles sector)

Particulars	*Statistics*	*Hindustan Motors Ltd*	*Mahindra & Mahindra Ltd*	*Maruti Udyog Ltd*	*Total*
Inventory to Current Assets Ratio (%)	Mean	47.00	32.07	29.27	36.11
	CV	0.14	0.19	0.38	0.17
	t	9.13 *	-2.72 **	-4.01 *	
Inventory to Total Assets Ratio (%)	Mean	24.13	15.80	15.40	18.44
	CV	0.19	0.33	0.31	0.22
	t	7.28 *	-3.23 *	-5.20 *	

*Significant at 0.01 level; ** Significant at .0.05 level

Source: Computed from the annual reports of the respective units

Table 4.38

Statistical Values of Ratios Relating to the Size of Inventory

(Two- and three-wheelers sector)

Particulars	*Statistics*	*Bajaj Auto Ltd*	*LML Ltd*	*Maharashtra Scooters Ltd*	*TVS Motor Company Ltd*	*Kinetic Motors Ltd*	*Hero Honda Motors Ltd*	*Kinetic Engineering Ltd*	*Majestic Auto Ltd*	*Scooters India Ltd*	*Total*
Inventory to current assets ratio (%)	Mean	11.00	43.13	7.47	39.93	55.47	30.27	27.13	30.87	44.27	32.17
	CV	0.81	0.21	0.67	0.19	0.62	0.54	0.19	0.20	0.39	0.20
	t	-16.04 *	2.86 **	-10.46 *	3.01 *	3.10 *	-0.59	-3.29 *	-0.69	3.78 *	
Inventory to total assets ratio (%)	Mean	6.93	22.53	3.60	18.67	31.20	15.73	16.53	13.93	37.53	18.52
	CV	0.77	0.13	0.75	0.25	0.27	0.51	0.25	0.29	0.42	0.25
	t	-15.81 *	2.89 **	-11.59 *	0.19	-9.17 *	-2.60 **	-2.22 **	-4.60 *	6.37 *	

* Significant at 0.01 level; ** Significant at 0.05 level

Source: Computed from the annual reports of the respective units.

Table 4.39

Statistical Values of Composition of Inventory

(Total Industry)

Particulars	*Statistics*	*Commercial vehicles sector*	*Passengers cars and multiutility vehicles sector*	*Two- and three-wheelers sector*	*Total industry*
Ratio of raw materials to total inventory	Mean	49.84	52.08	46.48	49.46
	CV	0.18	0.14	0.22	0.14
Ratio of stores and spares to total inventory	Mean	3.34	9.38	10.12	7.61
	CV	0.17	0.29	0.15	0.09
Ratio of semi-finished goods to total inventory	Mean	11.56	8.61	14.39	11.52
	CV	0.11	0.32	0.31	0.17
Ratio of finished goods to total inventory	Mean	34.09	28.95	28.74	30.60
	CV	0.27	0.32	0.31	0.27
Ratio of other inventory to total inventory	Mean	1.17	0.98	0.27	0.81
	CV	1.26	0.59	1.18	0.79

Source: Computed from the annual reports of the respective units.

Table 4.40

Statistical Values of Composition of Inventory

(Commercial vehicles sector)

Particulars	*Statistics*	*Ashok Leyland Ltd*	*Tata Motors Ltd*	*Bajaj Tempo Ltd*	*Eicher Motors Ltd*	*Swaraj Mazda Ltd*	*Total*
Ratio of raw materials to total inventory	Mean	46.12	34.21	55.93	57.00	55.92	49.84
	CV	0.26	0.26	0.25	0.17	0.15	0.18
Ratio of stores and spares to total inventory	Mean	5.03	1.77	5.89	2.99	1.03	3.34
	CV	0.43	0.19	0.17	0.61	0.28	0.17
Ratio of semi-finished goods to total inventory	Mean	13.90	17.58	14.01	6.37	5.90	11.56
	CV	0.14	0.37	0.16	0.38	0.17	0.11
Ratio of finished goods to total inventory	Mean	34.96	46.44	24.70	27.80	37.15	34.09
	CV	0.34	0.31	0.50	0.37	0.23	0.27
Ratio of other inventory to total inventory	Mean	–	–	–	5.84	–	1.17
	CV	–	–	–	7.61	–	1.26

Source: Computed from the annual reports of the respective units.

cars and multiutility vehicles sector and 3.60 per cent to 37.53 per cent in the two- and three-wheelers sector. The mean value of this ratio in all the selected units except TVS Motors Company Ltd in two and three wheelers sector varies significantly from sector mean. The high CV value of this ratio indicates more fluctuations in this ratio in all the selected units during the study period.

To conclude, it may be said that the size of inventory in automobile industry of India has been quite large and has constituted a very high proportion of current assets (35.79 per cent) and total assets (21.09 per cent).

Table 4.41

Statistical Values of Composition of Inventory

(Passenger cars and multiutility vehicles sector)

Particulars	*Statistics*	*Hindustan Motors Ltd*	*Mahindra & Mahindra Ltd*	*Maruti Udyog Ltd*	*Total*
Ratio of raw material to total inventory	Mean CV	59.99 0.07	36.97 0.13	59.28 0.24	52.08 0.14
Ratio of stores and spares to total inventory	Mean CV	5.34 0.32	6.18 0.29	16.10 0.38	9.38 0.29
Ratio of semi-finished goods to total inventory	Mean CV	14.56 0.26	6.59 0.52	3.83 0.40	8.61 0.32
Ratio of finished goods to total inventory	Mean CV	20.11 0.30	45.35 0.18	20.79 0.87	28.95 0.32
Ratio of other inventory to total inventory	Mean CV	– –	4.91 0.59	– –	0.98 0.59

Source: Computed from the annual reports of the respective units.

Composition of Inventory

In the automobile industry of India, the major component of inventory includes raw materials, stores and spares, semi-finished goods, finished goods, and other inventory. Tables 4.39 to 4.42 contain the statistical values (mean and co-efficient of variation) of proportionate share of these components to total inventory during the study period.

It is evident from the table that industry average for raw material proportion works out to 49.46 per cent as against which the commercial vehicles sector had this share to the tune of 49.84 per cent, the passenger cars and multiutility vehicles sector 52.08 per cent and two- and three-wheelers sector 46.48 per cent in total inventory. The CV value for raw materials further indicates that variations in this ratio have been moderate. Among the commercial vehicles sector the mean values of raw material proportion have fluctuated between 34.21 per cent to 57.00 per cent. In the passenger cars and multiutility vehicles sector the mean value of raw material proportion have fluctuated between 36.97 per cent and 59.99 per cent. In the two- and three-wheelers sector the mean value of raw material proportional have fluctuated between 33.64 per cent and 59.95 per cent. The CV value indicates that moderate variation has taken place in this proportion in all the selected units during the study period.

The table further points out that mean value of stores and spares proportion to total inventory have been higher in the two- and three-wheelers sector than in the commercial vehicles sector and the passenger cars and multiutility vehicles sector. The two- and three-wheelers sector average for stores and spares proportion work out to 10.12 per cent as against which commercial vehicles sector, has this share to the tune of 3.34 per cent, passenger cars and multiutility vehicles sector 9.38 per cent and industry 7.61 per cent in total inventory. Among the commercial vehicles sector units, the mean values of stores and spares proportion have fluctuated between 1.03 per cent and 5.89 per cent. Among the passenger cars and multiutility vehicles sector units, the mean values of stores and spares proportion have fluctuated between 5.34 per cent and 16.10 per cent. In the two- and three-wheelers sector units, the mean values of stores and spares proportion have fluctuated between 2.94 per cent and 21.21 per cent.

Among the units, Kinetic Motors Ltd have maintained a low proportion of stores and spares in total inventory in comparison

Table 4.42: Statistical Values of Composition of Inventory

(Two- and three-wheelers sector)

Particulars	*Statistics*	*Bajaj Auto Ltd*	*LML Ltd*	*Maharashtra Scooters Ltd*	*TVS Motor Company Ltd*	*Kinetic Motors Ltd*	*Hero Honda Motors Ltd*	*Kinetic Engineering Ltd*	*Majestic Auto Ltd*	*Scooters India Ltd*	*Total*
Ratio of raw material to total	Mean	46.78	51.13	38.05	35.98	56.02	59.38	37.43	59.95	33.64	46.48
inventory	CV	0.37	0.12	0.65	0.40	0.27	0.10	0.23	0.17	0.44	0.22
Ratio of stores and spares to	Mean	9.97	21.21	4.38	13.30	2.94	12.93	7.31	4.56	14.51	10.12
total inventory	CV	0.40	0.20	0.60	0.58	0.29	0.20	0.39	0.89	0.17	0.15
Ratio of semi-finished goods to total	Mean	9.22	10.53	24.77	15.63	9.26	7.43	18.09	18.53	16.04	14.39
inventory	CV	0.28	0.21	0.87	0.52	0.56	0.29	0.29	0.40	0.25	0.31

(Contd...)

(Contd...)

Particulars	*Statistics*	*Bajaj Auto Ltd*	*LML Ltd*	*Maharashtra Scooters Ltd*	*TVS Motor Company Ltd*	*Kinetic Motors Ltd*	*Hero Honda Motors Ltd*	*Kinetic Engineering Ltd*	*Majestic Auto Ltd*	*Scooters India Ltd*	*Total*
Ratio of finished goods to total	Mean	34.03	17.13	32.80	34.92	31.78	20.26	35.44	16.84	35.41	28.74
inventory	CV	0.48	0.45	0.87	0.41	0.49	0.41	0.36	0.50	0.49	0.31
Ratio of other inventory to	Mean -	-	-	0.17	-	-	1.73	0.12	0.40	0.27	
total inventory	CV	-	-	-	3.88	-	-	3.88	4.00	0.53	1.18

Source: Computed from the annual reports of the respective units.

with the other units. However, all the units have registered a considerable improvement in this component as a proportion to total inventory during the period, leading to high CV values.

The Table 4.39 also shows that the industry average for semi-finished goods proportion works out to 11.52 per cent as against which the commercial vehicles sector has this share to the tune of 11.56 per cent, the passenger cars and multiutility vehicles sector 8.61 per cent and the two- and three-wheelers sector 14.39 per cent. Among the commercial vehicles sector, the mean values of semi-finished goods proportion have fluctuated between 5.90 per cent and 17.58 per cent. In the passenger cars and multiutility vehicles sector, the mean values of semi-finished goods proportion have fluctuated between 3.83 per cent and 14.56 per cent. Among the two- and three-wheelers sector the mean values of semi-finished goods proportion have fluctuated between 7.43 per cent and 24.77 per cent. The CV value indicates that high variation had taken place in this proportion in all the selected units during the study period.

Table 4.39 further points out that mean values of finished goods proportion to total inventory have been higher in the commercial vehicles sector than in the passenger cars and multiutility vehicles sector and the two- and three-wheelers sector. The commercial vehicles sector average for finished goods proportion works out to 34.09 per cent as against which passenger cars and multiutility vehicles sector has this share to the tune of 28.95 per cent, two and three wheeler units 28.74 per cent and industry 30.60 per cent in total inventory. The average proportion of finished goods ranged between 24.70 per cent and 46.44 per cent among commercial vehicles sector, 20.11 per cent and 45.35 per cent among the passenger cars and multiutility vehicles sector and 16.84 per cent to 35.44 per cent among two- and three-wheeler units. Pointing towards high variations in the ratio during the period under study the CV has been relatively high in all the selected sectors.

Other inventory also occupy an important place in inventory in the industry with 0.81 per cent mean value. This share has relatively been less in the two- and three-wheelers sector than in the commercial vehicles sector and the passenger cars and multiutility vehicles sector. The CV has been relatively high fluctuation in this component of inventory during the study period.

Table 4.43

Statistical Values of Ratios Relating to Movement of Inventory

(Total Industry)

Particulars	*Statistics*	*Commercial vehicles sector*	*Passengers and cars multiutility vehicles*	*Two- and three-wheelers sector sector*	*Total industry*
Holding period of raw material (No. of days)	Mean	54.86	54.05	46.72	51.87
	CV	0.38	0.35	0.26	0.29
	t	1.27	0.85	-2.06 ***	
Holding period of work-in-progress (No. of days)	Mean	9.15	6.76	8.43	8.11
	CV	0.25	0.51	0.25	0.25
	t	3.56 **	-2.87 **	0.55	
Holding period of finished goods (No. of days)	Mean	24.06	16.27	16.29	18.87
	CV	0.31	0.17	0.26	0.19
	t	4.28 *	-4.98 *	-2.39 **	
Holding period of debtors (No. of days)	Mean	50.41	30.13	31.69	37.41
	CV	0.27	0.33	0.25	0.14
	t	4.64 *	-4.08 *	-2.35 **	

* Significant at 0.01 level; ** Significant at 0.05 level; *** Significant at 0.10 level

Source: Computed from the annual reports of the respective units.

To sum up, raw material inventory had a large share in aggregate inventory. Similarly, the relative share of finished goods in total inventory had also improved in all the units during the period under review.

Circulation of Inventory

Circulation of inventory directly affects profitability of a firm. Other things remaining the same, the faster the circulation, the

Table 4.44

Statistical Values of Ratios Relating to Movement of Inventory

(Commercial vehicles sector)

Particulars	*Statistics Leyland Ltd*	*Ashok Motors Ltd*	*Tata Tempo Ltd*	*Bajaj Motors Ltd*	*Eicher Mazda Ltd*	*Swaraj Total*	
Holding period of raw material (No. of days)	Mean	60.69	32.12	88.79	36.86	55.85	54.86
	CV	0.45	0.41	0.34	0.62	0.42	0.38
	t	2.55 **	-8.35 *	8.58 *	-4.52 *	0.43	
Holding period of work-in-progress (No. of days)	Mean	12.41	10.99	14.51	2.98	4.89	9.15
	CV	0.29	0.53	0.19	0.41	0.26	0.25
	t	8.26 *	1.80 **	7.11 *	-14.25 *	-13.24 *	
Holding period of finished goods (No. of days)	Mean	28.73	25.28	24.30	12.18	29.80	24.06
	CV	0.39	0.60	0.56	0.53	0.38	0.31
	t	3.42 **	0.43	0.08	-6.11 *	2.41 **	
Holding period of debtors (No. of days)	Mean	86.06	54.31	19.03	33.36	59.30	50.41
	CV	0.51	0.75	0.61	0.34	0.38	0.27
	t	4.38 *	0.51	-5.31 *	-7.23 *	1.10	

* Significant at 0.01 level ; ** Significant at 0.05 level

Source: Computed from the annual reports of the respective units.

larger the profits. Each turnover adds to the volume of profits. In order to judge the velocity with which inventory and its components have circulate in the selected units during the period under study, ratios, namely, holding period of raw material, holding period of work-in-progress, holding period of finished goods and holding period of debtors has been computed. The statistical values (mean, co-efficient of variation and 't' value) relating to these ratios has been presented in Tables 4.43 to 4.46.

Table 4.45

Statistical Values of Ratios Relating to Movement of Inventory

(Passenger cars and multiutility vehicles sector)

Particulars	*Statistics*	*Hindustan Motors Ltd*	*Mahindra & Mahindra Ltd*	*Maruti Udyog Ltd*	*Total*
Holding period of raw material (No. of days)	Mean	85.93	36.23	39.98	54.05
	CV	0.43	0.32	0.47	0.35
	t	5.68 *	-5.88 *	-4.68 *	
Holding period of work-in-progress (No. of days)	Mean	14.05	4.57	1.65	6.76
	CV	0.54	0.60	0.36	0.51
	t	6.70 *	-7.07 *	-5.98 *	
Holding period of finished goods (No. of days)	Mean	16.77	25.88	6.17	16.27
	CV	0.50	0.21	0.49	0.17
	t	0.29	7.75 *	-8.36 *	
Holding period of debtors (No. of days)	Mean	39.74	35.38	15.28	30.13
	CV	0.43	0.35	0.51	0.33
	t	3.70 **	3.36 **	-6.72 *	

* Significant at 0.01 level; ** Significant at 0.05 level

Source: Computed from the Annual reports of the respective units.

The average raw material holding period for the industry as a whole comes to 51.87 days and it seems to be considerably high. Among the commercial vehicles sector units, Bajaj Tempo Ltd have the highest raw material holding period. The mean values to raw material holding period have also been quite high among all the commercial vehicles sector units, ranging between 32.12

days and 88.79 days. The CV values which oscillate between 0.34 and 0.62 also confirm that the variations in this ratio during the period have been relatively high. Among the passenger cars and multiutility vehicles sector units it ranged between 36.23 days and 85.93 days accompanied by relatively high variations. In the two and three wheelers sector units it ranged between 16.29 days and 100.35 days accompanied by relatively high variations.

It has been observed from the table that the average holding period of work-in-progress for the industry as a whole comes to 8.11 days, as against 9.15 days in the commercial vehicles sector, 6.76 days in the passenger cars and multiutility vehicles sector and 8.43 days in the two- and three-wheelers sector. Among the commercial vehicles sector, it ranged between 2.98 days and 14.51 days. In the passenger cars and multiutility vehicles sector, it ranged between 1.65 days to 14.05 days. Among the two- and three-wheelers sector, it ranged between 2.42 days and 19.32 days. The high CV values of all the units confirm that variations in this ratio during the period have been relatively high. Similarly the holding period of work-in-progress in all the two- and three-wheelers sector are significant from sector mean except Maharashtra Scooters Ltd and Majestic Auto Ltd.

It has been observed from the table that the average holding period of finished goods for the industry as a whole comes to 18.87 days, as against 24.06 days in the commercial vehicles sector, 16.27 days in the passenger cars and multiutility vehicles sector and 16.29 days in two and three wheelers sector. Among the commercial vehicles sector units, it ranged between 12.18 days to 29.80 days, among the passenger cars and multiutility vehicles sector units, it ranged between 6.17 days to 25.88 days and in the two- and three-wheelers sector units, it ranged between 5.79 days and 34.23 days. The high CV values of all the units confirm that variations in this ratio during the period have been relatively high. The 't' values further bring to light that the mean values for holding period of finished goods in all the two- and three-wheelers sector units except LML Ltd and Maharastra Scooters Ltd vary significantly from sector mean.

It has also been observed from the table that the average holding period of debtors for industry comes to 37.41 days as

Table 4.46: Statistical Values of Ratios Relating to Movement of Inventory

(Two- and three-wheelers sector)

Particulars	*Statistics*	*Bajaj Auto Ltd*	*LML Ltd*	*Maharashtra Scooters Ltd*	*TVS Motor Company Ltd*	*Kinetic Motors Ltd*	*Hero Honda Motors Ltd*	*Kinetic Engineering Ltd*	*Majestic Auto Ltd*	*Scooters India Ltd*	*Total*
Holding period	Mean	31.69	87.46	16.29	20.38	48.13	23.83	56.79	35.51	100.35	51.87
of raw material	CV	0.79	0.29	1.26	0.31	0.15	0.44	0.33	0.38	0.58	0.29
(No. of days)	t	-3.78 **	6.28 *	-5.08 *	-12.53 *	0.37	-10.19 *	3.08 ***	-2.49	4.40 *	
Holding period	Mean	3.21	9.36	6.07	6.20	6.26	2.42	14.75	8.27	19.32	8.11
of work-in-	CV	0.54	0.23	1.04	0.67	0.56	0.68	0.30	0.69	0.47	0.25
progress	t	-9.74 *	2.27 **	-1.54	-2.37 **	-2.17 **	-10.49 *	7.51 *	-0.13	5.16 *	
(No. of Days)											
Holding period	Mean	8.48	15.19	13.75	11.34	22.03	5.79	28.69	7.12	34.23	18.87
of finished	CV	0.19	0.42	0.90	0.40	0.58	0.75	0.44	0.44	0.40	0.19
goods	t	-7.64 *	-0.78	-0.86	-6.34 *	2.29 **	-5.12 *	4.81 *	-6.77 *	6.22 *	
(No. of days)											
Holding period	Mean	14.17	19.98	26.81	15.35	35.97	8.78	88.57	49.44	26.17	37.41
of debtors	CV	0.21	0.48	0.69	0.59	0.44	0.60	0.48	0.39	0.51	0.14
(No. of days)	t	-7.24 *	-2.99 ***	-1.40	-4.29 *	1.49	-7.95 *	6.25 *	4.31 *	-2.31 **	

* Significant at 0.01 level; ** Significant at 0.05 level; *** Significant at 0.10 level

Source: Computed from the annual reports of the respective units.

against 50.41 days in the commercial vehicles sector, 30.13 days in passenger cars and multiutility vehicles sector and 31.69 days in two- and three-wheelers sector. Among the commercial vehicles sector units, the average holding period of debtors has been high in all the units. It ranged between 19.03 days and 86.06 days, accompanied by relatively high variations. Among the passenger cars and multiutility vehicles sector units, it ranged between 15.28 days and 39.74 days with the high variations. In the two- and three-wheelers sector units, it ranged between 8.78 days and 88.57 days with the high variation during the period under study. The 't' values further bring to light that the mean values for holding period of debtors in all the two- and three-wheeler units except Maharashtra Scooters Ltd and Kinetic Motors Ltd vary significantly from sector mean.

To sum up, it may be said that there is overstocking in industry. Ficher Motors Ltd in the commercial vehicles sector, Maruti Udyog Ltd in the passenger cars and multiutility vehicles sector and Hero Honda Motors Ltd in the two- and three-wheelers sector seems to have done fairly well in maintaining all inventory components in proper balance. Its holding periods for all the components are below the industry's average.

Growth Trends in Inventory and Sales

The sales of a concern directly affect profits and holding of inventory involves cost. Every increase in inventory is expected to be accompanied by adequate increase in sales so that increased cost of inventory may be recovered from increased profits. For the purpose of comparing the growth in sales with the growth in inventory during the period under review, the progressive base year growth rates have been computed and presented in Table 4.47.

Table 4.47 points out that in the industry as a whole, the overall average growth rates of inventory have been lower than growth rates of sales during the period under review as against the average growth rate of 12.74 per cent of the inventory and 15.92 per cent of sales in the industry. The commercial vehicles sector has 7.45 per cent and 16.49 per cent, the passenger cars and multiutility vehicles sector has 6.07 per cent and 13.85 per cent and two- and three-wheelers sector 9.11 per cent and 17.49 per cent respectively. In all the sectors, the growth in sales are higher than the growth in inventory during the study period.

It is evident from the table that, among commercial vehicles sector units, one out of five units (Bajaj Tempo Ltd) and among two and three wheelers sector units, four out of nine units (LML Ltd, Maharashtra Scooters Ltd, Kinetic Motors Ltd and Hero Honda Motors Ltd), the average growth rate of inventory has been more than the growth rate of sales during the period of study comparatively has improved on this account

Table 4.47

Average Growth Rates in Inventory and Sales

(During the years 1992-93 to 2006-07)

Units	*Inventory*	*Sales*
Ashok Leyland Ltd	9.85	15.52
Tata Motors Ltd	6.47	17.22
Bajaj Tempo Ltd	9.42	8.09
Eicher Motors Ltd	8.65	21.31
Swaraj Mazda Ltd	·9.61	15.36
Commercial vehicles sector	7.45	16.49
Hindustan Motors Ltd	-6.76	-1.39
Mahindra and Mahindra Ltd	8.41	14.99
Maruti Udyog Ltd	7.08	15.02
Passenger cars and multiutility vehicles sector	6.07	13.85
Bajaj Auto Ltd	3.96	16.00
LML Ltd	6.55	4.37
Maharashtra Scooters Ltd	-8.59	-15.50
TVS Motor Company Ltd	20.38	21.80
Kinetic Motors Ltd	4.11	2.83
Hero Honda Motors Ltd	14.51	9.21
Kinetic Engineering Ltd	2.41	2.92
Majestic Auto Ltd	0.20	2.02
Scooters India Ltd	5.71	13.44
Two- and three-wheelers sector	9.11	17.49
Industry (Total)	12.74	15.92

Source: Computed from the annual reports of the respective units.

Relationship between Inventory and Sales – Regression Analysis

The achievement of the maximum possible profit is the goal of any enterprise. This object can be achieved by accelerating sales to the extent poss:ble in order to have uninterrupted flow of production and sales, inventories are to be made available, whenever needed. Thus, the volume of sales and size of inventory holdings are related to each other. For the purpose of having in depth insight into the extent of relationship between inventory and sales, the values of co-efficient of correlation (r), co-efficient of determination (R^2), 't' value (to test of significance of correlation) and linear regression equation have been computed and presented in Table 4.48.

Table 4.48: Inventory and Sales - Regression Analysis

(Y= a + bX)

Units	*Linear regression equation*	*Pearson correlation co-efficient*	R^2	*t- Value*
Ashok Leyland Ltd	Y = 223.80 + 0.11X	0.88	0.77	6.512 *
Tata Motors Ltd	Y = 524.88 + 6.92X	0.97	0.93	13.609 *
Bajaj Tempo Ltd	Y = 102.40 + 0.10X	0.55	0.31	2.400 **
Eicher Motors Ltd	Y = 7.79 + 8.21X	0.98	0.96	18.170 *
Swaraj Mazda Ltd	Y = 19.06 + 0.12X	0.92	0.85	8.587 *
Commercial vehicles sector	Y = 177.82 + 1.60X	0.97	0.93	13.436 *
Hindustan Motors Ltd	Y = -12.14 + 0.26X	0.88	0.77	6.515 *
Mahindra and Mahindra Ltd	Y = 222.23 + 7.34X	0.97	0.94	13.416 *
Maruti Udyog Ltd	Y = 388.28 + 3.68X	0.60	0.36	2.726 **
Passenger cars & multiutility vehicles sector	Y = 265.83 + 1.58X	0.78	0.61	4.510 *
Bajaj Auto Ltd	Y = 181.21 + 1.14X	0.63	0.40	2.913 **
LML Ltd	Y = 44.19 + 0.13X	0.77	0.59	4.353*
Maharastra Scooters Ltd	Y = -21.66 + 0.33X	0.45	0.20	1.822***
TVS Motor				

(Contd...)

(Contd...)

Company Ltd	Y = -15.09 + 9.66X	0.97	0.94	13.921 *
Kinetic Motors Ltd	Y = 8.92 + 0.14X	0.78	0.61	4.470 *
Hero Honda Motors Ltd	Y = 69.50 + 2.13X	0.91	0.83	8.051 *
Kinetic Engineering Ltd	Y = 11.40 + 0.14X	0.58	0.34	2.590
Majestic Auto Ltd	Y = 15.80 + 2.22X	0.24	0.06	0.904
Scooters India Ltd	Y = 16.13 + 0.14X	0.75	0.56	4.095 *
Two and three wheelers sector	Y = 46.24 + 3.90X	0.91	0.83	8.095 *
Industry (Total)	Y = 171.53 + 3.94X	0.92	0.85	8.630 *

Y - Working Capital; X - Sales;

*Significant at 0.01 level;**Significant at 0.05 level; *** Significant at 0.10 level

Source: Computed from the annual reports of the respective units.

The value of correlation co-efficient between sales and inventories is 0.92 in the industry, as against 0.97 in the commercial vehicles sector, 0.78 in the passenger cars and multiutility vehicles sector and 0.91 in two and three wheelers sector. This is an indication of high positive correlation between them. The 't' values indicates that the relationship between inventory and sales has been significant in all the selected units of commercial vehicles sector and passenger cars and multiutility vehicles sector. Among the two and three wheelers sector all the have significant relationship between inventory and sales except Kinetic Engineering Ltd and Majestic Auto Ltd. Because these two units have failed to maintain inventory level as per the operative requirements.

The correlation is stronger in the commercial vehicles sector units and the passenger cars and multiutility vehicles sector units than in the two- and three-wheelers sector. It reflects on the effectiveness of management in controlling inventory in relation to sales. The linear regression equation given in the table, may be used for the purpose of future projections. The values of parameter 'b' indicate the sensitivity with which inventory in a concern changes for a unit increase / decrease in sales. The two- and three-wheelers sector (3.90) are more sensitive than the commercial vehicles sector (1.60) and the passenger cars and multiutility vehicles sector (1.58) for change in inventory as a result change in sales. Among the commercial vehicles sector units, the sales elasticity of inventories varies from 0.10 units to 8.21 units, the passenger cars and multiutility vehicles sector units, it varies from 0.26 units to 7.34 units and in the two- and three-wheelers sector units, it varies from 0.13 units to 9.66 units.

Receivables Management

The receivables represented an important component of current assets next to inventories and constitute a substantial portion of current assets in most of the business houses. Trade credit is considered to be an important marketing tool, acting as a bridge for the movement of goods from production and distribution stages to customers finally. Granting credit and creating receivables amount to the blocking of the firm's funds. The interval period between the date of sale and the date receipt of payment has been financed out of working capital funds. As substantial amounts are tied up in receivables, they need a careful analysis and proper management.

The receivables in the strict accounting sense arise out of delivery of goods or rendering of services on credit and include book debts, notes and bills and accrued receivables. However, in a broader sense, the term 'receivables' is used to include further any pre-payments made against purchase and expenses contract and advances to subsidiaries, employees and officers. In the present context, the term 'receivables' has been used in its broader sense, that is, to include trade debtors and loan and advances in its purview.

The basic objective of receivable management is to maximize the value of the firm by achieving a trade off between liquidity (risk) and profitability.[13] The purpose of credit management is not sale maximization. But efficient and effective credit management does help to expand sales and can prove to be an effective tools of marketing. Thus, the objective of receivables management is to promote sales and profits until that point is reached where the return on investment in further funding of receivables is less than the cost of funds raised to finance that additional credit. (i.e. cost of capital)

In order to evaluate and examine the receivables management performance in the automobile industry of India, an attempt has been made in this part to analyse the size, composition, receivables collection period, growth of receivables and its relationship with sales.

Size of Receivables

The total investment in receivables in industry average has increased from Rs.232.89 crores in 1992-93 to Rs.1,103.96 crores in 2006-07. i.e., by 4.74 times during the period under study. The growth in size of receivables has been more in the two- and three-wheelers sector (7.44 times) than in the commercial vehicles sector (4.98 times) and the passenger cars and multiutility vehicles sector (3.77 times). In the commercial vehicles sector units, the aggregate investment in receivables had risen from Rs.353.42 crores in 1992-93 to Rs.1,760.38 crores in 2006-07. Among the passenger cars and multiutility vehicles sector units, the aggregate investment in receivables had risen from Rs.276.96 crores in 1992-93 to Rs.1,043.42 crores in 2006-07. The two- and three-wheelers sector units the receivables had increased from Rs.68.29 crores in 1992-93 to Rs.508.09 crores in 2006-07 during the same period.

Among the commercial vehicles sector all the units have experienced relatively better growth in their respective investments in receivables. Tata Motors Ltd maintained large size (in absolute figures) of receivables than any other units under the commercial vehicles sector units. On the whole, the increase in receivables size in Ashok Leyland Ltd, Tata Motors Ltd, Bajaj Tempo Ltd, Eicher Motors Ltd and Swaraj Mazda Ltd have been recorded as 2.50, 5.38, 3.64, 14.83 and 43.65 times respectively during the period. Among the passenger cars and multiutility vehicles sector units Mahindra and Mahindra Ltd have maintained larger size (in absolute figures) of receivables than any other units in the sector. The increase in receivables size is the highest in Mahindra and Mahindra Ltd followed by Hindustan Motors Ltd and Maruti Udyog Ltd. Among the two- and three-wheelers sector units Kinetic Engineering Ltd have maintained large size (in absolute figures) of receivables than any other units in the sector. The increase in receivables size is the highest in Kinetic Engineering Ltd followed by Bajaj Auto Ltd, LML Ltd, Maharashtra Scooters Ltd, TVS Motor Company Ltd, Kinetic Motors Ltd, Hero Honda Motors Ltd, Majestic Auto Ltd and Scooters India Ltd.

Tables 4.49 to 4.52 which contain the statistical value (mean, co-efficient of variation and 't' values) of ratios concerning the size of receivables indicate that the receivables have constituted quite a considerable proportion of total assets in the industry i.e., 31.09 per cent.

Table 4.49

Statistical Values of Ratios Relating to the Size of Receivables

(Total industry)

Particulars	*Statistics*	*Commercial vehicles sector*	*Passengers and cars multiutility vehicles sector*	*Two- and Three-wheelers sector*	*Total industry*
Receivables to	Mean	56.57	47.31	47.21	50.37
current assets	CV	0.29	0.13	0.11	0.12
ratio (%)	t	2.02	-1.63	-2.36	
Receivables to	Mean	41.89	23.89	27.51	31.09
total assets	CV	0.68	0.13	0.22	0.34
ratio (%)	t	2.28 **	-2.90 *	-1.46	
Receivables to	Mean	31.40	21.09	28.50	27.00
Sales (%)	CV	0.49	0.20	0.11	0.19
	t	1.56	-4.50 *	0.83	

* Significant at 0.01 level; ** Significant at 0.05 level

Source: Computed from the annual reports of the respective units.

The commercial vehicles, the passenger cars and multiutility vehicles and the two- and three-wheelers sector have relatively high mean values i.e., 41.89 per cent, 23.87 per cent and 27.51 per cent respectively for the ratio receivables to total assets.

Table 4.50

Statistical Values of Ratios Relating to the Size of Receivable

(Commercial vehicles sector)

Particulars	*Statistics*	*Ashok Leyland Ltd*	*Tata Motors Ltd*	*Bajaj Tempo Ltd*	*Eicher Motors Ltd*	*Swaraj Mazda Ltd*	*Total*
Receivables to current assets ratio (%)	Mean	53.20	60.07	53.87	61.20	54.53	56.57
	CV	0.26	0.17	1.46	0.20	0.27	0.29
	t	-0.70	0.83	-0.17	0.94	-0.36	
Receivables to total assets ratio (%)	Mean	32.87	30.00	23.07	34.07	89.47	41.89
	CV	0.30	0.31	0.23	0.12	1.54	0.68
	t	-1.19	-1.69	-2.60**	-1.05	1.68	
Receivables to Sales (%)	Mean	39.07	32.13	15.47	19.47	50.87	31.40
	CV	0.49	0.39	0.17	0.22	1.56	0.49
	t	1.37	0.16	-3.87*	-2.82*	1.16	

* Significant at 0.01 level; ** Significant at 0.05 level;

Source: Computed from the annual reports of the respective units.

Comparatively, the commercial vehicles sector has the highest relative proportion to total assets in the form of receivables. Moreover, the mean values for the ratio of receivables to current asset show that the commercial vehicles sector has the largest share of its working capital blocked in receivables i.e., 56.57 per cent, as against 47.31 per cent in the passenger cars and multiutility vehicles sector, 47.21 per cent in the two- and three-wheelers sector and 50.37 per cent in industry.

Table 4.51

Statistical values of ratios relating to the size of receivable

(Passenger cars and multiutility vehicles sector)

Particulars	*Statistics*	*Hindustan Motors Ltd*	*Mahindra & Mahindra Ltd*	*Maruti Udyog Ltd*	*Total*
Receivables to current assets ratio (%)	Mean	44.40	51.07	46.47	47.31
	CV	0.09	0.17	0.28	0.13
	t	-1.55	2.29 **	-0.37	
Receivables to total assets ratio (%)	Mean	22.40	24.33	24.87	23.87
	CV	0.07	0.19	0.20	0.13
	t	-1.67	0.82	1.44	
Receivables to Sales (%)	Mean	22.20	23.27	17.80	21.09
	CV	0.10	0.29	0.47	0.20
	t	0.94	1.81 ***	-2.65 **	

** Significant at 0.05 level; *** Significant at 0.10 level

Source: Computed from the Annual reports of the respective units.

Among the commercial vehicles sector, Tata Motors Ltd and Bajaj Tempo Ltd have comparatively low mean values for receivables to total assets ratio, the values varied significantly at 5 per cent level from sector mean. Similarly Ashok Leyland Ltd and Bajaj Tempo Ltd have comparatively low mean values for receivables to current assets ratio. Moreover, the CV values for these ratios which fluctuate between 0.12 and 1.55 among the commercial vehicles sector. Among the passenger cars and multiutility vehicles sector Hindustan Motors Ltd have comparatively low mean values for receivables to total assets ratio. Similarly the

Table 4.52

Statistical Values of Ratios Relating to the Size of Receivable

(Two and three wheelers sector)

Particulars	*Statistics*	*Bajaj Auto Ltd*	*LML Ltd*	*Maharashtra Scooters Ltd*	*TVS Motor Company Ltd*	*Kinetic Motors Ltd*	*Hero Honda Motors Ltd*	*Kinetic Engineering Ltd*	*Majestic Auto Ltd*	*Scooters India Ltd*	*Total*
Receivables to current assets ratio (%)	Mean	54.40	37.80	56.80	47.20	47.13	30.80	68.47	64.53	17.80	47.21
	CV	0.22	0.29	0.42	0.19	0.28	0.42	0.10	0.08	0.33	0.11
	t	3.21*	-4.01*	1.94***	0.05	1.37*	-7.57*	10.44	10.37*	-12.23*	
Receivables to total assets ratio (%)	Mean	34.40	21.20	31.87	29.33	30.07	16.20	41.20	28.47	14.87	27.51
	CV	0.18	0.45	0.68	1.06	0.26	0.29	0.08	0.20	0.37	0.22
	t	6.20*	-3.38*	0.99	0.26	0.82	-10.08*	9.18*	0.53	-5.81*	
Receivables to Sales (%)	Mean	44.53	20.87	58.40	10.80	19.67	7.13	52.77	27.33	15.33	28.50
	CV	0.26	0.50	0.34	0.30	0.61	0.37	0.25	0.34	0.41	0.11
	t	4.63*	-2.69**	6.38	-13.84	-3.10*	-18.48*	8.40*	-0.56	-9.78*	

* Significant at 0.01 level; *** Significant at 0.10 level

Source: Computed from the annual reports of the respective units.

Hindustan Motors Ltd also have comparatively low mean values for receivables to current assets ratio. Moreover the CV values for these ratios which fluctuate between 0.09 and 0.28 in that units. Among the two- and three-wheelers sector only Scooters India Ltd and Hero Honda Motors Ltd have comparatively low mean values for receivables to total assets ratio and also in receivable to current assts ratio, the values varying significantly at 1 per cent and 10 per cent level from sector mean.

Table 4.53

Statistical Values of Ratios Relating to Composition of Receivables

(Total Industry)

Particulars	*Statistics*	*Commercial vehicles sector*	*Passengers and cars multiutility vehicles sector*	*Two- and three-wheelers sector*	*Total Industry*
Debts to	Mean	97.87	87.74	93.78	93.13
Receivables (%)	CV	0.02	0.11	0.03	0.04
	CAGR	-0.07	0.51	0.51	0.33
Loans and	Mean	2.13	12.26	6.22	6.87
advances to	CV	0.88	0.81	0.43	0.14
receivables (%)	CAGR	4.48	-3.46	-6.58	-4.14

Source: Computed from the annual reports of the respective units.

The receivables to sales ratio of the commercial vehicles sector (31.40 per cent), the passenger cars and multiutility vehicles sector (21.09 per cent), the two- and three-wheelers sector (28.50 per cent), resemble the industry closely (27.00 per cent) as far as this ratio is concerned. However all the sectors have recorded gradual improvements in the ratio during the period under study. That is why the values of CV are high in these sectors. Among the commercial vehicles sector Bajaj Tempo Ltd and Eicher Motors Ltd have low mean values for the ratio of receivables to sales and the variations are statistically significant at 1 per cent level. The CV values which oscillate between 0.17 and 1.56 also demonstrate that the variations in the ratio have been more than in the

Table 4.54

Statistical Values of Ratios Relating to Composition of Receivables

(Commercial vehicles sector)

Particulars	*Statistics*	*Ashok Leyland Ltd*	*Tata Motors Ltd*	*Bajaj Tempo Ltd*	*Eicher Motors Ltd*	*Swaraj Mazda Ltd*	*Total*
Debts to Receivables (%)	Mean	99.92	89.82	99.65	99.95	100	97.87
	CV	0.01	0.11	0.01	0.01	–	0.02
	CAGR	0.07	-0.55	0.20	0.07	–	-0.07
Loans and advances to receivables (%)	Mean	0.08	10.18	0.35	0.05	–	2.13
	CV	2.25	0.94	2.74	3.80	–	0.88
	CAGR	–	–	–	–	–	4.48

Source: Computed from the annual reports of the respective units.

commercial vehicles sector. Among the passenger cars and multiutility vehicles sector, only Maruti Udyog Ltd has low mean value of this ratio, values varying significantly at 5 per cent level from the sector mean. In the two- and three-wheeler units, Hero Honda Motors Ltd has low mean value of this ratio, values varying significantly at 1 per cent level from the sector mean.

To conclude, it may be said that investments in receivables, which have constituted a considerably high proportion of total assets and current assets in the automobile industry of India have been on regular increase during the period. Among two out of five units (Tata Motors Ltd and Bajaj Tempo Ltd) in the commercial vehicles sector, one out of three units (Hindustan Motors Ltd) in the passenger cars and multiutility vehicles sector and two out of nine units (Hero Honda Motors Ltd and Scooters India Ltd) in the two- and three-wheelers sector top in the effective utilisation of receivables fund in terms of their sales.

Composition of Receivables

After considering the size of receivables, it is proposed to examine the relative importance of the various components of receivables. Tables 4.53 to 4.56 which contain the statistical values (mean, co-efficient of variations and average trend) relating to the composition of receivables in the selected units during the period under study are a pointer to the fact that receivables in the automobile industry comprise debts and loans and advances. Moreover, debts have constituted a large proportion of receivables than loans and advances.

Tables 4.53 to 4.56 reveal that on the whole 93.13 per cent of receivables in industry were debts and the balance loans and advances during the period under study. However, in the commercial vehicles sector, the average share of debts was high as 97.87 per cent, whereas it was 87.74 per cent in the passenger cars and multiutility vehicles sector and 93.78 per cent in the two- and three-wheelers sector in this regard. The CV values are high in case of loans and advances, indicating more fluctuations in this components during the study period.

Table 4.55
Statistical Values of Ratios Relating to Composition of Receivables
(Passenger cars and multiutility vehicles sector)

Particulars	*Statistics*	*Hindustan Motors Ltd*	*Mahindra & Mahindra Ltd*	*Maruti Udyog Ltd*	*Total*
Debts to receivables (%)	Mean	99.95	82.61	80.65	87.74
	CV	0.01	0.14	0.27	0.11
	CAGR	–	-0.41	2.12	0.51
Loans and advances to receivables (%)	Mean	0.05	17.39	19.35	12.26
	CV	3.20	0.69	1.13	0.81
	CAGR	–	1.92	-8.36	-3.46

Source: Computed from the annual reports of the respective units.

Among the commercial vehicles sector units, the mean values of debt receivables ratio range between 89.82 per cent and 100 per cent. The high CV values depict that fluctuation in the composition of receivables have been less in all the commercial vehicles sector units except Tata Motors Ltd. Among the passenger cars and multiutility vehicles sector units the mean values of debt to receivables ratio range from 80.65 per cent to 99.95 per cent. The higher values depict that fluctuation in the composition of receivables have been more in all the passenger cars and multiutility vehicles sector units. In the two- and three-wheelers sector units, the mean values of debt receivables ratio range between 86.17 per cent and 100 per cent. The CV values indicate that fluctuations in these composition of receivables have been consistent in all the units in that sector.

Among the commercial vehicles sector units, the mean values of loans and advances to receivables ratio ranged between 0.05 per cent and 10.18 per cent. In passenger cars and multiutility vehicles sector units, the mean values of loans and advances to receivables ratio ranged between 0.05 per cent and 19.35 per cent. In the two- and three-wheelers sector, this ratio ranged between 0.64 per cent and 13.83 per cent. The CV values depict that fluctuations in these

Table 4.56

Statistical Values of Ratios Relating to Composition of Receivables

(Two and three wheelers sector)

Particulars	*Statistics*	*Bajaj Auto Ltd*	*LML Ltd*	*Maharashtra Scooters Ltd*	*TVS Motor Company Ltd*	*Kinetic Motors Ltd*	*Hero Honda Motors Ltd*	*Kinetic Engineering Ltd*	*Majestic Auto Ltd*	*Scooters India Ltd*	*Total*
Debts to Receivables (%)	Mean	86.17	91.91	91.98	92.09	89.84	94.26	99.36	100	98.41	93.78
	CV	0.13	0.15	0.14	0.08	0.19	0.06	0.02	–	0.02	0.03
	CAGR	1.28	2.46	2.83	-0.20	-0.07	-0.41	-0.34	–	0.26	0.51
Loans and Advances to Receivables (%)	Mean	13.83	8.09	8.02	7.91	10.16	5.74	0.64	–	1.59	6.22
	CV	0.70	1.75	1.56	0.90	1.64	1.04	2.41	–	1.05	0.43
	CAGR	–	-5.47	–	5.40	9.40	–	–	–	–	-6.58

Source: Computed from the annual reports of the respective units.

composition of receivables have been consistent in all the selected units of Indian automobile industry.

From the analysis, it is evident that debt proportion have constituted the bulk of the total receivables in all the units, under the commercial vehicles, the passenger cars and multiutility vehicles and two- and three-wheelers sector units selected for the study.

Receivables Collection Period

The computation of average collection period also helps in the determination of the quality of receivables as it points towards the rapidity or sluggishness of their collectability. Tables 4.57 to 4.60 depict the statistical values relating to average collection period of receivables (in aggregate) and debts separately in the selected units during the period under study.

Table 4.57

Statistical Values of Ratios Relating to Receivable Collection Period

(Total industry)

Particulars	*Statistics*	*Commercial vehicles sector*	*Passengers and cars multiutility vehicles sector*	*Two and three wheelers sector*	*Total industry*
Receivable	Mean	26.93	24.87	16.53	22.67
Collection	CV	0.30	0.37	0.23	0.24
Period (in days)	t	4.02 *	1.70	-4.33 *	
Debt Collection	Mean	2.13	10.80	7.53	6.82
Period (in days)	CV	1.42	1.14	0.81	0.81
	t	–2.97 *	2.10 **	0.67	

* Significant at 0.01 level; ** Significant at 0.05 level

Source: Computed from the annual reports of the respective units.

Tabled 4.57 to 4.60 demonstrate that, on an average, the receivables have remained outstanding in the commercial vehicles sector, the passenger cars and multiutility vehicles sector and the two- and three-wheelers sector for 26.93, 24.87 and 16.53 days as against 22.67 days in the industry taken together. Here the mean values of the commercial vehicles sector and the two- and three-

Table 4.58

Statistical Values of Ratios Relating to Receivable Collection Period

(Commercial vehicles sector)

Particulars	*Statistics*	*Ashok Leyland Ltd*	*Tata Motors Ltd*	*Bajaj Tempo Ltd*	*Eicher Motors Ltd*	*Swaraj Mazda Ltd*	*Total*
Receivable Collection Period (in days)	Mean	86.07	54.33	19.27	35.20	57.53	26.93
	CV	0.51	0.75	0.62	0.28	0.35	0.30
	t	5.53 *	2.58 **	-2.25 **	2.27 **	5.74 *	
Debt Collection Period (in days)	Mean	0.15	10.27	0.18	0.03 –	2.13	
	CV	2.27	1.48	2.89	4.33 –	2.42	
	t	-2.54 **	2.59 **	-2.39 **	-2.67 **	–	

* Significant at 0.01 level; ** Significant at 0.05 level

Source: Computed from the annual reports of the respective units.

wheelers sector vary significantly at 1 per cent level from industry mean. Similarly the mean values of debt collection period in commercial vehicles sector, the passenger cars and multiutility vehicles sector and the two- and three-wheelers sector for 2.13, 10.80 and 7.53 days against 6.82 days in the industry mean. Here the mean value of commercial vehicles sector and the passenger cars and multiutility vehicles sector vary significantly from the industry mean. The high CV values indicate more fluctuations in these periods in all the units during the study period.

Table 4.59

Statistical Values of Ratios Relating to Receivable Collection Period

(Passenger cars and multiutility vehicles sector)

Particulars	*Statistics*	*Hindustan Motors Ltd*	*Mahindra & Mahindra Ltd*	*Maruti Udyog Ltd*	*Total*
Receivable	Mean	43.47	35.47	15.20	24.87
collection period	CV	0.30	0.34	0.52	0.37
(in days)	t	4.76 *	4.23 *	-15.53 *	
Debt collection					
period (in days)	Mean	0.04	14.63	17.72	10.80
	CV	3.50	0.74	1.66	1.14
	t	-3.37 *	1.85 ***	1.51	

* Significant at 0.01 level; *** Significant at 0.10 level

Source: Computed from the annual reports of the respective units.

Tables 4.57 to 4.60 highlight that in the case of the commercial vehicles sector units, the receivables collection period ranged between 19.27 days and 86.07 days. The values vary significantly in Ashok Leyland Ltd, Swaraj Mazda Ltd, Tata Motors Ltd, Bajaj Tempo Ltd and Eicher Motors Ltd from the sector mean. The debt collection period of the commercial vehicles sector units ranged between 0.03 days and 10.27 days. The values vary significantly in all the units from the sector mean.

Among the passenger cars and multiutility vehicles sector, the receivable collection period ranged between 15.20 days and 43.47 days and values vary significantly in all the units from sector mean. Similarly the debt collection period in the passenger cars and multiutility vehicles sector units ranged between 0.04 days and 17.72 days and the variations in the mean values are significantly differ from sector mean in Hindustan Motors Ltd and Mahindra and Mahindra Ltd.

In the two- and three-wheelers sector units, the receivable collection period ranged between 8.87 days and 88.07 days and the variations in means values are significant from the sector mean in Bajaj Auto Ltd, Hero Honda Motors Ltd, Majestic Auto Ltd, TVS Motor Company Ltd and Kinetic Engineering Ltd. The high CV values indicate more fluctuations in these periods in all the units during the study period. Comparatively in the case of the commercial vehicles sector units, the debt collection period is relatively low.

Growth of Receivables

With the increase in sales, an increase in receivables size is also expected. But, an effective control over receivables does not allow faster growth of receivables than the sales growth. Table 4.61 shows the progressive base year percentage growth in receivables and sales in the selected units during the study period.

Table 4.61 points out that in the industry as a whole, the overall average growth rates of receivables have been lower than growth rates of sales during the period under review. As against the average growth of 10.93 per cent of receivables and 15.92 per cent of sales in the industry, the commercial vehicles sector has 11.31 per cent and 16.49 per cent, the passenger cars and multiutility vehicles sector has 9.25 per cent and 13.85 per cent and the two- and three-wheelers sector has 14.32 per cent and 17.49 per cent respectively. Comparatively the growth in receivables than the growth in sales are lower in the passenger cars and multiutility vehicles sector than in the other sectors. This indicates that the passenger cars and multiutility vehicles sector could exercise relatively more effective control over the growth of its receivables than the commercial vehicles sector and the two- and three-wheelers sector.

It is evident from the table that, among commercial vehicles sector units one out of five units (Bajaj Tempo Ltd) and among the two- and three-wheelers sector units 7 out of 9 units (Bajaj

Table 4.60

Statistical Values of Ratios Relating to Receivable Collection Period

(Two and three wheelers sector)

Particulars	*Statistics*	*Bajaj Auto Ltd*	*LML Ltd*	*Maharashtra Scooters Ltd*	*TVS Moior Company Ltd*	*Kinetic Motors Ltd*	*Hero Honda Motors Ltd*	*Kinetic Engineering Ltd*	*Majestic Auto Ltd*	*Scooters India Ltd*	*Total*
Receivable	Mean	13.60	19.67	26.93	15.33	36.13	8.87	88.07	50.00	26.67	16.53
collection period	CV	0.30	0.48	0.68	0.59	0.45	0.59	0.48	0.39	0.52	0.23
(in days)	t	-2.37 **	1.70	2.07 **	-0.71	4.18 *	-8.44 *	6.45 *	6.62 *	2.72 **	
Debt collection	Mean	22.13	9.74	20.41	2.87	8.65	1.87	1.47	-0.66	7.53	
period (In days)	CV	0.78	2.16	1.75	0.97	2.13	1.16	2.56	-1.23	0.81	
	t	3.58 *	0.52	1.66	-2.39 **	0.22	-3.95 *	-2.19 **	-4.76 *	-4.88	

* Significant at 0.01 level; *** Significant at 0.05 level

Source: Computed from the annual reports of the respective units.

Auto Ltd, Maharashtra Scooters Ltd, Kinetic Motors Ltd, Hero Honda Motors Ltd, Kinetic Engineering Ltd, Majestic Auto Ltd and Scooters India Ltd) the average growth rate of receivables has been more than the growth rate of sales in during the period for the study. From the above analysis, it may be inferred that in the automobile industry of India is expected that effective management of receivables must lead towards restricted growth of receivable, keeping it below the growth rates of sales units could achieve this to some extent. A lot more is expected from the industry in this regard.

Table 4.61

Average Growth Rates in Receivables and Sales

Units	*Receivables*	*Sales*
Ashok Leyland Ltd	6.30	15.52
Tata Motors Ltd	11.87	17.22
Bajaj Tempo Ltd	9.00	8.09
Eicher Motors Ltd	19.70	21.31
Swaraj Mazda Ltd	12.57	15.36
Commercial vehicles sector	11.31	16.49
Hindustan Motors Ltd -	2.44	-1.39
Mahindra and Mahindra Ltd	11.62	14.99
Maruti Udyog Ltd	9.21	15.02
Passenger cars and multiutility vehicles sector	9.25	13.85
Bajaj Auto Ltd	17.53	16.00
LML Ltd	-2.42	4.37
Maharashtra Scooters Ltd	-14.23	-15.50
TVS Motor Company Ltd	16.68	21.80
Kinetic Motor Ltd	10.77	2.83
Hero Honda Motors Ltd	20.44	9.21
Kinetic Engineering Ltd	6.44	2.92
Majestic Auto Ltd	5.30	2.02
Scooters India Ltd	13.75	13.44
Two and three wheelers sector	14.32	17.49
Industry (Total)	10.93	15.92

Source: Computed from the annual reports of the respective units.

Relationship between Receivables and Sales–Regression Analysis

With a view to studying more accurately the behaviour of receivables in relation to sales in the selected units, the values of co-efficient of correlation (r), co-efficient of determination (R^2), t value (to test the significance of correlation) and linear regression equation have been computed and presented in Table 4.62.

Table 4.62: Receivables and Sales – Regression Analysis

Units	*Linear Regression Equation*	*Pearson correlation co-efficient*	R^2	*t- Value*
Ashok Leyland Ltd	Y= 791.38 + 1.73X	0.11	0.01	0.410
Tata Motors Ltd	Y= 564.16 + 0.22X	0.87	0.75	6.297 *
Bajaj Tempo Ltd	Y= -26.41 + 0.20X	0.94	0.89	10.262 *
Eicher Motors Ltd	Y= 3.11 + 0.18X	0.99	0.97	20.754 *
Swaraj Mazda Ltd	Y= -49.12 + 0.54X	0.92	0.85	8.429 *
Commercial vehicles sector Y=	251.75+ 3.75X	0.87	0.75	6.247 *
Hindustan Motors Ltd	Y= 25.29 + 0.19X	0.97	0.94	13.874 *
Mahindra and Mahindra Ltd	Y= 410.47 + 0.10X	0.78	0.60	4.438 *
Maruti Udyog Ltd	Y= 513.10 + 8.07X	0.79	0.63	4.713 *
Passenger cars and multiutility vehicles sector Y=	335.68+ 3.03X	0.83	0.68	5.284 *
Bajaj Auto Ltd	Y= 419.79 + 0.32X	0.91	0.82	7.666 *
LML Ltd	Y= 66.74 + 4.39X	0.49	0.24	2.011 ***
Maharastra Scooters Ltd	Y= 3.30 + 0.50X	0.86	0.74	6.045 *
TVS Motor Company Ltd	Y= 36.40 + 7.04X	0.93	0.86	8.878 *
Kinetic Motors Ltd	Y= 16.85 + 0.12X	0.41	0.17	1.618
Hero Honda Motors Ltd	Y= 21.90 + 4.95X	0.98	0.96	16.558 *
Kinetic Engineering Ltd	Y= -12.71 + 0.59X	0.84	0.70	5.461 *
Majestic Auto Ltd	Y= 20.34 + 0.13X	0.77	0.60	4.378 *
Scooters India Ltd	Y= -4.34 + 0.20X	0.80	0.63	4.739 *
Two and three wheelers sector	Y= 90.98 + 1.65X	0.93	0.86	8.797 *
Industry (Total)	Y= 234.71 + 9.49X	0.93	0.86	9.012 *

* Significant at 0.01level; *** Significant at 0.10 level

Source: Computed from the annual reports of the respective units.

The value of correlation co-efficient between sales and receivables was 0.93 in the industry, as against 0.87 in the commercial vehicles sector, 0.83 in the passenger cars and multiutility vehicles sector, 0.93 in the two- and three-wheelers sector. This as an indication of correlation is much stronger in the two- and three-wheelers sector than in the commercial vehicles sector and the passenger cars and multiutility vehicles sector. The 't' values indicate that the relationship between receivables and sales has been significant at 1 per cent level in all the industry.

Among the commercial vehicles sector units, except Ashok Leyland Ltd, all the units have significant relationship between receivables and sales. In Tata Motors Ltd, Bajaj Tempo Ltd, Eicher Motors Ltd and Swaraj Mazda Ltd., the relationship is significant at 1 per cent level. Among the passenger cars and multiutility vehicles sector units, all the units have significant relationship between receivables and sales at 1 per cent level. In the two- and three-wheelers sector units all the units have significant relationship between receivables and sales. The correlation is stronger in the two- and three-wheelers sector units than in the passenger cars and multiutility vehicles and the commercial vehicles sector units. This shows the effectiveness of management in controlling receivables in relation to sales.

The linear regression equations, given in the table indicate the sensitivity with which receivables in a concern change for a unit increase or decrease in sales. The table inferred that the commercial vehicles sector (3.75) is more sensitive than the passenger cars and multiutility vehicles sector (3.03) and the two- and three-wheelers sector (1.65) for change in receivables and result of change in sales. Among the commercial vehicles sector units, the sales elasticity of receivables is the highest in Ashok Leyland Ltd followed by Tata Motors Ltd, Bajaj Tempo Ltd, Eicher Motors Ltd and Swaraj Mazda Ltd. In the passenger cars and multiutility vehicle sector units, the sales elasticity of receivables is the highest in Maruti Udyog Ltd followed by Hindustan Motors Ltd and Mahindra and Mahindra Ltd. It is also inferred from the table that among the two- and three-wheelers sector units, the sales elasticity of receivables is the highest in TVS Motor Company Ltd followed by Bajaj Auto Ltd, LML Ltd, Maharastra

Scooters Ltd, Kinetic Motors Ltd, Hero Honda Motors Ltd, Kinetic Engineering Ltd, Majestic Auto Ltd and Scooters India Ltd. From this analysis, it may be said that the receivables management in the two- and three-wheelers sector is much better compared with that of the passenger cars and multiutility vehicles and commercial vehicles sector.

Cash Management

Cash is a vital component of working capital because it is the cash which keeps a business going. It is the hub around which all other financial matters centre.[14] There is no denying the fact that cash is the life-blood of a business enterprise. Steady and healthy circulation of cash in the entire business operation is the basis for business solvency.[15] Cash is the basic input needed to keep the business running on a continuous basis. Ultimately, every transaction in a business results in either an inflow or an outflow of cash. Therefore, effective management of cash is the key determinant of efficient working capital management. There should be sufficient cash with a firm all the time to meet the needs of the business. Both the excess and inadequate cash situations are undesirable from the point of view of profitability and liquidity. Inadequate cash may degenerate a firm into a state of technical insolvency and even lead to its liquidation.

In an efficiently managed business, static cash balance situation generally does not exist. A firm should keep sufficient cash, neither more or less. Cash shortage will disrupt the firm's operations, while excessive cash will simply remain idle, without contributing any thing towards the firm's profitability. Therefore, for its smooth running and maximum profitability, proper and effective cash management in a business is of paramount importance. Thus, the aim of cash management is to maintain an equilibrium between liquidity and profitability of an undertaking so as to facilitate the realization of business objectives. In order to make a proper evaluation of cash management performance in the selected units in the automobile industries of India, an attempt has been made in this section to analysis size, composition, and its adequacy.

Size of Cash

The size of cash in industry average has shown fluctuating trend during the study period. The total investment in cash in the Indian automobile industry has increased from Rs.38.31 crores in 1992-93 to Rs.205.12 crores in 2006-07, i.e., by 5.35 times during the study period under study. The growth in size of cash has been more in the commercial vehicles sector than in the passenger cars and multiutility vehicles sector and the two- and three-wheelers sector. In commercial vehicles sector, the aggregate investment in cash has risen from Rs. 24.71 crores in 1992-93 to Rs. 266.57 crores in 2006-07, the passenger cars and multiutility vehicles sector from Rs.83.95 crores in 1992-93 to Rs.316.08 crores in 2006-07 and the two- and three-wheelers sector from Rs.6.27 crores to Rs.32.72 crores in 2006-07, i.e., by 10.79, 3.77 and 5.22 times during the same period.

To achieve the objectives of maximum profitability and liquidity in a concern, the firm has to employ its cash resources to the fullest extent possible. The opportunity cost of holding excess cash and liquidity risk of inadequate cash are two forces which affect the determination of size of cash in an enterprise. On the basis of past experiences and by comparing the company's own cash balances with those of similar firms in the industry, a management can decide what proportion of current assets should be kept in cash form. Besides this, cash to sales ratio and cash to current liabilities ratio are other tools for such comparison.

The analysis of these ratios is based on the assumption that there should be significant variations in the computed values of these ratios of an enterprise over a period of time as well as in comparison with other similar enterprises in the field. The statistical values (mean, co-efficient of variation and 't' values) relating to these ratios are presented in Tables 4.63 to 4.66.

Tables 4.63 to 4.66 brings out that the mean values for cash to current assets ratio of the industry comes to 9.32 per cent against which it is 7.32 per cent for commercial vehicles sector, 11.69 per cent for the passenger cars and multiutility vehicles sector and 8.96 per cent the for two- and three-wheelers sector. Among the commercial vehicles sector units, Ashok Leyland Ltd has the highest proportion of current assets in cash, followed by Tata Motors Ltd, Bajaj Tempo Ltd, Eicher Motors Ltd and Swaraj

Mazda Ltd. The mean values of cash to current assets ratio varies significantly in Ashok Leyland Ltd and Swaraj Mazda Ltd from the sector mean. Among the passenger cars and multiutility vehicles sector units, this ratio is the highest in Mahindra and Mahindra Ltd, followed by Hindustan Motors Ltd and Maruti Udyog Ltd. The mean values of this ratio varies significantly in Hindustan Motors Ltd and Mahindra and Mahindra Ltd from the sector mean. In the two- and three-wheelers sector units, Scooters India Ltd has the highest proportion of current assets in cash, followed by Bajaj Auto Ltd, LML Ltd, Maharastra Scooters Ltd, TVS Motor Company Ltd, Kinetic Motors Ltd, Hero Honda Motors Ltd, Kinetic Engineering Ltd and Majestic Auto Ltd. The mean values of cash to current assets ratio varies significantly in all the units from the sector mean except TVS Motor Company Ltd.

Table 4.63

Statistical Values of Ratios Relating to the Size of Cash

(Total industry)

Particulars	*Statistics*	*Commercial vehicles sector*	*Passengers and cars multiutility vehicles sector*	*Two- and three-wheelers sector*	*Total industry*
Cash to current Assets ratio	Mean	7.23	11.69	8.96	9.32
	CV	0.43	0.58	0.22	0.33
	t	-2.96 *	2.29 **	-0.26	
Cash to sales ratio	Mean	3.68	5.18	5.71	4.86
	CV	0.50	0.60	0.17	0.40
	t	-3.37 *	1.00	2.98 *	
Cash to current liabilities ratio	Mean	13.01	35.73	18.91	22.31
	CV	0.46	0.64	0.49	0.48
	t	-6.56 *	2.04 **	3.46 **	

* Significant at 0.01 level; ** Significant at 0.05 level

Source: Computed from the annual reports of the respective units.

The commercial vehicles sector units has comparatively low proportion of current assets in cash form. It is suggestive of the fact that the commercial vehicles sector units have exercised better

Table 4.64

Statistical Values of Ratios Relating to the Size of Cash

(Commercial vehicles sector)

Particulars	Statistics	Ashok Leyland Ltd	Tata Motors Ltd	Bajaj Tempo Ltd	Eicher Motors Ltd	Swaraj Mazda Ltd	Total
Cash to Current Assets ratio	Mean	11.13	7.93	5.87	7.00	4.67	7.32
	CV	0.92	0.89	1.40	0.66	0.48	0.44
	t	1.84 ***	0.46	-0.70	-0.24	-2.74 **	
Cash to Sales ratio	Mean	6.40	3.93	2.93	2.67	2.47	3.68
	CV	0.83	0.75	1.33	0.67	0.50	0.50
	t	2.57 **	0.42	-0.70	-1.66	-2.97 *	
Cash to Current Liabilities ratio	Mean	28.40	14.20	7.40	9.20	5.87	13.01
	CV	0.89	0.93	1.57	0.78	0.67	0.46
	t	3.03 *	0.53	-1.83	-1.44	-3.75 **	

* Significant at 0.01 level; ** Significant at 0.05 level; *** Significant at 0.10 level

Source: Computed from the annual reports of the respective units.

control over cash balance than the passenger cars and multiutility vehicles sector units and the two- and three-wheelers sector units.

Table 4.65

Statistical Values of Ratios Relating to the Size of Cash

(Passenger cars and multiutility vehicles sector)

Particulars	*Statistics*	*Hindustan Motors Ltd*	*Mahindra & Mahindra Ltd*	*Maruti Udyog Ltd*	*Total*
Cash to current assets ratio	Mean	6.47	14.93	13.67	11.69
	CV	0.33	0.60	0.96	0.58
	t	-2.59 **	2.57 **	0.97	
Cash to sales ratio	Mean	3.07	6.93	5.53	5.18
	CV	0.33	0.57	0.83	0.60
	t	-2.81 **	2.86 **	0.31	
Cash to current liabilities ratio	Mean	9.07	39.20	59.00	35.76
	CV	0.44	0.54	1.07	0.64
	t	-4.23 *	0.62	2.18 **	

* Significant at 0.01 level; ** Significant at 0.05 level

Source: Computed from the annual reports of the respective units.

The ratio of cash to sales, which provide a deep insight into the cash balance held by the companies, is a pointer to the fact, on an average, 4.86 per cent of sales in the industry, have remained as cash during the study period. The two- and three-wheelers sector had higher proportion of cash in relation to sales than the industry mean, while it is other wise in case of the commercial vehicles sector and passenger cars and multiutility vehicles sector. Among the commercial vehicles sector units, this ratio ranged between 2.47 per cent and 6.40 per cent and its mean value of this ratio varies significantly in Ashok Leyland Ltd and Swaraj Mazda Ltd. In the passenger cars and multiutility vehicles sector units, it ranged between 3.07 per cent and 6.93 per cent. Its mean value significantly varies at 5 per cent level from the sector mean in all the select units except Maruti Udyog Ltd. Among the two- and three-wheelers sector units, it ranged between 1.27 per cent and

Table 4.66

Statistical Values of Ratios Relating to the Size of Cash

(Two and three wheelers sector)

Particulars	*Statistics*	*Bajaj Auto Ltd*	*LML Ltd*	*Maharashtra Scooters Ltd*	*TVS Motor Company*	*Kinetic Motors Ltd*	*Hero Honda Motors*	*Kinetic Engi-neering*	*Majestic Auto Ltd*	*Scooters India Lt*	*Total*
Cash to current assets ratio	Mean	2.73	14.87	2.13	10.87	3.93	5.00	1.53	2.87	36.73	8.96
	CV	0.96	0.41	0.61	0.72	1.32	1.09	0.65	0.45	0.36	0.23
	t	-6.95*	4.32*	-10.51*	1.14	-3.34**	-2.84**	-14.76*	10.96*	8.71*	
Cash to sales ratio	Mean	2.00	8.93	2.27	2.47	1.73	1.27	1.73	1.27	29.73	5.71
	CV	0.76	0.40	0.51	0.76	0.96	0.47	1.33	0.36	0.40	0.24
	t	-6.29*	3.73*	-8.50*	-5.87*	-6.42*	-11.34*	-6.45*	-13.13*	8.62*	
Cash to current liabilities ratio	Mean	14.26	20.09	6.65	16.11	8.17	7.42	4.92	4.19	81.92	18.19
	CV	0.46	0.47	0.85	0.76	1.33	0.84	1.03	0.67	0.85	0.49
	t	6.09*	-3.56*	2.87**	-4.36*	-5.34*	2.55**	-5.87*	-7.29*	2.31**	

* Significant at 0.01 level; ** Significant at 0.05 level

Source: Computed from the Annual reports of the respective units.

29.73 per cent. Its mean value significantly varies at 1 per cent level from the sector mean in all the selected units. Moreover, the values of CV indicated of the fact that the two- and three-wheelers sector had a better control over cash than any of the commercial vehicles sector and passenger cars and multiutility vehicles sector.

Another way of looking at the variations in cash balances is to compare with current liabilities. The table under discussion further depicts that cash balances, on an average, have constituted 22.31 per cent of current liabilities in industry, against 13.01 per cent for the commercial vehicles sector, 35.73 per cent for the passenger cars and multiutility vehicles sector and 18.19 per cent for the two- and three-wheeler units. Among the commercial vehicles sector units, it ranged between 5.87 per cent and 28.40 per cent. Its mean value significantly varies in Ashok Leyland Ltd and Swaraj Mazda Ltd from sector mean. In the passenger cars and multiutility vehicles sector units, this ratio ranged between 9.07 per cent and 59.00 per cent and its mean value significantly varies in Hindustan Motors Ltd and Maruti Udyog Ltd from sector mean. Among the two- and three-wheelers sector units, it ranged between 4.19 per cent and 81.92 per cent and its mean value significantly varies in Bajaj Auto Ltd, LML Ltd, Maharashtra Scooters Ltd, TVS Motor Company Ltd, Kinetic Motors Ltd, Kinetic Engineering Ltd, Majestic Auto Ltd, Hero Honda Motors Ltd and Scooters India Ltd from sector mean. The CV value further indicates that the commercial vehicles sector have exercised an effective control over this ratio than the passenger cars and multiutility vehicles sector and the two- and three-wheelers sector. On the whole, its may be concluded that the passenger cars and multiutility vehicles sector has the largest amount the cash in relations to current assets, with high variations, whereas the commercial vehicles sector has the minimum size of cash with relatively low variations during the period under study.

Composition of Cash Balance

Tables 4.67 to 4.70 disclose that cash at bank has constituted a major proportion of total cash balance in all the units. On an average, cash at bank has formed 76.35 per cent of total cash in the industry, as against 79.09 per cent in the commercial vehicles sector, 60.66 per cent in the passenger cars and multiutility vehicles sector and 89.32 per cent in the two- and three-wheelers sector. The study also brings to light that all the selected units have preferred to save cash with bank. In the commercial vehicles sector, the percentage of bank balance to total cash ranged from 53.10 per cent to 96.86 per cent, whereas in the passenger cars and multiutility vehicles sector, it ranged from 41.39 per cent to 84.01 per cent and the two- and three-wheelers sector, it ranged from 75.10 per cent to 99.97 per cent during the same period.

Table 4.67

Statistical Values of Composition of Cash

(Total industry) *(% to total cash)*

Particulars	*Statistics*	*Commercial vehicles sector*	*Passengers and cars multiutility vehicles sector*	*Two- and three-wheelers sector*	*Total industry*
Cash in hand	Mean	20.93	39.34	10.68	23.65
	CV	0.37	0.36	0.38	0.20
Cash at bank	Mean	79.07	60.66	89.32	76.35
	CV	0.12	0.23	0.05	0.07

Source: Computed from the annual reports of the respective units.

Adequacy of Cash

Every business concern is expected to keep adequate cash balance to meet its daily operational requirements, as also continually maintain its liquidity and solvency on which hinges the very existence of an enterprise. The sufficiency of cash in terms of operational requirements is judged by the computation of cash in terms of number of days of operational requirements ratio. Further more, to ascertain the liquidity and solvency position of a concern, current and quick ratios have been studied. But, some modern financial experts like James E.Walker[16] suggest that in order to draw conclusions about liquidity and solvency, currently maturing obligations should be matched with the net cash flows. Besides this, current liabilities coverage ratio should also be analysed. Keeping this in view, an attempt has been made to measure the adequacy of cash in terms of operational requirements and then in terms of liquidity and solvency.

Table 4.68

Statistical Values of Composition of Cash

(Commercial vehicles sector) *(% to total cash)*

Particulars	*Statistics*	*Ashok Leyland Ltd*	*Tata Motors Ltd*	*Bajaj Tempo Ltd*	*Eicher Motors Ltd*	*Swaraj Mazda Ltd*	*Total*
Cash in hand	Mean	3.14	10.44	46.90	39.94	4.23	20.93
	CV	1.55	1.34	1.78	0.99	0.62	0.37
Cash at bank	Mean	96.86	89.56	53.10	56.06	95.77	79.07
	CV	0.05	0.16	0.72	0.75	0.03	0.12

Source: Computed from the annual reports of the respective units.

Table 4.69

Statistical Values of Composition of Cash

(Passenger cars and multiutility vehicles sector)

(% to total cash)

Particulars	*Statistics*	*Hindustan Motors Ltd*	*Mahindra & Mahindra Ltd*	*Maruti Udyog Ltd*	*Total*
Cash in hand	Mean	58.61	43.43	15.99	39.34
	CV	0.45	0.40	1.35	0.36
Cash at bank	Mean	41.39	56.55	84.01	60.66
	CV	0.63	0.31	0.26	0.23

Source: Computed from the annual reports of the respective units.

Operational Adequacy of Cash

The adequacy level of cash differs from firm to firm owing to variations in volume of output and other operational activities. Therefore, it is very difficult to lay down any norm concerning the adequacy of cash in any industry. However, James E. Walker[17] has observed that a business enterprise should kept its cash and near cash reserves below the requirements of one months normal expenditure. If the cash and near cash reserves happen to be more than this limit, it should be concluded that excessive cash is being held by the firm. The actual position of the automobile industry of India under study is shown in Tables 4.71 to 4.74.

It is apparent from the table that industries, by and large, held adequate cash balances to support their operational requirements. On an average industries have kept cash balances sufficient for 20 days requirements of normal expenditure. The passenger cars and multiutility vehicles sector had slightly more cash in terms of operational needs than the commercial vehicles sector and two and three wheelers sector. The overall average of the ratio of cash in terms of number of days of operating expenses amounts to 16 days in the commercial vehicles sector, 23 days in the passenger cars and multiutility vehicles sector and 22 days in the two- and three-wheelers sector. The high CV value of the passenger cars and multiutility vehicles sector indicates that the passenger cars

Table 4.70

Statistical Values of Composition of Cash

(Two and three wheelers sector) *(% to total cash)*

Particulars	*Statistics*	*Bajaj Auto Ltd*	*LML Ltd*	*Maharashtra Scooters Ltd*	*TVS Motor Company*	*Kinetic Motors Ltd*	*Hero Honda Motors*	*Kinetic Engineering*	*Majestic Auto Ltd*	*Scooters India Lt*	*Total*
Cash in hand	Mean	18.88	24.90	0.03	0.96	1.89	18.72	14.32	14.43	2.01	10.68
	CV	1.07	0.83	2.67	1.44	1.15	1.12	0.89	1.01	1.27	0.38
Cash at bank	Mean	81.12	75.10	99.97	99.04	98.11	81.28	85.68	85.57	97.99	89.32
	CV	0.24	0.28	0.01	0.01	0.02	0.26	0.15	0.17	0.03	0.05

Source: Computed from the annual reports of the respective units.

and multiutility vehicles sector had experienced the more fluctuations in the ratio during the study period.

Table 4.71

Statistical Values and Ratios Relating to Adequacy of Cash in Terms of Liquidity and Solvency

(Total industry)

Particulars	*Statistics*	*Commercial vehicles sector*	*Passengers and cars multiutility vehicles sector*	*Two- and three-wheelers sector*	*Total industry*
Cash in terms of no. of days of operating expenses	Mean	16.00	23.00	22.00	20.00
	CV	0.42	0.52	0.25	0.29
	t	-3.52 *	1.41	1.40	
Current ratio	Mean	1.38	1.38	1.32	1.36
	CV	0.12	0.18	0.11	0.07
	t	0.44	0.35	-1.16	
Quick ratio	Mean	0.53	0.64	0.60	0.59
	CV	16.81	0.33	0.27	0.20
	t	-1.87 ***	1.67	0.53	
Net cash flows to current liability	Mean	1.33	4.06	0.53	3.40
	CV	1.80	0.02	2.37	1.99
	t	-1.80 ***	1.54	-1.46	
% cover of current liability	Mean	14.42	31.89	12.83	19.54
	CV	0.67	0.82	0.37	0.56
	t	-2.90 **	2.85 **	-2.28 **	

*Significant at 0.01 level; ** Significant at 0.05 level; *** Significant at 0.10 level

Source: Computed from the annual reports of the respective units.

Among the commercial vehicles sector, cash in terms of numbers of days of operating expenses varied from 11 days to 28 days. Its mean value significantly varies in Ashok Leyland Ltd and Swaraj Mazda Ltd from sector mean. In the passenger cars and multiutility vehicles sector, it varied from 13 days to 31 days. Its mean value significantly varies in Hindustan Motors Ltd and Mahindra and Mahindra Ltd.

Table 4.72

Statistical Values and Ratios Relating to Adequacy of Cash in Terms of Liquidity and Solvency

(Commercial vehicles sector)

Particulars	*Statistics*	*Ashok Leyland Ltd*	*Tata Motors Ltd*	*Bajaj Tempo Ltd*	*Eicher Motors Ltd*	*Swaraj Mazda Ltd*	*Total*
Cash in terms of no. of days of operating expenses	Mean	28.00	17.00	12.00	11.00	11.00	16.00
	CV	0.85	0.86	1.50	0.71	0.54	0.42
	t	2.47**	0.28	-0.83	-1.54	-2.50**	
Current ratio	Mean	2.16	1.07	1.27	1.25	1.20	1.38
	CV	0.21	0.21	0.17	0.17	0.17	0.12
	t	9.42*	-5.49*	-1.54	-3.94*	-3.01*	
Quick ratio	Mean	0.95	0.45	0.25	0.50	0.50	0.53
	CV	0.32	0.49	0.56	0.28	0.36	16.81
	t	6.99*	-1.59	-6.49*	-1.10	-0.48	
Net cash flows to current liability	Mean	3.67	1.47	-1.27	1.33	1.48	1.33
	CV	0.06	5.24	-6.17	5.95	0.77	1.80
	t	0.64	0.66	-1.68	0.53	0.37	
% cover of current liability	Mean	29.47	12.10	9.04	11.53	6.82	14.42
	CV	0.84	0.86	1.31	0.73	0.59	0.67
	t	3.09**	-2.39**	-1.22	-0.79	-2.97*	

* Significant at 0.01 level; ** Significant at 0.05 level

Source: Computed from the annual reports of the respective units.

Among the two- and three-wheelers sector, it varied from five days to 108 days. Its mean value statistically significant from sector mean in all the units. From this, it may be inferred that the automobile industry of India has been able to maintain its cash balances in relatively sufficient quantity as per the operational requirements.

Table 4.73: Statistical Values and Ratios Relating to Adequacy of Cash in Terms of Liquidity and Solvency

(Passenger cars and multiutility vehicles sector)

Particulars	*Statistics*	*Hindustan Motors Ltd*	*Mahindra & Mahindra Ltd*	*Maruti Udyog Ltd*	*Total*
Cash in terms of	Mean	13.00	31.00	24.00	23.00
no. of days of	CV	0.47	0.58	1.01	0.52
operating expenses	t	-2.53 **	3.05 *	0.38	
Current ratio	Mean	1.17	1.54	1.56	1.38
	CV	0.20	0.21	0.49	0.18
	t	-2.12 ***	1.71	0.86	
Quick ratio	Mean	0.39	0.72	0.80	0.64
	CV	0.28	0.33	0.85	0.33
	t	-3.27 *	1.33	1.32	
Net cash flows to	Mean	-3.00	5.87	9.33	4.06
current liability	CV	-2.37	0.04	0.03	0.02
	t	-1.96 ***	-0.44	-0.26	
% cover of current	Mean	11.90	32.80	37.00	31.89
liability	CV	0.53	0.60	1.17	0.82
	t	-2.50 **	0.31	1.14	

* Significant at 0.01 level; ** Significant at 0.05 level; *** Significant at 0.10 level

Source: Computed from the annual reports of the respective units.

Adequacy of Cash in Terms of Liquidity and Solvency

As already said, the adequacy of cash in terms of liquidity and solvency may be judged on the basis of current ratio and liquid ratio and also by computation of percentage of cash flows to current liabilities and current liabilities coverage ratios.

Analysis of Current Ratio and Liquid Ratio

To test firm's liquidity and solvency, Generally current ratio and quick ratio are analyzed over a period of time. Traditionally, 2:1 for current ratio and 1:1 for liquid ratio are taken as satisfactory standards for the purpose. The former gives and idea of the extent of soundness of current financial position of the firm and the degree of safety provided to the creditors while the later denotes the ability of the firm to settle all its current obligations on a particular date which ability is an evidence of the firms strong liquid position.

It is evident from the table that the industry's overall average for current ratio and liquid ratio had been 1.36 and 0.59 respectively. Commercial vehicles sector mean values of current ratio and liquid ratio were 1.38 and 0.53 respectively. These values significantly vary at 10 per cent level from the industry mean. Among the passenger cars and multiutility vehicles sector mean values of current ratio and liquid ratio stood at 1.38 and 0.64 respectively. Among the two- and three-wheelers sector mean values of current ratio and liquid ratio were 1.32 and 0.60 respectively.

Among the commercial vehicles sector units, the current ratio ranged between 1.07 and 2.16. The mean values of current ratio significantly vary at 1 per cent level from sector mean in all the selected units except Bajaj Tempo Ltd. Similarly, the liquid ratio ranged between 0.25 and 0.95. The mean values of liquid ratio in Ashok Leyland Ltd and Bajaj Tempo Ltd vary significantly at 1 per cent level from the sector mean. In the passenger cars and multiutility vehicles sector units the mean values of current ratio ranged between 1.17 and 1.56 and vary significantly from sector mean in Hindustan Motors Ltd at 10 per cent level. The mean values of liquid ratio ranged between 0.39 and 0.80 and vary significantly from the sector mean in Hindustan Motors Ltd at 1 per cent level.

Among the two- and three-wheelers sector units, the mean values of current ratio ranged between 1.03 and 1.87 and vary significantly from sector mean in Bajaj Auto Ltd, LML Ltd, TVS Motor Company Ltd and Majestic Auto Ltd at 1 per cent level and in Maharashtra Scooters Ltd at 10 per cent level. The mean values of liquid ratio ranged between 0.29 and 0.95 and vary significantly from the sector mean in Bajaj Auto Ltd, LML Ltd and TVS Motor Company Ltd at 1 per cent level; in Kinetic Motors Ltd and Majestic Auto Ltd at 5 per cent level, and in Maharashtra Scooters Ltd at 10 per cent level. These ratios trend to suggest that all the firms in the automobile industry of India experienced adequacy of cash in terms of liquidity and solvency. Comparatively the commercial vehicles sector is said to have a high current ratio at any time during the period under study. The passenger cars and multiutility vehicles sector is said to have a high liquid ratio at any time during the period under review.

Analysis of Actual Liquidity and Solvency

Usually a going concern meets its current obligations mostly with cash coming from operations. To dispose of the current assets with a view to paying off current obligations seems to be a remote possibility in a manufacturing concern. By doing so, it will not only have smaller quantum of production but also gain less profits than it has bargained for. It is needless to recall that the actual liquidity of a business enterprise can be found by calculating the percentage of net cash flows to current liabilities and by determining the coverage of current liabilities provided by profits.

Percentage of Cash Flows to Current Liabilities

In a going concern, net cash flows are very important because these provide the necessary wherewithal to meet the current liabilities. It is on the view that any positive net cash flows will provide added safety to current creditors. Keeping in view that every firm maintaining positive net cash flows to current liabilities ratio may be considered liquid and solvent. However, the higher the ratio, the greater the degree of liquidity and solvency of the firm.

The table under discussion also demonstrates that the overall average of net cash flows to current liabilities ratio for industry work out to 3.40 per cent as against 1.33 per cent for the commercial vehicles sector, 4.06 per cent for the passenger cars and multiutility vehicles sector and 2.00 per cent for the two- and three-wheelers sector. The mean value of this ratio significantly varies from industry mean at 10 per cent level in the commercial vehicles sector units only. In the commercial vehicles sector units, it is the highest in Ashok Leyland Ltd followed by Tata Motors

Table 4.74

Statistical Values and Ratios Relating to Adequacy of Cash in Terms of Liquidity and Solvency

(Two and three wheelers sector)

Particulars	*Statistics*	*Bajaj Auto Ltd*	*LML Ltd*	*Maharashtra Scooters Ltd*	*TVS Motor Company*	*Kinetic Motors Ltd*	*Hero Honda Motors*	*Kinetic Engineering*	*Majestic Auto Ltd*	*Scooters India Lt*	*Total*
Cash in terms of no. of days of operating expenses	Mean	11.00	37.00	7.00	11.00	6.00	5.00	5.00	5.00	108.00	22.00
	CV	0.87	0.48	0.52	0.80	1.29	0.74	1.14	0.48	0.45	0.25
	t	-3.79*	3.78*	-7.85*	-4.34*	-5.49*	-8.59*	-7.48*	-11.36*	7.61*	
Current ratio	Mean	1.87	0.91	1.57	1.10	1.20	1.32	1.43	1.03	1.54	1.32
	CV	0.16	0.25	0.40	0.18	0.29	0.29	0.20	0.23	0.64	0.11
	t	6.76*	-6.95*	1.76***	-4.04*	-1.16	-0.06	1.32	-3.42*	1.02	
Quick ratio	Mean	0.95	0.29	0.85	0.37	0.44	0.76	0.51	0.45	0.78	0.60
	CV	0.38	0.41	0.78	0.46	0.30	0.67	0.45	0.22	0.81	0.27
	t	4.37*	-5.36*	1.77***	-4.07*	-2.65**	1.42	1.17	2.92**	1.41	
Net cash flows to current liability	Mean	8.67	-4.67	-3.73	2.53	-3.80	6.67	2.40	-9.33	7.40	2.00
	CV	0.64	-0.02	-0.69	0.06	-0.03	1.07	1.35	-0.18	0.01	2.37
	t	0.29	-0.25	-0.64	0.57	-1.15	0.22	NIL	-0.88	2.53**	
% cover of current liability	Mean	14.26	20.09	6.65	16.11	8.17	7.42	4.91	4.19	81.92	12.83
	CV	0.91	0.53	0.68	0.91	1.27	0.74	0.84	0.47	0.71	0.37
	t	0.47	3.04**	-3.57*	1.16	-1.57	-2.80**	-4.29*	-7.53*	4.62*	

* Significant at 0.01 level; ** Significant at 0.05 level; *** Significant at 0.10 level

Source: Computed from the annual reports of the respective units.

Ltd, Bajaj Tempo Ltd, Eicher Motors Ltd and Swaraj Mazda Ltd. Among the passenger cars and multiutility vehicles sector units, it is the highest in Maruti Udyog Ltd, followed by Hindustan Motors Ltd, Mahindra and Mahindra Ltd. In the two- and three-wheelers sector units, it is the highest in Bajaj Auto Ltd, followed by other the two- and three-wheelers sector. Further the value of CV indicates that changes in this ratio have been relatively lower in the passenger cars and multiutility vehicles sector than the commercial vehicles sector and the two- and three-wheelers sector during the study period. It is suggestive of the fact that the passenger cars and multiutility vehicles sector have registered better liquidity position than the commercial vehicles sector and the two- and three-wheelers sector.

Coverage of Current Liabilities Ratio

This ratio establishes the relationship between net profits and current liabilities. It is evident from Table 4.71 that the average coverage of current liabilities for industry comes to 19.54 per cent as against 14.42 per cent for the commercial vehicles sector, 31.89 per cent for the passenger cars and multiutility vehicles sector and 12.83 per cent for the two- and three-wheelers sector. Moreover, the mean value of this ratio of all three sectors significantly varies from industry mean at 5 per cent level. Among the commercial vehicles sector units, it is the highest for Ashok Leyland Ltd, followed by Tata Motors Ltd, Bajaj Tempo Ltd, Eicher Motors Ltd and Swaraj Mazda Ltd. Its mean values significantly vary in Ashok Leyland Ltd, Tata Motors Ltd and Swaraj Mazda Ltd at 5 per cent level from sector mean. In the passenger cars and multiutility vehicles sector units, it is the highest in Maruti Udyog Ltd, followed by Hindustan Motors Ltd and Mahindra and Mahindra Ltd. Its mean value varies significantly in Hindustan Motors Ltd at 5 per cent level from the sector mean. Among the two- and three-wheelers sector units, it is highest in Scooters India Ltd, followed by Bajaj Auto Ltd, LML Ltd, Maharashtra Scooters Ltd, TVS Motor Company Ltd, Kinetic Motors Ltd, Hero Honda Motors Ltd, Kinetic Engineering Ltd and Majestic Auto Ltd. Its means value varies significantly in Maharashtra Scooters Ltd, Kinetic Engineering Ltd, Majestic Auto Ltd and Scooters India Ltd at 1 per cent level from sector mean and in LML Ltd and Hero Honda Ltd at 5 per cent level from the sector mean. Moreover, the values of CV are indicative of the fact that two- and three-wheelers sector had a better control over this ratio than the commercial vehicles sector and the passenger cars and multiutility vehicles sector.

The computation of actual liquidity and solvency position reveals that the passenger cars and multiutility vehicles sector have good liquidity and solvency position with regard to actual liquidity and solvency as per the current ratio and liquid ratio.

REFERENCES

1. Clarkson, G.P.E., and Elliot, (1972), *Managing Money and Finance, Hents:* The Gower Press Ltd, p.98.
2. Charles O., Kroncke et. al, (1978), *Managerial Finance: Essentials,* Minnesota: West Publishing Company, p.108.
3. Gitman, L.J., (1976), *Principles of Managerial Finance,* New York : Harper and Row Publishers, p.xvii.
4. Kreps Cliften, H. and Richard F.Wacht, (1975), *Financial Administration,* Housdale : Illinois, p.45.
5. Gitman, L.J., (1976), op. cit., p.52.
6. Ibid., p.52.
7. Chapman Findlay, M. and Edward F.Williams., (1970), *An Integrated Analysis for Managerial Finance,* New Delhi: Prentice Hall, Inc., p.70.
8. Gitman, L.J, (1976), op. cit., p.53.
9. Kuchhal, S.C., (1980), *Financial Management, An Analytical and Conceptual Approach,* p.162.
10. Man Mohan and Goyal, (1979), *Principles of Management Accounting, Agra:* Sahitya Prakash, p.368.
11. Walker, E.W., Towards a theory of working capital in Wolf and Richardson's, *Reading in Finance,* p.238.
12. Viyyanna Rao, K. and Prasad, G., (Aug., 1981), Inventory Management in Andhra Pradesh Public Sector Undertakings. *Lok udyog,* p.34.
13. Bolten S.E., (1976), *Managerial Finance, Boston:* Houghton Mifflin Co., p.446.
14. Joseph F.Bradely, (1969), *Administrative Financial Management, New York:* Holt, Rinehart and Winston Inc., p.196.
15. Howard, B.B, and Upton, M., (1953) *Introduction to Business Finance,* New York; Hill Book Co, Inc., p.188.
16. As quoted by Ram Kumar Mishra, (1975), *Problems of Working Capital, Bomba;* Somaiya Publications Pvt. Ltd, p.127.
17. Ibid., p.128.

5

Assessment of Liquidity Position

Assessment of Liquidity Position

Working capital management is sometimes referred to as liquidity management. More specifically, the management of net working capital is nothing but the management of short-term liquidity.[1] Liquidity is defined as the ability to realise value in money, the most liquid of assets.[2] In short, it refers to the ability to pay in cash the obligations that are due. The corporate liquidity has two dimensions, viz., quantitative and qualitative concepts. The quantitative concept includes the quantum, structure and utilisation of liquid assets, and in the qualitative concept, it is the ability to meet all present and potential demands on cash from any source in a manner that minimises cost and maximises the value of the firm. In the former sense, liquidity is specific objective and limited in its purview, and its management covers structure and utilisation of cash and its equivalents. In the latter sense, liquidity explores all possible means of raising sources and utilising them in such a way that all the obligations are met without putting the firm at a disadvantages.

Thus, corporate liquidity is a vital factor in business. Excess liquidity, through a guarantor of solvency would reflect lower profitability, deterioration in managerial efficiency through complacency, increased speculation and unjustified expansion, extension of too liberal credit and dividend policies. Too little liquidity they may lead to frustration of business objections, reduced rate of return, business opportunity missed and weakening of morale. If sufficient liquidity is not maintained, the enterprise is technically insolvent and atleast faces the financial embracement of renegotiating its obligations to creditors.[3] The control of liquidity requires active working capital management.

Therefore, in the present section an attempt has been made to assess the liquidity position and its relationship with the profitability in the selected automobile industries in India during 1992-93 to 2006-07.

Net Working Capital Position

There are several measures with the help of which the short–term liquidity of an enterprise may be assessed. Among them, net working capital itself provides the one which indicates a 'margin of safety' of protection provided to creditors.' The Accounting Principles Board (APB) of American Institute of Certified Public Accountant (AICPA)[4] states that "Net working capital identifies the relatively liquid portion of total enterprise capital which constitute the margin or buffer for maturing obligations within the ordinary operating cycle of the business." Net working capital has also been viewed as absolute measure of liquidity.[5] Such a margin or cushion of protection provided by the Automobile Industry of India is shown in the Table 5.1.

Table 5.1 indicates that almost all the industries have positive networking capital. A negative networking capital has been observed for Tata Motors Ltd in the years 1999-2000, 2000– 2001, 2001-2002 and 2002-2003, Bajaj Tempo Ltd in 2005-2006 and 2006-2007, Eicher Motors Ltd in 2002-2003, 2005-2006 and 2006-2007 and Swaraj Mazda Ltd in 1992-1993, 1993-1994, and 1994-1995 among the commercial vehicles sector units. Hindustan Motors Ltd in 2003-2004, 2004-2005, 2005-2006 and 2006-2007 and Maruti Udyog Ltd in 1993-1994, 1994-1995 and 1995-1996 among the passenger cars and multiutility vehicles sector units. LML Ltd in 1992-1993, 1993-1994 and 2001-2007, Maharashtra Scooters Ltd in 2006-2007, TVS Motor Company Ltd in 1992-1993, 1993-1994, 1995-1996, 1998-1999, 2002-2003 and 2003-2004, Kinetic Motors Ltd in 2005-2006 and 2006-2007, Hero Honda Motors Ltd in 1999-2000 and 2001-2002, Kinetic Engineering Ltd in 2005-2006, Majestic Auto Ltd in 1999-2000, 2000-2004, 2005-2006 and 2006-2007, Scooters India Ltd in 1992-1993, 1993-1994, 1994-1995 and 1995-1996 among the two- and three wheelers sector units. The negative networking capital shows the risky approach adopted by

Table 5.1

Net Working Capital of the Selected Units

Year	*Commercial vehicles sector*					*Passenger cars & multiutility vehicles sector*			*Two- and three-wheelers sector*									
	Ashok Leyland Ltd	*Tata Motors Ltd*	*Bajaj Tempo Ltd*	*Eicher Motors Ltd*	*Swaraj Mazda Ltd*	*Hind-ustan Motors Ltd*	*Mah & Mah Ltd*	*Maruti Udyog Ltd*	*Bajaj Auto Ltd*	*LML Ltd*	*Maha-rashtra Scoot-ers Ltd*	*TVS Motors Company Ltd*	*Kinetic Motors Ltd*	*Hero Honda Motors Ltd*	*Kinetic Eng., Ltd*	*Maj-estic Auto Ltd*	*Sco-oters India Ltd*
1992-93	479.03 (100)	605.43 (100)	45.32 (100)	9.80 (100)	-3.54 (100)	30.24 (100)	212.20 (100)	241.77 (100)	155.69 (100)	-29.47 (100)	27.32 (100)	-18.63 (100)	10.09 (100)	33.88 (100)	26.71 (100)	1.09 (100)	-219.96 (100)
1993-94	408.03 (85)	559.79 (92)	46.44 (102)	13.32 (136)	-7.03 (199)	73.26 (242)	401.60 (189)	-99.31 (-41)	245.05 (157)	-32.92 (112)	30.30 (111)	-6.60 (35)	20.38 (202)	19.62 (58)	25.59 (96)	2.78 (255)	-313.06 (142)
1994-95	859.06 (179)	507.62 (84)	58.07 (128)	23.59 (241)	-6.64 (188)	80.69 (267)	333.96 (157)	-681.71 (-282)	603.61 (388)	1.46 (-5)	49.27 (180)	13.88 (-75)	18.41 (182)	11.89 (35)	23.40 (88)	5.55 (509)	-399.35 (182)
1995-96	883.82 (185)	227.93 (38)	36.72 (81)	29.62 (302)	14.14 (-399)	108.96 (360)	159.53 (75)	-12.50 (-5)	553.71 (356)	15.42 (-52)	25.97 (95)	-2.06 (11)	14.33 (142)	0.59 (2)	21.40 (80)	22.99 (2109)	-488.53 (222)
1996-97	1046.00 (218)	1219.90 (201)	45.21 (100)	36.43 (372)	28.14 (-795)	177.78 (588)	733.31 (346)	246.70 (102)	896.81 (576)	9.67 (-33)	20.66 (76)	36.69 (-197)	13.11 (130)	0.1[illegible] (1)	37.44 (140)	5.51 (506)	5.89 (-3)
1997-98	1227.28 (256)	911.57 (151)	47.05 (104)	28.34 (289)	21.36 (-603)	165.21 (546)	876.72 (413)	144.02 (60)	1136.80 (730)	17.17 (-58)	12.29 (45)	97.30 (-522)	18.72 (186)	53.26 (157)	52.90 (198)	22.89 (2100)	27.40 (-12)
1998-99	728.57 (152)	217.68 (36)	38.75 (86)	28.82 (294)	29.21 (-825)	109.71 (363)	907.33 (428)	727.41 (301)	1393.70 (895)	85.13 (-289)	21.50 (79)	-7.74 (42)	25.60 (254)	17.49 (52)	54.28 (203)	10.15 (931)	33.86 (-15)
1999-00	698.87 (146)	-361.07 (-60)	57.56 (127)	27.30 (279)	25.95 (-733)	131.52 (435)	819.09 (386)	57.00 (24)	1990.60 (1279)	56.14 (-190)	33.60 (123)	80.48 (-432)	23.94 (237)	-45.91 (-136)	81.83 (306)	-10.92 (-1002)	49.83 (-23)
2000-01	854.13 (178)	-1049.70 (-173)	56.44 (125)	22.01 (225)	43.10 (-1218)	77.46 (256)	567.45 (267)	177.30 (73)	1061.30 (682)	16.88 (-57)	38.52 (141)	63.80 (-342)	24.56 (243)	203.71 (601)	80.29 (301)	-22.44 (-205[illegible])	55.17 (-25)

(Contd...)

(Contd...)

2001-02	860.51 (180)	-752.26 (-124)	46.29 (102)	4.54 (46)	11.94 (-337)	38.52 (127)	533.24 (251)	300.00 (124)	1509.20 (969)	-44.62 (151)	47.24 (173)	77.22 (-414)	18.94 (188)	-343.75 (-1015)	105.60 (395)	-34.69 (-3183)	67.62 (-31)
2002-03	710.59 (148)	-831.31 (-137)	67.96 (150)	-0.61 (-6)	24.49 (-692)	53.66 (177)	493.84 (233)	1140.20 (472)	1307.00 (839)	-33.46 (114)	57.45 (210)	-9.06 (49)	60.90 (604)	550.36 (1624)	71.97 (269)	-32.83 (-3012)	65.80 (-30)
2003-04	605.97 (126)	204.93 (34)	74.31 (164)	46.30 (472)	37.51 (-1060)	-3.80 (-13)	157.88 (74)	1988.20 (822)	1124.40 (722)	-66.32 (225)	65.21 (239)	-12.06 (65)	18.94 (188)	808.75 (2387)	29.03 (109)	-17.40 (-1596)	55.92 (-25)
2004-05	1126.05 (235)	761.09 (126)	51.20 (113)	48.65 (496)	43.95 (-1242)	-19.66 (-65)	422.06 (199)	2719.60 (1125)	3975.95 (2554)	-42.35 (144)	17.88 (65)	45.65 (-245)	4.06 (40)	1077.25 (3180)	25.14 (94)	9.45 (867)	56.76 (-26)
2005-06	1078.88 (225)	1908.64 (315)	-39.28 (-87)	-4.78 (-49)	74.24 (-2097)	-37.59 (124)	886.16 (418)	3501.20 (1448)	4757.62 (3056)	-72.10 (245)	16.60 (61)	113.76 (-611)	-30.93 (-307)	1288.12 (3802)	-14.11 (-52.83)	-0.49 (-45)	59.19 (-27)
2006-07	697.57 (146)	916.79 (151)	-15.60 (-34)	-20.57 (210)	38.43 (-1086)	-8.04 (-27)	1044.94 (495)	2474.55 (1024)	5008.02 (3217)	-151.91 (515)	-1.75 (-6)	193.88 (-1041)	-55.79 (-553)	1354.52 (3998)	28.76 (108)	-4.15 (-381)	74.06 (-34)
Mean	817.62	336.44	41.10	19.52	23.98	65.19	569.95	861.63	1714.63	-18.09	30.80	44.43	12.32	335.33	43.35	-2.83	-57.96

Figures in parentheses denote growth index

Source : Computed from the Annual reports of the respective units.

the industry. Table 5.1 also shows that average net working capital varied widely from one industry to another. The average networking capital is largest for Ashok Leyland Ltd followed by Tata Motors Ltd, Bajaj Tempo Ltd, Eicher Motors Ltd and Swaraj Mazda Ltd in the commercial vehicles sector units and in the passenger cars and multiutility vehicles sector units, it is the highest for Maruti Udyog Ltd followed by Hindustan Motors Ltd and Mahindra and Mahindra Ltd, whereas in two- and three-wheelers sector units, it is the highest for Bajaj Auto Ltd followed by LML Ltd, Maharashtra Scooters Ltd, TVS Motor Company Ltd, Kinetic Motors Ltd, Hero Honda Motors Ltd, Kinetic Engineering Ltd , Majestic Auto Ltd and Scooters India Ltd. The average net working capital computed across the years in the commercial vehicles sector indicates that it increased from Rs. 227.21 crores in 1992-93 to Rs. 330.49 crores in 2006-07. In the passenger cars and multiutility vehicles sector, it increased from Rs.161.40 crores in 1992-93 to Rs. 1170.48 crores in 2006-07. In two- and three-wheelers sector, it increased from Rs. -1.48 crores in 1992-93 to Rs. 716.18 crores in 2006-07 during the study period. For the whole industry, the average net working capital across the years increased from Rs. 94.53 crores in 1992-93 to Rs.682.91 crores in 2006-07.

In order to indicate whether or not there has been a growth in net working capital in individual industry, the growth index are computed and presented in Table 5.1. It is evident from the table that there has been a growth in net working capital over a period of time in all the industries under the commercial vehicles sector, the passenger cars and multiutility vehicles sector and the two- and three-wheelers sector. The growth in networking capital is the highest for Eicher Motors Ltd followed by Ashok Leyland Ltd, Tata Motors Ltd, Bajaj Tempo Ltd and Swaraj Mazda Ltd in the commercial vehicles sector units, in the passenger cars and multiutility vehicles sector units, it is the highest for Maruti Udyog Ltd followed by Hindustan Motors Ltd and Mahindra and Mahindra Ltd and in the two- and three-wheelers sector units, it is the highest for Hero Honda Motors Ltd followed by Bajaj Auto Ltd, LML Ltd, Maharashtra Scooters Ltd, TVS Motor Company Ltd, Kinetic Motors Ltd, Kinetic Engineering Ltd, Majestic Auto Ltd and Scooters India Ltd in 2006-07 over 1992-93.

Quick Net Working Capital Position

The measure of net working capital does not indicate true ability to pay the current debts when they become due. The net working capital is the excess of current assets over current liabilities comprised illiquid inventories, these inventories cannot be easily converted into cash. Therefore, while dealing with liquidity, the measure of Quick Net Working Capital (QNWC) has been assumed as more relevant than the measure of net working capital. The QNWC [(CA – INV) – CL] figures computed for the selected industry are presented in Table 5.2 which clearly shows that all the industries have negative 'Margin of safety' of protection provided to creditors from the quick assets.

The number of industries for which positive quick networking capital has been noticed to be three (Ashok Leyland Ltd, Maharashtra Scooters Ltd and Kinetic Engineering Ltd) in 1992-1993, five (Ashok Leyland Ltd, Mahindra and Mahindra Ltd, Bajaj Auto Ltd, Maharashtra Scooters Ltd and Kinetic Engineering Ltd) in 1993-94, three (Ashok Leyland Ltd, Bajaj Auto Ltd and Maharashtra Scooters Ltd) in 1994-95, three (Ashok Leyland Ltd, Bajaj Auto Ltd and Maharashtra Scooters Ltd) in 1995-96, Seven (Ashok Leyland Ltd, Tata Motors Ltd, Eicher Motors Ltd, Mahindra and Mahindra Ltd, Bajaj Auto Ltd, Maharashtra Scooters Ltd and Kinetic Engineering Ltd) in 1996-97, Seven (Ashok Leyland Ltd, Eicher Motors Ltd, Mahindra and Mahindra Ltd, Bajaj Auto Ltd, TVS Motor Company Ltd, Kinetic Engineering Ltd and Majestic Auto Ltd) in 1997-98, Seven (Ashok Leyland Ltd, Eicher Motors Ltd, Mahindra and Mahindra Ltd, Maruti Udyog Ltd, Bajaj Auto Ltd, Kinetic Engineering Ltd and Scooters India Ltd) in 1998-99, Six (Ashok Leyland Ltd, Mahindra and Mahindra Ltd, Bajaj Auto Ltd, Maharashtra Scooters Ltd, Kinetic Engineering Ltd and Scooters India Ltd) in 1999-2000, Seven (Ashok Leyland Ltd, Mahindra and Mahindra Ltd, Bajaj Auto Ltd, Maharashtra Scooters Ltd, Hero Honda Motors Ltd, Kinetic Engineering Ltd and Scooters India Ltd) in 2000-01, Six (Ashok Leyland Ltd, Mahindra and Mahindra Ltd, Baja Auto Ltd, Maharashtra Scooters Ltd, Kinetic Engineering Ltd and Scooters India Ltd) in 2001- 02, Eight (Ashok Leyland Ltd, Mahindra and Mahindra Ltd, Maruti Udyog Ltd, Bajaj Auto Ltd, Maharashtra Scooters Ltd, Hero Honda Motors Ltd, Kinetic Engineering Ltd

Table 5.2

Quick Net Working Capital of the Selected Units

Year	Commercial vehicles sector					Passenger cars & multiutility vehicles sector							Two and three wheelers sector				
	Ashok Leyland Ltd	Tata Motors Ltd	Bajaj Tempo Ltd	Eicher Motors Ltd	Swaraj Mazda Ltd	Hind-ustan Motors	Mah & Mah Ltd	Maruti Udyog Ltd	Bajaj Auto Ltd	LML Ltd	Maha-rashtra Scoot-	TVS Motors Company	Kinetic Motors Ltd	Hero Honda Motors	Kinetic Eng., Ltd	Maj-estic Auto	Sco-oters India
1992-93	217.29	-371.79	-51.04	-17.56	-29.58	-146.57	-49.20	-83.97	-16.99	-69.09	24.00	-43.19	-9.24	-2.26	7.38	-10.40	-236.58
1993-94	153.93	-179.39	-59.26	-10.43	-34.99	-95.45	82.36	-443.61	83.72	-75.54	28.82	-35.98	-5.06	-22.83	1.00	-10.18	-328.85
1994-95	554.87	-270.68	-95.50	-7.15	-33.67	-101.79	-17.95	-1253.19	348.77	-56.97	45.59	-38.09	-9.64	-61.79	-3.46	-11.05	-423.76
1995-96	478.40	-773.57	-118.15	-12.15	-34.31	-101.70	-232.26	-734.22	334.33	-73.45	20.21	-54.51	-32.74	-59.54	-12.76	-6.76	-517.42
1996-97	393.03	76.80	-125.42	1.82	-29.12	-53.69	285.83	-351.82	663.46	-95.61	7.34	-24.66	-28.60	-68.05	7.72	-18.17	-29.61
1997-98	569.68	-54.38	-146.38	1.62	-16.47	-89.70	361.85	-424.86	903.51	-94.43	-9.57	44.52	-25.83	-36.91	21.70	3.45	-1.30
1998-99	300.82	-638.43	-152.91	10.68	-13.04	-274.85	470.34	149.81	1221.10	-46.00	-215.59	-98.61	-26.65	-118.50	27.16	-9.85	1.86
1999-00	441.12	-1351.93	-132.64	-5.84	-1.88	-206.04	303.54	-933.20	1729.37	-65.17	9.70	-38.31	-21.63	-215.27	37.08	-32.31	22.89
2000-01	336.48	-2154.80	-126.96	-10.15	-18.31	-134.00	14.91	-688.20	807.87	-146.77	30.76	-88.23	-25.35	5.14	34.48	-40.77	15.98
2001-02	265.20	-1739.76	-86.01	-28.96	-3.42	-128.19	63.20	-381.10	1330.10	-175.61	44.67	-71.57	-29.73	-522.11	48.97	-59.05	31.46
2002-03	300.11	-1990.60	-80.19	-36.66	-47.89	-159.83	37.06	653.20	1099.02	-178.58	53.94	-223.13	-5.17	349.48	2.86	-53.11	35.41
2003-04	99.03	-942.40	-77.84	-79.95	-35.85	-162.14	-341.82	1548.40	921.84	-227.28	60.62	-228.72	-22.37	620.55	-39.16	-38.41	28.84
2004-05	578.70	-754.93	-133.87	-112.60	-51.05	-122.93	-257.06	2069.50	3810.14	-162.54	15.69	-187.58	-29.03	873.46	-27.37	-11.91	26.46
2005-06	196.93	-21.45	-253.12	-166.01	-47.19	-123.45	79.65	2635.50	4549.67	-183.57	10.19	-244.14	-55.53	1065.12	-61.09	-19.00	16.72
2006-07	-368.97	-1584.16	-237.34	-189.48	-28.93	-69.27	166.46	1564.40	4755.67	-254.48	-2.62	-202.68	-91.17	1083.76	1.13	-15.97	35.89
Mean	301.11	-850.10	-125.11	-44.19	-28.38	-131.31	64.46	221.78	1502.77	-127.01	8.25	-102.33	-27.85	192.68	3.04	-22.23	-88.13

Source : Computed from the annual reports of the respective units.

and Scooters India Ltd) in 2002–03, Six (Ashok Leyland Ltd, Maruti Udyog Ltd, Bajaj Auto Ltd, Maharashtra Scooters Ltd, Hero Honda Motors Ltd and Scooters India Ltd) in 2003-04, Six (Ashok Leyland Ltd, Maruti Udyog Ltd, Bajaj Auto Ltd, Maharashtra Scooters Ltd, Hero Honda Motors Ltd and Scooters India Ltd) in 2004-05, Seven (Ashok Leyland Ltd, Mahindra and Mahindra Ltd, Maruti Udyog Ltd, Bajaj Auto Ltd, Maharashtra Scooters Ltd, Hero Honda Motors Ltd and Scooters India Ltd) in 2005-06, Six (Mahindra and Mahindra Ltd, Maruti Udyog Ltd, Bajaj Auto Ltd, Hero Honda Motors Ltd, Kinetic Engineering Ltd and Scooters India Ltd) in 2006-07. It is also noticed that none of the industries covered current liabilities from the quick assets throughout the period from 1992-93 to 2006-07. Thus, the capability to pay current debts out of quick assets by the selected industries goes much lower. However, in the recent years, three industries, namely, Ashok Leyland Ltd in commercial vehicles sector units, Mahindra and Mahindra Ltd in the passenger cars and multiutility vehicles sector units, Bajaj Auto Ltd in the two- and three-wheelers sector units which have covered current liabilities from their quick assets as indicated by their positive quick net working capital.

However, nothing concrete can be concluded depending solely upon the net working capital or quick net working capital, while assessing the liquidity position of the selected enterprises. The problem is that they do not show the extent of margin of safety provided to the current creditors. Due to this, the Current Ratio (CR) and Quick Ratio (QR) are regarded as better measures of liquidity.

Current Ratio

The most widely used measure to liquid position of a firm is the current ratio. It gives an idea of the liquidity position and short term financial strength of a concern. According to Walker and Boughn. "A good current ratio may mean a good umbrella for creditors against the rainy day, but to the management it reflects bad financial planning or presence of idle assets or over capitalisation." The current ratios of the selected automobile industries of India for the period of study are presented in Table 5.3.

A relatively high value of the current ratio is considered as an indication that the firm is liquid and has the ability to pay its bills. On the other hand a relatively low value of the current ratio is considered as an indication that the firm will find difficulty in paying its bills. As a conventional rule, a current ratio of 2:1 or more is considered to be satisfactory. But the size of current ratio depends upon many factors, a standard of common current ratio cannot be designated as appropriate for all types of business. Therefore, as regards the industrial firms with larger investment in fixed assets and a slower operating cycle, the standard of this ratio may fall around 1.5:1.

The selected automobile industries have an average current ratio greater than 1.5, i.e., Ashok Leyland Ltd in the commercial vehicles sector units, Mahindra and Mahindra Ltd and Maruti Udyog Ltd in the passenger cars and multiutility vehicles sector units, and Bajaj Auto Ltd, Maharashtra Scooters Ltd and Scooters India Ltd in the two- and three-wheelers sector units. The number of industries for which current ratio are less than 1.5 have been noticed to be fourteen (except Ashok Leyland Ltd, Hero Honda Motors Ltd and Kinetic Engineering Ltd) in 1992-93, thirteen (except Ashok Leyland Ltd, Mahindra and Mahindra Ltd, Bajaj Auto Ltd and Kinetic Motors Ltd) in 1993 -94, thirteen (except Ashok Leyland Ltd, Mahindra and Mahindra Ltd, Bajaj Auto Ltd and Kinetic Motors Ltd) in 1994-95, fifteen (except Ashok Leyland Ltd and Bajaj Auto Ltd) in 1995-96, twelve (except Ashok Leyland Ltd, Hindustan Motors Ltd, Mahindra and Mahindra Ltd, Bajaj Auto Ltd and Kinetic Engineering Ltd) in 1996-97, ten (except Ashok Leyland Ltd, Eicher Motors Ltd, Mahindra and Mahindra Ltd, Bajaj Auto Ltd, TVS Motor Company Ltd, Kinetic Engineering Ltd and Scooters India Ltd) in 1997-98, eleven (except Ashok Leyland Ltd, Eicher Motors Ltd, Mahindra and Mahindra Ltd, Bajaj Auto Ltd, Kinetic Engineering Ltd and Scooters India Ltd) in 1998-99, twelve (except Ashok Leyland Ltd, Mahindra and Mahindra Ltd, Bajaj Auto Ltd, Kinetic Engineering Ltd and Scooters India Ltd) in 1999-2000, twelve (except Ashok Leyland Ltd, Bajaj Auto Ltd, Maharashtra Scooters Ltd, Kinetic Engineering Ltd and Scooters India Ltd) in 2000-01, twelve (except Ashok Leyland Ltd, Bajaj Auto Ltd, Maharashtra Scooters Ltd, Kinetic Engineering Ltd and Scooters India Ltd) in 2001-02, twelve (except Ashok Leyland Ltd, Maruti Udyog Ltd, Bajaj Auto Ltd,

Maharashtra Scooters Ltd and Scooters India Ltd) in 2002-03, twelve (except Ashok Leyland Ltd, Maruti Udyog Ltd, Maharashtra Scooters Ltd, Hero Honda Motors Ltd and Scooters India Ltd) in 2003-04, eleven (except Ashok Leyland Ltd, Maruti Udyog Ltd, Bajaj Auto Ltd, Maharashtra Scooters Ltd, Hero Honda Motors Ltd and Scooters India Ltd) in 2004-05, ten (except Ashok Leyland Ltd, Bajaj Tempo Ltd, Maruti Udyog Ltd, Bajaj Auto Ltd, Maharashtra Scooters Ltd, Hero Honda Motors Ltd and Scooters India Ltd) in 2005-06 and thirteen (except Maruti Udyog Ltd, Bajaj Auto Ltd, Hero Honda Motors Ltd and Scooters India Ltd) in 2006-07.

The average current ratio is the highest for Ashok Leyland Ltd, followed by Bajaj Tempo Ltd, Eicher Motors Ltd, Swaraj Mazda Ltd and Tata Motors Ltd in the commercial vehicles sector units, it is the highest for Mahindra and Mahindra Ltd followed by Maruti Udyog Ltd and Hindustan Motors Ltd in the passenger cars and multiutility vehicles sector units, and in the two- and three-wheelers sector units, it is the highest for Bajaj Auto Ltd followed by Maharashtra Scooters Ltd, Scooters India Ltd, Kinetic Engineering Ltd, Hero Honda Motors Ltd, Kinetic Motors Ltd, TVS Motor Company Ltd, Majestic Auto Ltd and LML Ltd. Thus, average current ratio of commercial vehicles sector of Indian automobile industries ranged from 1.07 times to 2.16 times, in the passenger cars and multiutility vehicles sector, it ranged from 1.17 times to 1.54 times, whereas in the two- and three-wheelers sector, it ranged from 0.91 times to 1.87 times. Comparatively, the commercial vehicles sector in automobile industries have maintained a higher current ratio than the passenger cars and multiutility vehicles sector and the two- and three-wheelers sector during the study period.

Within the industries also, the current ratio fluctuated widely. It fluctuated from 1.35 to 3.05 for Ashok Leyland Ltd, 0.73 to 1.35 for Tata Motors Ltd, 0.86 to 1.44 for Bajaj Tempo Ltd, 0.97 to 1.60 for Eicher Motors Ltd, and 0.91 to 1.49 for Swaraj Mazda Ltd in the commercial vehicles sector units. In the passenger cars and multiutility vehicles sector units, it fluctuated from 0.76 to 1.64 for Hindustan Motors Ltd, 0.97 to 2.00 for Mahindra and Mahindra Ltd and 0.64 to 2.85 for Maruti Udyog Ltd and in the two- and three-wheelers sector units, it fluctuated from 1.44 to

Table 5.3

Current Ratio of the Selected Units

	Commercial vehicles sector					Passenger cars & multiutility vehicles sector					Two and three wheelers sector							
Year	Ashok Leyland Ltd	Tata Motors Ltd	Bajaj Tempo Ltd	Eicher Motors Ltd	Swaraj Mazda Ltd	Hind-ustan Motors	Mah & Mah Ltd	Maruti Udyog Ltd	Bajaj Auto Ltd	LML Ltd	Maha-rashtra Scoot-	TVS Motors Company	Kinetic Motors Ltd	Hero Honda Motors	Kinetic Eng., Ltd	Maj-estic Auto	Sco-oters India	Mean
1992-93	2.67	1.35	1.44	1.21	0.91	1.10	1.42	1.23	1.44	0.62	1.15	0.75	1.46	1.57	1.66	1.04	0.99	1.29
1993-94	2.23	1.35	1.28	1.29	0.98	1.27	2.00	0.64	1.54	0.65	1.33	0.91	1.84	1.22	1.47	1.07	0.08	1.24
1994-95	2.98	1.25	1.27	1.37	0.91	1.27	1.62	0.74	1.97	1.01	1.48	1.15	1.53	1.09	1.42	1.09	0.08	1.31
1995-96	2.17	1.06	1.17	1.35	1.19	1.36	0.97	0.99	1.64	1.07	1.19	0.96	1.26	1.00	1.29	1.47	0.08	1.19
1996-97	2.12	1.34	1.19	1.45	1.39	1.64	1.96	1.19	1.90	1.04	1.16	1.25	1.18	1.00	1.51	1.08	0.54	1.35
1997-98	3.05	1.27	1.20	1.60	1.43	1.47	1.90	0.95	1.89	1.07	1.09	1.61	1.22	1.30	1.57	1.44	1.66	1.51
1998-99	2.03	0.86	1.17	1.52	1.49	1.18	1.94	1.45	1.89	1.31	1.14	0.91	1.41	1.06	1.63	1.17	1.78	1.41
1999-00	1.84	0.83	1.27	1.43	1.43	1.26	1.84	1.03	2.07	1.22	1.22	1.17	1.35	0.87	1.91	0.86	2.54	1.42
2000-01	2.19	0.73	1.27	1.32	1.25	1.19	1.48	1.08	1.69	1.05	1.76	1.16	1.34	1.44	1.71	0.77	2.21	1.39
2001-02	2.15	0.77	1.25	1.04	1.43	1.11	1.44	1.17	1.88	0.86	1.98	1.12	1.19	0.61	1.71	0.66	2.87	1.37
2002-03	2.14	0.76	1.33	0.99	1.08	1.15	1.34	1.67	1.64	0.84	2.36	0.98	1.38	1.49	1.43	0.68	2.73	1.41
2003-04	1.71	1.04	1.29	1.13	1.14	0.99	1.05	2.28	1.47	0.82	3.32	0.97	0.84	1.64	1.16	1.13	2.13	1.42
2004-05	1.97	1.13	1.19	1.11	1.13	0.90	1.29	2.69	2.44	0.83	1.84	1.09	0.70	1.72	1.01	1.21	2.09	1.43
2005-06	1.77	1.26	1.91	0.98	1.11	0.84	1.47	2.77	2.36	0.71	1.68	1.18	0.62	1.83	0.89	0.99	1.75	1.42
2006-07	1.35	1.06	0.86	0.97	1.09	0.76	1.35	2.85	2.16	0.49	0.92	1.27	0.62	1.92	1.10	0.86	1.63	1.25
Mean	2.16	1.07	1.27	1.25	1.20	1.17	1.54	1.52	1.87	0.91	1.57	1.10	1.20	1.32	1.43	1.03	1.54	

Source : Computed from the annual reports of the respective units.

2.44 for Bajaj Auto Ltd, 0.49 to 1.31 for LML Ltd, 0.92 to 3.32 for Maharashtra Scooters Ltd, 0.91 to 1.61 for TVS Motor Company Ltd, 0.62 to 1.84 for Kinetic Motors Ltd, 0.61 to 1.92 to Hero Honda Motors Ltd, 0.89 to 1.91 for Kinetic Engineering Ltd, 0.66 to 1.47 for Majestic Auto Ltd and 0.08 to 2.87 for Scooters India Ltd.

Liquid Ratio

This ratio is a more vigorous and penetrating test of the liquidity position of firm. The fundamental object of calculating this ratio is to enable the finance officer to ascertain as to what would happen if the current creditors pressed for immediate payment. Though the current ratio of 2:1 is generally acceptable, the precise definition of an acceptable ratio is greatly dependent on the industry in which firm operates.[7] The acceptability of a current ratio is highly dependent on the predictability of the firm's cashflows. The more predictable the cashflows, the lower the current ratio required. The high current ratio need not indicate a higher liquidity, because current assets comprise of inventories which cannot be converted into cash easily. It affects the capability of the enterprises to pay their current debts. The basic assumption of the quick ratio is that inventory is generally the least liquid current assets and should therefore be ignored.[8] Viewed in this way, liquid ratio is considered more relevant than current ratio.

The liquid ratios computed for the selected automobile industries presented in Table 5.4. The problem with the measure of Quick Net Working Capital (QNWC) is that it does not show to what extent the margin of safety provided in the form of quick assets to the current creditors is sufficient. The QNWC as a measure is good enough to indicate whether it is positive or negative. But a liquid ratio as a measure shows the extension of 'cushion' of protection provided from the quick assets to the current creditors and hence it is a better measure.

If the standard liquid ratio is to be taken as 1:1, the majority of the all selected automobile industries have average quick ratios of less than 1. The industries for which liquid ratios are less than 1 have been noticed to be sixteen (except Ashok Leyland Ltd) in 1992-93, sixteen (except Mahindra and Mahindra Ltd) in 1996-97, sixteen (except Ashok Leyland Ltd) in 1997-98, fifteen (except Ashok Leyland Ltd and Mahindra and Mahindra Ltd) in 1998 -

99, sixteen (except Scooters India Ltd) in 1999-2000, fifteen (except Ashok Leyland Ltd and Scooters India Ltd) in 2000-01, fourteen (except Bajaj Auto Ltd, Maharashtra Scooters Ltd and Scooters India Ltd) in 2001-02, fourteen (except Maharashtra Scooters Ltd, Hero Honda Motors Ltd and Scooters India Ltd) in 2002-03, thirteen (except Maruti Udyog Ltd, Maharashtra Scooters Ltd, Hero Honda Motors Ltd and Scooters India Ltd) in 2003-04, eleven (except Ashok Leyland Ltd, Maruti Udyog Ltd, Bajaj Auto Ltd, Maharashtra Scooters Ltd, Hero Honda Motors Ltd and Scooters India Ltd) in 2004-05, thirteen (except Maruti Udyog Ltd, Bajaj Auto Ltd, Maharashtra Scooters Ltd and Hero Honda Motors Ltd) in 2005-06, fourteen (except Maruti Udyog Ltd, Bajaj Auto Ltd and Hero Honda Motors Ltd) in 2006-07. The average liquid ratios are less than one for all the selected automobile industry during the study period.

The average liquid ratio is the highest for Ashok Leyland Ltd, followed by Eicher Motors Ltd, Swaraj Mazda Ltd, Tata Motors Ltd and Bajaj Tempo Ltd in the commercial vehicles sector units and it is the highest for Maruti Udyog Ltd, followed by Mahindra and Mahindra Ltd and Hindustan Motors Ltd in the passenger cars and multiutility vehicles sector units. In the two- and three-wheelers sector units, it is the highest for Bajaj Auto Ltd, followed by Maharashtra Scooters Ltd, Scooter India Ltd, Hero Honda Motors Ltd, Kinetic Engineering Ltd, Majestic Auto Ltd, Kinetic Motors Ltd, TVS Motor Company Ltd and LML Ltd. Thus, average liquid ratio of commercial vehicles sector ranged from 0.25 times to 0.95 times. In the passenger cars and multiutility vehicles sector it ranged from 0.39 times to 0.80 times, whereas in the two- and three-wheelers sector it ranged from 0.29 times to 0.95 times. Comparatively, commercial vehicles sector and two and three wheelers sector automobile industries have maintained higher liquid ratio than the passenger cars and multiutility vehicles sector during the study period.

Within the industries also quick ratio fluctuated widely. It fluctuated from 0.52 to 1.76 for Ashok Leyland Ltd, 0.15 to 0.80 for Tata Motors Ltd, 0.07 to 0.49 for Bajaj Tempo Ltd, 0.28 to 0.77 for Eicher Motors Ltd and 0.13 to 0.79 for Swaraj Mazda Ltd in the commercial vehicles sector units, 0.20 to 0.57 for Hindustan Motors Ltd, 0.26 to 1.14 for Mahindra and Mahindra Ltd and 0.16

Table 5.4

Liquid Ratio of the Selected Units

	Commercial vehicles sector					*Passenger cars & multiutility vehicles sector*						*Two and three wheelers sector*						
Year	*Ashok Leyland Ltd*	*Tata Motors Ltd*	*Bajaj Tempo Ltd*	*Eicher Motors Ltd*	*Swaraj Mazda Ltd*	*Hindustan Motors*	*Mah & Mah Ltd*	*Maruti Udyog Ltd*	*Bajaj Auto Ltd*	*LML Ltd*	*Maharastra Scoot-*	*TVS Motors Company*	*Kinetic Motors Ltd*	*Hero Honda Motors*	*Kinetic Eng., Ltd*	*Majestic Auto*	*Scooters India*	*Mean*
1992-93	1.16	0.63	0.11	0.42	0.13	0.39	0.48	0.16	0.42	0.20	0.44	0.24	0.40	0.75	0.57	0.43	0.01	0.41
1993-94	0.84	0.71	0.40	0.48	0.29	0.46	0.70	0.20	0.68	0.25	0.59	0.29	0.62	0.54	0.50	0.38	0.02	0.47
1994-95	0.92	0.60	0.34	0.55	0.33	0.43	0.65	0.40	0.92	0.31	0.75	0.34	0.55	0.36	0.33	0.37	0.01	0.48
1995-96	0.52	0.49	0.07	0.56	0.28	0.47	0.26	0.47	0.72	0.32	0.46	0.19	0.27	0.38	0.25	0.47	0.03	0.37
1996-97	0.84	0.80	0.11	0.75	0.45	0.57	1.07	0.47	0.94	0.30	0.39	0.47	0.47	0.35	0.54	0.48	0.20	0.52
1997-98	1.10	0.69	0.10	0.59	0.45	0.53	0.90	0.24	0.83	0.37	0.27	0.91	0.61	0.45	0.67	0.70	0.81	0.60
1998-99	1.76	0.46	0.12	0.77	0.55	0.38	1.14	0.80	0.84	0.55	0.27	0.27	0.44	0.32	0.80	0.60	0.89	0.64
1999-00	0.78	0.29	0.20	0.56	0.79	0.42	0.91	0.22	0.92	0.48	0.28	0.42	0.60	0.11	0.81	0.41	1.46	0.57
2000-01	1.06	0.19	0.18	0.48	0.61	0.38	0.67	0.34	0.69	0.31	0.88	0.36	0.51	0.81	0.73	0.43	1.09	0.57
2001-02	0.88	0.20	0.34	0.46	0.71	0.42	0.70	0.47	1.01	0.24	1.32	0.47	0.49	0.25	0.84	0.30	1.54	0.63
2002-03	0.85	0.15	0.44	0.31	0.45	0.36	0.62	0.97	0.77	0.20	1.60	0.31	0.48	1.21	0.51	0.33	1.56	0.65
2003-04	0.82	0.54	0.49	0.47	0.60	0.29	0.42	1.57	0.72	0.16	2.64	0.23	0.32	1.30	0.31	0.41	1.28	0.74
2004-05	1.19	0.52	0.33	0.40	0.62	0.25	0.66	1.87	1.64	0.32	1.39	0.36	0.26	1.42	0.21	0.50	1.29	0.78
2005-06	0.95	0.27	0.29	0.28	0.66	0.23	0.86	1.98	1.67	0.23	1.09	0.28	0.27	1.52	0.12	0.48	0.97	0.71
2006-07	0.53	0.18	0.25	0.36	0.64	0.20	0.79	1.90	1.45	0.04	0.45	0.40	0.27	1.58	0.46	0.45	0.91	0.64
Mean	0.95	0.45	0.25	0.50	0.50	0.39	0.72	0.80	0.95	0.29	0.85	0.37	0.44	0.76	0.51	0.45	0.78	

Source : Computed from the annual reports of the respective units.

to 1.98 for Maruti Udyog Ltd in the passenger cars and multiutility vehicles sector units and 0.42 to 1.67 for Bajaj Auto Ltd, 0.04 to 0.55 for LML Ltd, 0.27 to 2.64 for Maharashtra Scooters Ltd, 0.19 to 0.91 for TVS Motor Company Ltd, 0.26 to 0.62 for Kinetic Motors Ltd, 0.11 to 1.58 for Hero Honda Motors Ltd, 0.12 to 0.81 for Kinetic Engineering Ltd, 0.33 to 0.70 for Majestic Auto Ltd, and 0.01 to 1.54 for Scooters India Ltd in two- and three-wheelers sector units. Table 5.4 also shows that the average liquid ratio has improved over a period of time. This is obviously due to increase in the liquid assets of majority of the selected automobile industries.

Analysis of Variance (F-Test)-Current Ratio

With a view to testing the significance of variation in the current and liquid ratios between various automobile industries and between various years covered under the study, the 'F' test based on a two-way classification has been applied.

Total Industry

It can be seen from Table 5.5 that the calculated value of 'F' ratio of the current ratio between the years is 0.71.

Table 5.5: Analysis of Variance (F- Test) – Current Ratio

Total Industry

Source of variance	*Sum of squares*	*d.f*	*Mean square variance*	*F ratio (Calculated value)*	*Critical values of F at 5% level*
Between years	1.811	14	0.129	0.71	1.74
Between industries	24.140	16	0.509	8.26	1.69
Residual	40.935	224	0.182		
Total	60.886	254			

Commercial vehicles sector

Source of variance	*Sum of squares*	*d.f*	*Mean square variance*	*F ratio (Calculated value)*	*Critical values of F at 5% level*
Between years	1.556	14	0.111	1.61	1.87
Between industry	11.432	4	2.858	41.29	2.54
Residual	3.876	56	0.069		
Total	16.864	74			

Passenger cars and multiutility vehicles sector

Source of variance	*Sum of squares*	*d.f*	*Mean square variance*	*F ratio (Calculated value)*	*Critical values of F at 5% level*
Between years	1.383	14	0.099	0.31	2.06
Between industry	1.305	2	0.652	2.04	3.34
Residual	8.937	28	0.319		
Total	11.624	44			

Two- and three-wheelers sector

Source of variance	*Sum of squares*	*d.f*	*Mean square variance*	*F ratio (Calculated value)*	*Critical values of F at 5% level*
Between years	2.604	14	0.186	0.85	1.78
Between industry	11.117	8	1.389	6.38	2.02
Residual	24.390	112	0.218		
Total	38.111	134			

Sources : Computed

Since the calculated value of 'F' (0.71) between the years are less than the table value of 'F' (1.74) at 5 per cent level of significance, the difference in the current ratio between the industries among the different years are not significant. Similarly, the calculated value of 'F' ratio between the industries is 8.26. The calculated value of 'F' (8.26) between the industries are more than the table value of 'F' (1.69) at 5 per cent level of significance, the current ratio between the years among the selected automobile industries is significant. On the basis of this analysis it may be concluded that the performance of individual industries are significantly different with the standards of industry.

Commercial Vehicles Sector

In the commercial vehicles sector, the calculated value of F ratio of current ratio in between the years is 1.61. The calculated value of 'F' (1.61) is less than the table value of 'F' (1.87) at 5 per cent level of significance. Thus, the differences in the current ratio in between the years among the commercial vehicles sector are not significant. Similarly, the calculated value of 'F' ratio in between the industries in commercial vehicles sector is 41.29. The calculated value of 'F' (41.29) much more than the table value 'F' (2.54) at 5 per cent level of significance, the differences in the current ratio in between the industries are significant.

Passenger Cars and Multiutility Vehicles Sector

In the passenger cars and multiutility vehicles sector, the calculated value of 'F' ratio of current ratio in between the years is 0.31. The calculated value 'F' (0.31) is less than the table value of 'F' (2.06) at 5 per cent level of significance. Thus, the differences in current ratio in between the years among the passenger cars and multiutility vehicles sector are not significant. The calculated value of 'F' ratio in between the industries in passenger cars and multiutility vehicles sector is 2.04. The calculated value of 'F' (2.04) between the industries are less than the table value of 'F' (3.34) at 5 per cent level of significance. Thus, the differences in the current ratio in between the industries among different years are not significant.

Two- and Three-Wheelers Sector

In the two- and three-wheelers sector, the calculated value of 'F' ratio of current ratio in between the years is 0.85. The calculated value of 'F' (0.85) is less than the table value of 'F' (1.78) at 5 per cent level of significance. Thus, the differences in the current ratio in between the years among the two- and three-wheelers sector are not significant. Similarly, the calculated value of 'F' ratio in between the industries in the two- and three-wheelers sector is 6.38. Since the calculated value of 'F' (6.38) is more than the table value of 'F' (2.02) at 5 per cent level of significance, the differences in the current ratio in between the industries are significant.

It is concluded from the analysis that all the selected units, the current ratio in between the years among the industries are not significant. But in between the industries among the different years are significant except the passenger cars and multiutility vehicles sector.

Analysis of Variance (F- Test) - Liquid Ratio

Total industry

It can also be seen from Table 5.6 that the calculated value 'F' ratio of liquid ratio between the years is 2.10. Since the calculated value of 'F' (2.10) between the years are more than the table value of 'F' (1.74) at 5 per cent level of significance, thus the difference in the liquid ratio between the industries among different years are significant. Similarly, the calculated value of 'F' ratio between the industries is 6.77. Since the calculated value of 'F' (6.77) between the industries are more than table value of 'F' (1.69) at 5 per cent level of significance, the liquid ratio between the years among the selected automobile industries are significant. On the basis of this analysis it may be concluded that the differences in liquid ratio between the years among selected industries and liquid ratio between the industries among different years are significant.

Commercial vehicles sector

In the commercial vehicles sector, the calculated value of 'F' ratio of liquid ratio in between the years is 0.93. Similarly, the calculated value of 'F' (0.93) is less than the table value of 'F' (1.87) at 5 per cent level of significance, thus the differences in the liquid ratio in between the years among the commercial vehicles sector units are not significant. Similarly, the calculated value of 'F' ratio in between the industries in the commercial vehicle sector is 23.02. The calculated value of 'F' (23.02) is more than the table value of 'F' (2.54) at 5 per cent level of significance. Thus, the differences in the liquid ratio in between the industries are significant.

Passenger Cars and Multiutility Vehicles Sector

In the passenger cars and multiutility vehicles sector, the calculated value of 'F' ratio of liquid ratio in between the years is 0.69. The calculated value of 'F' (0.69) is less than the table value of 'F' (2.06) at 5 per cent level of significance. Thus, the differences in the liquid ratio in between the years among the passenger cars and multiutility vehicles sector units are not significant. Similarly, the calculated value of 'F' ratio in between the industries in the passenger cars and multiutility vehicle sector is 3.75.

Table 5.6

Analysis of Variance (F- Test)-Liquid Ratio

Total industry

Source of variance	*Sum of squares*	*d.f*	*Mean square variance*	*F ratio (Calculated value)*	*Critical values of F at 5% level*
Between years	3.408	14	0.243	2.10	1.74
Between industry	12.530	16	0.7831	6.77	1.69
Residual	25.915	224	0.116		
Total	41.853	254			

Commercial vehicles sector

Source of variance	*Sum of squares*	*d.f*	*Mean square variance*	*F ratio (Calculated value)*	*Critical values of F at 5% level*
Between years	0.551	14	0.039	0.93	1.87
Between industry	3.897	4	0.974	23.02	2.54
Residual	2.370	56	0.042		
Total	6.818	74			

Passenger cars and multiutility vehicles sector

Source of variance	*Sum of squares*	*d.f*	*Mean square variance*	*F ratio (Calculated value)*	*Critical values of F at 5% level*
Between years	1.912	14	0.137	0.69	2.06
Between industry	1.477	2	0.738	3.75	3.34
Residual	5.506	28	0.197		
Total	8.895	44			

Two- and three-wheelers sector

Source of variance	*Sum of squares*	*d.f*	*Mean square variance*	*F ratio (Calculated value)*	*Critical values of F at 5% level*
Between years	3.338	14	0.238	1.71	1.78
Between industry	6.775	8	0.847	6.06	2.02
Residual	15.646	112	0.140		
Total	25.758	134			

Sources: Computed

The calculated value of 'F' (3.75) is more than the table value of 'F' (3.34) at 5 per cent level of significance. Thus, the differences in the liquid ratio in between the industries are significant.

Two- and Three-Wheelers Sector

In the two and three wheeler sector, the calculated value of 'F' ratio of liquid ratio in between the years is 1.71. The calculated value of 'F' (1.71) is less than the table value of 'F' (1.78) at 5 per cent level of significance. Thus, the differences in the liquid ratio in between the years among the two- and three-wheelers sector units are not significant. Similarly, the calculated value of 'F' ratio in between the industries in two- and three-wheelers sector is 6.06. The calculated value of 'F' (6.06) is more than the table value of 'F' (2.02) at 5 per cent level of significance. Thus, the differences in the current ratio in between the industries are significant.

It is concluded from the analysis that in all the selected units, the liquid ratio in between the years among the industries are not significant but between the industries among different years are significant

Analysis of Cash Position Ratio

While dealing with liquidity, an additional ratio which measures cash adequacy should be mentioned. The ratio is to compute the proportion of cash to current liabilities (Cash position ratio) which shows how much cash is available to pay current obligations. These ratios computed for the selected automobile industries and presented in Table 5.7. The table shows that the ratio is highest for Ashok Leyland Ltd followed by Tata Motors Ltd, Eicher Motors Ltd, Baja Tempo Ltd and Swaraj Mazda Ltd in the commercial vehicles sector units and highest in Maruti Udyog Ltd, followed by Mahindra and Mahindra Ltd and Hindustan Motors Ltd in the passenger cars and multiutility vehicles sector units. In the two- and three-wheelers sector units, the ratio is the highest in Bajaj Auto Ltd followed by Maharashtra Scooters Ltd, Hero Honda Motors Ltd, Scooters India Ltd, LML Ltd, TVS Motor Company Ltd, Kinetic Motors Ltd, Kinetic Engineering Ltd and Majestic Auto Ltd. However, the ratio had fluctuated over a period of time for the majority of the selected automobile industries. The average ratio of cash to current liabilities had

Table 5.7

Cash to current liability ratio

Year	Commercial vehicles sector					Passenger cars & multiutility vehicles sector			Two and three wheelers sector									Mean
	Ashok Leyland Ltd	Tata Motors Ltd	Bajaj Tempo Ltd	Eicher Motors Ltd	Swaraj Mazda Ltd	Hindustan Motors	Mah & Mah Ltd	Maruti Udyog Ltd	Bajaj Auto Ltd	LML Ltd	Maharastra Scoot-	TVS Motors Company	Kinetic Motors Ltd	Hero Honda Motors	Kinetic Eng., Ltd	Majestic Auto	Scooters India	
1992-93	0.32	0.06	0.03	0.05	0.05	0.07	0.17	0.03	0.25	0.11	0.28	0.01	0.10	0.35	0.15	0.03	0.01	0.12
1993-94	0.10	0.03	0.36	0.09	0.03	0.10	0.42	0.17	0.52	0.11	0.54	0.08	0.22	0.39	0.16	0.03	0.02	0.20
1994-95	0.27	0.08	0.31	0.13	0.03	0.12	0.42	0.36	0.77	0.18	0.68	0.14	0.29	0.25	0.05	0.05	0.01	0.24
1995-96	0.02	0.06	0.02	0.14	0.02	0.10	0.13	0.39	0.59	0.20	0.40	0.05	0.01	0.25	0.04	0.05	0.02	0.15
1996-97	0.02	0.10	0.02	0.20	0.04	0.16	0.89	0.30	0.79	0.16	0.22	0.23	0.06	0.21	0.09	0.04	-0.22	0.19
1997-98	0.02	0.18	0.02	0.05	0.05	0.15	0.43	0.09	0.71	0.23	0.20	0.51	0.02	0.28	0.03	0.06	0.72	0.22
1998-99	0.01	0.14	0.02	0.25	0.12	0.07	0.58	0.67	0.70	0.36	0.20	0.09	0.02	0.23	0.03	0.04	0.71	0.25
1999-00	0.12	0.07	0.06	0.13	0.16	0.07	0.49	0.02	0.82	0.29	0.23	0.06	0.05	0.03	0.07	0.02	1.02	0.22
2000-01	0.31	0.06	0.02	0.02	0.05	0.06	0.18	0.05	0.62	0.25	0.72	0.05	0.03	0.72	0.04	0.02	0.86	0.24
2001-02	0.49	0.09	0.03	0.01	0.09	0.10	0.22	0.05	0.90	0.13	1.10	0.22	0.02	0.14	0.01	0.01	1.29	0.29
2002-03	0.37	0.06	0.04	0.01	0.04	0.08	0.22	0.60	0.69	0.14	1.54	0.21	0.02	1.09	0.02	0.04	1.41	0.39
2003-04	0.41	0.46	0.06	0.10	0.05	0.05	0.18	1.18	0.67	0.12	2.52	0.12	0.01	1.27	0.01	0.02	1.06	0.49
2004-05	0.84	0.45	0.05	0.07	0.06	0.16	0.40	1.53	1.57	0.29	1.26	0.29	0.01	1.36	0.01	0.03	1.07	0.56
2005-06	0.66	0.18	0.04	0.05	0.05	0.04	0.58	1.67	1.59	0.28	0.92	0.21	0.01	1.42	0.01	0.02	0.68	0.49
2006-07	0.30	0.11	0.03	0.08	0.04	0.03	0.57	1.74	1.32	0.03	0.45	0.28	0.06	1.36	0.01	0.01	0.57	0.41
Mean	0.28	0.14	0.07	0.09	0.06	0.09	0.39	0.59	0.83	0.19	0.75	0.17	0.06	0.62	0.05	0.03	0.62	

Source : Computed from the annual reports of the respective units.

fluctuated from 0.12 times in 1992-93 to 0.56 times in 2004-05. It shows that automobile industries have been trying to operate with lower level of cash.

Assessment of Liquidity Position – A Bivariate Discriminant Analysis

The application of discriminant analysis to two category (dichotomous) classification problems in empirical financial research has substantially increased in the recent years.[9] A number of studies[10] have shown the usefulness of discriminant analysis while determining the financial information the rating agencies employ to rate. One should evaluate liquidity on the basis of current and quick ratios but this is not always possible. It is difficult particularly when some industries have high current ratio but low quick ratio and other industries have low current ratio but high quick ratio. In such cases, it is difficult to state which of these industries are good risks. The risks refer to good and poor risks indicating good and poor liquidity position respectively. The need for the use of the discriminant analysis is felt in this study due to the fact that it takes into account the effect of both of the ratios in order to distinguish good risks from the poor ones.

In this study, the following two variables as reliable indicators of liquidity behaviour have been considered for the selected automobile industries.

X_1 = The Current Ratio (CR)
X_2 = The Liquid Ratio (QR)

The object is to determine weights for X_1 and X_2 that is the values of 'a' and 'b' in the equation

$$Z = aX_1 + bX_2$$

where, Z is the discriminant index.

Grouping of the selected industries

First of all, the selected automobile industries have been classified into two groups. The industries which have current and liquid ratios of 1.5:1 and 1:1 or more respectively have been classified as good risk and the remaining industries as poor risk. As per this rule, the selected industries falling in the good and poor risks groups are presented in Table 5.8. On the basis of current and quick ratios, the industries which have been classified as 'poor' risks in all the selected years have thus appeared to be Tata Motors Ltd, Bajaj Tempo Ltd, Eicher Motors Ltd and Swaraj Mazda Ltd in the commercial vehicles sector, Hindustan Motors Ltd in the passenger cars and multiutility vehicles sector and LML Ltd, TVS Motor Company Ltd, Kinetic Motors Ltd, Kinetic Engineering Ltc and Majestic Auto Ltd in the two- and three-wheelers sector. In the years 1993-94, 1994-95, 1995-96 and 1997-98, all industries had be appeared in 'poor' risk.

Estimation of the Discriminant Co-efficient and Discriminate Score

After classifying the selected automobile industries into the good and poor risk classes, the values 'a' and 'b' in the discriminant functions are estimated. The discriminant functions of the selected years are presented in Table 5.9 where the co-efficient for 'a' and 'b' indicate values for current and quick ratios respectively. It is evident from the table that current ratios appeared to be stronger than liquid ratios from 1992-93 to 2006-07, except in the years 1993-94, 1994-95, 1995-96 and 1997-98.

Estimating the Cut-off Values

With the help of the discriminant score given in Table 5.10, the cut off value was calculated as follows.

$$\text{Cut of Value} = \frac{n_1 Z_1 + n_2 Z_2}{n_1 + n_2}$$

where n_1 and n_2 are the size of samples and z_1 and z_2 are mean of the discriminant score of Group A and Group B respectively. The cut-off values have also been presented in Table 5.10. Actual Z scores of the individual industries were then compared with the discriminating Z scores. If the Z scores were found to be more than the discriminating Z scores, it can said that such industries have good liquidity position.

Table 5.8

Good and Poor Risk Units in Terms of Current and Quick Ratio

(Good risk consists of those units where CR > 1.5 and LR >1)

Year	*92-93*	*93-94*	*94-95*	*95-96*	*96-97*	*97-98*	*98-99*	*99-00*	*00-01*	*01-02*	*02-03*	*03-04*	*04-05*	*05-06*	*06-07*
Group A	ALL				MML		MML	SIL	ALL	BAL	MSL	MUL	ALL	MUL	MUL
									SIL	MSL	SIL	MSL	MUL	BAL	BAL
										SIL		HHML	BAL	MSL	HHML
												SIL HHML	MSL	HHML	
													SIL		
	$n_1=1$	$n_1=0$	$n_1=0$	$n_1=0$	$n_1=1$	$n_1=0$	$n_1=1$	$n_1=1$	$n_1=2$	$n_1=3$	$n_1=2$	$n_1=4$	$n_1=6$	$n_1=4$	$n_1=3$
Group	TML	ALL	ALL	ALL	ALL	ALL	ALL	ALL	TML	ALL	ALL	ALL	TML	ALL	ALL
B	BTL	TML	TML	TML	TML	TML	TML	TML	BTL	TML	TML	TML	BTL	TML	TML
	EML	BTL	BTL	BTL	BTL	BTL	BTL	BTL	EML	BTL	BTL	BTL	EML	BTL	BTL
	SML	EML	EML	EML	EML	EML	EML	EML	SML	EML	EML	EML	SML	EML	EML
	HML	SML	SML	SML	SML	SML	SML	SML	HML	SML	SML	SML	HML	SML	SML
	MML	HML	HML	HML	HML	HML	HML	HML	MML	HML	HML	HML	MML	HML	HML
	MUL	MML	MML	MML	MUL	MML	MUL	MML	MUL	MML	MML	MML	LMLL	MML	MML
	BAL	MUL	MUL	MUL	BAL	MUL	BAL	MUL	BAL	MUL	MUL	BAL	TMCL	LMLL	LMLL
	LMLL	BAL	BAL	BAL	LMLL	BAL	LMLL	BAL	LMLL	LMLL	BAL	LMLL	KML	TMCL	MSL
	MSL	LMLL	LMLL	LMLL	MSL	LMLL	MSL	LMLL	MSL	TMCL	LMLL	TMCL	KEL	KML	TMCL

(Contd...)

(Contd...)

TMCL	MSL	MSL	MSL	TMCL	MSL	TMCL	MSL	TMCL	KML	TMCL	KML	MAL	KEL	KML
KML	TMCL	TMCL	TMCL	KML	TMCL	KML	TMCL	KML	HHML	KML	KEL		MAL	KEL
HHML	KML	KML	KML	HHML	KML	HHML	KML	HHML	KEL	HHML	MAL		SIL	MAL
KEL	HHML	HHML	HHML	KEL	HHML	KEL	HHML	KEL	MAL	KEL				SIL
MAL	KEL	KEL	KEL	MAL	KEL	MAL	KEL	MAL		MAL				
SIL	MAL	MAL	MAL	SIL	MAL	SIL	MAL							
	SIL	SIL	SIL		SIL									
n_2 =16	n_2=17	n_2 =17	n_2 =17	n_2 =16	n_2 =17	n_2 =16	n_2 =16	n_2 =15	n_2 =14	n_2 =15	n_2 =13	n_2 =11	n_2 =13	n_2 =14

ALL – Ashok Leyland Ltd; TML – Tata Motors Ltd; BTL – Bajaj Tempo Ltd; EML – Eicher Motors Ltd; SML – Swaraj Mazda Ltd; HML – Hindustan Motors Ltd; MML – Mahindra and Mahindra Ltd; MUL – Maruti Udyog Ltd; BAL – Bajaj Auto Ltd; LMLL – LML Ltd; MSL – Maharashtra Scooters Ltd; TMCL – TVS Motor Company Ltd; KML – Kinetic Motors Ltd; HHML – Hero Honda Motors Ltd; KEL – Kinetic Engineering Ltd; MAL – Majestic Auto Ltd; SIL – Scooters India Ltd.

Source: Computed

Table 5.9

Discriminant Functions for the Period 1992-93 to 2006-07

Year	*Function*	*Remark*
1992-93	Z = 3.933 a – 0.246 b	a > b
1993-94	Z = -2.645 a + 0.165 b	b > a
1994-95	Z = -2.435 a + 0.152 b	b > a
1995-96	Z = -3.587 a + 0.224 b	b > a
1996-97	Z = 2.196 a – 0.137 b	a > b
1997-98	Z = -1.402 a + 0.088 b	b > a
1998-99	Z = 2.345 a – 0.147 b	a > b
1999-00	Z = 3.376 a – 0.211 b	a > b
2000-01	Z = 2.715 a – 0.362 b	a > b
2001-02	Z = 3.327 a – 0.713 b	a > b
2002-03	Z = 3.281 a – 0.438 b	a > b
2003-04	Z = 2.409 a – 0.741 b	a > b
2004-05	Z = 3.632 a – 1.981 b	a > b
2005-06	Z = 2.783 a – 0.856 b	a > b
2006-07	Z = 4.232 a – 0.907 b	a > b

Note: The expression *b* >*a* is to be read "*b* is stronger than *a*".

Source: Computed.

The good risk industries as indicated by Z values are Ashok Leyland Ltd, Tata Motors Ltd, Baja Tempo Ltd, Mahindra and Mahindra Ltd, Bajaj Auto Ltd, Kinetic Motors Ltd, Hero Honda Motors Ltd and Kinetic Engineering Ltd in 1992-93; Swaraj Mazda Ltd, Maruti Udyog Ltd, LML Ltd, TVS Motor Company Ltd, Hero Honda Motors Ltd, Majestic Auto Ltd and Scooters India Ltd in 1993-94; Tata Motors Ltd, Bajaj Tempo Ltd, Swaraj Mazda Ltd, Hindustan Motors Ltd, Maruti Udyog Ltd, LML Ltd, TVS Motor Company Ltd, Hero Honda Motors Ltd, Majestic Auto Ltd and Scooters India Ltd in 1994-95; Tata Motors Ltd, Bajaj Tempo Ltd, Mahindra and Mahindra Ltd, Maruti Udyog Ltd, LML Ltd, Maharashtra Scooters Ltd, TVS Motor Company Ltd, Hero Honda Motors Ltd and Scooters India Ltd in 1995-96; Ashok Leyland Ltd,

Eicher Motor Ltd, Swaraj Mazda Ltd, Hindustan Motors Ltd, Mahindra and Mahindra Ltd, Bajaj Auto Ltd, and Kinetic Engineering Ltd in 1996-97; Tata Motors Ltd, Bajaj Tempo Ltd, Swaraj Mazda Ltd, Hindustan Motors Ltd, Maruti Udyog Ltd, LML Ltd, Maharashtra Scooters Ltd, Kinetic Motors Ltd, Hero Honda Motors Ltd and Majestic Auto Ltd in 1997-98; Ashok Leyland Ltd, Eicher Motors Ltd, Swaraj Mazda Ltd, Mahindra and Mahindra Ltd, Maruti Udyog Ltd, Bajaj Auto Ltd, Kinetic Motors Ltd, Kinetic Engineering Ltd and Scooter India Ltd in 1998-99; Ashok Leyland Ltd, Eicher Motors Ltd, Mahindra and Mahindra Ltd, Bajaj Auto Ltd, Kinetic Engineering Ltd and Scooter India Ltd in 1999-2000; Ashok Leyland Ltd, Mahindra and Mahindra Ltd, Bajaj Auto Ltd, Maharashtra Scooters Ltd, Hero Honda Motors Ltd, Kinetic Engineering Ltd and Scooters India Ltd in 2000-01; Ashok Leyland Ltd, Swaraj Mazda Ltd, Mahindra and Mahindra Ltd, Bajaj Auto Ltd, Maharashtra Scooters Ltd, Kinetic engineering Ltd and Scooters India Ltd in 2001-02; Ashok Leyland Ltd, Maruti Udyog Ltd, Bajaj Auto Ltd, Maharashtra Scooters Ltd, Hero Honda Motors Ltd, Kinetic Engineering Ltd and Scooters India Ltd in 2002-03; Ashok Leyland Ltd, Maruti Udyog Ltd, Bajaj Auto Ltd, Maharashtra Scooters Ltd, Hero Honda Motors Ltd and Scooters India Ltd in 2003-04; Ashok Leyland Ltd, Bajaj Tempo Ltd, Maruti Udyog Ltd, Bajaj Auto Ltd, Maharashtra scooters Ltd and Scooters India Ltd in 2004-05; Ashok Leyland Ltd, Bajaj Tempo Ltd, Mahindra and Mahindra Ltd, Maruti Udyog Ltd, Bajaj Auto Ltd, Maharashtra Scooters Ltd, Hero Honda Motors Ltd and Scooters India Ltd in 2005-06; and Ashok Leyland Ltd, Mahindra and Mahindra Ltd, Maruti Udyog Ltd, Bajaj Auto Ltd, TVS Motor Company Ltd, Hero Honda Motors Ltd and Scooters India Ltd in 2006-07. The rest of the companies are the poor risks in all the years.

Classification Matrix

The number of good and poor risk industries as per the criteria of current and liquid ratio and as per the discriminant score are presented in Table 5.11. It is clear from the table that the misclassification does not occur in the year 2004-05. It means that there is no difference between the criteria of current and liquid ratio and the criteria of discriminant score in that year.

Table 5.10
Discriminant Z scores

Units	*92-93*	*93-94*	*94-95*	*95-96*	*96-97*	*97-98*	*98-99*	*99-00*	*2000-01*	*2001-02*	*2002-03*	*2003-04*	*2004-05*	*2005-06*	*2006-07*
Ashok Leyland Ltd	10.22	-5.76	-7.12	-7.67	4.54	-4.18	4.50	6.05	5.56	6.52	6.65	3.51	4.80	4.11	5.23
Tata Motors Ltd	5.15	-3.45	-2.95	-3.69	2.83	-1.72	1.95	2.74	1.91	2.42	2.43	2.11	3.07	3.28	4.32
Bajaj Tempo Ltd	5.64	-3.32	-3.04	-4.18	2.60	-1.67	2.73	4.25	3.38	3.92	4.17	2.74	3.67	5.07	3.41
Eicher Motors Ltd	4.66	-3.33	-3.25	-4.72	3.08	-2.19	3.45	4.71	3.41	3.13	3.11	2.37	3.24	2.49	3.78
Swaraj Mazda Ltd	3.55	-2.54	-2.17	-4.21	2.99	-1.97	3.41	4.66	3.17	4.25	3.35	2.30	2.88	2.52	4.03
Hindustan Motors Ltd	4.23	-3.28	-3.03	-4.77	3.52	-2.01	2.71	4.17	3.09	3.39	3.62	2.17	2.77	2.14	3.03
Mah & Mah Ltd	5.47	-5.17	-3.85	-3.42	4.16	-2.58	4.38	6.02	3.78	4.29	4.12	2.22	3.38	3.35	5.00
Maruti Udyog Ltd	4.80	-1.66	-1.74	-3.45	2.55	-1.31	3.28	3.43	2.81	3.56	5.05	4.33	6.07	6.01	10.34
Bajaj Auto Ltd	5.56	-3.06	-4.66	-5.72	4.04	-2.58	4.31	6.79	4.34	5.53	5.04	3.01	5.61	5.14	7.83
LML Ltd	2.39	-1.68	-2.41	-3.77	2.24	-1.47	2.99	4.02	2.74	2.69	2.67	1.86	2.38	1.78	2.04
Maharastra Scooters Ltd	4.41	-3.42	-3.49	-4.17	2.49	-1.50	2.63	4.06	4.46	5.64	7.04	6.04	3.93	3.74	3.49
TVS Motor Co., Ltd	2.89	-2.36	-2.75	-3.40	2.68	-2.18	2.09	3.86	3.02	3.39	3.08	2.17	3.25	3.04	5.01
Kinetic Motors Ltd	5.64	-4.76	-3.64	-4.46	2.53	-1.66	3.24	4.43	3.45	3.61	4.32	1.79	2.03	1.49	2.38
Hero Honda Motors Ltd	5.99	-3.14	-2.60	-3.50	2.15	-1.78	2.44	2.91	3.62	1.85	4.36	2.99	3.43	3.79	6.69
Kinetic Eng., Ltd	6.39	-3.81	-3.41	-4.57	3.24	-2.14	3.70	6.28	4.38	5.09	4.47	2.56	3.25	2.37	4.24
Majestic Auto Ltd	3.98	-2.77	-2.60	-5.17	2.31	-1.96	2.66	2.82	1.93	1.98	2.09	2.42	3.40	2.34	3.23
Scooters India Ltd	3.89	-0.21	-0.19	-0.28	1.21	-2.26	4.04	8.27	5.61	8.45	8.27	4.18	5.04	4.04	6.07
Cut of Z Value	4.99	-3.21	-3.11	0.96	0.37	-2.07	3.21	4.67	3.57	4.10	4.34	2.87	3.66	3.34	4.71

Source: Computed

Misclassification of industries is noticed for the remaining years. Generally, the industries with lower current and liquid ratios in the good risk group and the industries with higher current and liquid ratios in the poor risk group have been misclassified under the criteria of discriminant score.

Table 5.11

Classification Matrix

Year	*As per CR and LR*		*As per discriminant score*	
	Good	*Poor*	*Good*	*Poor*
1992-93	1	16	8	9
1993-94	0	17	7	10
1994-95	0	17	10	7
1995-96	0	17	9	8
1996-97	1	16	7	10
1997-98	0	17	10	7
1998-99	1	16	9	8
1999-00	1	16	6	11
2000-01	2	15	7	10
2001-02	3	14	7	10
2002-03	2	15	7	10
2003-04	4	13	6	11
2004-05	6	11	6	11
2005-06	4	13	8	9
2006-07	3	14	7	10

Source: Computed

It is to be criteria of discriminant score. Such industries are Tata Motors Ltd, Bajaj Tempo Ltd, Mahindra and Mahindra Ltd, Bajaj Auto Ltd, Kinetic Motors Ltd, Hero Honda Motors Ltd and Kinetic Engineering Ltd in 1992-93; Swaraj Mazda Ltd, Maruti Udyog Ltd, LML Ltd, TVS Motor Company Ltd, Hero Honda Ltd, Majestic Auto Ltd and Scooters India Ltd in 1993-94; Tata Motors Ltd, Bajaj Tempo Ltd, Swaraj Mazda Ltd, Hindustan Motors Ltd, Maruti Udyog Ltd, LML Ltd, TVS Motor Company Ltd, Hero Honda Motors Ltd, Majestic Auto Ltd and Scooters India Ltd in 1994-95; Tata Motors Ltd, Bajaj Tempo Ltd, Mahindra and

Mahindra Ltd, Maruti Udyog Ltd, LML Ltd, Maharashtra Scooters Ltd, TVS Motor Company Ltd, Hero Honda Motors Ltd and Scooters India Ltd in 1995-96; Ashok Leyland Ltd, Eicher Motors Ltd, Swaraj Mazda Ltd, Hindustan Motors Ltd, Bajaj Auto Ltd and Kinetic Engineering Ltd in 1996-97; Tata Motors Ltd, Bajaj Tempo Ltd, Swaraj Mazda Ltd, Hindustan Motors Ltd, Maruti Udyog Ltd, LML Ltd, Maharashtra Scooters Ltd, Kinetic Motors Ltd, Hero Honda Motors Ltd and majestic Auto Ltd in 1997-98; Ashok Leyland Ltd, Eicher Motors Ltd, Swaraj Mazda Ltd, Maruti Udyog Ltd, Bajaj Auto Ltd, Kinetic Motors Ltd, Kinetic Engineering Ltd and Scooters India Ltd in 1998-99; Ashok Leyland Ltd, Eicher Motors Ltd, Mahindra and Mahindra Ltd, Bajaj Auto Ltd and Kinetic Engineering Ltd in 1999-2000; Mahindra and Mahindra Ltd, Bajaj Auto Ltd, Maharashtra Scooters Ltd, Hero Honda Motors Ltd and Kinetic Engineering Ltd in 2000-01; Ashok Leyland Ltd, Swaraj Mazda Ltd, Mahindra and Mahindra Ltd and Kinetic Engineering Ltd in 2001-02; Ashok Leyland Ltd, Maruti Udyog Ltd, Bajaj Auto Ltd, Hero Honda Motors Ltd and Kinetic Engineering Ltd in 2002-03; Ashok Leyland Ltd and Bajaj Auto Ltd in 2003-04; Bajaj Tempo Ltd in 2004-05; Ashok Leyland Ltd, Bajaj Tempo Ltd, Mahindra and Mahindra Ltd and Scooters India Ltd in 2005-06 and Ashok Leyland Ltd, Mahindra and Mahindra Ltd, TVS Motor Company Ltd and Scooters India Ltd in 2006-07.

Liquidity and Profitability Tangle

Generally it is assumed that there is always a negative relationship between liquidity and profitability. But it cannot be denied that unless there is a minimum level of investment in the current assets, which provide a promising vehicle for increasing profitability, output and sales cannot be maintained up to a certain level, one is complementary to the other. Maintenance of a sound liquidity position enhances profits, provided that the established liquidity level harmonises with the nature of the enterprise. By keeping this short run position secure by maintaining liquidity, the finance manager is able to plan for profitability in the long run. In this senses liquidity is not competing with profitability; rather it is a means towards the end-profits.[11] Gentry[12] hypothesised a relationship between liquidity and profitability as perceived by business managers. According to him, the relationship between the two may not be continuously positive but rather have the shape of an inverted cup; up to certain level, increase in liquidity leads to increase in profitability, beyond that profitability remains constant with the increase in liquidity up to a certain point.

Table 5.12

Correlation Co-efficient between Liquidity and Owners' Profitability

Units	*Correlation co-efficient*
Ashok Leyland Ltd	-0.414 (-1.639)
Tata Motors Ltd	0.182 (0.668)
Bajaj Tempo Ltd	0.314 (1.192)
Eicher Motors Ltd	-0.053 (-0.191)
Swaraj Mazda Ltd	0.422 (1.677)
Commercial vehicles sector	-0.236 (-0.878)
Hindustan Motors Ltd	0.779 (4.476)*
Mahindra and Mahindra Ltd	-0.020 (-0.072)
Maruti Udyog Ltd	0.112 (0.405)
Passenger cars and multiutility vehicles sector	0.128 (0.467)
Bajaj Auto Ltd	-0.102 (-0.370)
LML Ltd	0.385 (1.506)
Maharashtra Scooters Ltd	-0.641 (-3.012)
TVS Motor Company Ltd	0.102 (0.370)
Kinetic Motors Ltd	0.637 (2.978)**
Hero Honda Motors Ltd	0.477 (1.954)***
Kinetic Engineering Ltd	0.502 (2.094)***
Majestic Auto Ltd	-0.171 (-0.627)
Scooters India Ltd	-0.163 (-0.597)
Two- and three-wheelers sector	0.699 (-3.527)*
Industry (Total)	-0.227 (-0.838)

Figures in Brackets show 't' value

* Significant at 0.01 level; ** Significant at 0.05 level; *** Significant at 0.10 level

Source: Computed from the annual reports of the respective units.

Thereafter, any further attempt to hold more current assets will lead to decline in profitability. For the purpose of establishing definite relationship between liquidity and profitability, Karl Pearson's correlation co-efficient can be applied.

Table 5.12 shows the correlation co-efficient of the units in between liquidity and owners profitability. It is evident from the table that as a whole the liquidity and profitability were adversely correlated, as the correlation co-efficient of overall liquidity and profitability was found to be -0.227. Negative correlation indicates that changes in liquidity had opposite reaction on profitability that is, increase in liquidity resulted in decrease in profitability and vice versa. The correlation co-efficients of overall liquidity and profitability of commercial vehicles sector, the passenger cars and multiutility vehicles sector and the two- and three-wheelers sector in automobile industries were found to be -0.236, 0.128 and 0.699 respectively. In the commercial vehicles sector, liquidity and profitability were negatively correlated. But in the passenger cars and multiutility vehicles sector and the two- and three-wheelers sector, liquidity and profitability were positively correlated. It was statistically significant at 1 per cent level only in two and three wheelers sector as indicated by the 't' test. It is also inferred that such correlation was stronger in two and three wheelers sector than in the commercial vehicles sector and the passenger cars and multiutility vehicles sector.

Individually among commercial vehicles sector units, only two units namely Ashok Leyland Ltd and Eicher Motors Ltd liquidity and profitability were found to be adversely correlated. Among the passenger cars and multiutility vehicles sector units, only one unit namely Mahindra and Mahindra Ltd liquidity and profitability was found to be negatively correlated, other units are having positive correlation co-efficient. Among the two- and three-wheelers sector units 4 out of 9 units are negatively correlated, namely, Bajaj Auto Ltd, Maharashtra Scooters Ltd, Majestic Auto Ltd and Scooters India Ltd. Other units are positively correlated. However, such negative correlation was not statistically significant. In a nut shell it can this be concluded that in the cases mentioned above, growth in liquidity had reverse impact on profitability, through in some cases such impact was found to be negligible. It has also been observed that three units in the commercial vehicles sector (Tata Motors Ltd, Bajaj Tempo Ltd and Swaraj Mazda Ltd), two units in passenger cars and multiutility vehicles sector (Hindustan Motors Ltd and Maruti Udyog Ltd) and five units in two and three wheelers sector (LML Ltd, TVS Motor Company Ltd, Kinetic Motors Ltd, Hero Honda Motors Ltd and Kinetic Engineering Ltd), liquidity and profitability were positively correlated. These units did not satisfy the proposition of Van Horne[13] of "The higher the liquidity the lower the profitability".

References

1. John.D.Martin et.al.(1979), *Basic Financial Management*, New Jersy: Prentice Hall Inc, p.149.
2. Van Horne, J.C.(1988), *Financial Management and Policy*, New Delhi: Prentice Hall of India Pvt. Ltd, pp.324-325.
3. Burton A. Kolb (1983), *Principles of Financial Management*, Texas: Business Publications Inc, p.153.
4. Accounting Principles Board, 'Concepts and Objectives of Financial Statement', *AICPA*, New York, November 1978.
5. For example, see
   - i) Khan, M.Y. and Jain, P.K. (1984), *Financial Management*, New Delhi: Tata McGraw Hill, p.607.
   - ii) Kulashrestha, N.K. Auguest (1980), Corporate Liquidity – X Rayed, *The Management Accountant*, pp.331-34.
   - iii) Solomon, E. and Pringle, J.J.(1978), *Financial Management*, New Delhi: Prentice Hall of India, p.98.
   - iv) Mishra, R.K. (1975), *Problems of Working Capital* (With special Reference to selected Public Undertakings in India), Bombay: Somiya Publications Pvt. Ltd, p.12.
6. Walker, E.W. and Boughn, W.H.(1974), *Financial Planning and Policy*, Harper International, Students Edition, p.151.
7. Gitman, L.J.(1976), *Principles of Managerial Finance*, New York: Harper and Row Publishers, p.50.
8. Ibid., p.51.
9. Maurice Joy, O. and John O. Tollefson, (December 1975), on the Financial Applications of Discriminant Analysis. *The Journal of Financial and Quantitative Analysis*, pp.723-739.

10. For examples

i) Walter, J.E. (1959), A Discriminant Function for earnings price-ratios of Large Industrial Corporations, *Review of Economics and Statistics*, Vol.XLI, pp.44-52.

ii) Altman, E.I. (September 1963), Financial ratios, Discriminant analysis and the Prediction of Corporate Bankruptcy, *The Journal of Finance*, pp.589-609.

iii) Awh, R.Y. and Waters, D. (June, 1974), A Discriminant Analysis of Economic Demographic and Attitudinal Characteristics of Bank Charge Holders; A case study, *Journal of Finance*, Vol.XXIX, pp.973-980.

iv) Blum. M. (1974), Failing Company Discriminant analysis, *Journal of Accounting Reaearch*, Vol.12, No.1, p.3.

(v) Bhattacharyya, S.K. and Raghavachari, M. (March, 1977), Determinants of effective Working Capital Management: A Discriminant Analysis Approach, *Working paper No.151*, Indian Institute of Management, p.151.

11. Archer, S.H. et. al. (1969), *Business Finance: Theory and Management*, New Delhi: The Macmillan co.

12. Gentry, J.E. (1976), Management Perception of the working capital Process, *Faculty working paper*, College of Commerce and Business Administration, University of Illinois.

13. Van Horne, J.C.(1988), *Financial Management and Policy*, New Delhi: Prentice Hall of India Pvt. Ltd, p.401.

6

Impact of Working Capital Ratios on Profitability

In the conventional production function approach for determination of relationship between output and income or profit, fixed capital is taken into account as explanatory variable amongst others; the role of working capital is ignored (Dutta Majumdar 1968[1], Estrin et .al. 1987[2], Massell et. al. 1968[3] and Vittoria et. al. 1979.)[4] Even where capital employed that is fixed capital plus working capital has been used as regressor the significance of the relationship between fixed and working capital has not been properly emphasized (Jaffe, 1986)[5] It is therefore felt that there is the need to study the important role of working capital in profit generating process.

The two important aims of working capital management are short–term solvency and profitability. To ensure solvency, the enterprises should be very liquid. If the enterprises maintain a relative large investment of long-term funds in current assets, they will not face the risk of cash shortage or stocks-outs. However, there is a cost associated with maintaining a sound liquidity position. A considerable amount of the firm's funds will be tied up in current assets and to the extent the investment is idle, the firm's profitability will suffer.[6] To have higher profitability, the firms may sacrifice solvency and maintain a relatively low level of current assets. When the firms do so, their profitability will improve as less funds are tied up in idle current assets, but their solvency will be threatened.[7] Sarkar and Saha[8] have aptly observed that management of working capital has an important bearing on the profitability of an enterprise. Generally, the higher the working capital, the less the rate of return on capital employed while a lower value of working capital yields a higher rate of return.[9]

Hence, in this part, analysis is concerned with the study of association of profitability with working capital. The impact of working capital on profitability has been examined by computing co-efficients of correlation and regression between profitability ratio and working capital ratios, viz., current ratio, liquid ratio, working capital turnover ratio, inventory turnover ratio, receivables turnover ratio and cash turnover ratio.

Total Industry

The co-efficient of correlation between working capital ratios and profitability ratio for the selected automobile industries of India as a whole are presented in Table 6.1. Firstly, it is evident from the table that the co-efficient of correlation between profitability ratio and current ratio is +0.36. Secondly, it reveals a moderate degree of positive correlation which is insignificant. Similarly, the co-efficient of correlation between profitability ratio and liquid ratio stands at +0.50. It is also a positive correlation which is significant at 10 per cent level. Thirdly, the co-efficient of correlation between profitability and working capital turnover ratio is +0.91. It shows that positive correlation between the two variables. Fourthly, the co-efficient of correlation between profitability ratio and inventory turnover ratio is found to be +0.67 which is found to be significant at 1 per cent level. It shows that there is a high degree of positive correlation between the two variables. Fifthly, the co-efficient of correlation between profitability ratio and debtors turnover ratio indicates positive association of +0.61 which is significant at 5 per cent level. All these three turnover ratios conform with the assumption that higher the turnover increases the profitability of the selected automobile industry of India as a whole. Lastly, the co-efficient of correlation between profitability and cash turnover ratio is +0.12. This is low degree of positive correlation which is very insignificant. Thus, the study of the impact of working capital ratios on profitability showed all positive impacts.

Out of six independent working capital components ratios, three ratios, namely, LR, ITR and RTR, are found to have significant association with profitability ratio, while CR, WTR and

CTR are not found to have such significant association with the profitability ratio.

Table 6.1

Impact of Working Capital Ratios on Profitability—Simple Correlation Analysis

(Total Industry)

Year	*Working capital ratios*						*PBT to Total assets ratio*
	CR	*LR*	*WTR*	*ITR*	*RTR*	*CTR*	
1992-93	1.12	0.40	7.43	6.85	16.73	65.99	0.010
1993-94	1.28	0.47	1.41	7.59	18.55	59.85	0.058
1994-95	1.32	0.49	12.88	8.29	23.69	51.77	0.101
1995-96	1.20	0.37	-4.15	8.86	25.39	140.67	0.137
1996-97	1.43	0.57	230.52	8.73	21.08	68.68	0.138
1997-98	1.53	0.59	12.78	8.47	16.65	98.39	0.102
1998-99	1.43	0.68	5.57	8.66	15.28	53.43	0.076
1999-00	1.41	0.55	15.85	9.37	15.35	82.10	0.071
2000-01	1.35	0.54	12.34	8.60	14.29	85.74	0.007
2001-02	1.33	0.59	15.53	9.77	12.25	117.71	0.053
2002-03	1.38	0.62	-2.04	11.18	13.39	99.53	0.090
2003-04	1.40	0.72	-14.88	12.44	18.26	74.96	0.130
2004-05	1.46	0.79	9.62	13.16	22.39	65.75	0.142
2005-06	1.41	0.75	-31.67	11.88	19.77	90.44	0.158
2006-07	1.31	0.67	-11.57	12.34	18.65	54.44	0.166
Co-efficient of correlation (r)	0.36 (1.37)	0.50 (2.09)***	0.91 (0.33)	0.67 (3.28)*	0.61 (2.76)**	0.12 (0.04)	

Figures in brackets show 't' value

* Significant at 0.01 level; ** Significant at 0.05 level; *** Significant at 0.10 level

Source: Computed from the annual reports of the respective units

Commercial Vehicles Sector

The co-efficient of correlation between working capital ratios and profitability ratios for the commercial vehicles sector in the automobile industries of India are presented in Table 6.2.

Table 6.2

Impact of Working Capital Ratios on Profitability—Simple Correlation Analysis

(Commercial vehicles sector)

Year	*Working capital ratios*						*PBT to Total assets ratio*
	CR	*LR*	*WTR*	*ITR*	*RTR*	*CTR*	
1992-93	1.52	0.49	0.17	3.64	15.82	63.82	0.007
1993-94	1.43	0.54	2.67	4.72	18.32	115.05	0.030
1994-95	1.56	0.55	1.50	6.03	23.48	66.17	0.083
1995-96	1.39	0.38	13.73	6.13	21.73	225.43	0.105
1996-97	1.50	0.59	7.21	6.01	12.77	119.64	0.098
1997-98	1.71	0.59	6.97	5.11	11.74	203.47	0.030
1998-99	1.41	0.73	10.55	5.91	9.51	35.55	0.009
1999-00	1.36	0.52	2.14	7.66	10.15	54.74	0.014
2000-01	1.35	0.50	6.51	7.43	10.12	110.93	-0.031
2001-02	1.33	0.52	23.35	8.45	9.45	189.77	0.006
2002-03	1.26	0.44	17.16	10.25	11.08	165.76	0.068
2003-04	1.26	0.58	26.19	11.51	15.74	37.63	0.121
2004-05	1.31	0.61	19.90	10.82	17.29	36.28	0.112
2005-06	1.21	0.49	-67.64	9.25	16.67	37.46	0.124
2006-07	1.07	0.39	-21.67	9.58	18.53	45.96	0.135
Co-efficient of correlation (r)	-0.43 (-1.73)	-0.25 (-0.94)	0.30 (1.12)	0.52 (2.21)**	0.62 (2.84)**	0.22 (-0.81)	

Figures in brackets show 't' value

* Significant at 0.01 level; ** Significant at 0.05 level

Source: Computed from the annual reports of the respective units.

It is evident from the table that the co-efficient of correlation between profitability ratio and current ratio is -0.43. It shows a high degree of negative correlation between the variables. This correlation is very insignificant. Similarly, the co-efficient of correlation between profitability ratio and liquidity ratio stands at -0.25. It is also indicates that there is low degree of negative correlation between these two variables. The value of co-efficient of correlation is not found to be significant. Both the ratios current and liquid ratios conforms with the assumption that larger amount of current and liquid assets decreases risk as well as profitability.

The co-efficient of correlation between profitability ratio and working capital turnover ratio +0.30, inventory turnover ratio +0.52, and receivables turnover ratio +0.62 are found to have a positive association with profitability ratio. It reveals a moderate degree of correlation between the variables. The values of ITR and RTR are found to be significant at 5 per cent of level of significance, whereas the value of WTR is not found to be significant. Lastly, the co-efficient of correlation between profitability ratio and cash turnover ratio is +0.22. This is also positive correlation found to be insignificant.

Thus, the study of the impact of working capital ratios of profitability in the commercial vehicles sector in the automobile industries showed that CR and LR have shown a negative correlation with profitability ratio and WTR, ITR, RTR and CTR have shown positive correlation with profitability ratio. It is also inferred from the table that only ITR and RTR are significantly associated with profitability ratio.

Passenger Cars and Multiutility Vehicles Sector

The co-efficient of correlation between working capital ratios and profitability ratio for the passenger cars and multiutility vehicles sector in automobile industries of India are presented in Table 6.3. It is evident from the table that the co-efficient of correlation between profitability ratio and current ratio is +0.68. It shows a moderate degree of positive correlation between the variables. The value is also found to be significant at 1 per cent level of significance. Similarly, the co-efficient of correlation between profitability ratio and liquidity ratio stands at +0.69. It indicates that there is also positive correlation between these two variables. This correlation is significant at 1 per cent level.

Table 6.3

Impact of Working Capital Ratios on Profitability—Simple Correlation Analysis

(Passenger cars and multiutility vehicles sector)

Year	*Working capital ratios*						*PBT to Total assets ratio*
	CR	*LR*	*WTR*	*ITR*	*RTR*	*CTR*	
1992-93	0.75	0.34	9.59	5.74	17.42	62.80	0.011
1993-94	1.30	0.45	-2.97	6.37	22.22	25.49	0.058
1994-95	1.21	0.49	3.01	6.89	27.30	34.76	0.087
1995-96	1.11	0.40	-120.15	7.83	26.61	75.02	0.161
1996-97	1.60	0.70	11.12	8.53	22.26	30.09	0.179
1997-98	1.44	0.56	17.84	9.16	17.52	26.10	0.168
1998-99	1.52	0.77	7.70	8.87	14.93	15.84	0.111
1999-00	1.38	0.52	46.46	8.64	13.84	92.07	0.068
2000-01	1.25	0.46	20.28	7.92	10.52	51.22	-0.016
2001-02	1.24	0.53	17.79	8.61	8.39	48.17	0.015
2002-03	1.39	0.65	9.55	10.21	9.19	18.57	0.042
2003-04	1.44	0.76	-46.38	13.55	12.41	34.30	0.106
2004-05	1.63	0.93	-2.46	15.07	15.00	22.88	0.176
2005-06	1.69	1.02	0.56	13.02	13.31	22.58	0.199
2006-07	1.65	0.96	-12.17	13.66	16.07	26.80	0.210
Co-efficient of correlation (r)	0.68 (3.38) *	0.69 (3.41)*	0.34 (1.30)	0.60 (2.67)**	0.34 (1.29)	-0.35 (-1.34)	

Figures in brackets show 't' value

* Significant at 0.01 level; ** Significant at 0.05 level

Source: Computed from the annual Reports of the respective units

The co-efficient of correlation between profitability ratio and working capital turnover ratio +0.34, inventory turnover ratio +0.60 and receivables turnover ratio +0.34 are found to have a positive association with profitability ratio. It reveals moderate degree correlation between the variables. The value of ITR is found to be significant at 5 per cent level of significance, whereas the value of WTR and RTR is not found to be significant. Lastly, the co-efficient of correlation between profitability and cash turnover ratio is -0.35. This correlation is found to be insignificant.

Thus, the study of the impact of working capital ratios on profitability in the selected passenger cars and multiutility vehicle units in automobile industries showed that CTR only have shown negative correlation with profitability ratio and CR, LR, WTR, ITR and RTR have shown positive correlation with profitability ratio. It is also inferred from the table that CR, LR, and ITR in working capital ratios are significantly associated with profitability ratio.

Two- and Three-Wheelers Sector

The co-efficient of correlation between working capital ratios and profitability ratios for the selected two- and three-wheelers sector in automobile industries of India are presented in Table 6.4.

It is evident from the table that the co-efficient of correlation between profitability ratio and current ratio is +0.21. It shows positive correlation between the variables. The value is not found to be significant. Similarly, the co-efficient of correlation between profitability ratio and liquid ratio stands at +0.21. It is also positive correlation between these two variables. The value is found to be insignificant. The co-efficient of correlation between profitability ratio and working capital turnover ratio +0.26, inventory turnover ratio +0.49 and receivables turnover ratio +0.45 are found to have positive association with profitability ratio. It reveals moderate degree of correlation between the variables. The value of ITR and RTR are found to be significant at 10 per cent level of significance. Lastly, the co-efficient of correlation between profitability and cash turnover ratio is +0 23. This correlation is found to be insignificant.

Thus, the study of the impact of working capital ratios on profitability in two- and three-wheelers sector showed all positive impacts. Out of six independent working capital components ratios, two ratios, namely, ITR and RTR, are found to have significant association with profitability ratio, while CR, LR, WTR, and CTR is not found to have such significant association with the profitability ratio.

Table 6.4

Impact of Working Capital Ratios on Profitability—Simple Correlation Analysis

(Two- and three-wheelers sector)

Year	*Working capital ratios*						*PBT to Total assets ratio*
	CR	*LR*	*WTR*	*ITR*	*RTR*	*CTR*	
1992-93	1.09	0.38	12.54	11.16	16.96	71.34	0.016
1993-94	1.12	0.43	4.54	11.67	15.11	39.01	0.127
1994-95	1.20	0.44	34.12	11.96	20.30	54.37	0.166
1995-96	1.11	0.34	93.97	12.63	27.82	121.56	0.171
1996-97	1.18	0.42	673.24	11.65	28.22	56.32	0.185
1997-98	1.43	0.62	13.53	11.13	20.68	65.61	0.164
1998-99	1.37	0.55	-1.55	11.19	21.41	108.91	0.153
1999-00	1.48	0.61	-1.05	11.82	22.07	99.49	0.154
2000-01	1.46	0.65	10.24	10.44	22.24	95.08	0.092
2001-02	1.43	0.72	5.44	12.24	18.92	115.19	0.146
2002-03	1.50	0.77	-32.83	13.07	19.90	114.26	0.155
2003-04	1.50	0.82	-24.45	12.27	26.63	152.94	0.159
2004-05	1.44	0.82	11.43	13.60	34.87	138.08	0.153
2005-06	1.33	0.74	-27.93	13.38	29.32	211.29	0.169
2006-07	1.22	0.67	-0.87	13.78	21.36	90.55	0.175
Co-efficient of	0.21	0.25	0.26	0.49	0.45	0.23	
Correlation (r)	(0.76)	(0.92)	(0.95)	(2.02)***	(1.80)***	(0.84)	

Figures in brackets show 't' value

* Significant at 0.01 level; ** Significant at 0.05 level; *** Significant at 0.10 level

Source: Computed from the annual reports of the respective units.

Impact of Working Capital Ratios on Profitability—Multiple Regression Analysis

For the purpose of establishing definite relationship between working capital ratios and profitability ratio, Karl Pearson's correlation co-efficient can be applied. It implies that interdependence of the set of variables upon each other in such a way that changes in the one are in sympathy with changes in the other. In this section, in order to identify the working capital influence on profitability, a linear multiple regression model were used. In the analysis, working capital ratios, viz., CR, LR, WTR, ITR, RTR and CTR, are taken as the independent variables and Profit Before Tax (PBT) to total assets ratio is used as dependent variable.

For the purpose of selection of variables for the model, the co-efficient of correlation between the independent variables can be computed and presented in Table 6.5. It is evident from the table that there is a high degree of correlation between CR and LR (0.854) for the total industry. Similarly, both these variables are highly correlated all in the commercial vehicles sector (0.776), the passenger cars and multiutility vehicles sector (0.890) and the two- and three-wheelers sector (0.842). Therefore, current ratio is omitted for the analysis. The model used in this section was

$$PBT / TA = b_o + b_1 LR + b_2 WTR + b_3 ITR + b_4 RTR + b_5 CTR$$

where b_o, b_1, b_2, b_3, b_4 and b_5 are the parameters to be estimated.

Table 6.5: Correlation Matrix

Total Industry

Ratios	*CR*	*LR*	*WTR*	*ITR*	*RTR*	*CTR*	*PBT/TA*
CR	1.000						
LR	0.854	1.000					
WTR	0.281	0.266	1.000				
ITR	0.406	0.824	0.261	1.000			
RTR	-0.155	-0.140	0.300	0.085	1.000		
CTR	-0.098	-0.257	0.169	0.005	-0.066	1.000	
PBT/TA	0.355	0.501	0.843	0.673	0.607	0.012	1.000

Commercial vehicles sector

Ratios	*CR*	*LR*	*WTR*	*ITR*	*RTR*	*CTR*	*PBT/TA*
CR	1.000						
LR	0.776	1.000					

WTR	0.155	0.265	1.000				
ITR	-0.766	0.769	-0.238	1.000			
RTR	-0.028	-0.355	0.268	-0.065	1.000		
CTR	0.361	-0.337	-0.247	-0.278	-0.123	1.000	
PBT/TA	-0.432	-0.253	0.299	0.522	0.619	-0.220	1.000

Passenger cars and multiutility vehicles sector

Ratios	*CR*	*LR*	*WTR*	*ITR*	*RTR*	*CTR*	*PBT/TA*
CR	1.000						
LR	0.890	1.000					
WTR	-0.126	-0.207	1.000				
ITR	0.744	0.876	-0.050	1.000			
RTR	-0.217	-0.309	-0.132	-0.404	1.000		
CTR	-0.579	-0.602	0.426	-0.414	0.107	1.000	
PBT/TA	0.684	0.687	0.341	0.595	0.338	-0.347	1.000

Two- and three-wheelers sector

Ratios	*CR*	*LR*	*WTR*	*ITR*	*RTR*	*CTR*	*PBT/TA*
CR	1.000						
LR	0.842	1.000					
WTR	0.506	0.403	1.000				
ITR	0.040	0.684	0.251	1.000			
RTR	0.198	0.337	0.539	0.477	1.000		
CTR	0.441	0.634	0.451	0.539	0.606	1.000	
PBT/TA	0.207	0.246	0.257	0.489	0.446	0.226	1.000

Source: Computed

Total Industry

The pooled regression results of the model showing impact of working capital ratios on profitability for the total industry are presented in Table 6.6. The table indicates that the impact of liquid ratio, working capital turnover ratio, inventory turnover ratio, receivable turnover ratio and cash turn over ratio were statistically significant as seen from the values of regression co-efficient.

Table 6.6

Estimated Regression Results of Impact of Working Capital Ratios on Profitability

(Total industry)

$(PBT/TA = b_0 + b_1\,LR + b_2\,WTR + b_3\,ITR + b_4\,RTR + b_5\,CTR)$

Variables	*Beta co-efficients*	*t-value*
Constant	0.225	2.58 Significant**
Liquid ratio (LR)	-0.125	3.13 Significant*
Working capital ratio (WTR)	0.090	2.45 Significant**
Inventory turnover ratio (ITR)	0.009	3.04 Significant**
Receivable turnover ratio (RTR)	0.008	3.14 Significant **
Cash turnover ratio (CTR)	-0.006	0.59 Not Significant
$R^2 = 0.91$		
Adj $R^2 = 0.80$		

* Significant at 0.01 level; ** Significant at 0.05 level

Source: Computed

For a unit increase in liquid ratio, profitability decreased by -0.125 units which was statistically significant at 1 per cent level. When the working capital turnover ratio increased by one unit, profitability increased by 0.090 unit which was statistically significant at 5 per cent level of significance. When the inventory turnover ratio increased by one unit, profitability increased by 0.009 units which was statistically significant at 5 per cent level of significance. When the receivables turnover ratio increased by one unit, profitability increased by 0.008 units which was statistically significant at 5 per cent level of significance. For a unit increase in cash turnover ratio, profitability decreased by -0.006 units which was not statistically significant. The five independent variables contribute 91 per cent at the variations in the profitability of the selected automobile industries of India. Thus the overall results presented in the table are encouraging. The signs of all the co-efficients are as expected. The co-efficients are also statistically significant except cash turnover ratio.

Commercial Vehicles Sector

Table 6.7 shows the pooled regression results of the model indicating the impact of working capital ratios on profitability of selected commercial vehicles sector in automobile industries of India. The table indicates that the contribution of cash turnover ratio was not statistically significant as seen from the values of regression co-efficient. For a unit increase in liquid ratio, profitability decreased by -0.044 units and this was significant at 1 per cent level of significance. When working capital turnover ratio increased by one unit, profitability increased by 0.001 units which was significant at 10 per cent level of significance. When inventory turnover ratio increased by one unit, profitability increased by 0.014 units which was significant at 5 per cent level of significance.

Table 6.7

Estimated Regression Results of Impact of Working Capital Ratios on Profitability

(Commercial vehicles sector)

$(PBT/TA = b_0 + b_1\ LR + b_2\ WTR + b_3\ ITR + b_4\ RTR + b_5\ CTR)$

Variables	*Beta co-efficients*	*t-value*	
Constant	0.191	2.56	Significant**
Liquid ratio (LR)	-0.044	3.13	Significant*
Working capital ratio (WTR)	0.001	2.65	Significant***
Inventory turnover ratio (ITR)	0.014	3.04	Significant**
Receivable turnover ratio (RTR)	0.008	3.09	Significant **
Cash turnover ratio (CTR)	0.002	0.36	Not significant
R^2 = 0.93Adj			
R^2 = 0.78			

* Significant at 0.01 level; ** Significant at 0.05 level; *** Significant at 0.10 level

Source: Computed

When the receivables turnover ratio increased by one unit, profitability increased by 0.008 units which was statistically significant at 5 per cent level of significance, while the cash turnover ratio increased by one unit, profitability increased by 0.002 units which was not statistically significant. The five independent variables contribute 93 per cent of the variations in the profitability of the selected commercial vehicles sector in automobile industries of India.

Passenger Cars and Multiutility Vehicles Sector

The pooled regression results of the model showing the impact of working capital ratios on profitability for the passenger cars and multiutility vehicles sector in automobile industries are presented in Table 6.8. The table indicates that the contribution of liquid ratio, working capital turnover ratio, inventory turnover ratio and receivable turnover ratio were statistically significant as seen from the values of regression co-efficient. For a unit increase in liquid ratio, profitability decreased by -0.290 units and this was statistically significant. When the working capital turnover ratio increased by one unit, profitability increased by 0.002 units which was statistically significant at 5 per cent level. When the inventory turnover ratio increased by one unit, profitability increased by 0.004 units which was statistically significant at 5 per cent level of significance. When the receivables turnover ratio increased by one unit, profitability increased by 0.009 units which was statistically significant at 1 per cent level of significance. Similarly for a unit increased in cash turnover ratio, profitability increased by 0.001 units which was not statistically significant. The five independent variables contribute 97 per cent of the variations in the profitability of the selected passenger cars and multiutility vehicles sector in automobile industry of India.

Two- and Three-Wheelers Sector

Table 6.9 shows the pooled regression results of the model indicating the impact working capital ratios on profitability of selected two- and three-wheelers sector in Indian automobile industry. The table indicates that the contribution of cash turnover ratio was not statistically significant as seen from the values of regression co-efficient. For a unit increase in liquid ratio, profitability decreased by -0.001 units and this was significant at 5 per cent level of significance. When the working capital turnover ratio increased by one unit, profitability increased by 0.020 units which was significant at 1 per cent level of significance. When the inventory turnover ratio increased by one unit, profitability increased by 0.020 units which was significant at 5 per cent level of significance. While the receivable turnover ratio increased by one unit, profitability decreased by -0.001 units which was statistically significant at 5 per cent level of significance. For a unit increased in cash turnover ratio, profitability decreased by -0.004 units which was not statistically significant. The five independent variables contribute 90 per cent of the variations in the profitability of the selected two- and three-wheelers sector of automobile industries of India.

Table 6.8

Estimated Regression Results of Impact of Working Capital Ratios on Profitability

(Passenger cars and multiutility vehicles sector)

$(PBT/TA = b_0 + b_1\ LR + b_2\ WTR + b_3\ ITR + b_4\ RTR + b_5\ CTR)$

Variables	*Beta co-efficients*	*t-value*
Constant	0.282	4.79 Significant*
Liquid ratio (LR)	-0.290	2.77 Significant*
Working capital ratio (WTR)	0.002	3.01 Significant**
Inventory turnover ratio (ITR)	0.004	2.58 Significant**
Receivable turnover ratio (RTR)	0.009	5.56 Significant *
Cash turnover ratio (CTR)	0.001	0.24 Not Significant
$R^2 = 0.97$		
Adj $R^2 = 0.89$		

* Significant at 0.01 level; ** Significant at 0.05 level

Source: Computed

Thus, the overall results presented in Tables 6.6 to 6.9 are encouraging. The signs of all co-efficients are as expected except RTR in the two- and three-wheelers sector. The co-efficients are also statistically significant except CTR in all the sectors.

Table 6.9

Estimated Regression Results of Impact of Working Capital Ratios on Profitability

(Two and three wheelers sector)

$(PBT/TA = b_0 + b_1 LR + b_2 WTR + b_3 ITR + b_4 RTR + b_5 CTR)$

Variables	*Beta co-efficients*	*t-value*	
Constant	0.090	2.67	Significant*
Liquid ratio (LR)	-0.001	3.01	Significant**
Working capital ratio (WTR)	0.020	3.61	Significant*
Inventory turnover ratio (ITR)	0.020	2.59	Significant**
Receivable turnover ratio (RTR)	-0.001	3.06	Significant**
Cash turnover ratio (CTR)	-0.004	-0.94	Not Significant
$R^2 = 0.90$			
Adj $R^2 = 0.70$			

* Significant at 0.01 level; ** Significant at 0.05 level

Source: Computed

References

1. Dutta Majumdar, D.K. (1980), *Productivity of Labour and Capital in Indian Manufacturing Industries during 1951 to 1961,* Indian Statistical Institute Publication.
2. Estrin. Saul et. al. (March, 1987), The Productivity Effects of Workers Participations: Producer Co-operative in Western Economics, *Journal of Comparative Economics,* Vol.I, No.1, p.262.
3. Massell F. Benton and Jonson R.W.M (1968), Economics of Small Holder Farming in Rhodesia; A Cross-sectional Analysis of two areas Food Research Institute Studies in Agricultural Economics, *Trade and Development,* Vol.8, No.1, p.183.
4. Vittorio, et. al. (1979), The Translog Production Function; Some Evidence from Establishment Data, *Journal of Econometrics,* Vol.10, pp.193-99.
5. Jaffe Adam. B (December, 1986), Technological opportunity and spill govers of RSD; Evidence from Firms patents, Profit and Market Value, *The American Economic Review,* Vol.76, No.5, p.362.
6. Pandey, I.M. (1982), *Financial Management,* New Delhi: Vikas Publishing House Pvt. Ltd., p.337.

7. Ibid., pp.337.
8. Sarkar, J.B. and Saha, S.N. (May, 1987), Profitability crises and Working Capital Management in the Public Sector in India; Case study. *The Management Accountant*, p.329.
9. Rao, et.al. Impact of Working Capital on Profitability – An Empirical study of an Engineering Firm. *Indian Journal of Commerce*, Vol.39, p.56.

7

Estimating Demand Function of Working Capital

An interest in the study of the demand for working capital by Indian automobile industries has been stimulated by the empirical works on the demand for cash and inventories. A review of the empirical works on the demand for cash showed two distinct paths. Frazer, Nadiri, Kamtaprasad and Ashok Kumar Lahiri observed economics of scale therby supporting Baumol and Tobin, while Meltzer, Whalen, De Allessi and Bhole L.M. observed diseconomies of scale thereby supporting Friedman as far as the transaction demand for cash is concerned. Similarly there is no unanimous finding as regards the effect of capital costs on the demand for cash. Among others, De Allessi and Nadiri showed the statistically significant effect of capital costs on the demand for cash, while Friedman did not find the same. Like studies on the demand for cash, the earlier studies on the demand for inventories also did not present unanimous findings. Liu, Kuznets, Lieberman, Irvine and Akhtar observed significant effects of capital costs on the demand for inventories, while Robinson, Lovell, Joyce did not observe the same. Similarly, some reported economics of scale with respect to holding inventories, while others did not report the same. It has therefore become difficult to support one view or another in the context of selected automobile industries of India.

However, investigation in this section is not limited to the study of the demand for cash and inventories only. It has been extended to test whether models similar to those explaining the demand for cash and inventories, also explain the demand for receivables, gross working capital and net working capital. The analysis of this section determines empirically whether transactions of working capital balances including cash and inventories vary proportionately or less than in proportion to changes in the volume of sales (S_t) and one year lagged sales (S_{t-1}). It also describe the effect of capital costs on working capital holdings of the selected Indian automobile industry.

Sales (S_{t-1}) Effect on Demand Functions of Working Capital

The demand function of working capital and its various components (Y^*) has been simplified to assert that $Y^*=f(W)$. Then the statistical hypothesis may be expressed in logarithmic form as:

$$\log Y^* = b_0 + b_1 \log W_t$$

where, Y^* is the working capital components like cash, inventory, receivables, gross working capital and net working capital, b_0 is the intercept and b_1 is the elasticity of Y^* with respect to wealth (W) defined in terms of either S_t or S_{t-1}

Total Industry

The pooled regression results of the model showing the sales (S_{t-1}) effects on transactions demand for working capital and its components for the total industry are presented in the Table 7.1. It is to be noted that the figures in parentheses in the regression results indicate 't' values. These values marked with the asterisk sign (*) shows that the results are significant at the 1 per cent level of significance. The overall results presented in the tables are encouraging. The signs of all the co-efficients are as expected. The co-efficients are also statistically significant and the goodness of fit of the model is also satisfactory.

With respect to the demand for cash by the Indian automobile industries, the result as indicated by the table contradicts unitary or more than unitary sales elasticity (0.006) hypotheses of Friedman, Meltzer, Whalen, De Allessi and Bhole L.M. The findings are to some extent consistent with the conclusion of Baumol, Tobin, Frazer, Nadiri, Kamta Prasad and Ashok Kumar Lahiri. The result shows that transactions cash balances vary less than in proportion to changes in the volume of sales (S_{t-1}). Regarding the demand for inventories it may be stated that the results as indicated by Table 7.1 support the findings of Irvine and contradict unitary or more than unitary sales elasticities noticed in some of the equation of Lieberman.

The results indicated by Table 7.1 showed economics of scale with respect to investment in working capital and its components. The sales elasticity is less than unity in all the cases. It varies from 0.005 for inventory to 0.510 for gross working capital. Thus, economics of scale are highest for inventory (0.005) followed by cash (0.006), receivables (0.010), net working capital (0.200) and gross working capital (0.510).

Commercial Vehicles Sector

Table 7.2 indicates the pooled regression results of the model showing the sales (S_{t-1}) effects on transactions demand for working capital and its components for the commercial vehicles sector in the Indian automobile industry. The overall results presented in the table are encouraging. The signs of all the co-efficients are as expected. The co-efficients are also statistically significant and the goodness fit of the model is also satisfactory.

With respect to the demand for cash by the commercial vehicles sector in the Indian automobile industry, the result as indicated by the table contradicts unitary or more than unitary sales elasticity (0.020) hypotheses of Friedman, Meltzer, Whalen, De Allessi and Bhole L.M. The findings are to some extent consistent with the conclusion of Baumol, Tobin, Frazer, Nadiri, Kamta Prasad and Ashok Kumar Lahiri. The result shows that transactions cash balances vary less than in proportion to changes in the volume of sales (S_{t-1}). Regarding the demand for inventories it may be stated that the results as indicated by Table 7.2 support the findings of Irvine and contradict unitary or more than unitary sales elasticities noticed in some of the equation of Lieberman.

The results indicated by Table 7.2 showed economics of scale with respect to investment in working capital and its components. The sales elasticity is less than unity in all the cases. It varies from 0.02 for inventory to 0.46 for gross working capital. Thus, economics of scale are highest for inventory (0.02) followed by cash (0.02), receivables (0:05), net working capital (0.06) and gross working capital (0.46).

Table 7.1
Estimated Regression Results of Estimating Demand for Working Capital
(Total industry)
$[\log Y = b_0 + b_1 \log S_{t-1}]$

Particulars	*Constant*	*Sales* (S_{t-1})	R^2	*F*
Cash	106.19	0.006 (8.819)*	0.86	77.77
Inventory	164.83	0.005 (9.67)*	0.88	93.47
Receivables	217.49	0.010 (10.49)*	0.89	109.98
Gross working capital	1335.78	0.510 (16.62)*	0.96	276.26
Net working capital	-1237.12	0.200 (8.15)*	0.84	66.49

Figures in bracket show t value
* Significant at 0.01 level
Source: Computed

Table 7.2
Estimated Regression Results of Estimating Demand for Working Capital
(Commercial vehicles sector)
$[\log Y = b_0 + b_1 \log S_{t-1}]$

Particulars	*Constant*	*Sales* (S_{t-1})	R^2	*F*
Cash-60.23	0.02	0.60 (4.40)*	19.34	
Inventory	152.54	0.02 (17.05)*	0.96	290.68
Receivables	180.92	0.05 (7.23)*	0.80	52.22
Gross Working Capital	1371.61	0.46 (13.47)*	0.93	181.47
Net Working Capital	584.17	0.06 (1.87)***	0.61	13.48

Figures in bracket show t value
* Significant at 0.01 level; *** Significant at 0.10 level
Source: Computed

Passenger Cars and Multiutility Vehicles Sector

The pooled regression results of the model showing the sales (S_{t-1}) effects on transaction demand for working capital and its components of the passenger cars and multiutility vehicles sector in the automobile industry of India. The overall results presented in the table are encouraging. The signs of all the co-efficients are as expected. The co-efficients are also statistically significant and the goodness of fit of the model is also satisfactory.

With respect to the demand for cash by the passenger cars and multiutility vehicles sector in the Indian automobile industry, the result as indicated by the table contradicts unitary or more than unitary sales elasticity (0.040) hypotheses of Friedman, Meltzer, Whalen, De Allessi and Bhole L.M. The findings are to some extent consistent with the conclusion of Baumol, Tobin, Frazer, Nadiri, Kamta Prasad and Ashok Kumar Lahiri. The result shows that transactions cash balances vary less than in proportion to changes in the volume of sales (S_{t-1}). Regarding the demand for inventories it may be stated that the results as indicated by Table 7.3 support the findings of Irvine and contradict unitary or more than unitary sales elasticities noticed in some of the equation of Lieberman.

The results indicated by Table 7.3 showed economics of scale with respect to investment in working capital and its components. The sales elasticity is less than unity in all the cases. It varies from 0.02 for inventory to 0.38 for gross working capital. Thus, the economics of scale are the highest for inventory (0.02) followed by cash (0.04), receivables (0.04), net working capital (0.22) and gross working capital (0.38).

Two- and Three-Wheelers Sector

Table 7.4 indicates that the pooled regression results of the model showing the sales (S_{t-1}) effects on transaction demand for working capital and its components of the two- and three- wheelers sector in the Indian automobile industry. The signs of all the co-efficients are as expected. The co-efficients are also statistically significant except cash and the goodness of fit of the model is also satisfactory.

With respect to the demand for cash by the two- and three-wheelers sector units in the automobile industry of India, the results as indicated by table contradicts unitary or more than unitary sales elasticity (0.001) hypotheses of Friedman, Meltzer, Whalen, De Allessi and Bhole L.M. The findings are to some extent consistent with the conclusion of Baumol, Tobin, Frazer, Nadiri, Kamta Prasad and Ashok Kimar Lahiri. The results show that transactions cash balances vary less than in proportion to changes in the volume of sales (S_{t-1}). Regarding the demand for inventories it may be stated that the results as indicated by Table 7.5 support the findings of Irvine and contradict unitary or more than unitary sales elasticities noticed in some of the equation of Lieberman.

The results indicated by Table 7.5 showed economics of scale with respect to investment in working capital and its components. The sales elasticity is less than unity in all the cases. It varies from 0.001 for cash to 0.670 for gross working capital. Thus, economics of scale are highest for cash (0.001) followed by inventory (0.005), receivables (0.020), net working capital (0.340) and gross working capital (0.670).

Table 7.3

Estimated Regression Results of Estimating Demand for Working Capital

(Passenger cars and multiutility vehicles sector)

$[\log Y = b_0 + b_1 \log S_{t-1}]$

Particulars	*Constant*	*Sales (S_{t-1})*	R^2	*F*
Cash	307.28	0.04 (7.36)*	0.81	54.12
Inventory	266.93	0.02 (4.90)*	0.65	23.99
Receivables	319.42	0.04 (7.27)*	0.80	52.88
Gross working capital	783.71	0.38 (12.54)*	0.92	157.23
Net working capital	-828.49	0.22 (7.03)*	0.79	49.44

Figures in bracket show t value
* Significant at 0.01 level
Source: Computed

Table 7.4
Estimated Regression Results of Estimating Demand for Working Capital
(Two and three wheelers sector)
[$\log Y = b_0 + b_1 \log S_{t-1}$]

Particulars	*Constant*	*Sales (S_{t-1})*	R^2	*F*
Cash	11.09	0.001 (4.95)	0.65	24.51
Inventory	46.72	0.005 (8.12)*	0.84	66.00
Receivables	92.65	0.020 (8.97)*	0.86	80.45
Gross working capital	-327.18	0.670 (16.42)*	0.95	269.47
Net working capital	-282.15	0.340 (9.52)*	0.88	90.67

Figures in bracket show t value
* Significant at 0.01 level
Source: Computed

Sales (S_t) Effect on Demand Functions of Working Capital

So far the estimated results are based on (S_{t-1}) as a proxy for wealth (W). These results may not be directly comparable to the results of those earlier studies which used (S_t) as a proxy for (W). This applies mainly to the studies on the demand for cash and inventories. Therefore, it is felt necessary to use (S_t) as a proxy for (W) in order to see whether the functions using (S_t) produce results similar to the functions using (S_{t-1}).

Total Industry

Table 7.6 indicates the results of multiple regression model showing the sales (S_t) effects on the transactions demand for working capital and its components for the total industry. The result shows that transactions cash balances (0.005) vary less than in proportion to changes in the volume of sales in the automobile industries of India. Similarly, the transactions inventory balance (0.004) vary less than in proportion to changes in the volume of sales (S_t). The result indicated by the table showed economies of scale with respect to investment in working capital and its components. The sales elasticity is less than unity in all the cases. It varies from 0.004 for inventory to 0.430 for gross working capital. Thus, economies scale are highest for inventory (0.004) followed by cash (0.005), receivables (0.009), net working capital (0.160) and gross working capital (0.430). The table also shows that the signs of all the co-efficients are as expected and statistically significant. The goodness of fit of the model is also satisfactory.

Table 7.5

Estimated Regression Results of Estimating Demand for Working Capital

(Total industry)

$[\log Y = b_0 + b_1 \log S_t]$

Particulars	*Constant*	*Sales (S_{t-1})*	R^2	*F*
Cash	116.13	0.005 (7.49)*	0.81	56.06
Inventory	171.53	0.004 (8.63)*	0.85	74.48
Receivables	234.71	0.009 (9.01)*	0.86	81.22
Gross working capital	1741.75	0.430 (19.35)*	0.97	374.47
Net working capital	-1075.58	0.160 (8.35)*	0.84	69.78

Figures in bracket show t value

* Significant at 0.01 level

Source: Computed

Commercial Vehicles Sector

Table 7.7 shows that transactions cash balances (0.01) vary less than in proportion to changes in the volume of sales in the commercial vehicles sector automobile industries of India. Similarly, the transactions inventory balance (0.02) vary less than in proportion to changes in the volume of sales (S_t).

Table 7.6

Estimated Regression Results of Estimating Demand for Working Capital

(Commercial vehicle sector)

[$\log Y = b_0 + b_1 \log S_t$]

Particulars	*Constant*	*Sales* (S_{t-1})	R^2	F
Cash -43.45	0.01	0.60	19.82	
		(4.45)*		
Inventory	177.82	0.02	0.93	180.52
		(13.44)*		
Receivables	251.75	0.04	0.75	39.03
		(6.25)*		
Gross working capital	1906.06	0.35	0.92	139.45
		(11.81)*		
Net working capital	692.98	0.02	0.58	12.84
		(1.69)*		

Figures in bracket show t value

* Significant at 0.01 level

Source: Computed

The result indicated by the table showed economies of scale with respect to investment in working capital and its components. The sales elasticity is less than unity in all the cases. It varies from 0.01 for cash to 0.35 for gross working capital. Thus, economies scale are the highest for cash (0.01) followed by inventory (0.02), net working capital (0.02), receivables (0.04) and gross working capital (0.35). The table also shows that the signs of all the co-efficients are as expected and statistically significant. The goodness of fit of the model is also satisfactory.

Table 7.7: Estimated Regression Results of Estimating Demand for Working Capital

(Passenger cars and multiutility vehicles sector)

$[\log Y = b_0 + b_1 \log S_t]$

Particulars	*Constant*	*Sales* (S_{t-1})	R^2	*F*
Cash 323.52	0.03	0.69	28.53	
		(5.34)*		
Inventory	265.83	0.02	0.61	20.34
		(4.51)*		
Receivables	335.68	0.03	0.68	27.93
		(5.28)*		
Gross working capital	562.41	0.35	0.96	301.17
		(17.35)*		
Net working capital	-996.03	0.21	0.85	71.45
		(8.45)*		

Figures in bracket show t value

* Significant at 0.01 level

Source: Computed

Table 7.8: Estimated Regression Results of Estimating Demand for Working Capital

(Two and three wheeler sector)

$[\log Y = b_0 + b_1 \log S_t]$

Particulars	*Constant*	*Sales* (S_{t-1})	R^2	*F*
Cash	10.82	0.001	0.67	25.75
		(5.07)*		
Inventory	46.24	0.004	0.83	65.52
		(8.10)*		
Receivables	90.98	0.020	0.86	77.39
		(8.80)*		
Gross working capital	-425.49	0.580	0.96	323.82
		(18.00)*		
Net working capital	-931.52	0.290	0.88	96.53
		(9.83)*		

Figures in bracket show t value

* Significant at 0.01 level

Source: Computed

Passenger Cars and Multiutility Vehicles Sector

Table 7.8 shows that transactions cash balances (0.03) vary less than in proportion to changes in the volume of sales in the passenger cars and multiutility vehicles sector automobile industry of India. Similarly, the transactions inventory balance (0.02) vary less than in proportion to changes in the volume of sales (S_t). The result indicated by the table showed economies of scale with respect to investment in working capital and its components. The sales elasticity is less than unity in all the cases. It varies from 0.02 for inventory to 0.35 for gross working capital. Thus, economies scale are the highest for inventory (0.02) followed by cash (0.03), receivables (0.03), net working capital (0.21) and gross working capital (0.35). The table also shows that the signs of all the co-efficients are as expected and statistically significant. The goodness of fit of the model is also satisfactory.

Two- and Three-Wheelers

Table 7.9 shows that transactions cash balances (0.001) vary less than in proportion to changes in the volume of sales in the two and three wheelers sector in automobile industry of India. Similarly, the transactions inventory balance (0.004) vary less than in proportion to changes in the volume of sales (S_t). The result indicated by the table showed economies of scale with respect to investment in working capital and its components. The sales elasticity is less than unity in all the cases. It varies from 0.001 for cash to 0.580 for gross working capital. Thus, economies scale are the highest for cash (0.001) followed by inventory (0.004), receivables (0.020), net working capital (0.290) and gross working capital (0.580). The table also shows that the signs of all the co-efficients are as expected and statistically significant. The goodness of fit of the model is also satisfactory.

When the above results are compared with previous results it may be seen that the use of S_{t-1} or S_t produced similar results. The co-efficient of S_t are almost identical to the co-efficients of S_{t-1}. Most of the cases with S_{t-1} have slightly better values of t, R^2 and F. Due to this, only S_{t-1} are used for further analysis.

Sales and Capital Cost Effects on Demand Functions of Working Capital

It is inferred that the target levels of working capital and its components have been postulated not to depend solely on future expected sales. Theoretically, the levels of working capital and its components of an enterprise desires to hold depend on holding costs also. It is however surprising that there has been repeated failure of many of the earlier empirical studies to find any significant influence of holding cost on investment in cash and inventories. The role of the holding cost as a determinant of the demand for cash and inventories is controversial seems to cater on sign and magnitude of the interest elasticity of cash and inventory balances. In order to test it in the context of selected automobile industries of India, the short–term interest rate of commercial banks as proxy is included in the model.

The model can now be stated as $Y^{*}=f(w,i)$. Then the statistical hypothesis may be expressed in logarithmic form as:

$$\log Y^{*} = b_0 + b_1 \log w_t - b_2 \log i$$

where Y^{*} is the working capital components like cash, inventory, receivables, gross working capital and net working capital, b_0 is the intercept, b_1 is the elasticity of y^{*} with respect to wealth (w) defined in terms of S_{t-1} and b_2 is the elasticity of y^{*} with respect to short-term interest rate of commercial banks.

Total Industry

Table 7.10 indicates the sales and capital costs effects on the estimating demand function of working capital for the total industry. The overall results presented in the table are encouraging and provide an interest rate co-efficients with theoretically correct signs. Previously these co-efficients of capital cost measures used to be either positive or insignificant in many of the studies on the demand for cash and inventories. The co-efficients of sales are also highly significant and indicate higher sales, increase working capital and its components. The sales elasticity varies from 0.004 for cash to 0.550 for gross working capital. The sales elasticity is smaller for cash (0.004) followed by inventory (0.006), receivables (0.014), net working capital (0.230) and gross working capital (0.550).

With respect to the demand for cash by the total industry, the result as indicated by the table shows the sales elasticity of cash is consistently less than unity, suggesting economies of scale. This finding again seems to support theoretical propositions of Baumol, Tobin, Frazer, Nadiri, Kamta Prasad and Ashok Kumar Lahiri and contradicts the propositions of Friedman, Meltzer, Whalen, De Allessi and Bhole L.M. Similarly, the demand for inventories it may be stated that the results as indicated by Table 7.10 support the findings of Irvine and contradict unitary or more than unitary sales elasticities noticed in some of the equations of Lieberman. Contrary to previous studies, the table also show that fluctuations in cash and inventory levels depend in a significant manner on fluctuations in their financial carrying cost. The effect of capital cost and working capital shows that the sign of interest rate co-efficient is not only negative but also statistically significant in all these cases, except gross working capital and net working capital.

The estimated elasticities of the target levels of working capital and its components with respect to capital costs measure indicates that the target level of gross working capital is much more sensitive to capital cost fluctuations as compared to the target level of cash, inventory, receivables and net working capital. Among these, the target level of inventory is least sensitive to fluctuations in capital costs. It all can be seen from the interest rate elasticity of 18.99 for cash, 12.58 for inventory, 32.07 for receivables, 41.20 for gross working capital and 35.30 for net working capital.

Table 7.10 reveals further facts also, holding the sales constant, the result indicates that one percentage increase in interest rate leads on an average to about 18.99 per cent decline in the cash balances. Similarly this kind of decline is noticed to be about 12.58 per cent for inventories, 32.07 per cent for receivables, 41.20 per cent for gross working capital and 35.30 per cent for net working capital balances when there is one percentage point increase in interest rate. In the same way, holding the interest rate constant, one per cent point increase in sales leads on an average to about 0.004 per cent increase in cash balances. This kind of increase noticed about 0.006 per cent for inventory, 0.014 for receivables, 0.550 for gross working capital and 0.230 for networking capital balances. The table also indicates that the goodness fit of the model is satisfactory.

Commercial Vehicles Sector

The multiple regression results presented in Table 7.11 for the commercial vehicles sector in the automobile industries are encouraging and also provide an interest rate co-efficients with theoretically correct signs. The co-efficients of sales are statistically significant and indicates higher sales, increase working capital and its components. The sales elasticity varies from 0.012 for cash to 0.513 for gross working capital. The sales elasticity is the highest for gross working capital (0.513) followed by net working capital (0.110), receivables (0.068), inventory (0.024) and cash (0.012).

Table 7.9

Estimated Regression Results of Estimating Demand for Working Capital

(Total industry)

$[\log Y = b_o + b_1 \log S_{t-1} - b_2 \log i_2]$

Particulars	*Constant*	*Sales* (S_{t-1})	i_2	R^2	F
Cash	310.39	0.004	-18.99	0.91	60.56
		(4.86)*	(2.66) **		
Inventory	29.49	0.006	-12.58	0.91	62.00
		(8.69)*	(2.15)***		
Receivables	-127.49	0.014	-32.07	0.93	83.24
		(10.15)*	(2.62)**		
Gross working	-3948.02	0.550	-41.20		
capital		(11.88)*	(1.24)	0.96	144.47
Net working capital	-5622.	50	0.230	-35.30	
		(6.24)*	(1.19)	0.85	34.96

Figures in bracket show t Value

* Significant at 0.01level; ** Significant at 0.05 level; *** Significant at 0.10 level

Source: Computed

Table 7.10

Estimated Regression Results of Estimating Demand for Working Capital

(Commercial vehicles sector)

$[\log Y = b_0 + b_1 \log S_{t-1} - b_2 \log i_2]$

Particulars	*Constant*	*Sales (S_{t-1})*	i_2	R^2	*F*
Cash	217.82	0.012	-27.11	0.67	12.14
		(2.41)**	(1.61)		
Inventory	4.16	0.024	-14.47		
		(19.08) *	(3.30)*	0.98	261.24
Receivables	-739.25	0.068	-89.72	0.92	65.14
		(10.66)*	(4.05)*		
Gross working capital	-1483.91	0.513	-27.84	0.95	111.09
		(12.31)*	(1.91)***		
Net working capital	-2145.21	0.110	-25.12		
		(2.95)	(2.08)**	0.76	74.36

Figures in bracket show t value

* Significant at 0.01 level; ** Significant at 0.05 level; *** Significant at 0.10 level

Source: Computed

With respect to the demand for cash by the commercial vehicles sector in the automobile industries, the result as indicated by the table shows that sales elasticity of cash is consistently less than unity, suggesting economics of scale. Contrary to previous studies, the table also shows that fluctuations in cash and inventory levels depend in a significant manner on fluctuations in their financial carrying cost. However, the effect of capital costs in cash is not statistically significant. The effect of capital cost and working capital shows that the sign of interest rate co-efficient is not only negative but also statistically significant. Table 7.11 also indicates that the target level of receivables is much more sensitive to capital cost fluctuations and inventory is least sensitive to fluctuations in capital costs. It all can be seen from the interest rate elasticity of 27.11 for cash, 14.47 for inventory, 89.72 for receivables, 27.84 for gross working capital and 25.12 for net working capital. The goodness of fit of the model is also satisfactory except cash.

Passenger Cars and Multiutility Vehicles Sector

The pooled regression results of the model for the passenger cars and multiutility vehicles sector in the automobile industry are presented in Table 7.12. The results are encouraging and also provide interest rate co-efficient with theoretically correct signs. The co-efficients of sales are highly significant and indicate higher sales, increase working capital and its components. The sales elasticity varies from 0.023 for inventory to 0.370 for gross working capital. The sales elasticity is the highest for gross working capital (0.370) followed by net working capital (0.220), cash (0.030), receivables (0.029) and inventory (0.023).

With respect to the demand for cash by the passenger cars and multiutility vehicles sector in automobile industries, the result as indicated by the table shows that sales elasticity of cash is consistently less than unity suggesting economics of scale.

Table 7.11

Estimated Regression Results of Estimating Demand for Working Capital

(Passenger cars and multiutility vehicles sector)

$[\log Y = b_0 + b_1 \log S_{t-1} - b_2 \log i_2]$

Particulars	*Constant*	*Sales* (S_{t-1})	i_2	R^2	*F*
Cash	535.89	0.030	-20.36	0.82	27.82
		(3.89)**	(1.05)		
Inventory	65.44	0.023	-17.94	0.69	13.47
		(4.20)*	(3.30)*		
Receivables	580.67	0.039	-23.26		
		(3.77)*	(4.24)**	0.83	28.27
Gross working capital	1104.03	0.370	-28.52	0.92	72.93
		(7.50)*	(2.23)		
Net working capital	-608.50	0.220	-19.59	0.79	22.88
		(4.19)*	(0.15)**		

Figures in bracket show t Value

* Significant at 0.01 level; ** Significant at 0.05 level

Source: Computed

Table 7.12: Estimated Regression Results of Estimating Demand for Working Capital

(Two and three wheelers sector)

$[\log Y = b_0 + b_1 \log S_{t-1} - b_2 \log i_2]$

Particulars	*Constant*	*Sales* (S_{t-1})	i_2	R^2	*F*
Cash	27.97	0.001	-1.59	0.68	12.86
		(1.84) ***	(4.03)*		
Inventory	64.53	0.004	-1.67	0.84	31.47
		(3.84)*	(2.58)**		
Receivables	40.92	0.021	-4.86	0.86	37.81
		(5.10)*	(3.43)*		
Gross working capital	-3357.17	0.770	24.12	0.96	146.06
		(10.48) *	(4.41)**		
Net working capital	-3616.99	0.420	38.12	0.89	50.56
		(6.67)*	(1.48)***		

Figures in bracket show t value

* Significant at 0.01 level; ** Significant at 0.05 level; *** Significant at 0.10 level

Source: Computed

Contrary to previous studies, the table also shows that fluctuations in cash and inventory levels depend in a significant manner on fluctuations in their financial carrying cost. The effect of capital cost and working capital shows that the sign of interest rate co-efficient is not only by negative but also statistically significant in all these cases except gross working capital.

Table 7.12 also indicate that the target level of gross working capital is much more sensitive to capital cost fluctuations in capital casts. It all can be seen from the interest rate elasticity of 20.36 for cash, 17.94 for inventory, 23.26 for receivables, 28.52 for gross working capital, and 19.59 for net working capital. The goodness of fit of the model is also satisfactory.

Two- and Three-Wheelers Sector

The pooled regression results of the model for the two- and three-wheelers sector in the automobile industry are presented in the Table 7.13. The results are encouraging and also provide interest rate co-efficient with theoretically correct signs. The co-efficients of sales are highly significant and indicate higher sales, increase working capital and its components. The sales elasticity varies from 0.001 for cash to 0.770 for gross working capital. The sales elasticity is the highest for gross working capital (0.770) followed by net working capital (0.420), receivables (0.021), inventory (0.004) and cash (0.001).

With respect to the demand for cash by the two- and three-wheelers sector in the automobile industries, the results as indicated by the table shows that sales elasticity of cash is consistently less than unity, suggesting economics of scale. Contrary to previous studies, the table also shows that fluctuations in cash and inventory levels depend in a significant manner on fluctuations in their financial carrying cost. The effect of capital cost and working capital shows that the sign of interest rate co-efficient is not only negative but also statistically significant in all these cases. Table 7.13 also indicate that the target level of net working capital is much more sensitive to capital cost fluctuations and cash is least sensitive to fluctuations in capital costs. It all can be seen from the interest rate elasticity of 1.59 for cash, 1.67 for inventory, 4.86 for receivables, 24.12 for gross working capital and 38.12 for net working capital. The goodness of fit of the model is also satisfactory.

To sum up, the studies concerning the demand for cash and inventories by firms did not report unanimous findings. A lot of controversies exist with respect to the presence of economics of scale and role of capital costs to the desired cash and inventories. This chapter has investigated these various issues using the data of the automobile industry of India. The regression results suggest strongly that the demand for working capital and its components is a function of both sales and their holding costs. Further, the capital cost co-efficients are statistically significant with the theoretically correct signs. While going through the results, the question may rise as to why some of results are at variance with the findings of earlier studies. In this connection, it is worth while to note that the nature of data and the specification of the models may themselves be responsible for the difference in the results.

REFERENCES

1. Baumol, W. (November 1952), The Transaction Demands for Cash: An Inventory Theoretic Approach, *The Quarterly Journal of Economics,* pp. 545-566.
2. Tobin, J. (August 1956), The Interest Elasticity of Transactions Demand for Cash, *The Review of Economics and Statistics,* pp. 241-247.
3. Friedman, M. (August 1959), The Demand for Money: Some Theoretical and Empirical Results, *The Journal of Political Economy,* pp. 327-351.
4. Meltzer, A.H. (August 1963), The Demand for Money: A Cross Section study of Business firms, *The Quarterly Journal of Economics,* pp. 405-422.
5. Frazer, W.J. (April, 1964), Financial Structure of Manufacturing Corporations and the Demand for Money: Some Empirical Findings, *The Journal of Political Economy,* pp. 176-183.
6. Whalen, E.L. (September 1965), A Cross-Section Study of Business Demand for Cash, *The Journal Finance,* pp. 423-443.
7. Louis De Allessi (Auguest 1966), The Demand for Money: A Cross-Section study of British Business Firms, *Economica,* pp. 288-302.
8. Nadiri, M.I. (May, 1969), The Determinants of Real Cash Balance in the US Total Manufacturing Sector, *The Quarterly Journal of Economics,* pp. 173-196.
9. Bhole, L.M. (1979), An Empirical Study of Liquidity Preference of Corporate Sector in India, 1951-1974, *The Indian Economic Journal,* Vol. 27, No. 1, pp. 65-80.
10. Kamta Prasad and Sampath, R.K. (July-September 1979), Business Demand for Money in India-A Temporal Cross-Section Analysis, *The Indian Economic Journal,* Vol. 27, No. 1, pp. 43-62.
11. Ashok Kumar Lahiri (1981), Liquidity Behaviour on Indian Business Firms, *The Indian Economic Journal*, Vol. 29, No. 1, pp. 1-9.
12. Liu, T.C. (July 1963), An Exploratory Quarterly Model of Effective Demand in the Post-war US Economy, *The Econometrica,* pp. 301-308.
13. Kuznets, P.W. (1964), Financial Determinants of Manufacturing Inventory Behavour; A Quarterly Study Based on US Estimates, *Yale Economic Essays,* pp. 331-369.

14. Charles Lieberman (August 1980), Inventory Demand and Cost of Capital Effects, *The Review of Economics and Statistics*, pp. 348-356.
15. Qwen Irvine, F. (September 1981), Retail Inventory Investment and the Cost of C^pital, *The American Economic Review*, p. 633.
16. Akhtar, M.A. (June 1983), Effects of Interest Rates and Inflation on Aggregate Inventory Investment in US, *The American Economic Review*, pp. 319-328.

8

Profile of Indian Automobile Industry

Light Commercial Vehicles

Market Growth Rates

Year	*Growth Rates (%)*
1990-91 - 1996-97	8.4
1996-97 - 2001-02	-4.3
2001-02 - 2006-07	4.3
2006-07 - 2011-12	5.0

Demand: Past & Future

Year	*No*
1990 - 91	56
1991 - 92	54
1992 - 93	57
1993 - 94	81
1994 - 95	100
1995 - 96	137
1996 - 97	91
1997 - 98	71
1998 - 99	62
1999 - 00	68
2000 - 01	71
2001 - 02	73

2002 - 03	75
2003 - 04	78
2004 -05	81
2005 -06	85
2006 -07	90
2011 -12	115

Sensitivity Coefficient 11.6%

Strategic Alliances

Company	*Collaboration*
Ashok Leyland	IVECO, Italy
Bajaj Tempo	Mercedez Benz, Germany
Eicher	Mitsubishi, Japan
M&M	Nissan Motor Co., Japan
Swaraj Mazda	Mazda Motor Co., Japan

Market Structure

Market segmentation

Segment	*Share (%)*
North	18
East	9
West	33
South	40

Lead Players

Company	*Share*
Telco	52
Eicher Motors	.17
Swaraj Mazda	13
M&M	12
Bajaj Tempo	6
Ashok Leyland	1

Leading Brands

Dyna Clipper, Camter, Traveller, Chital, Matador, Cabking, Standard, Swaraj Mazda

PASSENGER CARS

Demand: Past & Future

Year	*No.*
1990-91	182
1991-92	166
1992-93	163
1993-94	207
1994-95	264
1995-96	375
1996-97	448
1997-98	448
1998-99	435
1999-00	662
2000-01	616
2001-02	678
2002-03	745
2003-04	827
2004-05	918
2005-06	1028
2006-07	1150
2011-12	2000

Market Growth Rates

Year	*Growth Rates (%)*
1990-91 - 1996-97	16.2
1996-97 - 2001-02	8.6

2001-02 - 2006-07	11.1
2006-07 - 2011-12	12.0

Sensitivity Coefficient 11.7%

Lead Players

Company	Share (%)
Maruti Udyog	61.0
Hyundai Motor	16.0
Telco	10.6
Hindustan Motors	3.0
Ford India	2.6
Fiat India	2.5
Deawoo Motors	1.8
Honda Siel	1.8
General Motors	1.5
Mercedez Benz	0.3

Market Structure

Market Segmentation

Segment	Share (%)
North	43.0
East	8.0
West	26.0
South	23.0
Over Rs 1.0 mn	0.8
Rs 5,01,000 to Rs 1.0 mn	3.2
Rs 3,01,000 to Rs 5,00,000	49
Under Rs 3,00,000	47

Strategic Alliances

Company	Collaboration
Hind. Motors	Mitsubishi, Japan
MUL	Suzuki, Japan
Honda Siel	Honda Motor Japan

Leading Brands

Maruti 800, Esteem, Omni, Lancer, Opel Astra, Opel Corsa, Mrecedez, E&S class, Uno, Ford, Ikon, Siera, Wagon R, Baleno, Alto, Zen, Altura, Opel Swing, Opel Astra Club, Indica, Sonata, Accord, Accent, Santro, Honda city, Matiz, Nexia, Palio, Versa

Multiutility Vehicles

Demand: Past & Future

Year	*No.*
1990-91	37
1991-92	32
1992-93	38
1993-94	49
1994-95	51
1995-96	68
1996-97	137
1997-98	137
1998-99	115
1999-00	128
2000-01	131
2001-02	140
2002-03	150
2003-04	162
2004-05	175
2005-06	190
2006-07	208
2011-12	335

Market Growth Rates

Year	*Growth Rates (%)*
1990-91 - 1996-97	24.4
1996-97 - 2001-02	0.4
2001-02 - 2006-07	8.2
2006-07 - 2011-12	10.0

Sensitivity Coefficient 5.8%

Product Variation

Type	*Share (%)*
Petrol	7
Diesel	93

Market Structure

Market Segmentation

Segment	*Share (%)*
North	36
East	11
West	33
South	20

Lead Players

Company	*Share (%)*
Mahindra & Mahindra	46
Toyota Kirloskar	24
TELCO	19
Maruti Udyog	4
Baja Tempo	4
Hindustan Motors	3

Strategic Alliances

Company	*Collaboration*
Maruti	Suzuki Motors, Japan
M&M	Willys Overland Corp. USA
	Mitsubishi, Japan
Toyota	Toyota Motor Co.
Kirloskar	Japan

LEADING BRANDS

Voyager, trax, Quadro, Qualis, Armada, Gypsy, Sumo, Pick Up, Safari, Bolero, Marshal, Sierra, Indo, Gurkha

TWO AND THREE WHEELERS

Demand: Past & Future

Year	*No.*
1990-91	1.82
1991-92	1.60
1992-93	1.50
1993-94	1.75
1994-95	2.19
1995-96	2.86
1996-97	2.98
1997-98	3.07
1998-99	3.37
1999-00	3.78
2000-01	3.83
2001-02	4.06
2002-03	4.30
2003-04	4.60
2004-05	4.92
2005-06	5.31
2006-07	5.73
2011-12	8.50

Market Growth Rates

Year	*Growth Rates*
1990-91 - 1996-97	8.6
1996-97 - 2001-02	6.4
2001-02 - 2006-07	7.1
2006-07 - 2011-12	8.2

Sensitivity Coefficient 6.2%

Lead Players

Company	Share (%)
Total Segment	
Hero Honda	33.0
Baja Auto	26.0
TVS Suzuki	20.0
LML	4.0
Kinetic Motors	3.0
Yamaha	5.0
Majestic Auto	2.0
Royal Enfield	0.5
Honda Motors	1.0
Maharastra Scooters	1.5
Kinetic Engineering	4.0
4-Stroke Hero Honda	72.0
Bajaj Auto	22.0
Yamaha	4.0
Kinetic	2.0

Market Structure

Market Segmentation

Segment	Share (%)
North	32
East	9
West	27
South	32

Product Variation

Type	Share (%)
Scooters	22.3
Motorcycles	66.1
Mopeds	11.6

Leading Brands

Bajaj, Super, Chetak, Classic, Bravo, Legend, Yamaha, Stride, LML, Vespa, Kawasaki Bajaj, Hero Honda, KineticHonda, Bullet 350, Shogun, Samurai, Caliber, Fiero

Current Status of the Automobile Industry

The industry over a period of time has installed a robust capacity as given in Table 1.1

Table 1.1

Installed Capacity in Different Segments of the Automobile Industry

Segment	*Installed capacity (in numbers)*
Commercial vehicles	410 000
Cars and multi utility vehicles	1146 000
Two-and three-wheelers	5 696 000
Grand Total	7 252 000

Further, actual production of Automobiles, sales values of automobile, export value of automobile and domestic sales of automobiles during the study period are presented in Table 1.2, 1.3, 1.4, and 1.5.

Auto Policy 2002

The New Auto policy was announced in March 2002 by the Government. It aims to establish a globally competitive automotive industry in India and double its contribution to the economy by 2010.

Measures to realize the policy objectives

- Initiatives relating to investment, traffic, duties and imposts will be the instruments to achieve the policy objectives. This is part of government's economic reform and are in harmony with the commitments made to WTO.
- Increased resource allocation to the highways sector to ensure collateral upgradation and development of road infrastructure in step with the increase in the population

of vehicles.

— An appropriate regulatory framework for smooth movement of traffic, safety and environmental aspects.

Foreign Direct Investment

Automatic approval for foreign equity investment upto 100 per cent of manufacture of automobiles and component is permitted.

Import Tariff

The incidence of import tariff will be fixed in a manner so as to facilitate development if manufacturing capabilities as opposed to mere assembly without giving undue protection; ensure balanced transition to open trade; promote increased competition in the market and enlarge purchase options to the Indian customer.

The Government will review the automotive tariff structure periodically to encourage demand, promote the growth of the industry and prevent India from becoming a dumping ground for international rejects.

In respect of items with bound rates viz. Buses, Trucks, Tractors, CBU and Auto components, Government will be give adequate accommodation to indigenous industry to attain global standards. In consonance with Auto Policy objectives, in respect of unbound items i.e., Motor Cars, MUVs, Motorcycles, Mopeds, Scooters and Auto Rickshaws, the import tariff shall be so designed as to give maximum fillip to manufacturing in the country without extending undue protection to domestic industry. The conditions for import of new Completely Built Units (CBUs), will be as per public notice issued by the Director General Foreign Trade (DGFT) having regard to environment and safety regulations.

Used vehicles imported into the country would have to meet CMVR, environmental requirements as per public notice issued by DGFT laying down specific standards and other criteria for such imports.

Appropriate measures including and dumping duties will be put in place to check dumping and unfair trade practices.

Table 1.2

Automobile Production (in 000' No's)

Category	*1992-93*	*1993-94*	*1994-95*	*1995-96*	*1996-97*	*1997-98*	*1998-99*	*1999-00*	*2000-01*	*2001-02*	*2002-03*	*2003-04*	*2004-05*	*2005-06*	*2006-07*
Passenger Cars	163.2	215.5	270.6	348.2	411.1	401.0	390.7	577.2	504.6	500.3	557.7	782.6	960.4	1046.1	1238.0
Multy Utility Vehicles	83.6	91.4	98.5	106.2	134.6	134.6	113.3	124.3	125.9	169.3	163.2	206.9	249.4	263.2	306.8
Total Passenger Vehicles	246.8	306.9	369.1	454.4	545.7	535.6	504.0	701.5	630.5	669.6	720.9	989.5	1209.8	13093	1544.8
M&HCVs	65.7	70.3	117.6	129.7	155.7	95.9	80.5	112.3	88.2	96.7	120.0	166.1	214.8	219.3	294.3
LCVs	62.3	69.7	76.2	87.8	84.9	65.0	55.3	61.2	63.8	65.7	82.9	108.9	138.9	171.7	275.7
Total Commercial Vehicles	128.0	140.0	193.8	217.5	240.6	160.9	135.8	173.5	152.0	162.4	202.9	275.0	353.7	391.0	520.0
Total Three Wheelers	69.4	92.4	150.2	176.4	221.6	234.8	209.0	205.5	203.2	212.7	271.2	356.2	374.4	434.4	556.1
Scooters	854.9	860.8	1287.5	1224.8	1312.9	1279.5	1315.0	1259.4	879.7	937.5	850.1	935.3	987.4	1021.0	943.9
Motorcycle	366.1	466.7	646.8	809.1	988.2	1125.9	1387.3	1794.1	2183.8	2906.3	3914.6	4355.1	5193.9	6207.7	7112.2
Mopeds	393.2	439.2	511.6	622.0	678.1	667.2	672.2	724.5	694.9	427.5	344.6	332.3	348.4	379.9	379.9
3lectric Two Wheelers															
Total Two Wheelers	1614.2	1766.7	2445.9	2655.9	2979.2	3072.6	3374.5	3778.0	3758.4	4271.3	5109.3	5622.7	6529.7	7608.6	8443.9
3rand Total	2058.4	2306.0	3159.0	3504.2	3987.1	4003.9	4223.3	4858.5	4744.1	5316.0	6304.3 I	7243.4	8467.6	9443.3	11056.

Table 1.3
Automobile Sales Value

(Rs. in Crores)

Category	*1992-93*	*1993-94*	*1994-95*	*1995-96*	*1996-97*	*1997-98*	*1998-99*	*1999-00*	*2000-01*	*2001-02*	*2002-03*	*2003-04*	*2004-05*	*2005-06*	*2006-07*
Passenger Cars	2823.5	3845.4	5688.5	8512.6	10354.4	10713.5	10606.1	16221.2	16954.3	17503.5	18744.5	23440.6	30287.8	33198.9	36463.2
Multi Utility vehicles	776.7	1136.1	1192.1	1811.0	2181.2	3944.1	3472.8	3786.7	4459.4	4968.6	4915.5	7182.1	7894.8	5947.1	7140.3
Total Passenger Vehicles	3600.2	4982.1	6880.6	10323.6	12535.6	14657.6	14078.9	20007.9	21413.7	22472.1	23660.0	30622.7	38182.6	39146.0	43603.5
M&HCVs	1460.0	2843.0	4163.0	5673.3	7022.0	4620.0	4418.3	6053.6	5098.8	5779.6	7946.9	10693.8	13761.0	15086.5	16942.3
LCVs	2451.6	1924.6	2748.6	3847.8	5289.3	2736.3	2500.8	2791.9	3000.3	2647.1	3655.3	5653.4	7711.3	9705.2	10813.1
Total Commercial Vehicles	3911.6	4767.6	6911.6	9521.1	12311.3	7356.3	6919.1	8845.5	8099.1	8426.7	11602.2	16347.2	21472.3	24791.7	27755.4
Total Three Wheelers	212.1	374.9	517.0	697.6	931.2	980.0	944.1	1148.6	1143.1	1531.7	1896.5	2348.7	2252.6	2506.5	3259.1
Scooters	1020.8	1211.6	1717.8	2330.6	2607.5	2502.2	3000.2	2944.0	2241.9	2251.2	2041.3	2270.7	2745.4	2834.4	3260.1
Motorcycle	809.910	1087.4	1682.9	2147.0	2678.0	3279.0	4010.8	5089.3	6249.6	8680.1	11148.4	13254.7	15784.5	19073.2	23816.8
Mopeds	318.5	409.4	491.0	651.8	808.3	872.3	823.6	902.7	1131.4	614.6	512.2	420.7	438.6	484.8	536.2
Total Two Wheelers	2149.2	2708.4	3891.7	5129.4	6093.8	6653.5	7834.6	8936.0	9622.9	11545.9	13701.9	15946.1	18968.5	22392.4	27613.1
Grand Total	9873.1	12833.0	18200.9	25671.7	31871.9	29647.4 (	29776.7	38938.0	40278.8	43976.4	50860.6	65264.7	80876.0	88836.6	102231.1

Table 1.4
Automobile Export Value

(Rs. in Crores)

Category	*1992-93*	*1993-94*	*1994-95*	*1995-96*	*1996-97*	*1997-98*	*1998-99*	*1999-00*	*2000-01*	*2001-02*	*2002-03*	*2003-04*	*2004-05*	*2005-06*	*2006-07*
Passenger Cars	214.8	278.6	455.9	591.1	799.0	599.5	516.2	408.2	400.8	332.6	883.1	962.4	898.7	968.7	1046.3
Vlulti Utility Vehicles	2.6	9.4	114.3	35.8	58.5	68.5	51.1	21.0	18.1	21.7	21.3	36.3	39.7	47.3	64.7
Total Passenger Vehicles	217.40	288.00	470.20	626.90	857.50	668.00	567.30	429.20	418.90	454.30	904.40	998.3	938.4	1016.0	4444.0
vI&HCVs	205 7	I 105.2	I 213.4	I 250.8	I 311.6	332.7	I 286.0	1 302.9	I 382.8	I 255.9	I 328.8	I 494.4	I 949.1	I 1040.3	1172.1
:CVs	21.3	39.5	52.8	56.1	62.5	106.7	125.7	103.4	227.6	134.4	71.4	141.2	428.6	569.5	615.3
Total Commercial Vehicles	227.0	144.7	410.9	306.9	374.1	439.4	411.7	406.3	610.4	390.3	400.20	635.60	1277.70	1609.80	1787.4
total Three Wheelers	13.4	27.5	54.7	102.4	73.8	78.2	86.5	80.5	109.5	131.7	258.7	17.61	31.6	1.9	8.3
wooters 5.8		26.5	44.2	52.5	58.2	76.6	71.3	54.6	47.9	98.2	64.3	88.2	11.2	23.1	6.9
dotorcycle	34.1	60.0	80.0	116.5	150.4	105.3	72.8	66.4	98.1	177.2	405.6	13.4	33.2	47.2	43.3
rlopeds	12.8	22.2	30.9	24.4	23.6	14.6	8.3	16.0	28.8	15.7	15.1	8.1	7.2	17.2	15.2
Cotal Two Wheelers	73.40	126.40	163.40	199.10	250.60	191.20	135.70	130.30	225.10	257.20	508.90	32.70	63.50	71.30	64.3
Grand Total	531.20	586.60	1099.20	123530	1556.00	1376.80	1201.20	104630	1363.40	1133.50	2072.20	1684.4	2311.2	2699.0	2971.0

Table 1.5

Automobile Domestic Value

(Rs. in Crores)

Category	1992-93	1993-94	1994-95	1995-96	1996-97	1997-98	1998-99	1999-00	2000-01	2001-02	2002-03	2003-04	2004-05	2005-06	2006-07
'assenger cxars	2617.3	3584.3	5257.2	7999.5	9634.4	10209.1	10145.7	15868.1	16596.5	17214.1	18096.9	23440.6	30287.8	33198.9	39462.7
Aulti Utility vehicls	774.2	1127.4	1178.5	1777.9	2123.2	3876.3	3423.2	3768.3	4443.7	4949.6	4903.5	7182.1	7894.8	5947.1	7689.3
Total Passenger Vehicles	3391.5	4711.7	6435.7	9777.4	11757.6	14085.4	13568.9	19636.4	21040.2	22163.7	23000.4	30662.7	38182.6	39146	47152.0
M&HCVs	1265.1	2773.1 I	39,70,8 I	5430.4	6725.0	4303.2	4163.7 I	5793.9	I14754.1 I	5581.3I	7686.3 I	10307.7 I	12949.4I	14138.1	17432.4
,CVs	2430.4	1885.0	2695.8	3791.7	5226.8	4369.3	2375.1	2688.5	2772.6	2512.8	3584.1	5512.6	7283.7	9137.0	10816.3
Total Commercial Vehicles	3695.5	4658.1	6666.6	9222.1	11951.8	8672.5	6538.8	8482.4	7526.7	8094.1	11270.4	15820.3	20233.1	23275.1	28248.7
Total Three Wheelers	198.7	347.5	462.3	595.2	857.4	901.8	857.6	1068.1	1033.8	1400.2	1638.1	2331.6	2221.2	2504.8	2916.4
Scooters	994.2	1167.4	1665.3	2272.4	2531.1	2431.2	2945.6	2896.3	2143.8	2187.0	1953.4	2259.7	2722.4	2827.6	2763.4
Motorcycle	775.9	1027.6	1603.0	2030.7	2528.1	3174.0	3938.8	5023.6	6152.3	8503.8	10743.8	13241.3	15751.4	19026.2	23089.1
Mopeds	305.7	387.3	460.1	627.4	784.6	857.8	815.3	886.7	1120.6	598.9	497.9	412.6	431.3	468.1	470.6
Total Two Wheelers	2075.8	2582.3	3728.4	4930.5	5843.8	6463	6884	8806.6	9416.7	11289.7	13195.1	15913.6	18905.1	22321.9	26323.1
Grand Total	9361.5	12299.6	17293	24525.2	30410.6	30122.7	27849.3	37993.5	39017.4	42947.7	49104 (	64688.2	79542	87247.8 I	104640.2

Excise Duty

Presently excise duty on commercial vehicles sold by a manufacturer whether as a chassis or with a complete body is 16 per cent. However, no duty is levied on the body that is built by an independent body builder on chassis bought from a manufacturer and is detrimental to safety standards. The duty imposed on the construction of bodies by an independent body builder, small or organized sector shall be equal to that of bodies built by a chassis manufacture.

The Government will encourage fabrication of bus body on bus chassis designed for better passenger comport instead of truck chassis as is the current practice.

Government will promote the use of multi axle vehicles for carriage of goods as they cause reduced environmental pollution and lesser wear and tear on road surface in comparison to the existing 2 – axle trucks.

Environmental Aspects

The automotive and oil industry have together to constantly fulfill environment imperatives. The Government will be continue to promote the use of low emission fuel auto technology. The Government after considering the recommendations of the Export Committee on Auto Fuel Policy headed by Dr. R.A. Mashelkar, have approved a road map for implementation for the auto fuel quality consistent with the required levels of vehicular emissions norms and environmental quality. The Government will formulate a comprehensive auto fuel policy covering the other related aspects and ensure availability of appropriate auto fuel/ fuel mixes at minimum social costs across the country. Suitable institutional mechanism will be put in place for certification, monitoring and enforcement of different technologies/fuel mixes. Appropriate fiscal measures will be devised to achieve milestones in the roadmap for implementation of auto fuel policy.

In the short run, the Government will encourage the use of short chain hydrocarbons along with other auto fuels of the quality necessary to meet the vehicular emissions norms.

There is prime need to support the development and introduction of vehicles propelled by energy sources other than hydrocarbons by promoting appropriate automotive technology.

Hybrid vehicles and vehicles operating with batteries and fuel cells are alternatives to the conventional automobile, which in their early beginnings, lie intreasured. As an impetus for the development of such vehicles, an appropriate long term fiscal structure shall be put in place to facilitate their acceptance vis a vis vehicles based on conventional fuels.

Internationally, the practice is to levy higher road tax on older vehicles in order to discourage their use. In India, the road tax on vehicles in nature and quantum among the states. Lifetime road tax is also in vogue. The endeavour will be to move to the international model.

Incentive for Research and Development

The Governmental shall promote Research and Development in automotive industry by strengthening the efforts of industry in this direction by providing suitable fiscal and financial incentives.

The current policy allows Weighted Tax Deduction under I.T. Act, 1961 for sponsored research and in house R&D expenditure. This will be improved further for research and development activities of vehicle and component manufactures from the current level of 125 per cent. In addition, Vehicle manufactures will also be considered for a rebate on the applicable excise duty for every 1 per cent of the gross turnover of the company expended during the year on Research and Development carried either in house under a district dedicated entity, faculty or division within the company assessed as competent and qualified for the purpose or in any other R & D institution in the country. This would include R&D leading to leading to adoption of low emission technologies and energy saving devices.

Government will encourage setting up of independent auto design firms by providing them tax breaks, concessional duty on plant/equipment imports and granting automatic approval. Allocations to automotive fewer funds created for R&D of automotive industry shall be increased and the scope of activities covered under it enlarged.

Automobile Industry: Future Projections

While the domestic auto industry now moving in step with the WTO covenants, the stage is set for it to make rapid strides domestically and internationally to attain its rightful place in the world trade.

Table 1.6

Manufacturers of Various Vehicle Category in India

Medium and heavy commercial vehicles	*Light commercial vehicles*
– Tata Group (engines in collaboration with Cummins)	– Tata Group – Bajaj Tempo Limited
– Ashok Leyland (in collaboration with IVECO, Italy)	– Eicher Motors Limited – Mahindra & Mahindra
– Volvo India Pvt. Ltd. (wholly owned subsidiary of Sweden)	– Swaraj Mazda – Hindustan Motors
– Defense Vehicle factory (in collaboration with MAN, Germany)	– Ashok Leyland Limited – Daewoo Motors (India) Limited
Passenger car and multi utility	*Two and three vehicles vehicles*
– Maruti Udyog Ltd.	– Bajaj Auto Ltd.
– Hindustan Motors Ltd.	– TVS Suzuki Ltd.
– Daewoo Motors (India) Ltd.	– LML Limited
– Premier Automobile Ltd.	– Hero Honda Motor Ltd.
– PAL Peugeot Ltd.	– Yamaha Motor India Ltd.
– General Motors (India) Ltd.	– Kinetic Engineering Ltd.
– Tata Group	– Maharashtra Scooters Ltd.
– Mahindra & Mahindra Ltd.	– Majestic Auto Ltd.
– Mercedes Benz (India) Ltd.	– Kinetic Honda Motors Ltd.
– Ford India Ltd	– Royal Enfield (India) Ltd.
– Hyundai India Ltd.	– Scooters (India) Ltd.
– Honda SIEL India Ltd.	– Greaves Ltd.
– Toyota India Ltd.	– Honda Motorcycle & Scooter
– Skoda India Ltd.	– India Pvt. Ltd.

A global recession for last two years notwithstanding, the industry has shown appreciable resilience and adjusted to the challenges of the environment. Based on the general growth projections indicated by the Planning Commission of India for the next five year period, automobile industry is expected to register growth pattern as given below. This growth estimate implies certain assumptions relating to segment wise growth rates based on a study conducted by the National Council of Applied Economic Research (NCAER).

Table 1.7

Projections of India's automobile industry, 2009–2012 (No.s')

Year	*Cars*	*MUVs*	*LCVs*	*MUVs & LCVs*	*Scooters*	*Motor Cycles*	*Three wheelers*	*Tractors*	*Total*
2009-10	1008804	179593	91255	137495	1157887	8208540	544850	361699	11690123
2010-11	1089508	186777	94905	144370	1193781	9686078	604783	392443	13392644
2011-12	1176669	194248	98701	151588	1230788	11429572	671309	425801	15378676

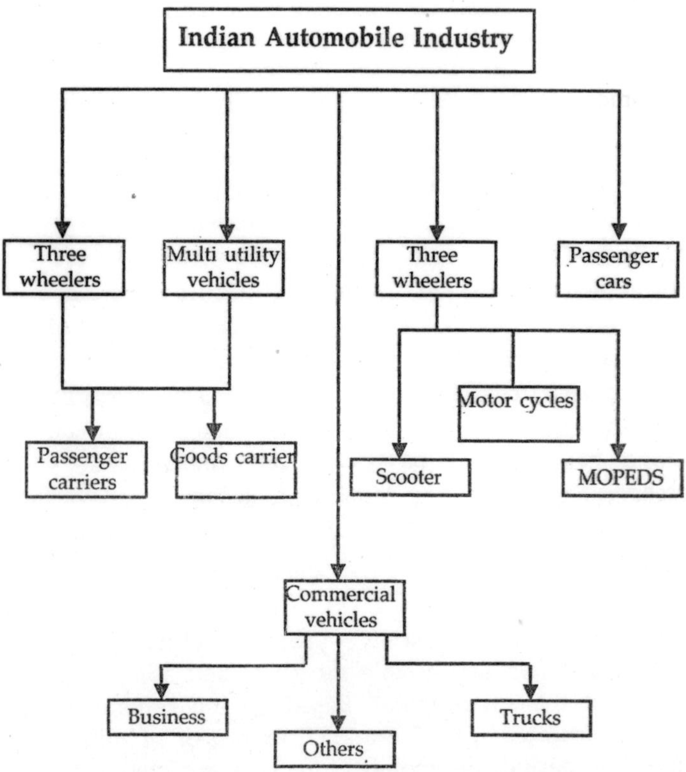

Figure 1: Range of Vehicles Made in India

9

Findings and Conclusion

The study in general aims at making a study of the management performance relating to working capital in the selected units of the automobile industry in India. Its specific objectives are: (1) To examine the structure, source and utilisation of working capital and its components; (2) To estimate the risk-return analysis of working capital position; (3) To assess the liquidity position; (4) To assess the impact of working capital ratios on profitability; and (5) To estimate transactions demand functions of working capital and its various components in utilisation of working capital in the selected units of the automobile industry of India.

This study covers seventeen major units in the automobile industry (five in the commercial vehicles sector, three in the passenger cars and multiutility vehicles sector and nine in the two- and three-wheelers sector). For the purpose of the study, necessary data on working capital and other related variables were collected for the period 1992-93 to 2006-07. The financial statements used were mainly the profit and loss accounts and balance sheets published in the annual reports of the respective units. The study used a variety of financial ratios to accomplish the objectives. It employed discriminant analysis to examine adequacy of working capital and the short-term liquidity position; multiple regression analysis was used to estimate the transactions demand functions of working capital and its various components.

This chapter epitomises the major findings of the study and offers a few suggestions for efficient management of working capital in the automobile industry of India.

Size of Working Capital

It is evident from the course of analysis that size of current assets in the automobile industry in India has increased 6.04 times whereas current liabilities increased by 5.61 times during the years 1992-93 to 2006-07. As the increase in CA is more than that of CL, the net working capital has increased by 7.22 times during the same period. It is observed that the increase in CA, CL and NWC sizes is more in the case of the two- and three- wheelers sector than in the passenger cars and multiutility vehicles sector and the commercial vehicles sector. Moreover the increase in the net working capital has been regular throughout the period except in the years 1993-94, 1998-99, 1999-2000 and 2000-01.

The decrease in NWC in all the selected automobile industries during the years 1993-94, 1998-99, 1999-2000 and 2000-01 was due to more decrease in finished goods component of current assets. It has been found in the course of the analysis that current assets constituted a considerably large proportion of total assets in the industry during the period under study. On an average 55.47 per cent of the total investment in the industry was committed in working capital alone.

Among the commercial vehicles sector units, three units (Ashok Leyland Ltd, Bajaj Tempo Ltd and Swaraj Mazda Ltd) had relatively high share of the total investment blocked in current assets. Similarly, among the passenger cars and multiutility vehicles sector units, two units (Hindustan Motors Ltd and Maruti Udyog Ltd) and in the two- and three-wheelers sector units, four units (Bajaj Auto Ltd, Kinetic Motors Ltd, Kinetic Engineering Ltd and Scooters India Ltd) had more current assets in their total assets. With all these variations, however, registered a continuous increase in almost all the units throughout the period except in the years 1993-94, 1998-99, 1999-2000 and 2000-2001.

The utilisation of the working capital, as reflected by the ratio of current assets in terms of number of days of sales, is certainly better in the two- and three-wheelers sector than in commercial vehicles sector and passenger cars and multiutility vehicles sector as its current assets to sales ratio had been found to be the lowest. Among the commercial vehicles sector units, this distinction goes to Ashok Leyland Ltd, among the passenger cars and multiutility vehicles sector units, it goes to Hindustan Motors Ltd and among two- and three-wheelers sector units, it goes to Maharashtra Scooters Ltd. The analysis of current and liquid ratio reveals that comparatively, the passenger cars and multiutility vehicles sector units stand at the top in terms of overall liquidity position during the period under study. Further, one unit (Ashok Leyland Ltd) in the commercial vehicles sector, two units (Mahindra and Mahindra Ltd and Maruti Udyog Ltd) in the passenger cars and multiutility vehicles sector and three units (Bajaj Auto Ltd, Maharashtra Scooters Ltd and Scooters India Ltd) in the two- and three- wheelers sector have very sound liquidity position during the study period. Moreover, the wide gap in CR and LR in all the units indicated that inventory forms quite a large proportion of total current assets in the automobile industry of India.

All these analyses lead to the conclusion that during the period under study, the passenger cars and multiutility vehicles sector units having enjoyed comparatively sound liquidity position and also effective utilisation of working capital funds, seem to have achieved a trade off in their liquidity and profitability.

Composition of Working Capital

Receivables, inventory, cash and bank and other current assets averaged 48.84 per cent, 35.61 per cent, 9.51 per cent and 5.96 per cent respectively of working capital in the automobile industry of India. These proportion were almost the same, with slight ups and down, in all the selected units in automobile industry. Among the selected units, Ashok Leyland Ltd in the commercial vehicles sector units, Maruti Udyog Ltd in the passenger cars and multiutility vehicles sector and Maharashtra Scooter Ltd in two- and three-wheelers sector have been able to make some reductions in inventory percentage to the total current assets as their average trend has been found to be the lowest.

Circulation of Working Capital

An analysis of the circulation of various current assets disclosed that different units have utilised their working capital with the varying degrees of efficiency in the selected automobile industry of India. It has been found from analysis that two units (Tata Motors Ltd and Eicher Motors Ltd) in the commercial vehicles sector, two units (Mahindra and Mahindra Ltd and Maruti Udyog

Ltd) in the passenger cars and multiutility vehicles sector and four units (Bajaj Auto Ltd, Maharashtra Scooters Ltd, TVS Motor company Ltd and Hero Honda Motors Ltd) in the two- and three-wheelers sector, have better inventory control than any other unit during the study period. As far as receivables management is concerned, the two- and three- wheelers sector units have better performance than the commercial vehicles sector and the passenger cars and the multiutility vehicles sector units.

Growth of Working Capital

The growth that has taken place in the size of current assets in relation to sales, points out that the automobile industry in India was recorded lower growth rates in current assets than in sales. This is an indication of sound working capital management. Further, the two- and three-wheelers sector have more average growth in current assets than in sales compared to the commercial vehicles sector and the passenger cars and multiutility vehicles sector units. However, such growth has been higher in the two- and three-wheelers sector than in the commercial vehicles sector and the passenger cars and multiutility vehicles sector units. It is inferred from the analysis that in the case of Ashok Leyland Ltd, Tata Motors Ltd, Bajaj Tempo Ltd and Eicher Motors Ltd among the commercial vehicles sector units, all the units of the passenger cars and multiutility vehicles sector and LML Ltd, TVS Motor Company Ltd, Hero Honda Motors Ltd and Scooters India Ltd among the two- and three-wheelers sector units, relatively good improvement in the working capital management has been noticed. Regression results further reveals that working capital and sales are functionally related concepts and a significant correlation has been found in all the selected units. The values of parameter 'b' bring out that working capital is more sensitive to the change in sales in the two- and three-wheelers sector than in the commercial vehicles sector and the passenger cars and multiutility vehicles sector. It is an index of the capability of the managements in controlling the sizes of their respective working capital funds by adjusting their sales volumes. The impact of the size of business on the magnitude of working capital has been analysed in this study by applying multiple correlation analysis. Individually, among the commercial vehicles sector units two out of five units (Ashok Leyland Ltd and Swaraj Mazda Ltd), the passenger cars and multiutility vehicles sector units two out of three units (Hindustan Motors Ltd and Maruti Udyog Ltd) and two- and three-wheelers sector units 4 out of 9 units (Bajaj Auto Ltd, Hero Honda Motors Ltd, Kinetic Engineering Ltd and Scooters India Ltd) multiple correlation co-efficients were high, remaining cases, it is low.

Adequacy of Working Capital

There is no standard by means of which the adequacy of working capital can be tested. However, sometimes the same is analysed by the relationship between current assets, liquid assets and current liabilities of a firm. Accepting current ratio of 2:1 as optimum, it was found that in the case of Ashok Leyland Ltd in the commercial vehicles sector and Bajaj Auto Ltd in the two- and three-wheelers sector, the average current ratio were found to be more than 2:1. Considering liquid ratio 1:1 as the measure of adequacy of working capital, it was found that in the case of Ashok Leyland Ltd in the commercial vehicles sector units and Bajaj Auto Ltd in the two- and three-wheelers sector, the liquid ratio were more than 1:1. In the remaining cases, liquid ratio was less than 1:1. On the whole, it could be said that only in few cases working capital were found to be adequate.

The operational adequacy of the working capital of the selected units has also been assessed by employing the discriminant analysis based on the size of working capital in terms of monthly operational requirements and sales requirements as independent variables. The construction of discriminate function suggests that the size of net working capital in terms of monthly operational requirements appeared to be stronger than sales requirements in all the years. The discriminate Z values were estimated and the good risk and poor risk enterprises may also be identified by computing the cut-off values.

The comparison of good and poor risk units as per the current ratio and as per the discriminant score shows that the misclassification of units is noticed in all the years. It can be concluded that in the years 1992-93 to 2006-07 Ashok Leyland Ltd in the commercial vehicles sector, Mahindra and Mahindra Ltd in the passenger cars and multiutility vehicles sector and Bajaj

Auto Ltd in the two- and three-wheelers sector units maintained adequate size of the working capital throughout the period under study.

Working Capital Trend

To analyse the working capital trend, the indices for different years, taking 1992-93 as base year, have been calculated for each unit of the automobile industry separately. The indices of the working capital shown an erratic trend in all the selected Indian automobile industry. Analysing the working capital trend, it has been assumed that the working capital trend will conform to the straight line calculated by the method of least squares. On the basis of chi-square test, it has been calculated that the progress of automobile industry with regard to working capital requirements cannot be approximated by the straight line method because the difference between the actual values and trend values of the working capital is significant in all the selected automobile industries of India.

On the basis of 'F' test (two-way analysis of variance), it has been calculated that the calculated value of 'F' between the year is less than the table value at 5 per cent level of significance. Thus the difference in the indices of working capital between the years among all the selected automobile industries is not significant. But the calculated value of 'F' between the companies is more than the table value at 5 per cent level of significance except the passenger cars and multiutility vehicles sector. Thus, the difference in the indices of working capital between the companies among different years are significant. On the basis of this analysis, it may be concluded that the performance of individual automobile companies is significantly differs from the standards of industry.

Financing of Working Capital

The proportion of working capital has been financed from long-term sources to the extent of 42.76 per cent in the commercial vehicles sector, 49.81 per cent in the passenger cars and multiutility vehicles sector and 72.65 per cent in the two- and three-wheelers sector. It is also inferred from the analysis that the average percentage of long term funds used for financing working capital in industry was 49.67 per cent, whereas in the commercial vehicles sector, passenger cars and multiutility vehicles sector and the two- and three-wheelers sector, it was 40.59 per cent, 40.75 per cent and 65.45 per cent respectively. The increasing dependence on the long-term sources of financing working capital in all the two- and three-wheelers sector units, Ashok Leyland Ltd and Tata Motor Ltd in commercial vehicles sector units and Maruti Udyog Ltd and Mahindra and Mahindra Ltd in the passenger cars and multiutility vehicles sector units depicts the incapability of the industry to make efficient management of its current assets namely inventories and receivables.

Risk-Return Analysis

The risk-return analysis of the working capital has been done on the basis of the proposition developed by E.W.Walkar which reads as if amount of working capital is varied relative to the fixed capital, the amount of risk that a firm assumes is also varied with opportunity for gain or loss increased by the same proportion. It has been found in the course of the analysis that overall working capital leverage of the automobile industry of India as a whole was very low which showed that changes in net working capital in relation to fixed capital has very low impacts over the profitability position, and also none of the selected automobile industry supports the proposition of E.W.Walker. In addition, in order to test the hypothesis of E.W.Walker of negative relationship between return on investment and working capital in relation to fixed capital, simple correlation in between these two has been computed. It was observed that there were negative correlations in Ashok Leyland Ltd and Eicher Motors Ltd under commercial vehicles sector and Bajaj Auto Ltd in two- and three-wheelers sector, which had satisfied the hypothesis of E.W.Walker. However, this negative correlation is significant only in Ashok Leyland Ltd in the commercial vehicles sector.

Inventory Management

The size of inventory in the automobile industry of India was large and formed, on an average, 35.79 per cent of current assets and 21.09 per cent of total assets during the study period. It has been found in the course of the analysis that the increase in inventory size, in absolute figures, has been noticed more in the two- and three-wheelers sector than in the commercial vehicles sector and the passenger cars and multiutility vehicles sector. In the automobile industries of India, the major components of inventory are raw materials, stores and spares, semi-finished goods, finished goods and other inventory which account 49.46 per cent 7.61 per cent, 11.52 per cent, 30.60 per cent and 0.81 per cent of the total inventory respectively. The same positions were also reflected in all the sectors of the automobile in industry in India. The computation of turnover ratios and average holding periods for inventory and its various components has spot lighted that all the units in the automobile industry of India were overstocked. Unit-wise analysis has revealed that Eicher Motors Ltd in the commercial vehicles sector and Maruti Udyog Ltd in the passenger cars and multiutility vehicles sector and Hero Honda Motors Ltd in the two- and three-wheelers sector seems to have done fairly well in maintaining all inventory components in proper balance. It's holding periods for all the components are below the industry's average.

The growth that has been taken place in inventory *vis-a-vis* sales in the automobile industry of India during the period also depicts that the average growth rate of inventory has been less than the growth rate of sales in all the selected units except among the commercial vehicles sector units, one out of five units (Bajaj Tempo Ltd) and among the two- and three-wheelers sector units, four out of nine units (LML Ltd, Maharashtra Scooters Ltd, Kinetic Motors Ltd and Hero Honda Motors Ltd). This shows better inventory management of the automobile industry of India. The correlation analysis are taken as a pointer to the fact that Tata Motors Ltd and Eicher Motors Ltd among the commercial vehicles sector units, Mahindra and Mahindra Ltd among the passenger cars and multiutility vehicles sector units and TVS Motor Company Ltd in the two and there wheelers sector units experienced relatively strong correlation between inventory and sales variables. The values of parameter 'b' indicated the sensitivity with which inventory in a concern changes for a unit increase or decrease in sales. The two- and three-wheelers sector (3.90) are more sensitive than the commercial vehicles sector (1.60) and the passenger cars and multiutility vehicles sector (1.58) for change in inventory as a result change in sales.

Receivables Management

Receivables accounted for the major use of the working capital in the automobile industry of India. On an average receivables worked out to 50.37 per cent of current assets and 31.09 per cent of total assets in the industry .Among the commercial vehicles sector automobile industries, two units (Tata Motor Ltd and Eicher Motor Ltd), one unit (Mahindra and Mahindra Ltd) in the passenger cars and multiutility vehicles sector and four units (Bajaj Auto Ltd, Maharashtra Scooters Ltd, Kinetic Engineering Ltd and Majestic Auto Ltd) in the two- and three-wheelers sector units had relatively large size of receivables. Efficiency in the use of receivables was awfully low in the industry. The ratio of receivables to sales proves that Hero Honda Motors Ltd and TVS Motor Company Ltd were able to have comparatively better utilisation of receivables, whereas remaining units showed very poor performance on this account. The study of composition of receivables points out that, contrary to the policy of making minimum invested in debts, the automobiles industry of India invested much of the amounts receivables in this very constituent on an average debts amounted to 93.13 per cent of the receivables in the industry. It is also evident that debts have constituted the bulk of the total receivables in all the units selected for the study.

The receivables collection period and debt collection period makes it evident that the receivables on an average have taken long period to be converted into cash. On an average, the receivables collection period in the industry was 22.67 days, whereas in the commercial vehicles sector, passenger cars and multiutility vehicles sector and two- and three-wheelers sector, it worked out as 26.93 days, 24.87 days and 16.53 days respectively. As the automobile industry has been operating in the sellers market, it is expected that an effective management of receivables must lead to restricted growth of receivables in relation to growth of sales. However among the commercial vehicles sector units four out of five units (Ashok Leyland Ltd, Tata Motors Ltd, Eicher Motors Ltd and Swaraj Mazda Ltd), all the passenger cars and multiutility vehicles sector and among the two- and three-wheelers sector units two out of nine units (LML Ltd and TVS Motor Company Ltd) in the industry has been able to achieve this objective. The regression results demonstrate that receivables and sales are significantly correlated in all the units expect Ashok Leyland Ltd in the commercial vehicles sector, but the sensitivity to change in receivables is not very high for a unit change in sales. This confirms that credit facility is not properly availed of as a marketing force in the industry.

Cash Management

It is evident from the analysis that on an average cash worked out to 9.32 per cent of the total working capital in the industry during the study period. The size of cash in all the selected automobiles industry remained, in general, growing during the period, a few fluctuations notwithstanding. It has been found from the analysis that the passenger cars and multiutility vehicles sector had the largest amount of cash in relations to current assets with high variations, whereas commercial vehicles sector has the minimum size of cash with relatively low variations during the period under study.

Every business concern is expected to keep adequate cash balance to meet its daily operational requirements, as also constantly to maintain liquidity and solvency, on which hinge the very existence of an enterprise. It has been found from the analysis that the automobile industry of India by and large holds inadequate cash balances to support its operational requirements. Only Ashok Leyland Ltd and Tata Motors Ltd among the commercial vehicles sector units, Mahindra and Mahindra Ltd and Maruti Udyog Ltd in the passenger cars and multiutility vehicles sector units and LML Ltd and Scooters India Ltd among the two- and three-wheelers sector units were able to maintain their cash balances in relatively sufficient quantity, whereas the remaining units had too little size of cash balances to be sufficient to meet the operational needs.

It has been inferred from the analysis that all the units in the automobile industry of India experienced adequacy of cash in terms of liquidity and solvency. Analysis of current ratio, Liquid ratio, net cash flows to current liabilities ratio and current liability coverage ratio brings out that as far as actual liquidity position among the firms was concerned, the passenger cars and multiutility vehicles sector units, in particular, had good liquidity and solvency position with regard to actual liquidity and solvency.

Assessment of Liquidity Position

Among the various measures of short-term liquidity, net working capital itself provides the one which indicates a 'margin of safety' of production provided to creditors. It has been found in the course of the analysis that almost all the selected automobile units of India have positive net working capital. The negative net working capital has been observed for Tata Motors Ltd in 1999-2000, 2000-2001, 2000-2002 and 2002-03, Bajaj Tempo Ltd in 2005-06 and 2006-07 and Swaraj Mazda Ltd in 1992-93, 1993-94 and 1994-95 among the commercial vehicles sector units. Hindustan Motors Ltd in 2003-04, 2004-05, 2005-06 and 2006-07 and Maruti Udyog Ltd in 1993-94, 1994-95 and 1995-96 among the passenger cars and Multiutility vehicles sector unit and LML Ltd in 1992-93, 1993-94 and 2001-2007, Maharashtra scooters Ltd in 2006-07, TVS Motors Company Ltd in 1992-93, 1993-94, 1995-96, 1998-99, 2002-03 and 2003-04, Kinetic Motors Ltd in 2005-06 and 2006-07, Hero Honda Motors Ltd in 1999-2000 and 2001-02, Kinetic Engineering Ltd in 2005-06, Majestic Auto Ltd in 1999-2000, 2000-2004, 2005-06 and 2006-07, Scooters India Ltd in 1992-93, 1993-94, 1994-95 and 1995-96 among the two- and three-wheelers sector units. This shows the negative approach adopted by the industry. In addition, liquid assets are compared with current liabilities. It is revealed that the former is insufficient to cover current liabilities on many occasions. It is also inferred that none of the industries cover current liabilities from the liquid assets throughout the period from 1992-93 to 2006-07. This shows lack of capability to pay current debts from liquid assets.

By analysing the current ratio and liquid ratio, it has been found that comparatively, the commercial vehicles sector have maintained higher current and liquid ratio than the passenger cars and multiutility vehicles sector and the two- and three-wheelers sector of the Indian automobile industry during the study period. On the basis of 'F' test in current ratio, it has been found that the differences in the current ratio between the industries among the different years are not significant. Similarly, the current ratio between the years among the selected automobile industries are significant at 5 per cent level. Further, the differences in the liquid ratio between the industries among different years and between the years among the selected automobile industries are significant at 5 per cent level. On the basis of this analysis it may be concluded that the performance of individual industries are significantly different with the standards of industry.

It is inferred from the analysis of cash position ratio that this ratio has declined over a period of time for the majority of the selected automobile industry. It shows that automobile industry has been trying to operate with lower level of cash.

The liquidity position of the selected automobiles industries of India has also been assessed by employing the discriminate analysis based on current and liquid ratios. The construction of the discriminant function suggests that current ratios appeared to be stronger than liquid ratios from 1992-93 to 2006-07 except in the years 1993-94, 1994-95, 1995-96 and 1997-98. The good risk and poor risk units may also be identified by computing the cut-off values. The number of good risk and poor risk units as per the current and liquid ratio and as per the discriminant score are compared. Misclassification of industries is noticed in all the years except in the year 2004-05.

For the purpose of establishing definite relationship between liquidity and profitability, Karl Pearson's correlation co-efficient can be applied. It has been found from the analysis that the liquidity and profitability of the automobile industry of India were adversely correlated. In a nutshell, it can thus be concluded that Ashok Leyland Ltd and Eicher Motors Ltd among the commercial vehicles sector units, Mahindra and Mahindra Ltd in the passenger cars and multiutility vehicles sector units and among the two- and three-wheelers sector units, four out of nine units namely Bajaj Auto Ltd, Maharashtra Scooters Ltd, Majestic Auto Ltd and Scooters India Ltd growth in liquidity had reverse impact on profitability. These units satisfy the proposition of Van Horne of "The higher the liquidity, the lower the profitability".

Impact of Working Capital on Profitability

The impact of the working capital on profitability has been examined by computing co-efficient of correlation and regression between profitability ratio (PBT to total assets ratio) and working capital ratios (CR, LR, WTR, ITR, RTR and CTR). The study of the impact of working capital ratios on profitability of Indian automobile industry showed both negative and positive impacts.

All the working capital ratios have shown positive association with profitability. In the commercial vehicles sector CR and LR, in the passenger cars and multiutility vehicles sector CTR have shown negative correlation and in the two and three-wheelers sector all the working capital ratios have shown positive correlation with profitability ratio.

The pooled regression results of the modes showing the impact of working capital ratios on profitability for the automobile industry of India as a whole are encouraging. The five independent variables contribute 91 per cent of the variations in the profitability of the automobile industry of India. It has been found from the analysis that for a unit increase in LR and CTR the profitability decreased by 0.125 units and 0.006 units respectively. Whereas WTR, ITR and RTR, increased by one unit, the profitability increased by 0.090, 0.009 and 0.008 units respectively

In the commercial vehicles sector, the five independent variables contribute 93 per cent of the variations in the profitability of the Indian automobile industry. It is inferred from the analysis that for one unit increase in LR, the profitability decreased by 0.044 units, whereas for one unit increase in WTR, ITR, RTR and CTR, the profitability increased by 0.001, 0.014, 0.008 and 0.002 units respectively. In the passenger cars and multiutility vehicles sector, the five independent variables contribute 97 per cent of the variations in the profitability of the selected passenger cars and multiutility vehicles sector of the Indian automobile industry. It has been found from the analysis that for one unit increase in LR, the profitability decreased by 0.290 units, whereas one unit increase in WTR, ITR, RTR and CTR the profitability increased by 0.002, 0.004, 0.009 and 0.001 units respectively. In the two- and three-wheelers sector, the five independent variables contribute 90 per cent of the variations in the profitability of the selected two- and three-wheelers sector of Indian automobile industry. It is inferred from the analysis that for one unit increase in LR, RTR and CTR, the profitability decreased by 0.001, 0.001 and 0.004 units respectively, whereas one unit increase in WTR and ITR, the profitability increased by 0.020 and 0.020 units respectively. The overall results of the model showing impact of working capital on profitability are encouraging.

Estimating Demand Function of Working Capital

In all the sectors of automobile industry, the pooled regression results of this study contradicts unitary or more than unitary sales elasticity hypothesis of Friedman, Meltzer, Whalen, De Allessi and Bhole L.M with respect to the demand for cash. The presence of economics of scale in cash holdings is consistent with the conclusion of Baumol, Tobin, Frazer, Nadiri, Kamta Prased and Ashok Kumar Lahiri. The demand for inventories holdings showed economics of scale thereby supporting the findings of Irvine and contradict to the unitary or more than unitary sales elasticities noticed in some of the equation of Lieberman. The study also showed the presence of economics of scale with respect to investment in working capital and its components.

The regression results also shows that the level of working capital and its components of an enterprise's desire to hold depend not only on sales but on holding cost also. The capital cost co-efficient are all statistically significant except gross working capital and net working capital elasticity in the automobile industry of India with the theoretically correct signs. In all the selected sector of automobile industries also, the capital cost co-efficient are all statistically significant with the theoretically correct signs except cash elasticity in the commercial vehicles sector and cash and gross working capital in the passenger cars and multiutility vehicles sector.

Thus, it has been found from the analysis that the demand for working capital and its components is a function of both sales and their holdings cost. Further, the capital cost co-efficients are statistically significant with the theoretically correct signs.

SUGGESTIONS

Keeping in view the above observations relating to the study, the following measures are suggested which would go a long way to improve management of working capital in the automobile industry of India.

1. The problem of surplus investments in inventory and receivables in the selected units can largely be tackled through improved coordination in the functioning of some strategic departments such as purchase, production,

marketing and finance. For coordination, strengthening up of management information system in the units is essential. The organisations need to adopt weekly reporting system in respect of inventory and receivables. Moreover, the responsibility for arranging funds to meet the working capital requirements should not be thrust upon the finance managers only, rather it should be made a collective responsibility of all the departmental managers.

2. There is an urgent need to bring about a change in the attitude of the management towards the working capital. During the course of the investigation, it has been found that the managements normally consider the liquidity aspects of the working capital managements to be important and do not play much attention to the profitability of funds employed in it. That is why the main problem of the working capital in the automobile industry of India is over investments in various current assets. To overcome this difficulty, the managements should regard both the facts of working capital as equally important and realise that only proper balancing of liquidity and profitability would ensure efficient working capital management.

3. With a view to lowering investments in receivables, the selected units should administer their receivables on certain well established principles of receivables management. Allocation of authority pertaining to credit and collection to some specific departments, selection of proper credit terms and laying down of sound collection policies and procedures would go a long way to improve collections.

4. Cash management in the selected units can be streamlined by proper planning and control of cash. The firms must increasingly adopt objective methods rather than intuitive methods of cash forecasting. Moreover, cash inflows and outflows must be assiduously regularised. Quick disposal of documents and letters relating to sales would surely speed up the inflow of money. For efficient performance of this function, it is suggested that cash section can be placed under the charge of finance experts.

5. As the management of working capital involves frequent decision-making, it is proposed that every organisation should set up a separate 'cell' to keep an eye on the environmental conditions and economic trends. So far, no unit under study has been able to create such a section in the organisation.
6. To deal with overstocking in stores and spares components of inventory, ancillary units should be developed, internal repair facilities created and classification of stores and spares made according to the nature of consumption such as fast-moving, slow-moving and non-moving items.
7. The Automobile industry is impeded by the poor state of the road infrastructure in the country. The poor state is manifest in the fact that the National and State highways which constitute 8 per cent of the total road length in our country carry 80 per cent of the total road traffic. The loss by way of higher operating costs on account of bad road conditions has been estimated at Rs.15,000 crores per annum. Because of the road condition the penetration level of commercial vehicles in India would have been much above its current level of three vehicles / 1000 persons which is very low compared to other developing countries even. It is suggested to take road building seriously and start massive project for roads in the next 10 years is imperative. The automobile market will stagnate soon if this is not done.
8. The cost of fuel is an impediment for the user of automobiles. Altering of fuel ratio will go a long way in encouraging the demand of vehicles. Not only is the cost of fuel is high but also quality is low and this is not only detrimental for the engine of car but also for the environmental health. The high prices of fuel prevent the people from buying new cars despite the availability of attractive financial schemes. Under these circumstances scrapping of old vehicles in favour of new ones will become difficult. It suggested that the Indian cost of fuel is important and at the same this fuel quality needs to be improved in terms of gumming tendency and dust contamination.

9. The Indian automobile industry production is based on the assembly of different components in a knock down condition. The MNC's have not been improving the quality of produce in India rather they have been in a sense "importing" high quality products into the country. It is suggested that the inverted duty structure of customs duty on raw materials, components and finished goods needs to be corrected. This is pending for more than five years.
10. The government failed to realise that by allowing the assembly of vehicles, i.e., employment is created in Europe, Australia, Korea or Japan. This is to say that one manufacturing creates one job in India and 10 in Korea or Japan. It suggested that the country has already permitted too many companies to come here for the limited market of passenger cars. Therefore, to create employment the local manufacturer has to be encouraged.
11. Our economy was indiscriminately opened up to give a chance to one per cent of Indians to choose from 16 or more different models of passenger cars. Wastage of capital due to overcapacity in the passenger cars and auto component industry has meant loss of not only foreign capital but much more of domestic capital in the form of bad loans given by Indian financial institutions and banks. It is suggested that the prices of cars are high in terms of the purchasing power of the people, in spite of finance schemes being available. This will make scrapping of old vehicles, in favour of new ones, rarer if the price of vehicle is high.
12. All local constraints like the outdated Industrial Disputes Act, Factories Act and the like which make local manufacturing far more difficult, should be modified without further delay.

Conclusion

In conclusion it may be said that the adoption of above measures will undoubtedly help the selected units improve their overall performances in the management of the working capital. A lot of funds now invested in inventory and receivables can be released for alternative uses. Ultimately liquidity and profitability of the concerns will be promoted. The industry will be able to generate funds increasingly from internal sources, thus breaking the vicious circle of financial stringencies. It is common knowledge that the function of fixed assets is to create capacity and that of current assets to make the utilisation of capacities possible. The problem of under utilisation of capacities of the industry will be solved to a large extent with the improvement in the management of the working capital. Thus, the dream of our planners to accelerate the economic growth in the country by effecting increased automobile vehicles production at reasonable costs are still possible to be translated into reality.

Appendix-II

Current Assets, Current Liabilities and Net Working Capital on the selected units from 1992-93 to 2006-07

(Commercial vehicles sector) *(Rs. in crores)*

Particulars		*Ashok Leyland Ltd*	*Tata Motors Ltd*	*Bajaj Tempo Ltd*	*Eicher Motors Ltd*	*Swaraj Mazda Ltd*
1992-93	CA	765.97	2344.40	146.94	56.32	36.43
	CL	286.94	1738.97	101.62	46.52	39.97
	NWC	479.03	605.43	45.32	9.80	-3.54
1993-94	CA	739.55	2144.00	211.37	59.12	56.21
	CL	331.52	1584.21	164.93	45.80	63.24
	NWC	408.03	559.79	46.44	13.32	-7.03
1994-95	CA	1292.78	2559.30	274.58	87.47	66.95
	CL	433.72	2051.68	216.51	63.88	73.59
	NWC	859.06	507.62	58.07	23.59	-6.64
1995-96	CA	1636.40	3356.53	255.62	113.33	86.83
	CL	752.58	3129.10	218.90	83.71	72.69
	NWC	883.82	227.43	36.72	29.62	14.14
1996-97	CA	1978.90	4795.20	249.88	116.92	100.89
	CL	932.90	3575.30	238.67	80.49	72.75
	NWC	1046.00	1219.90	45.21	36.43	28.14
1997-98	CA	1825.15	4119.57	278.94	75.48	70.75
	CL	597.87	3208.00	231.89	47.14	49.39
	NWC	1227.28	911.57	47.05	28.34	21.36
1998-99	CA	1438.60	4426.08	266.07	84.59	86.22
	CL	710.03	4208.40	227.32	55.77	57.82
	NWC	728.57	217.68	38.75	28.82	28.40
1999-00	CA	1530.40	3003.13	270.20	90.77	97.30
	CL	831.53	3364.20	212.64	63.47	68.09
	NWC	698.87	-361.07	57.56	27.30	29.21
2000-01	CA	1574.80	2790.10	266.42	90.87	127.77
	CL	720.67	3839.80	209.98	68.86	101.82
	NWC	854.13	-1049.70	56.44	22.01	25.95

2001-02	CA	1611.60	2749.54	230.86	106.89	142.81
	CL	751.09	3501.80	184.57	102.35	99.71
	NWC	860.51	-752.26	46.29	4.54	43.10
2002-03	CA	1331.60	3076.38	276.73	119.18	159.34
	CL	621.01	3907.69	208.77	119.79	147.40
	NWC	710.59	-831.31	67.96	-0.61	11.94
2003-04	CA	1459.34	5074.70	330.33	391.47	205.80
	CL	553.37	4869.77	256.30	345.17	181.31
	NWC	905.97	204.93	74.31	46.30	24.49
2004-05	CA	2334.83	7472.78	324.68	505.08	323.68
	CL	1208.78	6711.69	273.48	456.43	286.17
	NWC	1126.05	761.09	51.20	48.65	37.51
2005-06	CA	2522.74	9577.97	385.35	487.44	439.86
	CL	1443.86	7669.33	424.63	492.22	395.91
	NWC	1078.88	1908.64	-39.28	-4.78	43.95
2006-07	CA	2723.91	10146.49	420.56	613.11	486.36
	CL	2026.34	9229.70	436.16	633.68	412.12
	NWC	697.57	916.79	-15.60	-20.57	74.24

Appendix III

Current Assets, Current Liabilities and Net Working Capital on the selected units from 1992-93 to 2006-07

(Passenger cars and multiutility vehicles sector) *(Rs. in crores)*

Particulars		*Hindustan Motors Ltd*	*Mahindra & Mahindra Ltd*	*Maruti Udyog Ltd*
1992-93	CA	331.63	623.99	738.89
	CL	301.39	411.79	497.12
	NWC	30.24	212.20	241.77
1993-94	CA	348.86	804.31	1152.59
	CL	275.60	402.71	1251.90
	NWC	73.26	401.60	-99.31
1994-95	CA	377.69	868.99	1869.29
	CL	297.00	535.30	2551.00

	NWC	80.69	333.96	-681.71
1995-96	CA	412.70	964.72	2050.40
	CL	303.74	805.19	2062.90
	NWC	108.96	159.53	-12.50
1996-97	CA	455.80	1500.80	1577.30
	CL	278.02	767.49	1330.60
	NWC	177.78	733.31	246.70
1997-98	CA	518.06	1850.70	1577.82
	CL	352.85	973.98	1433.80
	NWC	165.21	876.72	144.02
1998-99	CA	713.39	1874.60	2344.50
	CL	603.68	967.27	1617.09
	NWC	109.71	907.33	727.41
1999-00	CA	642.85	1793.80	2029.10
	CL	511.33	974.71	1972.10
	NWC	131.52	819.09	57.00
2000-01	CA	485.07	1711.85	2265.50
	CL	407.61	1144.40	2088.25
	NWC	77.46	567.45	177.30
2001-02	CA	387.69	1732.04	2111.80
	CL	349.17	1198.80	1811.80
	NWC	38.52	533.24	300.00
2002-03	CA	421.05	1611.60	2782.80
	CL	367.39	1117.76	1642.60
	NWC	53.66	493.84	1140.20
2003-04	CA	326.28	1500.58	3538.90
	CL	330.08	1342.70	1550.70
	NWC	-3.80	157.88	1988.20
2004-05	CA	265.46	226.71	4351.70
	CL	285.12	1844.65	1632.10
	NWC	-19.66	422.06	2719.60
2005-06	CA	198.05	2976.84	5504.20
	CL	235.64	2090.68	2003.00
	NWC	-37.59	889.16	3501.20
2006-07	CA	212.12	3732.28	4621.39
	CL	220.16	2687.34	2146.84
	NWC	-8.04	1044.94	2474.55

APPENDIX IV

Current Assets, Current Liabilities and Net Working Capital on the selected units from 1992-93 to 2006-07

(Two and three wheelers sector)

(Rs. in crores)

Particulars		*Bajaj Auto Ltd*	*LML Ltd Ltd*	*Maharastra Scooters Ltd*	*TVS Motors Ltd*	*Kinetic Motors*	*Hero Honda Motors Ltd*	*Kinetic Engineering Ltd*	*Majestic Auto Ltd*	*Scooters India Ltd*
1992-93	CA	505.76	127.18	106.50	59.17	31.97	93.18	64.05	32.23	22.45
	CL	350.07	156.65	79.18	77.80	21.88	59.30	40.34	31.14	242.41
	NWC	155.69	-29.47	27.32	-18.63	10.09	33.88	26.71	1.09	-219.96
1993-94	CA	702.86	148.65	121.24	66.51	44.38	107.14	80.53	42.18	26.12
	CL	457.81	181.57	90.94	73.11	24.00	87.52	54.94	39.40	339.18
	NWC	245.05	-32.92	30.30	-6.60	20.38	16.62	25.59	2.78	-313.06
1994-95	CA	1226.10	178.46	151.23	108.78	52.90	141.89	78.60	64.88	34.25
	CL	622.49	177.00	101.96	94.90	34.49	130.00	55.20	59.33	433.60
	NWC	603.61	1.46	49.27	13.88	18.41	11.89	23.40	5.55	-399.35
1995-96	CA	1425.00	227.73	142.00	148.80	69.78	146.19	94.03	71.68	45.50
	CL	871.29	212.31	116.03	150.86	55.45	145.60	72.63	48.69	534.03
	NWC	553.71	15.42	25.97	-2.06	14.33	0.59	21.40	22.99	-488.53

(Contd...)

(Contd...)

1996-97	CA	1893.40	251.97	149.74	184.37	87.52	186.55	110.60	70.89	56.83
	CL	996.59	242.30	129.08	147.68	74.41	186.42	73.16	65.38	50.94
	NWC	896.81	9.67	20.66	36.69	13.11	0.13	37.44	5.51	5.89
1997-98	CA	2410.50	268.64	152.32	257.63	105.54	232.76	146.44	75.01	66.62
	CL	1273.70	251.47	140.03	160.33	86.82	179.50	93.54	52.12	39.22
	NWC	1136.80	17.17	12.29	97.30	18.72	53.26	52.90	22.89	27.40
1998-99	CA	2969.10	355.73	172.87	255.80	88.61	326.14	140.05	69.66	77.34
	CL	1575.40	270.60	151.37	263.54	63.01	308.65	85.77	59.51	43.48
	NWC	1393.70	85.13	21.50	-7.74	25.60	17.49	54.28	10.15	33.86
1999-00	CA	3843.20	306.44	188.79	329.17	92.24	313.95	171.70	67.65	81.11
	CL	1852.60	250.30	155.19	248.69	68.30	359.86	89.87	78.57	31.28
	NWC	1990.60	56.14	33.60	80.48	23.94	-45.91	81.83	-10.92	49.83
2000-01	CA	2608.70	324.22	89.34	378.58	97.36	663.83	193.42	74.47	100.72
	CL	1547.40	307.34	50.82	314.78	72.80	460.12	113.13	96.91	45.55
	NWC	1061.30	16.88	38.52	63.80	24.56	203.71	80.29	-22.44	55.17
2001-02	CA	3220.90	267.36	95.66	410.15	130.31	536.46	254.17	68.50	102.03
	CL	1711.70	312.24	48.42	332.93	111.87	880.21	148.57	103.19	34.41
	NWC	1509.20	-44.62	47.24	77.22	18.44	-343.75	105.60	-34.69	67.62

(Contd...)

2002-03	CA	3349.40	286.17	99.83	448.76	142.33	1666.60	239.96	70.49	103.86
	CL	2042.40	319.63	42.38	457.82	81.43	1116.24	167.99	103.32	38.06
	NWC	1307.00	-33.46	57.45	-9.06	60.90	550.36	71.97	-32.83	65.80
2003-04	CA	3505.00	299.87	93.37	457.48	113.38	2068.80	212.16	68.76	105.21
	CL	2380.60	366.19	28.16	469.54	94.44	1260.05	183.07	86.16	49.29
	NWC	1124.40	-66.32	65.21	-12.06	18.94	808.75	29.09	-17.40	55.92
2004-05	CA	6826.28	282.46	39.05	553.45	102.32	2577.72	200.86	55.32	107.00
	CL	2852.33	324.81	21.17	507.80	98.26	1500.47	175.72	45.87	50.24
	NWC	3975.95	-42.35	17.88	45.65	4.06	1077.25	25.14	9.45	56.76
2005-06	CA	8367.38	246.18	41.07	734.78	75.77	2854.47	153.83	60.00	130.00
	CL	3809.76	318.28	24.47	621.02	106.70	1566.35	167.94	60.49	70.81
	NWC	4557.62	-72.10	16.60	113.76	-30.93	1288.12	-14.11	-0.49	59.19
2006-07	CA	9420.59	164.45	20.70	924.77	93.55	2838.50	147.27	68.10	146.18
	CL	4412.57	316.36	22.45	730.89	149.34	1483.98	118.51	72.25	72.12
	NWC	5008.02	-151.91	-1.75	193.88	-55.79	1354.52	28.76	-4.15	74.06

Appendix-B

Appendix 1

Size of Inventory (Rs. in crores)

Year	Commercial vehicles sector	Passenger cars and multiutility vehicles sector	Two- and three-wheelers sector	Total
1992-93	277.74	254.65	38.12	190.17
1993-94	230.14	277.42	39.58	182.38
1994-95	258.76	368.62	59.84	229.07
1995-96	335.80	441.39	62.94	280.04
1996-97	411.70	425.82	68.00	301.84
1997-98	376.31	446.22	70.38	297.63
1998-99	307.01	466.38	100.44	291.28
1999-00	340.62	614.44	92.60	349.22
2000-01	376.52	543.17	103.19	340.96
2001-02	359.03	438.95	90.63	296.20
2002-03	362.76	385.74	106.38	284.96
2003-04	398.62	365.95	103.40	289.32
2004-05	520.86	509.90	102.37	377.71
2005-06	676.20	615.27	123.09	471.52
2006-07	813.02	616.62	133.14	520.93

APPENDIX II

Size of Inventory

(Rs. in crores)

Year	*Ashok Leyland Ltd*	*Tata Motors Ltd*	*Bajaj Tempo Ltd*	*Eicher Motors Ltd*	*Swaraj Mazda Ltd*	*Total*
1992-93	261.74	977.19	96.36	27.36	26.04	277.74
1993-94	254.10	739.19	105.70	23.75	27.96	230.14
1994-95	304.19	778.28	153.57	30.74	27.03	258.76
1995-96	432.41	1001.50	154.86	41.77	48.45	335.80
1996-97	652.92	1143.10	170.63	34.61	57.26	411.70
1997-98	657.60	965.95	193.43	26.72	37.83	376.31
1998-99	427.75	856.11	191.66	18.14	41.40	307.01
1999-00	457.80	990.86	190.20	33.14	31.09	340.62
2000-01	517.67	1105.10	183.40	32.16	44.26	376.52
2001-02	595.35	987.50	132.30	33.50	46.52	359.03
2002-03	410.46	1159.29	148.15	36.05	59.83	362.76
2003-04	506.94	1147.40	152.15	126.25	60.34	398.62
2004-05	568.04	1601.36	185.07	161.25	88.56	520.86
2005-06	902.56	2012.24	213.84	161.23	91.14	676.20
2006-07	1070.33	2500.95	221.74	168.91	103.17	813.02

Appendix III

Size of Inventory
(Passenger cars and multiutility vehicles)

(Rs. in crores)

Year	*Hindustan Motors Ltd*	*Mahindra and Mahindra Ltd*	*Maruti Udyog Ltd*	*Total*
1992-93	176.81	261.40	325.74	254.65
1993-94	168.71	319.24	344.30	277.42
1994-95	182.48	351.91	571.48	368.62
1995-96	210.66	391.79	721.72	441.39
1996-97	231.47	447.48	598.52	425.82
1997-98	254.91	514.87	568.88	446.22
1998-99	384.56	436.99	577.59	466.38
1999-00	337.56	515.55	990.20	614.44
2000-01	211.46	552.54	865.50	543.17
2001-02	166.71	469.04	681.10	438.95
2002-03	213.49	456.74	487.00	385.74
2003-04	158.34	499.70	439.80	365.95
2004-05	103.27	759.84	666.60	509.90
2005-06	85.86	878.74	881.20	615.27
2006-07	61.23	878.48	910.15	616.62

APPENDIX IV

Size of Inventory (Two and three wheelers) *(Rs. in crores)*

Year	Bajaj Auto Ltd	LML Ltd	Maharastra Scooters Ltd	TVS Motor Company Ltd	Kinetic Motors Ltd	Hero Honda Motors Ltd	Kinetic Engineering Ltd	Majestic Auto Ltd	Scooters India Ltd	Total
1992-93	172.68	39.62	3.32	24.56	19.33	36.14	19.34	11.49	16.62	38.12
1993-94	161.33	42.62	1.48	29.38	25.44	42.45	24.59	12.96	15.94	39.58
1994-95	254.84	58.43	3.68	51.97	28.05	73.68	26.86	16.60	24.41	59.84
1995-96	219.34	88.87	5.76	52.45	47.07	60.13	34.16	29.75	28.89	62.94
1996-97	233.39	105.28	13.32	61.35	41.71	68.18	29.63	23.68	35.50	68.00
1997-98	233.39	111.60	21.56	52.78	44.55	90.17	31.20	19.44	28.70	70.38
1998-99	177.50	131.13	237.09	90.87	52.25	135.99	27.12	20.00	32.00	100.44
1999-00	261.13	121.31	23.90	118.79	45.57	169.57	44.75	21.39	26.95	92.60
2000-01	253.43	163.65	7.76	152.03	49.91	198.57	45.81	18.33	39.19	103.19
2001-02	179.10	130.99	2.57	148.79	58.67	178.36	56.63	24.36	36.16	90.63
2002-03	207.98	145.12	3.51	214.07	66.07	200.92	69.11	20.28	30.39	106.38
2003-04	202.56	160.96	4.59	216.66	41.31	188.20	68.19	21.01	27.08	103.40
2004-05	224.17	120.19	2.19	233.23	33.09	204.26	52.51	21.36	30.30	102.37
2005-06	272.93	111.47	6.41	357.90	24.60	226.55	46.98	18.51	42.47	123.09
2006-07	309.70	102.57	0.87	396.56	35.38	275.58	27.63	11.82	38.17	133.14

Appendix V

Size of Receivables *(Rs. in crores)*

Year	*Commercial vehicles sector*	*Passenger cars and multiutility vehicles sector*	*Two and three wheelers sector*	*Total*
1992-93	353.42	276.96	68.29	232.89
1993-94	386.45	420.78	84.45	297.23
1994-95	539.99	609.95	121.93	423.96
1995-96	737.18	446.68	163.58	449.15
1996-97	975.91	490.36	183.32	549.86
1997-98	806.30	685.93	239.04	577.09
1998-99	845.68	761.50	299.09	635.42
1999-00	618.30	714.31	320.05	550.88
2000-01	519.50	854.01	280.83	551.45
2001-02	467.37	868.88	297.25	544.50
2002-03	529.99	799.97	306.13	545.36
2003-04	584.70	752.91	294.32	543.98
2004-05	989.07	761.07	345.38	698.50
2005-06	1565.32	875.09	388.07	942.82
2006-07	1760.38	1043.42	508.09	1103.97

APPENDIX VI

Size of Receivables (Commercial vehicles) *(Rs. in crores)*

Year	*Ashok Leyland Ltd*	*Tata Motors Ltd*	*Bajaj Tempo Ltd*	*Eicher Motors Ltd*	*Swaraj Mazda Ltd*	*Total*
1992-93	415.35	1267.90	48.60	26.73	8.54	353.42
1993-94	451.20	1376.50	47.10	31.34	26.12	386.45
1994-95	869.51	1691.50	53.05	48.29	37.60	539.99
1995-96	1189.10	2304.50	95.80	59.82	36.66	737.18
1996-97	1304.30	3363.20	104.75	66.51	40.77	975.91
1997-98	1159.45	2714.50	80.95	46.38	30.22	806.30
1998-99	940.52	3128.00	69.47	52.37	38.03	845.68
1999-00	972.39	1947.00	67.26	49.39	55.44	618.30
2000-01	835.94	1546.20	79.74	57.22	78.41	519.50
2001-02	648.29	1435.40	93.35	72.78	87.04	467.37
2002-03	693.80	1671.56	108.83	82.21	93.53	529.99
2003-04	603.23	1788.20	163.64	232.08	136.37	584.70
2004-05	774.66	3513.37	125.38	312.80	219.12	989.07
2005-06	684.80	6359.18	155.86	297.12	329.62	1565.32
2006-07	1036.97	6818.78	176.91	396.48	372.78	1760.38

APPENDIX VII

Size of Receivables
(Passenger cars and multiutility vehicles)

(Rs. in crores)

Year	*Hindustan Motors Ltd*	*Mahindra and Mahindra Ltd*	*Maruti Udyog Ltd*	*Total*
1992-93	134.41	294.06	402.41	276.96
1993-94	152.20	402.69	707.45	420.78
1994-95	160.94	461.21	1207.70	609.95
1995-96	172.31	541.46	626.28	446.68
1996-97	180.84	527.75	762.49	490.36
1997-98	209.36	973.04	875.38	685.93
1998-99	287.37	1075.30	921.82	761.50
1999-00	270.32	879.90	992.70	714.31
2000-01	249.44	1014.70	1297.90	854.01
2001-02	186.65	1072.40	1347.60	868.88
2002-03	179.47	914.03	1306.40	799.97
2003-04	152.25	767.57	1338.90	752.91
2004-05	133.46	873.75	1276.00	761.07
2005-06	103.32	1055.15	1466.80	875.09
2006-07	92.26	1527.74	1510.27	1043.42

APPENDIX VIII

Size of Receivables (Two and three wheelers)

(Rs. in crores)

Year	*Bajaj Auto Ltd*	*LML Ltd*	*Maharastra Scooters Ltd*	*TVS Motor Company Ltd*	*Kinetic Motors Ltd*	*Hero Honda Motors Ltd*	*Kinetic Engineering Ltd*	*Majestic Auto Ltd*	*Scooters India Ltd*	*Total*
1992-93	296.44	71.94	99.76	33.55	10.34	36.99	41.71	19.76	4.15	68.29
1993-94	421.09	88.02	88.62	31.61	13.53	38.10	46.97	27.87	4.20	84.45
1994-95	721.40	90.86	88.79	43.56	14.87	39.24	48.73	45.20	4.75	121.93
1995-96	971.74	100.70	132.17	90.04	22.23	55.53	56.72	39.59	3.51	163.58
1996-97	1089.30	108.41	110.14	89.77	41.54	88.03	74.49	44.50	3.70	183.32
1997-98	1483.50	98.92	112.00	122.44	59.41	101.92	112.89	52.27	8.00	239.04
1998-99	1965.40	128.08	119.73	140.51	34.92	129.90	111.30	47.43	14.52	299.09
1999-00	2076.30	112.63	132.07	195.00	42.96	135.06	120.92	44.86	20.62	320.05
2000-01	1786.90	82.65	45.89	210.64	45.47	135.54	143.55	54.34	22.45	280.83
2001-02	1785.50	96.33	39.71	187.09	70.08	238.52	196.37	43.16	18.53	297.25
2002-03	1917.10	94.13	31.15	152.23	75.02	251.26	167.90	46.55	19.80	306.13
2003-04	1771.10	95.33	17.95	201.37	72.01	283.67	142.05	39.31	26.12	294.32
2004-05	2256.88	62.69	10.09	204.55	61.31	332.67	127.03	32.50	20.69	345.38
2005-06	2481.90	58.21	12.25	273.37	50.93	435.97	106.49	40.53	32.94	388.07
2006-07	3344.76	51.01	9.82	339.28	47.99	601.91	106.56	42.81	28.71	508.09

APPENDIX IX

Size of cash *(Rs. in crores)*

Year	*Commercial vehicles sector*	*Passenger cars and multiutility vehicles sector*	*Two and three wheelers sector*	*Total*
1992-93	24.71	83.95	6.27	38.31
1993-94	17.29	57.85	8.50	27.88
1994-95	35.66	53.39	21.63	36.89
1995-96	14.06	33.81	12.51	20.13
1996-97	48.43	183.11	15.87	82.47
1997-98	90.20	153.53	30.86	91.53
1998-99	105.94	392.92	23.89	174.25
1999-00	26.80	110.63	19.56	52.33
2000-01	58.00	85.46	22.88	55.45
2001-02	123.32	81.93	33.18	79.48
2002-03	98.76	418.10	26.33	181.06
2003-04	230.37	163.07	26.03	139.82
2004-05	572.29	554.87	39.91	389.02
2005-06	356.31	713.59	42.55	370.82
2006-07	266.57	316.08	32.72	205.12

APPENDIX X

Size of cash (Commercial vehicles) *(Rs. in crores)*

Year	*Ashok Leyland Ltd*	*Tata Motors Ltd*	*Bajaj Tempo Ltd*	*Eicher Motors Ltd*	*Swaraj Mazda Ltd*	*Total*
1992-93	79.79	37.68	1.98	2.23	1.85	24.71
1993-94	3.48	18.47	58.32	4.03	2.13	17.29
1994-95	85.13	18.53	63.86	8.44	2.32	35.66
1995-96	2.55	50.53	3.78	11.74	1.72	14.06
1996-97	6.54	212.89	4.08	15.80	2.86	48.43
1997-98	2.51	439.12	4.29	2.38	2.70	90.20
1998-99	62.16	441.97	4.67	14.08	6.82	105.94
1999-00	37.28	65.27	12.47	8.21	10.77	26.80
2000-01	164.93	115.46	3.01	1.49	5.10	58.00
2001-02	274.89	326.63	5.21	0.61	9.25	123.32
2002-03	221.92	245.53	19.44	0.92	5.98	98.76
2003-04	324.98	770.49	14.13	33.14	9.09	230.37
2004-05	796.68	2005.04	12.72	31.03	16.00	572.29
2005-06	602.88	1119.43	14.14	26.09	19.03	356.31
2006-07	434.94	826.76	13.02	47.72	10.41	266.57

APPENDIX XI

Size of cash

(Passenger cars and multiutility vehicles)

(Rs. in crores)

Year	*Hindustan Motors Ltd*	*Mahindra and Mahindra Ltd*	*Maruti Udyog Ltd*	*Total*
1992-93	20.30	125.68	105.87	83.95
1993-94	27.73	44.99	100.84	57.85
1994-95	34.10	35.96	90.11	53.39
1995-96	29.67	31.47	40.29	33.81
1996-97	43.32	409.23	96.79	183.11
1997-98	53.62	273.41	133.56	153.53
1998-99	41.29	320.56	816.91	392.92
1999-00	34.80	265.39	31.70	110.63
2000-01	24.17	144.61	87.60	85.46
2001-02	33.28	140.60	71.90	81.93
2002-03	24.04	240.87	989.40	418.10
2003-04	15.69	233.31	240.20	163.07
2004-05	11.23	623.98	1029.40	554.87
2005-06	8.87	730.30	1401.60	713.59
2006-07	6.24	640.25	301.74	316.08

Appendix XII

Size of cash (Two and three wheelers) *(Rs. in crores)*

Year	Bajaj Auto Ltd	LML Ltd	Maharastra Scooters Ltd	TVS Motor Company Ltd	Kinetic Motors Ltd	Hero Honda Motors Ltd	Kinetic Engineering Ltd	Majestic Auto Ltd	Scooters India Ltd	Total
1992-93	24.95	15.62	3.42	1.06	2.30	5.77	0.62	0.98	1.68	6.27
1993-94	21.67	18.01	4.67	5.52	5.41	11.42	2.47	1.35	5.98	8.50
1994-95	134.22	22.34	2.25	12.75	9.98	4.26	0.69	3.08	5.09	21.63
1995-96	54.58	24.40	4.07	6.31	0.48	6.36	0.97	2.34	13.10	12.51
1996-97	40.83	31.71	4.48	32.74	4.27	6.00	2.48	2.71	17.63	15.87
1997-98	92.51	55.13	4.03	76.90	1.58	12.66	1.74	3.30	29.92	30.86
1998-99	54.08	93.42	1.88	24.42	1.39	5.23	1.58	2.23	30.82	23.89
1999-00	35.95	70.89	1.40	15.38	3.66	9.32	4.48	1.40	33.53	19.56
2000-01	21.32	74.65	4.48	15.91	1.93	45.09	1.66	1.80	39.08	22.88
2001-02	25.20	38.57	0.66	74.27	1.56	108.96	1.09	0.98	47.34	33.18
2002-03	30.02	40.15	0.46	82.46	1.24	24.33	1.00	3.66	53.67	26.33
2003-04	79.37	43.55	0.74	18.00	0.29	37.12	1.05	2.15	52.01	26.03
2004-05	108.69	99.58	0.75	73.87	0.26	17.60	0.99	1.44	56.01	39.91
2005-06	82.09	61.28	0.40	24.35	0.24	158.72	0.36	0.96	54.59	42.55
2006-07	83.47	10.87	0.51	86.56	10.18	35.78	13.08	0.45	53.61	32.72

Bibliography

Books

Agarwal, N.K. *Management of Working Capital,* (New Delhi: Steeling Publishers Private Limited, 1983).

Archer, S.H. et. al. *Business Finance: Theory and Management,* (New Delhi: The Macmillan co. 1969).

Bhattcharya, S.K. and Raghavachari, M. *Determinants of effective Working Capital Management:* A Discriminant Analysis Approach, Working paper No. 151, (Indian Institute of Management, Ahmedabad, March 1977).

Bolten S.E., *Managerial Finance,* (Boston: Houghton Mifflin Co., 1976), 446.

Burton A. Kolb *Principles of Financial Management,* (Texas : Business Publications Inc, 1983), 153.

Chapman Findlay, M. and Idward F.Williams., *An Integrated Analysis for Managerial Finance,* (New Delhi: Prentice Hall, Inc., 1970), 70.

Charles O., Kroncke et. al, *Managerial Finance: Essentials,* (Minnesota: West Publishing Company, 1978), 108.

Clarkson, G.P.E., and Elliot, *Managing Money and Finance,* (Hents: The Gower Press Ltd, 1972), 98.

Cohn, R.A. and Pringle, J.J. *Steps Towards an Integration of Corporate Financial Theory, in Management of Working Capital: A Reader, Keith V. Smith (ed.),* (New York: West Publishing Co., 1975), 369.

Donnell, O. and Goldberg *Elements of Financial Administration,* (New Delhi: Prentice Hall of India Pvt. Ltd., (1964), 55.

Dutta Majumdar, D.K., *Productivity of Labour and Capital in Indian Manufacturing Industries during 1951 to 1961,* (Indian Statistical Institute Publication, 1980).

Fred Weston, J. and Brigham, E.F, *Managerial Finance*, (New York: The Dryden Press, 1981), 185.

Gitman, L.J., *Principles of Managerial Finance*, (New York : Harper and Row Publishers, 1976).

Hampton, J.J., *Financial Decision Making*, (New Delhi: Prentice Hall of India Pvt. Ltd, June 1983), 18.

Hampton, J.J. and Wagner, C., *Working Capital Management*, (New York: John Wiley & Sons., 1989).

Howard, B.B, and Upton, M., *Introduction to Business Finance*, (New York; Hill Book Co, Inc., 1953) 188.

Howard, L.R., *Working Capital – Its Management and Control*, (London: Mac Donald & Evans Ltd, 1971), 2.

John.D.Martin et. al. *Basic Financial Management*, (New Jersy: Prentice Hall Inc, 1979), 149.

John Maynard Keynes, The *General Theory of Employment*, (Harcount Brace and Company, 1936), 201.

Joseph F.Bradely., *Administrative Financial Management*,
(New York: Holt, Rinehart and Winston Inc., 1969), 196.

Khan, M.Y. and Jain, P.K., *Financial Management*, (New Delhi : Tata McGraw Hill, 1984), 607.

Keown,A.J. et al., *Basic Financial Management*, (New Delhi: Prentice Hall of India Pvt. Ltd, 1985), 131.

Kreps Cliften, H. and Richard F.Wacht, *Financial Administration*, (Housdale : Illinois, 1975), 45.

Kuchhal, S.C., *Financial Management*, (An Analytical and Conceptual Approach, 1980) 162.

Lovell, M.C., *Determinants of Inventory Behaviour*, (In Models of Income Behaviour (Ed.) Edward F. Denison and Lawrence R. Klein, New York, 1964).

Man Mohan and Goyal, *Principles of Management Accounting*, (Agra: Sahitya Prakash, 1979) 368.

Mishra R.K., *Problems of Working Capital (With special reference to selected public undertakings in India)*, (Bombay: Somaiya Publications Pvt. Ltd, 1975).

Mukherjee, A.K., *Management of Working Capital in Public Enterprises*, (Vohra publishers & Distributors, Allahabad, 1988).

Pandey, I.M. (2005), *Financial Management, (9th Edition)*, (New Delhi: Vikas publishing House Pvt Ltd., 2005), 579-592.

Pandey, I.M., *Financial Management*, (New Delhi: Vikas Publishing House Pvt. Ltd., 1982), 337.

Panda, J. and Satapathy, A.K., *Working capital structure of Private Enterprises: A study of cement industry,* New Delhi, Discover Publishing House, 1988).

Pradhan, R.S., *Management of Working Capital,* (New Delhi: National Book Organisation, 1986), 86-94.

Ramamoorthy, V.E., *Working Capital Management,* (Institute of Financial Management Research, Madras, 1978).

Ram Kumar Mishra, *Problems of Working Capital,* (Bombay; Somaiya Publications Pvt. Ltd, 1975), 127.

Smith, K.V., *State of the Art of Working Capital Management, in Issues in Managerial Finance, Eugene F. Brigham and Ramom E.Johnson, (ed.),* (Illinois: The Dryden Press, 1976), 63.

Solomon, E. and Pringle, J.J., *Financial Management,* (New Delhi: Prentice Hall of India, 1978), 98.

Verma, H.L., *Management of Working Capital,* (New Delhi: Deep & Deep Publications, 1989).

Van Horne, J.C., *Financial Management and Policy,* (New Delhi: Prentice Hall of India Pvt. Ltd, 1988), 324-325.

Walker, E.W. and Boughn, W.H., *Financial Planning and Policy,* (Harper International, Students Edition, 1974), 151.

Articles

Agarwal, J.D. (1991), Goal programming Model for Working Capital Management, in Working Capital Management (Analysis & Cases), Jaipur: *Research Development Association,* pp. 67-80.

Akhtar, M.A. (June 1983), Effects of Interest Rates and Inflation on Aggregate Inventory Investment in US, *The American Economic Review,* pp. 319-328.

Amir Jafar and Debasish Sur (2006), Efficiency of Working Capital Management in Indian Public Enterprises during the post liberalisation Era, A case study of NTPC, *The ICFAI Journal of Management Research,* Vol. V, No.6, pp.56- 63.

Amit K. Chakraborty (2005), Working Capital Management: An Empirical Study, *Southern Economist,* Vol. 43, No.19, pp. 23-27.

Amit K.Mallik, Debasish Sur and Debdas Rakshit (2005), Working Capital and Profitability: A study on their relationship with reference to selected companies in Indian Pharmaceutical Industry, *GITAM Journal of Management,* Vol.3, No:2, pp. 51-62.

Anand, M. (2001), Working capital performance of corporate India: An Empirical Survey, *Management & Accounting Research,* Vol. 4, pp. 35-65.

Arindam Ghosh, (January 2007), Working Capital Management Practices in some selected industries in India, *The Management Accountant*, pp. 60-67.

Ashok Kumar Lahiri (1981), Liquidity Behaviour on Indian Business Firms, *The Indian Economic Journal*, Vol. 29, No. 1, pp. 1-9.

Azhagaiah, R. and Gejalakshmi, S. (2007), Working – Capital Management – Efficiency, *UDYOG PRAGAN*, Vol.31, No.3, pp. 15-20

Banerjee, B. (July 1982), Corporate Liquidity and Profitability in India. Research Bulletin, *Institute of Cost Works Accountant of India*, pp. 225-234.

Banerjee, D and Hazra, M.K (May, 1999), Working capital Management in Grasim Industries Limitied: A case study, *The Management Accountant*, pp. 336-340.

Bardia, S.C. (2004), Liquidity Management – A case study o: Steel Authority of India Ltd, *The Management Accountant*, pp. 463-467.

Basu, S.N. (May 1992), Working Capital Management – Type Companies, *The Management Accountant*, pp. 331-333.

Baumol, W. (November 1952), The Transaction Demands for Cash: An Inventory Theoretic Approach, *The Quarterly Journal of Economics*, pp. 545-566.

Bhole, L.M. (1979), An Empirical Study of Liquidity Preference of Corporate Sector in India, 1951-1974, *The Indian Economic Journal*, Vol. 27, No. 1, pp. 65-80.

Bierman, H., et al. (March 1975), Ruin considerations: Optimal Working Capital and Capital Structure, *The Journal of Financial and Quantitative Analysis*, pp. 119-128.

Chakraborthy, S.K. (August 1973), Use of Operating Cycle Concept for Better Management of Working Capital, *The Economic and Political Weekly*, pp. 69- 76.

Chakraborty, P.K. (2004), Managing Corporate Liquidity and Financial Flexibility: Different Approach, *The Management Accountant*, Vol.39, No.8, pp. 653-655.

Chakraborty, P.K. (2004), Managing Corporate Liquidity and Financial Flexibility: Different Approach, *The Management Accountant*, Vol.39, No.8, pp. 653-655.

Chang, C.H., Dandapani, K and Prakash, A .J (1995), Aspects of Financial Management in Europe and Asia, *Management International Review*, Vol.35, special issue No. 2, pp. 105-117.

Charles Lieberman (August 1980), Inventory Demand and Cost of Capital Effects, *The Review of Economics and Statistics*, pp. 348-356.

Chore, K.B. (1979), Report of the Working Group to Review the System of Cash Credit, *Bombay: Reserve Bank of India,* pp. 26-52.

Cossaboom, R.A. (May 1971), Let's Reassess the Profitability-Liquidity Trade off, *Financial Executive,* pp. 46-51.

Debasish Sur, (June 2001), Liquidity Management: An overview of four companies in Indian Power Sector, *The Management Accountant,* pp. 407-412.

Debasish Sur, Joydeep Biswas and Prasenjit Ganguly (2001), Liquidity Management in Indian Private Sector Enterprises: A case study of Indian Aluminum producing industry, *Indian journal of accounting,* Vol.32, pp.68-76.

Dehejia, V.T. (November 1969), Report of the Committee. Reserve Bank of India Bulletin, *Bombay: Reserve Bank of India,* pp. 1972-1978.

Frazer, W.J. (April, 1964), Financial Structure of Manufacturing Corporations and the Demand for Money: Some Empirical Findings, *The Journal of Political Economy,* pp. 176-183.

Fred Weston, J. and Engene Brigham, F. (1975), Managerial Finance, *New York: The Dryden Press,* pp.185.

Friedman, M. (August 1959), The Demand for Money: Some Theoretical and Empirical Results, *The Journal of Political Economy,* pp. 327-351.

Garai, S. and Mallik, A. (July, 1988), Role of Working Capital in Manufacturing Industries-Case Study in Indian perspective, *Research Bulletin,* pp. 46-54.

Ghosh and Maji (2004), Working Capital Management Efficiency: A study on the Indian Cement Industry, *The Management Accountant,* Vol. 39, No.5, pp. 363-372.

Ghosh, S.K and Maji, S.G. (2003), Utilisation of current assets and operating profitability: An Empirical study on Cement and Tea industries in India, *Indian Journal of Accounting,* pp. 52-55.

Gupta, S.P. (1991), Working Capital Control through Variance Analysis, in Working Capital Management (Analysis & Cases), *Jaipur: Research Development Association,* pp. 143-145.

Indrasena Reddy, P. and Someswar Rao, K. (1996), Working capital Management in Public Sector Undertaking – A case study, *The Management Accountant,* Vol.31, No. 9, pp. 643-645.

Ioannis Lazaridis and Dimitrios Tryfonidis (2006), Relationship between Working Capital Management and Corporate profitability, *Journal of Financial Management and Analysis,* Vol. 19, No.1, pp. 26-35.

Jhon Sagan, (May 1955), Towards a Theory of Working Capital Management, *The Journal of Finance,* pp. 121-129.

Johnson, J.M, Campbell, D.R. and Savoie, I.M. (October 1983), Corporate liquidity: A comparison of two recessions, *Financial Executive,* pp. 18-22.

Joyce, J.M. (October 1973), Cost of Capital and Inventory Investment: Further Evidence, *The Southern Economic Journal,* pp. 323-329.

Kamta Prasad and Sampath, R.K. (July-September 1979), Business Demand for Money in India-A Temporal Cross-Section Analysis, *The Indian Economic Journal,* Vol. 27, No. 1, pp. 43-62.

Kannadhasan, M. (2007), Working capital management in a Public Limited Company – A case study, *The ICFAI Journal of Management Research,* Vol. VI, No.5, pp. 20-33.

Kaushik Chakraborty, G. (2008), Working Capital and Profitability: An Empirical Analysis of their Relationship with Reference to Selected Companies in the Indian Pharmaceutical Industry, *The Icfai University Press,* pp.41-59.

Khatik, S.K and Pradeep Kumar Singh (2003), Liquidity Management in EICHER Ltd., – A case study, *The Management Accountant,* pp. 217-220.

Khatik, S.K and Singh, P.K. (January 2004), Working Capital Management in Indian Farmers Fertiliser Cooperative Limited – A case study, *The Management Accountant,* pp. 19-25.

Kulshreshta, N.K. (August 1980), Corporate Liquidity – X Rayed, *The Management Accountant,* Vol. 15, No. 8, pp. 331-34.

Kuznets, P.W. (1964), Financial Determinants of Manufacturing Inventory Behaviour; A Quarterly Study Based on US Estimates, *Yale Economic Essays,* pp. 331-369.

Lambrix, R.L. and Singhvi, S.S. (June, 1979), Managing the Working Capital Cycle, *Financial Executive,* pp. 32-41.

Liu, T.C. (July 1963), An Exploratory Quarterly Model of Effective Demand in the Post-war US Economy, *The Econometrical,* pp. 301-308.

Louis De Allessi (Auguest 1966), The Demand for Money: A Cross-Section study of British Business Firms, *Economic,* pp. 288-302.

Mall, C.P. and S.K.Singh, (April-June, 1989), Management of Working Capital in a Public Sector Corporation – A Case Study, *IPE Journal,* pp. 23-33.

Mallik, A. K. and Sur, D. (1999), Working Capital Management: A Case Study of Hindustan Lever Ltd, *Finance India,* pp. 857-871.

Mallik, A.K and Sur, D. (1998), Working capital and profitability: A case study in inter relation, *The Management Accountant*, pp. 805-809.

Manoj Anand and Gupta, C.P (January-June 2003), Working Capital Management of Corporate India: An Empirical Survey for the year 2000-2001, *Management & Accounting Research*, pp. 11-45.

Manoj Anand and Keshav Malhotra, (January 2007), Working Capital Management Performance of Corporate India: An Empirical Study, *Applied Finance*, pp. 46-80.

Marathe, S.S. (1983), Report of the Committee to Review the Working of the Credit Authorisation Scheme, *Bombay: Reserve Bank of India*, pp. 20-27.

Meltzer, A.H. (August 1963), The Demand for Money: A Cross Section study of Business firms, *The Quarterly Journal of Economics*, pp. 405-422.

Merville, J. and Tavis, L.A. (January, 1973), Optimum Working Capital Policies: A Chance Constrained Programming Approach, *The Journal of Financial and Quantitative Analysis*, pp. 47-59.

Mishra, M. (October 1980), Problems of Working Capital Management during Inflation, *The Chartered Accountant*, pp.298-302.

Mukherjee, A.K (Jan-March 1985), Management of Working Capital of Central Government Undertakings in India, *IPE journal*, pp.36-48.

Mukhopadhyay, D (2004), Working Capital Management in Heavy Engineering Firms – A case study, *The Management Accountant*, pp.317-323.

Nadiri, M.I. (May, 1969), The Determinants of Real Cash Balance in the US Total Manufacturing Sector, *The Quarterly Journal of Economics*, pp. 173-196.

Nalini Ambegaokar (October 1969), Working capital requirements and availability of bank credit (Indian Processing and Manufacturing Industries), *Reserve Bank of India Bulletin*, pp. 1535-1553.

Nand Kishore Sharma, (May 2007), Current Assets Accounting and Control, *The Chartered Accountant*, pp. 1706-1712.

Narware, P.C. (June 2004), Working Capital and Profitability – An empirical analysis, *The Management Accountant*, pp. 491 –495.

Narware, P.C. and Vivek Sharma (2004), Liquidity Management of Hindustan Petroleum Corporation Ltd., - An empirical study, *The Management Accountant*, Vol.39, No.3. pp. 201-203

Pancras, U. (November 1981), Time Adjusted Current Ratio, *The Management Accountant,* pp. 524-526.

Panigrahi, J. (October 1990), Working capital management of large Indian companies *The Management Accountant,* pp. 653-656.

Parasuram, N.R. (2004), Working Capital Practices in Leading Pharmaceutical Companies – A view of the credit policy and profitability, *The Management Accountant,* Vol. 39, No. 12, pp. 998-1005.

Parmar (2003), Performance evaluation through inventory management (A comparative study of G.S.F.C & G.N.F.C), *Indian Journal of Accounting,* Vol.xxxiii, June, pp.64-68.

Patel, D.M (January 2005), Analysis of Working Capital (A Case study of Colour- Chem Limited), *ACCST Research Journal,* pp. 13-21.

Pathak, J.N. (1983), Report of the Committee, Reserve Bank of India Bulletin. *Bombay, Reserve Bank of India,* pp. 15-22.

Paul Welter (1970), How to calculate savings possible through reduction of working capital? *Financial Executive,* pp. 50-58.

Pradeep Singh (2008), Inventory and Working Capital Management: An Empirical Analysis, *The Icfai Journal of Accounting Research,* Vol.VII, No.2, April, pp.53-73.

Prakash Tandon (1974), Report of the Study Group to Frame Guidelines for Follow- up of Bank Credit, *Bombay: Reserve Bank of India,* pp. 20-21.

Qwen Irvine, F. (September 1981), Retail Inventory Investment and the Cost of Capital, *The American Economic Review,* p. 633.

Rabiul Alam, S.M. and Syed Zabid Hossain (2001), Aspects of Inventory Management in shipbuilding industry in Bangladesh, *The Management Accountant,* September, pp.699-706.

Rabiul Alam, S.M. and Zabid Hossain, S. (February 2004), Management of Working Finance: A study on the Shipbuilding Industry in Bangladesh, *The Management Accountant,* pp. 111-117.

Rais Abmad and Ali Ghufran (June-December 2005), Analytical study of Working Capital Management of Marketing Cooperative Societies, *Management & Account Research,* pp. 35-51.

Rajendran, P. and Ramesh, D. (March 2006), Liquidity Management of Tamilnadu Tourism Development Corporation Ltd – An Empirical Study, *The Management Accountant,* pp. 205-208.

Rao, K.V. and Chinta Rao (April-June 1991), Evaluating Efficiency of Working Capital Management – Are the conventional techniques adequate?, *Decision,* Vol. 18, No. 2, pp. 81-98.

Reddy, B.R. (January and July 1988), Working Capital Management in Co-operative Sugar Mills in Tamil Nadu, *Research Bulletin,* pp. 37-45.

Reddy, Y.V. and Patkar S.B. (2004), Working Capital and Liquidity Management in Factoring: A comparative study on SBI and Canbank Factors, *The Management Accountant,* Vol. 39, No.5, pp. 373-378.

Sahu, R.K.(November 2002), A Simplified model for liquidity analysis of Paper companies, *The Management Accountant,* pp. 805-808.

Sam Luther, C.T. (2007), Liquidity, risk and profitability analysis – A case study of Madras Cements Ltd, *The Management Accountant,* Vol.42, No.10, pp. 784-789.

Sanjay J. Bhayani (2004), Working capital and Profitability Relationship (A case study of Gujarat Ambuja Cement ltd), *SCMS Journal of Indian Management,* Vol.1, No.2, pp. 98-107

Sanjay, J.Bhayani (2006), Assets Turnover and Profitability, *Indian Journal of Accounting,* Vol.xxxvi (2), pp. 1-7.

Santanu Kr.Ghosh and Santi Gopal Maji, (May 2004), Working Capital Management Efficiency: A study on the Indian Cement Industry, *The Management Accountant,* pp. 363-372.

Santimoy Patra (2005), Liquidity Vs Profitability, *Indian Journal of Accounting,* Vol.xxxv(2), pp.39-43.

Sarkar, J.B. and Saha, S.N. (1987), Profitability crisis and working capital management in the public Sector in India: A Case Study, *The Management Accountant,* pp. 328-333.

Sarvanan, P. (2001), A study of Working Capital Management in Non-Banking Finance Companies, *Finance India,* Vol.XV, No.3, pp. 987-994.

Sathyamoorthi, C.R. (2002), Management of Working Capital in Selected Co- operatives in Botswana, *Finance India,* Vol.16, No.3, pp.105-125.

Satyanarayana Chary and Venkateshwarlu (2003), Working Capital Analysis (A case study of Sri Venkata Narasimha Solvent Oils Ltd), *Udyog Pragati,* Vol.27, No.3, pp.38-50.

Shankar, K. (1996), Developments in Working Capital Finance, *The Management Accountant,* Vol.31, No. 9, pp. 689-694.

Shanmugam, R. (July-September 2006), Liquidity – Profitability International ships: A Sectoral Analysis, *Udyog Pragati – The Journal for Practicing Managers,* pp. 38-43.

Sharma, K.K and Agarwal, R.K (January 1986), Working Capital Management in State Transport Undertaking, *Journal of Transport Management,* pp. 17-20.

Sharma, S.N. and Reddy, A.V. (Auguest 1985), Corporate Liquidity; A Case Study, *The Management Accountant*, pp. 415-419.

Singh, P.K. (2004), Working Capital Management in Lupin Laboratories Ltd – A Case Study, *The Management Accountant*, pp.534-539.

Subhas Chandra Sarkar and Amalendu Bhunla (2004), Liquidity Trend Analysis: A case study of TISCO, *Southern Economist*, Vol.43, No.9, pp.15-17.

Subir Nath Sarkar (July 1987), Liquidity Management in the Public Sector – a Case Study of a Government of West Bengal Undertaking, *The Management Accountant*, pp. 496-498.

Subramanya, Sarma.M and Thiruvengala Chary (1999), Working Capital Management in VST – An Appraisal, *Finance India*, Vol.XIII, No.1, March 1999, pp.71-79.

Sudarsana Reddy, G., Sivarami Reddy, C., and Mohan Reddy, P. (2004), Debtors' management: A case study of Andhara Pradesh paper industry, *The Management Accountant*, pp. 265-274.

Sudarshan, R. (2004), Analysis of inventory behaviour-an application model for Chemicals and Pharmaceutical enterprises, *The Management Accountant*, pp.868-872.

Sudipta Ghosh (2005), Performance Appraisal through Inventory Management (A case of study of Stewarks and Lloyds of India Ltd), *The Management Accountant*, pp. 560-562.

Sukhdev Singh (2006), Inventory Control Practices in IFFCO, *The Management Accountant*, July, Vol.41, No.7, pp.577-580.

Surendra S.Yadav, Jain P.K. and Ashish K.Rastogi, (July 2001), Working Capital Management in oil industry in India, *The Management Accountant*, pp.511-516.

Sushil.K.Jain (May, 1991), Working Capital Management, *The Management Accountant*, pp. 507-509.

Sushma Vishnani and Bhupesh Kr Shah (2006), Liquidity Vs Profitability – A detailed study in perspective of Indian consumer electronics industry, *Pranjana*, Vol.9, No.2, pp.13-19.

Tobin, J. (August 1956), The Interest Elasticity of Transactions Demand for Cash, *The Review of Economics and Statistics*, pp. 241-247.

Van Horne, J.C. (Winter 1969), A Risk-Return Analysis of a firm's Working Capital Position, *The Engineering Economist*, pp. 71-88.

Vijaya Saradhi, S.P. (June-December 1980), Problems of Working Capital Management in Public Enterprises, *The Indian Journal of Accounting*, Vol. X, pp. 65-75.

Vijayakumar, A. (April-June 1996), The Transactions Demand for Working Capital in Indian PSUs: Some theoretical and empirical results, *IPE Journal,* pp. 92-100.

Vijayakumar, A. and Venkatachalam, A. (1995), Working capital and profitability – An empirical analysis, *The Management Accountant,* pp. 748-750.

Vijayakumar, A., Sivasubramanian, K. and Venkatachalam, A. (April 1994), Working Finance in National Cooperative Sugar Mills Ltd, Tamilnadu – A case study, *Management & Labour Studies,* Vol. 19, No. 2. pp. 132-143.

Walker, E.W. (Winter 1964), Towards a Theory of Working Capital, *The Engineering Economist,* pp. 21-35.

Whalen, E.L. (September 1965), A Cross-Section Study of Business Demand for Cash, *The Journal Finance,* pp. 423-443.

Yadav, R.A. (1986), Working Capital Management – A Parametric Approach. *The Chartered Accountant,* pp. 952-955.

Yardeni, E.E. (May, 1978), A Portfolio-Balance Model of Corporate Working Capital, *The Journal of Finance,* pp. 535-552.

Unpublished Thesis

Khan Mohd Amir (1985), Working Capital Management at Escorts Ltd, Unpublished thesis, Aligarh Muslim University, Aligarh.

Sivaram Prasad R.(1999), Working Capital Management in Indian Paper Industry, Unpublished thesis, Nagarjuna University, Nagarjuna Nagar.

Harbir Singh (1990), Management of Working Capital: A case study of Modi Sugar Mills, Modinagar, Ph.D. Dissertation, Meerut University, Published in A survey of Research in Commerce and Management, pp. 477-483.

Asha Jain, (1981). Price- Cost Margin in Indian Manufacturing Industries: An Econometric Analysis, Ph.D thesis, IIT, Kanpur.

Kadirvelu,S. (2002). Profitability Analysis of Selected Indian Public Sector Manufacturing Enterprises- before and after Liberalisation, Unpublished thesis,Bharathiar University, Coimbatore.

Krishnaveni, M. (2004). Performance Appraisal of an Indian Chemical Industry after Liberalisation (199192 to 2001-02),Unpublished thesis, Bharathiar University, Coimbatore.

Kulshreshtha, R.S.(1973). Profitability in India's Steel Industry-During the decade 1960-70 (A thesis submitted for the degree of Ph.D., Dept. of E.A.F.M. University of Rajashthan), p. 83.

Maninder S.Sarkaia, Shergil U.S. (2004). Market Structure and Financial Performance-An Indian Evidence with Enhanced Controls, Ph.D Thesis Submitted to the Guru Nanak Dev University.

Reports

Annual Reports of the Indian Automobile Industry

Basic statistics relating to Indian Economy, Center for Monitoring Indian Economy, Mumbai,Sep 1994.

Government of India, Annual Survey of Industries (Series), Central Statistical Organisation.

Kothari's Industrial Directory of India

RBI Bulletin, RBI, Mumbai.

UNIDO (1996). Industrial Development : Global Report.

Select On-line Newspapers

Business Line

Business Standard

Business-Standard.com

Deccan Chronicle

DeccanHerald.com

ExpressIndia.com

Financial Express

Hindustan Times Online

India Today

IndiaDaily.com

IndiaDirect.com

IndiaExpress.com

IndiaInfoline.com

IndiaPress.org

NewsIndia-Times.com

PatrikaOnline.com

The Economic Times

The Hindu

The Times of India

Select Business Magazines

Banking & Finance-Bi-monthly magazine on banking & finance.

Business Barons-Bi-monthly business magazine.

Business Today—A fortnightly business magazine.

Business Weekly News—International weekly business reports.

Capital Market—A business magazine focused on the stock market.

Dhan—An online business & financial news magazine

Domex Information-Fortnightly industrial & business bulletin.

Fortune—A financial magazine from pathfinder

India Investors—Weekly newsletter on stock markets.

India Times—Online business magazine

Industrial Economist—Online business magazine

Industrial Magazine Online—Industry news, events, press releases, etc.

Select Search Engines and Websites

http://did.nic.in

http://finmin.nic.in

http://www.altavista.com

http://www.bisnetindia.com

http://www.bseindia.com

http://www.cmie.org

http://www.economictimes.com

http://www.gadnet.com/india.html

http://www.indiainfoline.com

http://www.indiamart.com/assocham

http://www.indianindustry.com

http://www.indiastat.com

http://www.indiatimes.com

http://www.india-yp.com

http://www.indous.org

http://www.nic.in

http://www.nic.in/bicp/

http://www.nic.in/delnet

http://www.nic.in/icar

http://www.nic.in/lawmin/

http://www.nsdl.com

http://www.nseindia.com
http://www.rbi.org.in
http://www.rediff.com
http://www.sebi.com
http://www.usibc.com
http://www.yahoo.com

Index